AF575948

Hasan-i-Sabah

Advance Praise for Hasan-i-Sabah

First, let me congratulate you on an overwhelming undertaking. You are dealing with a subject that is not well-understood and has been a magnet for a great deal of disinformation over the centuries. You have had to start at rock bottom and work your way up through layers of flawed data that have accumulated (and hardened) to such an extent that one would need a pile driver to punch through.

I hope your readers understand that and, as you mention in your opening, it isn't necessary to wade through the background and historical narrative—as valuable as it is—for those who want to get right to the heart of the subject matter, which is Hasan himself.

Hasan comes through your work as a complex, three-dimensional human being in spite of all the mythology surrounding him and the Assassins. Importantly, Islam is shown to be a multi-faceted faith with a complicated history, something that not many modern commentators understand.

In addition, the translations at the end are well worth the cover price as they are not available anywhere else and they do help to clear up some misconceptions about Hasan and the Ismailis.

Thus, I whole-heartedly endorse this project.

—Peter Levenda, author of *Dark Lord* and *Tantric Temples*

Jim Wasserman presents a compelling portrait of Hasan-i-Sabah and the Nizari Ismaili branch of Shia Islam. Hasan-i-Sabah, the founder of the renowned Order of Assassins, exemplifies all the spiritual richness and political complexity of Islam, and Wasserman is a skilled storyteller who illuminates the events of history with both scholarship and mystical insight. This valuable book also includes, for the first time in English, medieval Persian texts describing the life of Hasan-i-Sabah, and Wasserman's explication makes these fascinating texts accessible.

—James H. Cumming, author of *Torah and Nondualism*

NEARLY NINE HUNDRED YEARS AFTER HIS DEATH, Hasan-i-Sabah, founder of the mysterious sect known as the "Assassins," continues to exert his influence across the Middle East and the West. Mystic, heretic, pious Muslim, master of politics, war, scholar, and prolific author, Hasan is a mystery not easily penetrated; yet, Wasserman takes us carefully by the hand through the labyrinth of legend and history that compose our understanding of a man thought to be pivotal in transforming the Knights Templar into an esoteric body, as well as in the transmission of Hermetic doctrines to the West. The Byzantine complexity of the medieval Islamic world is revealed, and with it, deep insights into the present world conflict—the "war on terrorism." This book is essential reading for anyone wishing to know more about secret societies, Islam, and their combined role in a historical and contemporary context.

—MARK STAVISH, director of the Institute of Hermetic Studies

I HAVE BEEN ABLE TO GO BACK NINE HUNDRED years and get a feel for this legendary leader. The unfolding history was also great. So much stays the same. Despite the darkness and constant fighting, it was the eternal striving for realization that shines through most in your book. This is an outstanding effort. —CLAIRE DEEM, pianist

JAMES WASSERMAN ESCORTS READERS ON a kaleidoscopic journey from the first stirrings of human civilization to a hurricane millennia later: the birth of the fearsome Assassins. Wasserman's passionate knowledge illuminates the myth, mystery, life and teachings of the semi-mythical Assassin master Hasan-i-Sabah, and shows how these echo through the ages and inform the unrest that continues to reverberate in the Fertile Crescent today. —RICHARD KACZYNSKI, author of *Perdurabo: The Life of Aleister Crowley.*

In 1256, the Mongol invaders destroyed Alamut and its library, thus making it seemingly impossible to distinguish truth from fantasy in understanding the nature of the Assassins and the mystical gnosis that shaped their philosophy. What little we do know has been assumed to be all we could know. But in this essential book, James Wasserman has tirelessly examined all the available evidence and provided a serious and sober assessment of the initiatory society that may well have played a decisive role in the shaping of European history with its influence on the Knights Templar during the Crusades. This book, which I believe is destined to become an essential reference book in this field, stands out for its inclusion of the first English translation of *The Biography of Our Master* by Rashid al-Din, and even more significantly, for the author's lucid and extensive presentation of the mysterious *Qiyama* Doctrine that earned this Order the unrelenting hatred of the Orthodox authorities of their day (such as the Seljuk Sunnis and the Twelver Shiites). I thought there was no more that could be said about the Nizari Ismalis. Thank you James Wasserman for proving me wrong.

—Jon Graham, writer, translator, and acquisitions editor

Also by James Wasserman

The Templars and the Assassins: The Militia of Heaven

An Illustrated History of the Knights Templar

Templar Heresy: A Story of Gnostic Illumination

In the Center of the Fire: A Memoir of the Occult 1966–1989

The Egyptian Book of the Dead: The Book of Going Forth by Day

The Mystery Traditions: Secret Symbols and Sacred Art

The Temple of Solomon: From Ancient Israel to Secret Societies

The Secrets of Masonic Washington: A Guidebook to Signs, Symbols, and Ceremonies at the Origin of America's Capital

The Slaves Shall Serve: Meditations on Liberty

The Book of Days: Perpetual Calendar

To Perfect This Feast: A Performance Commentary on the Gnostic Mass (with Nancy Wasserman)

Pythagoras: His Life and Teachings (as editor) (by Thomas Stanley, with Manly P. Hall, Henry L. Drake, and J. Daniel Gunther)

Secret Societies: Illuminati, Freemasons, and the French Revolution (as editor) (by Una Birch)

Aleister Crowley and the Practice of the Magical Diary (as editor) (by Aleister Crowley and Frater Achad)

AHA! The Sevenfold Mystery of the Ineffable Love (as editor) (by Aleister Crowley, with Frater Achad, Israel Regardie, and J. Daniel Gunther)

The Weiser Concise Guide Series (as editor)

Hasan-i-Sabah
Assassin Master

James Wasserman

Foreword by
Tobias Churton

Including
The Biography of Our Master (*Sar-Guzasht-i-Sayyidna)* by
Rashid al-Din Tabib
Translated and annotated by
Aliasghar Taghipourteroujeni and James Wasserman

Ibis Press
Lake Worth, FL

First edition published 2020 by Ibis Press
An imprint of Nicolas Hays, Inc.
P. O. Box 540206
Lake Worth, FL 33454-0206
www.ibispress.net

Distributed to the trade by
Red Wheel/Weiser, LLC
65 Parker St. • Ste. 7
Newburyport, MA 01950
www.redwheelweiser.com

ISBN 978-0-89254-194-2
Ebook ISBN 978-0-89254-687-9

Library of Congress Cataloging-in-Publication Data
available upon request

Book design and typography by Studio 31
www.studio31.com

Imaginative portrait of Hasan-i-Sabah on the jacket by an unknown 19th century artist, colored by Nancy Wasserman
Background photo of Alamut by Alireza Javaheri

Printed and bound in the United States of America (mv)

Dedication

Glory be to the Living One who dieth not, who createth all creatures and decreeth to them death and who is the First, without beginning and the Last without End!

"and may Almighty Allah do vengeance upon the traitor to bread and salt!"

The Book of a Thousand Nights and a Night

Contents

Appendices

Maps

Foreword

Tobias Churton

Esotericism is at the core of spiritual history.

By the most curious of coincidences, I began writing this introduction in new year 2020, a few hours before a public announcement that the President of the United States had ordered the assassination of Iranian general Qassem Soleimani. This salient fact gave James Wasserman's new book both vivid contrast and alarming, unexpected context in real-time events of the twenty-first century, over nine hundred years after the heyday of the Nizari Ismaili state's founder, Hasan-i-Sabah: archetypal "assassin" and devotee of the One Imam, believed manifest to an enlightened faithful.

James Wasserman's account of "Assassin Master" Hasan-i-Sabah not only sheds light on this somewhat disturbing contemporary parallel but also helps us to understand that Islam is not a monolith of life-threatening, death-loving Jihadists wailing a perennially martial message in unison. Rather, the world's Muslim communities constitute a diverse civilization riven with internal political conflicts, doctrinal dissonances, and perceived deviances, set amid crucial spiritual distinctions between one community and another, operating in a psychological universe where politics and religion are most frequently inseparable and where internal and external conflict must thus seem inevitable. Similar remarks may of course be said of the surviving skeins of Christian civilization in the West, where critical distinctions between sects and parties have—though mostly in the past—most often thriven at civilization's expense.

All who worship—that is, *respect*—the God of Abraham will sooner or later arrive at the arguably illiberal doctrine that the object of worship is "no respecter of persons" (Acts 10:34; Romans 2:11), while also being the God who "desires mercy, not sacrifice" (Hosea 6:6; Matthew 9:13; *cf.* the Islamic Basmala). Followers' follies reflect tensions engendered in such paradoxes, especially when the presumption is that a person (un-respected) is "acting for God" (who desires mercy, not sacrifice).

In addition to helping us grasp the often-tangled structural history of Islam in its first six hundred years or so, James Wasserman opens up the question of the real nature of the followers of the legendary "Old Man of the Mountain" for careful inspection. This figure—almost more a literary than an historical character—emerged from the remarkably controversial career of Hasan-i-Sabah (c. 1050-1124) and the lives and teachings of Hasan's lineal successors; at least, that is, until Mongol invaders wiped out the Nizari Ismaili stronghold of Alamut in the Elburz Mountains of northern Iran in 1256.

The arresting qualities of the leader of the "Assassins" (a term probably derived from contemporary nickname "Hashishim") have entered popular mythology, in books and films frequently outside any specific Islamic milieu. One such example in Donald Cammell and Nicholas Roeg's inimitable movie *Performance* (1969-70), where Mick Jagger—playing reclusive, self-obscured counter-culture rock-star "Turner"—memorably invokes the name of the "Hashishim" and asks, intriguingly, *whether the mountains would be the same without the "bandits,"* while clutching a photograph of a deserted fastness resembling the distant terrain about Alamut—where, we may believe, this latter-day Alastor-Assassin belongs, and where the spirit still lives.

James Wasserman gives us a picture remarkably different to the broadly reported account of Alamut and its environs where, from the time of Marco Polo at least, tales were set of a strange, blood-soaked world dominated by dope-laden, sex-driven, antinomian, and fundamentally-deceived assassins: a picture Wasserman reveals as both travesty and romanticism. He presents us with a convincing, logical thesis as to how this arguably misleading portrait developed. It would certainly not be the first time a mystical movement of profound, far-reaching spiritual content was misrepresented as an anarchically subversive body of perverted obsessives. One thinks of the early Christian Gnostics (dwelling in "an abyss of madness and blasphemy" according to heresiologist Ireneaeus, c. 180 CE), the Moravian "Herrnhuter Brüdergemeine" of German Upper Lusatia (without whom the Methodist Church would never have existed), the sixteenth-century "Family of Love," and not least the Thelemite followers of Aleister Crowley in the twentieth century, whose adherents beyond that century include our author James Wasserman, whose experience lends insightful punch to his re-assessment of the Nizari Ismaili genesis in the twelfth and thirteenth centuries CE.

Personally speaking, I find this book's narrative of the persistence of persecuted knowledge-bearing minorities an inspiring one. Looking at today's Nizari Ismaili communities about the world, and the philanthropic scope of that community's famous leader, Karim al-Husayn Shah, Aga Khan IV (honored by believers as direct descendant of the Prophet Muhammad via his daughter, Fatima), ought to be a revelation to those who have absorbed an image of the Prophet's followers being somehow out of kilter, or even incompatible with the broader movement of liberal (that is, *generous*) human progress on the planet—arguably faltering at this moment—since the fading of the Middle Ages. Contemporary Nizari Ismailis appear, from all but distorted accounts, as a stirringly positive presence upon this insulted planet, now besmirched by incessant, electronically digitized propaganda.

Truth may appear hidden to us. Such hiddenness of Truth in our world bears some analogy to Hasan-i-Sabah's contention that the embodiment of the spirit of Muhammad's real teaching—the living person he believed to be the true Imam (al-Hadi ibn Nizar)—had to be bodily concealed at Alamut to protect him from the murderous corruption of those whose claimed to be faithful to the spirit of the Prophet Muhammad. To Hasan-i-Sabah, it was just that: *a claim*, and no more, for Hasan's enemies did not open themselves to the inner power of the one true Imam: living authority for interpreting doctrine. In his condemnation of those he believed denigrators of the true spirit, Hasan referred most pointedly to the Sunni-adhering leaders of the Seljuk Turks. The Seljuks had overrun Persia in the eleventh century and dominated Hasan's principal enemies, the Abbasid (Sunni) Caliphate, whose power-base, like Alamut, was exterminated by Mongol invaders in 1258.

Hasan-i-Sabah also had enemies in the Shia Ismaili Fatimid Caliphate in Egypt (who did not accept al-Hadi ibn Nizar as Imam), and the "Sevener" Shia Ismailis who regarded Muhammad ibn Ismail (775–813 CE) as the last visible Imam. Then there were the Shia "Twelvers" (today the largest Shia adherence in the Middle East, principally in Iran, with a majority in Iraq and Bahrain) who traced a different lineage of Imams from Ali ibn Abu Talib (600–661 CE) to Muhammad ibn al-Hasan who, though born in 869 CE, was held by Shia Twelvers to be in occultation as the expected Mahdi.

If we are to credit James Wasserman's interpretation of what is known of Hasan-i-Sabah's beliefs, along with his successor Hasan II's extraordinary proclamation of *Qiyama* (Resurrection) at Alamut in 1164, these "Assassin" leaders have a message for us: To believe in a God limited to low categories of human instincts and emotions is an insult to God in whose image Adam was first made. To fail to approach the true scope of Nature is to further insult the Creator. To insult knowledge or to suppress it is to insult the One who is source of all knowing and all truth, and who must therefore be the ultimate goal of knowledge. To stand in right relation to God means standing aside from the repressive and the reactionary-fearful, who, regardless of claims to speak with authority, have insufficient understanding of the depth and height of Him, and in "serving" His Greatness so inadequately do surely denigrate the Great Mystery and Majesty in which by His blessings we all live.

When the characteristics of the false ego are projected onto God, and God is "seen" through that distorting lens, there is hell to pay. Man's ordinary anger and frustration is transported onto "God" and appears as "God's will." Not surprisingly, it accords with the feelings of the ego-bound, delighted to have its God on its side, so to speak.

It was the belief of the Nizari Ismailis—and they are hardly alone in this—that religious scriptures have a meaning beyond the literal appearance of the words as text. To grasp this "esoteric" or deep spiritual meaning, the Nizaris believe the living Imam is required whose spirit is consonant with the spirit in which the words were first heard.

As I write these words, I become immediately aware of how closely they approximate to the spirit of the great stream of Sufi doctrines' approach to ultimate reality and the passing away of the false ego (*al fana*). Therefore it will be no surprise perhaps for readers to learn that after the barbaric Mongol devastation of the Middle East in the thirteenth century, and amid severe persecutions for "heresy," Nizari Ismailis were able to survive the torments of those and subsequent times by living closely amid the *turuk* (paths) of Sufi Masters, with whose doctrines of spiritual knowledge (*marifa*, or gnosis) the Nizari Ismailis find kinship.

Spiritual ideas associated with Nizari Ismailis (particularly the emphasis on *batin* or spiritual core meaning as distinct from *zahir* or outward form) may also be located in what is currently known of the mysticism present among the Mandaeans (Sabians) of Iraq, the Alawi of Syria, Lebanon, and Turkey, and the Kurdish Yezidis of northern Iraq, Armenia, Georgia, and Turkey. All of these communities have suffered baleful persecution over the centuries, while their still-living traditions further resonate with jñāna yoga in India, Sufism (as stated above), and with western Rosicrucian and Gnostic traditions and their offshoots, such as Aleister Crowley's Thelema system, currently represented internationally by Ordo Templi Orientis.

To take just one example, I found the conception of the proclamation of the *Qiyama* made by Hasan II at Alamut deeply akin to the early Christian Gnostics' and Egyptian Hermetists' idea of "realized resurrection" or "realized eschatology" (*palingenesia*, or *apolytrosis*). The "raising" of the spirit from the body of the believer may be accomplished in this life, but only by genuine Gnostic experience, when the individual directly experiences his or her formerly hidden being come alive to perception: a transcendent experience of bursting through the visible bonds of flesh into spiritual, living, transcendent being. This parallel made me wonder in fact whether the nickname "hashishim" might originally have been coined to describe ecstatic states of spiritual union enjoyed by close devotees of Hasan-i-Sabah, on account of common conceptions of the effects of hashish ingestion, which in the East was often linked to frenzies. The comparison would be neatly made with the view of onlookers at the Pentecost experience of Jesus' disciples after they received the Holy Spirit: The account in Acts tells us they saw fire about their heads, and on emergence into public space, were ridiculed for being "drunk" as they communicated in such an extraordinary manner that those who "got it" experienced a kind of "contact high," that is, they understood inwardly without conventional language, as the apostles "babbled" in ecstatic "tongues."

Likewise perhaps, that famous, or infamous, phrase associated with the "Old Man of the Mountains" that "Nothing is true; everything is permitted" (used by Mick Jagger in *Performance* in a libertine sense) seems to me to resonate first with what Renaissance sage Pico della Mirandola maintained in 1486 constituted the "dignity of Man," that is, that Man, spiritually enlightened, was free to fall down or rise up the Great Chain of Being, even unto the consciousness of the angels; and this is what distinguished the "great miracle of Man" from the lower orders of being. This of course is Hermetic Man who knows the bonds of ego, and has discarded them as he spiritually rises.

Secondly, the phrase "nothing is true" not only chimes in rather interestingly with John Lennon's famous visionary line "Nothing is real" in his lyric to "Strawberry Fields Forever" (1966) about recovering a lost childlike and childhood-known ecstasy of freedom from conventional categories of being, but is also of course a realization that beyond known "truth" is an unknown reality that so far transcends the known as to make our ordinary knowledge appear ultimately of little substance. When one has grasped this paradox of truth, one is indeed free to do everything. That does not mean, of course, that one will *choose* to do everything. One may choose liberty rather than license. Once one fully grasps that "everything is permitted," the wisdom that enabled one to understand the phrase's inner meaning will surely make one perspicacious in projecting the highest value from this freedom. Let it be clear: the "religious genius" has always attracted scorn for "breaking the law." The man or woman of truth may expect opposition. And the revelation offered in Hasan II's *Qiyama* might be expressed as, so to speak: "the *sharia* was made for man, not man for the *sharia*." Spiritual truth lies in greater abundance beyond regulations intended to keep bad or misguided people from wrecking the path that leads to ultimate Truth.

It is fascinating to note that among so much that was lost at the hands of Mongol invaders were the libraries of knowledge deliberately and assiduously assembled by Hasan-i-Sabah at Alamut and at other castles in Persia and the Levant under Nizari control. By all accounts, these were not at all sectarian in content but appeared open to all systems of knowledge, and scholars may now only dream about what was once the intellectual currency of those places. In this regard, I find it fascinating that when I have given ear in recent times to the voice of leaders of the Mandaeans, the Yezidis, and the Nizari Ismailis, their top priorities include provision of broad, high-level, modern and professional education facilities for their members, not bounded by sectarian or authoritarian dogmas. Education for these people is anything but indoctrination or even simply passing on what their parents knew. The belief is that knowledge of all arts and sciences opens the mind, and that is a spiritual benefit, for the spiritual person is not afraid of confronting truth; rather he or she is engaged in a lifelong search for it, with determined efforts made to refine that knowledge and see it put to beneficial use for the individual, the community, the world of humanity, and the whole environment in which we live and have our being. *Critical* apparatus is vital for the full development of the mind (reason is a gift of the spirit), and thus we find today in these communities that there appears a link once more between *scientia* (Latin for knowledge, thus "science") and *gnosis* (understood as the expansion of spiritual intelligence), not because one tradition or school "has it all" explicitly, but because God's revelation is in one sense unending, with more to come when the mind is fit, cleansed, and able to receive new wine. The paths to this state are understood as eternal and given, but the paths must be explored anew by every generation: ultimate truth is eternal and may be glimpsed at any point in time, but truth is dynamic, not static. God is limitless. Man then is, as it were, unfinished business as far as God is concerned. This approach to the joy of knowledge contrasts dramatically, even disturbingly, with the indoctrinations and repressions of the "fundamentalist" approach to life. We may seek our spiritual friends wherever they are, but we know where we are unwelcome. Truth is an unwelcome stranger at too many tables set in God's name.

If we seize on to the essential point of James Wasserman's book, we shall find its account inspirational. We sorely need a union of esoteric traditions—in spirit and, where possible, in body—because to use the conception of Hasan-i-Sabah, the truth is in the Imam, and at the point of critical decision, one must choose one door. The authoritative "Imam" is the state of mind in full spiritual union with God's expression, and this truth may take us beyond ordinary human passions and errors. The mind is to be expanded. How else can it even dream of approximating the enormity of the divine vista of things visible and invisible?

Man was made in God's image. Resurrection means being raised again to that image, whence we are fallen.

However, for all the inspiring mystical gnosis, we face the fact that the term most closely associated with the legacy of Hasan-i-Sabah is "Assassin," which, if it did not necessarily mean abusing individual integrity by ingestion of cannabinoids, and whatever may be its true etymology (which Wasserman examines), we know that the power of Hasan and his successors up until the Mongol conquest of Alamut in 1256 (two years before the fall of the Abbasid Caliphate in Baghdad) was politically and religiously targeted assassination.

James Wasserman makes a case for the seventy-five or so recorded assassinations by Hasan and his *fidai*, that is, that they served to exterminate extremely cruel, oppressive, murderous perpetrators of violence against his followers and other political enemies. Furthermore, the practice was used sparingly, with due warnings, and was not bloodthirsty or triumphalist, and undoubtedly saved many innocent lives. There were no "collateral" killings with impunity. Hasan did not have the military strength to oppose directly in the field the full numerical strength of the caliphates that rejected what he believed was the true Imamate, and so assassination might be seen as akin to those who believe it better for political opponents to have to face each other in single combat, rather than dragging hosts of humanity in general into their too-frequently selfish, myopic, sectarian ideological battles.

It is furthermore the case that followers of the Nizari community were willing to suffer the harsh consequences that often followed the elimination of targets, and many thousands consequently suffered death in merciless reprisals as martyrs to their cause. It is hard not to see a parallel here with today's "preachers of hate" who encourage suicide bombers to kill perfect strangers, all for promises of sweet scents of imagined paradise offered as a reward for alleged "services" to God. The Assassins' targets were specific, and their victims deeply involved in violent machinations against the faithful, as Hasan perceived them. Had Hasan the military might emanating from the Pentagon at his disposal, it is fairly certain he would not have resorted to assassination, except perhaps to save the lives of innocents in very rare and specific circumstances. It should also be noted that in the period under discussion, to remove the head of a political group was most often to send its entire following into long-term disarray. Nowadays, every job has a queue of would-be place-fillers behind it, though they might leave the queue if convinced they were next "for the chop." But there's always someone to take the place, though they might prove significantly weaker, or even willing to ameliorate causes for the most deadly opposition.

Civilized governments have in the past eschewed overt assassination as a policy because it opens the moral door for like-inspired reprisals, and leaders of "free nations" would be loath to step into the role were assassination the grammar of daily political discourse. There are doubtless extreme cases, but "hard cases make bad law."

A fact of life: all actions have consequences. The place today of Nizari Ismailis in the real world suggests their past leaders have survived the tumults of the Middle Ages and flourished in the modern world by having found wisdom of thought, word, and deed, finding thereby a rich, broad, and generous idea of humanity in the context of the One God, the compassionate, the merciful. The days of assassination—at least for them—are over.

—England
January 2020

Introduction

> Whether or not the Bible legend is true that it was Man's presumption in building the Tower of Babel which caused the multiplicity of languages in the world, the punishment was very severe; and it falls with especial severity upon historians.
>
> —Steven Runciman[1]

PERHAPS NOWHERE is a historian's objectivity or subjectivity more obvious to him or her self, or to the reader, than in seeking to understand a historical/legendary person of another era, culture, and language who lived nine hundred years ago. This is especially the case when his voluminous writings and carefully assembled library were ruthlessly destroyed by those who conquered his survivors some 130 years after his death. The intention of these attackers was to erase his and his followers' legacy from the pages of history. Add to this the controversies that have swirled around his name since he established his fortress and community in the year 1090, and you have a recipe for many conflicting opinions.

Hasan-i-Sabah has been idolized as a true man of God, a revolutionary religious genius, and a brilliant political organizer; and he has been widely despised as a heretic, a murderer, and a cynical manipulator. The sheer hatred dripping from the pages of Ata-Malik Juvaini's thirteenth-century account of Hasan is offset by the almost tender picture of Hasan presented in Jawad al-Muscati's excellent but obscure twentieth-century biography. While the truth may be elusive, this writer unashamedly embraces the more positive view of Hasan-i-Sabah, while clearly acknowledging (in fact celebrating) him for the heretic I believe he was.

By the word "heretic" I mean that Hasan was a religious and political innovator. He defined Truth as he understood it, and rejected all attempts to control his thought by the many who claimed to know

[1] Steven Runciman in his foreword to J. A. Boyle (trans. and ed.) and Ata-Malik Juvaini, *Genghis Khan: The History of the World Conqueror*, p. vii.

better. He carved out a headquarters for himself and his faithful by sheer force of will, and a command of the strategic and tactical levers of power that has rarely been equaled. I am grateful for the opportunity to know him better through this book.

It may be said that Hasan-i-Sabah founded and operated the world's most successful mystical secret society, while building a political territory in which to maintain his independence. The small empire he created would be home to him, his followers, and their descendants for 166 years. The religion he founded is alive and well today (though in far different form) under the leadership of the forty-ninth Imam. Originating in Persia, Hasan sent missionaries to extend the teachings of his sect to Syria, India, and Afghanistan. The Nizari Ismailis, or Assassins, survived and often flourished against the two most powerful dynasties of the medieval Muslim world of their day: the Abbasid Caliphate in Baghdad and the Seljuk Sultanate in Persia.

Hasan's circumstances called for the operation of a true conspiratorial apparatus at all levels. The Nizaris were surrounded by hostile Seljuk Sunnis and often almost equally hostile Twelver Shiites, no friend to the Ismaili schismatics. The precarious situation the Assassins faced has been characterized by historian and scholar Marshall Hodgson in these words:

> Our concern will be with the fate of an aspiring minority group, whose religious and social orientation had been rejected by the bulk of Islamic society; and who were faced with a steadily hardening pattern of orthodox life, hostile to them, and which they could not accept. Such were the Nizaris in the Twelfth Century in the countries of the Middle East.[1]

Those Ismailis (and, later, Nizari Ismailis) who attained to professional positions in education or government were forced to keep the truth of their spiritual and religious beliefs secret. The Assassins

---

1 Marshall G. S. Hodgson, *The Order of Assassins: The Struggle of the Early Nizari Ismailis Against the Islamic World*, p. 1.

were considered heretics, *malahida*, who rejected Sunni orthodoxy and Shia consensus, and who were rebellious political opponents of the rule of the state.

The story of Hasan and the Nizari Ismailis is filled with a great deal of myth and legend, some far less true than others; but they have all circulated in the literature for a very long time. Perhaps the least true, and most well-known and romantic, is the Garden of Paradise tale from Marco Polo (see appendix one). For eight hundred years it has captivated creative people who can intertwine romance with reality and lose neither rationality nor fascination. I am fully aware that it has also provided a rallying point for the cynical, the fearful, the disparaging, and the corrupt.

Myth, by definition, is imaginative, but it provides unique intuitive gateways to deeper truth. I offer extensive citations from the Quran describing the Garden of Paradise to contextualize the origins of the story, and which may help to explain why it has been so long-lived.

This book will spend time in Part One, chapters one and two, exploring the Mesopotamian and Persian milieux out of which Hasan and his community arose. In chapter three, we will explore some extremely important developmental issues in the growth of Islam, including some of the outer fringes of orthodoxy. This will help to better understand our subject: Hasan-i-Sabah was a Persian who was raised a Twelver Shiite; he converted to Ismailism; preached that doctrine far and wide for two decades; and then founded and nurtured the Nizari Ismaili schism to the end of his life. While all these terms and concepts will be carefully examined in Part One, I realize that many readers will want to make the immediate jump to Hasan's biography in Part Two.

It is important to realize that the Islam of his day was the product of only three to four centuries in a region of the world which had not only many thousands of years of history behind it, but a wealth of contrasting religious ideals to build upon. Sometimes when studying the belief systems attributed to the Nizaris, one becomes incredulous at the sophistication and almost multi-dimensional nature of the ideas attributed to them. However, by understanding their roots in the multiplicity of vibrant, multi-ethnic, and diverse spiritualities, religions, and cults of the Near East, it all becomes less foreign.

I acknowledge that Hasan and the Nizaris were exceedingly pious Muslims. This presents something of a quandary because the author is neither a Muslim, nor an Ismaili or Nizari Ismaili. I can say things, draw conclusions, even engage in imaginings (which will be carefully distinguished as such in the text) without violating my own beliefs. Therefore, I must apologize in advance to any Nizaris who believe I have transgressed their faith by celebrating Hasan as an all-inclusive transformative religious agent. How does one praise the Sufis, for example, without offending some of the pious Muslims who persecuted, reviled, and even killed them in past ages?

There are certain advantages an outsider's perspective can bring to such a book. Like Hasan, I was raised in a religion that did not serve my needs when I felt the call of the Holy Spirit in later adolescence. At that time in his life, Hasan explored Ismailism and gradually embraced it, later splintering off to establish the Nizari Ismailis. I came to Western Esotericism as a result of my spiritual awakening, and, in time, was inspired by the Law of Thelema and the teachings of Aleister Crowley. But again, like Hasan, my understanding of Thelema is intensely personal—the result of my culture, my personality, and the many and mysterious threads that weave themselves together to create a human being. I, thus, see in Hasan-i-Sabah a universality that transcends medieval Persia, or even Islam. If anything, I appreciate him as a Sufi, a Gnostic who danced to his own tune because of the intensity of the contact he felt with God. I find him an example, almost an archetype of independent thought, unrepentant courage, and religious creativity.

A second thematic factor to be noted here is the overarching combination of politics and religion in this story, and Islam in general. Many modern Westerners, proclaiming the "separation of Church and State," do not understand that, in Islam, the Church *is* the State. Shiism, and later Ismailism, and later still Nizari Ismailism, were all political revolutionary movements in addition to being religious and doctrinal reorganizations of Islam. They offered spiritual integrity in opposition to the corrupt state of ruling Sunni dynasties. They fought against the political machinations of the majority of Shiites. Their opposition extended even to the malfeasance of the Ismaili Fatimid dynasty in Egypt, where military strongmen and warlords inhibited the teachings of the legitimate Imam of his day. Further, the Shiite/Ismaili/Nizari proselytizing offered a home to non-Arabs. They conducted their efforts among the dispossessed and outsider groups within Persia, Syria, and Mesopotamia.

My interest in Hasan-i-Sabah was clearly stimulated by his being a mythic and mysterious character. Yet the more I filled in my visionary image with the facts, the more interesting he became. I was initially drawn to Hasan as a result of my interest in secret societies. Like him, I embrace a spiritual path that is new, controversial, and growing in influence as a result of a network of trained people reaching out to others. I, too, have written and published much, communicated extensively by all available media of my day, and traveled widely in an attempt to share a revolutionary spiritual doctrine. Psychologically I believe that, perhaps like Hasan, I have carved out a territory in which I can cultivate and practice my own spiritual path—having long ago dispensed with outside interpretations and authoritarian teachings that proved unsuccessful to my personal understanding. I, too, have raised a family and been associated with a community of others who share my beliefs. "Nothing is true, everything is permitted" is a statement (probably falsely) attributed to Hasan-i-Sabah. Yet when contemplating its meaning, I hear a conceptual ring to Crowley's "Do what thou wilt shall be the whole of the Law."

The possibility of greatest interest to the Western reader is, of course, the idea that is present in both history and legend crediting the Syrian Assassins as the initiators of the Knights Templar during the Crusades. If this is true, then Hasan-i-Sabah would be partly responsible for stimulating the European Renaissance that would reclaim the spiritual centrality of the Hermetic writings. While these had been lost to the West for some nine hundred years before being rediscovered and translated into Latin in Florence, they had been preserved by the Persians.

Another factor of interest is the concept of an initiatory society of graded spiritual ascent that is known to have been part of the Shia teaching, expanded upon by their Ismaili derivatives, and developed into an art form by the Nizaris. All these terms will be explained and explored as we go. However, whatever the truth of the content of Hasan's Seven or Nine Degrees of Wisdom, we know he administered an initiatory system. Peter Lamborn Wilson goes so far as to suggest that the Ninth Degree secret was openly revealed by Hasan II *ala dhikrhi al salam* (upon whose mention be peace) when he proclaimed the *Qiyama* in 1164.[1]

The *Qiyama* doctrine is so mysterious, esoteric, and controversial that it will be discussed at some length here. I believe it may have been one of the most profound and revolutionary concepts ever uttered and embraced by a religious community. The *Qiyama* declared the immanence of the "Inner Imam," what Crowley called the "True Will." The inner essence of an individual's spiritual reality and personal source of guidance was asserted to be superior to any rule-making or forced adherence to outer forms of behavior. Hasan II extended his revelation to the entire Nizari community. In my novel *Templar Heresy*, I make clear my belief that the truth of this revelation—first proclaimed by a white-robed Nizari Imam in the mountain fortress of Alamut—caused the heavens to reverberate ever since.

Finally, and meaning no disrespect, I think it is indisputable that Hasan's lasting fascination in Western culture must be attributed, in part, to his personification of the rebel and iconoclast, sworn to a more austere standard. Hasan lived outside the law of his day—though perhaps no one of his time was more observant of the higher law to which his life was dedicated. Stephen Knight, discussing Robin Hood, makes this point:

> The good outlaw: The idea attracts attention in every culture. Someone rejects conventional law, breaks it, is exiled from it,

---

[1] Peter Lamborn Wilson, *Scandal: Essays in Islamic Heresy*, pp. 50–52.

> is pursued and imprisoned by its agents, but somehow always escapes and somehow always represents a system of social and personal order that is better than what we have now. . . . Myths of this utopian kind can be personalized: a single figure can bear the meaning of the resistance to oppressive circumstances.[1]

So LET US NOW EMBARK on a journey through the Elburz Mountains of northern Persia at the southern end of the Caspian Sea. We will range far and wide through the Holy Land, the Mediterranean, Egypt, Arabia, Mesopotamia, India, and China. This journey has brought me closer to myself and it continues to fuel the passion for spiritual unity that has been the basis of my life. I hope it may have a similar effect for the reader.[2]

---

1 Stephen Knight, *Robin Hood: A Mythic Biography*, p. xi.

2 My 2001 book *The Templars and Assassins: The Militia of Heaven* covers some of the same ground in both the development of Islam and the history of the Nizari Ismailis. While that book is more widely focused to include the Knights Templar, the Crusades, European history, and more details on Hasan's successors and the history of the Nizaris after the loss of Alamut, this book is more narrowly concerned with Hasan-i-Sabah himself. However, the attentive reader will note that this book, of necessity, draws on much of my earlier research.

A Bibliographic Note

> On their way they [the Mongol invaders of 1256] destroyed the Assassins' sanctuary at Alamut and sacked its library of inestimable value, thus making it almost impossible for future generations to gain any in-depth knowledge of the doctrine and activities of the sect. —Amin Maalouf[1]

There are two primary sources for the life of Hasan-i-Sabah (ca. 1050–1124). The first is by Ata-Malik Juvaini (ca. 1226–1283), who finished his writing about 1260. The second is by Rashid al-Din Tabib (1247–1318), who completed his work between 1307 and 1316.

Juvaini was attached to the Mongol ruler Huelgu, a grandson of Genghis Khan. Huelgu conquered Alamut in 1256. Juvaini was assigned the task of exploring and then destroying the famed Alamut Library. He picked out certain works of interest and burned the rest.

Juvaini discovered (and preserved for a time) the manuscript of the *Sar-Guzasht-i-Sayyidna* (*The Biography of Our Master*), the story of Hasan-i-Sabah. The *Sar-Guzasht-i-Sayyidna* is autobiographical in the beginning and then is continued as a narrative by another hand. Extracts and a synopsis were published in Juvaini's classic history of the world of his day, *Ta-rikh-i-Jahan Gusha*, translated and published in English as *Genghis Khan: The History of the World Conqueror*.[2] Juvaini describes his editorial efforts regarding the manuscript of the *Sar-Guzasht-i-Sayyidna*, "From this work I have copied whatever was to the point and suitable for insertion in this history, adducing whatever was confirmed and verified."[3] Juvaini's hatred of Hasan-i-Sabah and the Assassins mirrored that of his Mongol employers and runs through nearly every page of his history of the group.

---

[1] Amin Maalouf (trans. John Rothschild), *The Crusades Through Arab Eyes*, p. 242.

[2] Ata-Malik Juvaini, J. A. Boyle (trans. and ed.), *Genghis Khan: The History of the World Conqueror (Ta-rikh-i-Jahan-Gusha).*

[3] Juvaini, *Genghis Khan*, p. 666.

Rashid al-Din was a Persian historian and politician who followed a generation after Juvaini. He published an equally ambitious world history known as the *Jami al-Tavarikh*, or *Collection of Histories*. In it, he offered an expanded version of the text of *Sar-Guzasht-i-Sayyidna*. This may have been derived from either Juvaini's unedited copy or his extensive notes, as Juvaini most likely destroyed the original Nizari manuscript. It is also possible that Rashid al-Din used additional sources, as his writings are more extensive. Rashid al-Din's grandfather, Muwaffaq al-Dawla Ali, had been a guest at Alamut for some time when the Nizaris surrendered to Huelgu. He then entered Huelgu's service, leaving open the possibility that he and Rashid al-Din had access to other Ismaili materials.[1] Like Juvaini, Rashid al-Din was working for the Mongol Ilkhanate dynasty, so his work retains, at times, an unsympathetic editorial slant, although he is far more objective, fair, and friendly than his predecessor.

Rashid al-Din's longer version of the text of *The Biography of Our Master* had not been translated into English before the present volume was able to correct that situation. With thanks to Aliasghar Taghipourteroujeni, a New York University Kevorkian Center scholar whose skilled and determined efforts have finally made this crucial text available to an English-speaking readership. We await a full English translation of Rashid al-Din's entire discussion of the Nizari Ismailis, which extends well past the death of Hasan until the destruction of Alamut. Again, the translation offered here is solely that of the biography of Hasan.

I also present a reputed letter exchange between Sultan Malikshah and Hasan-i-Sabah, first published in 1687–1688, which contains additional biographical details of Hasan. Although the authenticity of these two letters has been challenged, and they have been translated into English in two volumes of more limited availability,[2] I determined it best to include Aliasghar's new translation because of their interest.

---

[1] Farhad Daftary, *The Ismailis: Their History and Doctrines*, p. 329.

[2] Namely, Jawad al-Muscati, *Hasan Bin Sabbah*, and Dr. Ali Mohammad Rajput, *Hasan-i-Sabbah: His Life and Thought*. See bibliography.

I MAKE EXTENSIVE USE of five of the eight volumes of the superb *The Cambridge History of Iran*. After the initial mention with the full title, volumes are identified in footnotes as *CHI*. See bibliography.

Finally, the reader will note that, for our mutual convenience, I make almost no use of diacritical marks, choosing instead to render foreign terms as closely as possible to their general usage and pronunciation in English. An example of this is my use of the term "Ismaili" rather than "Ismā`īlī."

PART ONE

Historical Background

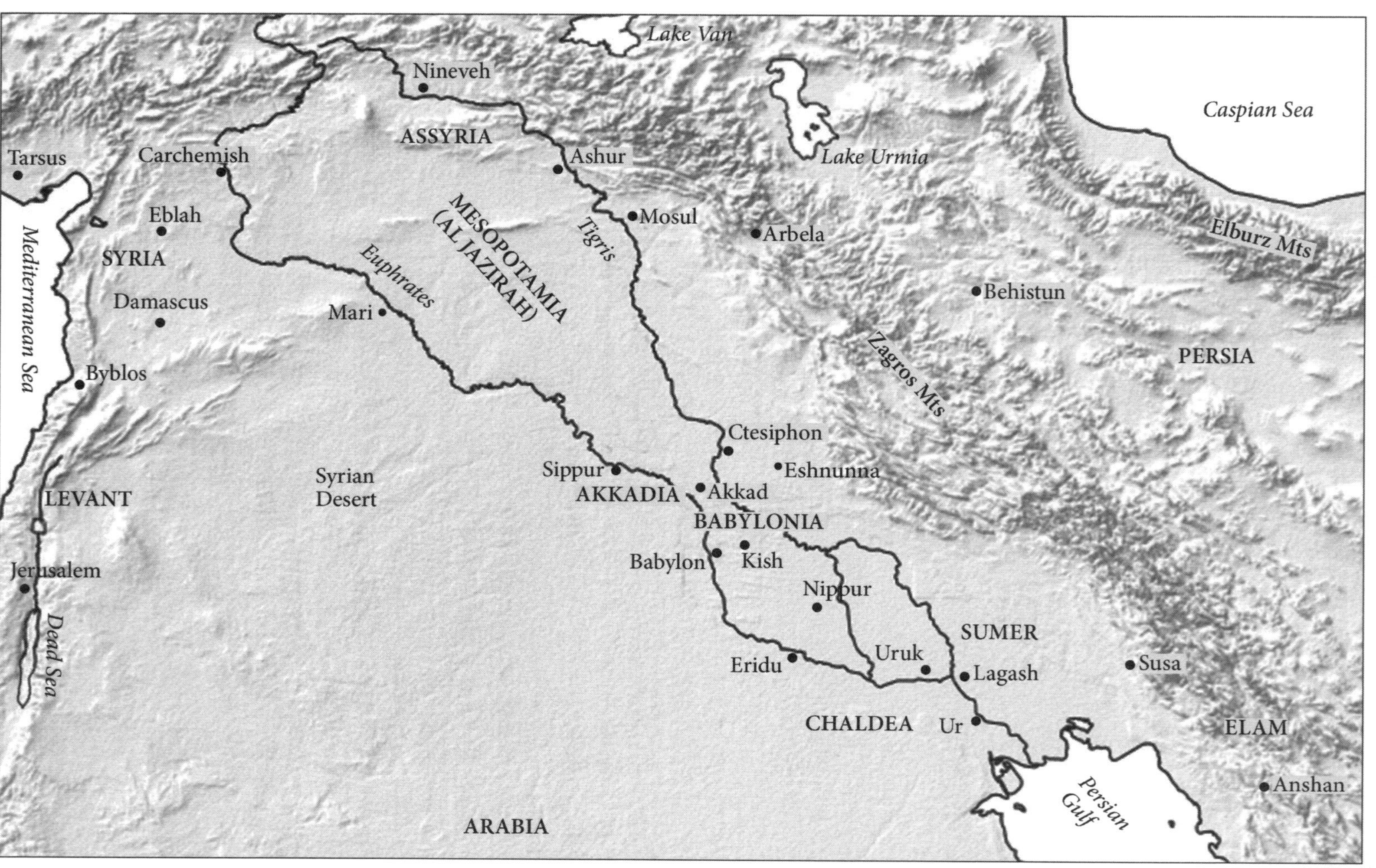
Lake Van
Nineveh
Caspian Sea
ASSYRIA
Lake Urmia
Tarsus
Carchemish
Ashur
Eblah
Mosul
Arbela
Mediterranean Sea
MESOPOTAMIA
(AL JAZIRAH)
Tigris
Elburz Mts
SYRIA
Euphrates
Behistun
Damascus
Mari
Byblos
Zagros Mts
PERSIA
Ctesiphon
Sippur
Eshnunna
Syrian
Desert
LEVANT
AKKADIA
Akkad
BABYLONIA
Babylon
Kish
Jerusalem
Nippur
Dead Sea
SUMER
Uruk
Eridu
Lagash
Susa
CHALDEA
Ur
ELAM
Persian
Gulf
Anshan
ARABIA

CHAPTER ONE

A Brief History of Mesopotamia

> God is He having the head of the Hawk. The same is the first, incorruptible eternal, unbegotten, indivisible, dissimilar: the dispenser of all good; indestructible; the best of the good, the Wisest of the wise; he is the Father of Equity and Justice, self-taught, physical, perfect, and wise—He who inspires the Sacred Philosophy. —*The Chaldean Oracles of Zoroaster*[1]

IN ORDER to contextualize the environment into which Hasan-i-Sabah was born and flourished, it will be helpful to review the history of Mesopotamia and Persia. Mesopotamia (modern Iraq) has long shared a most indefinite border with Persia (modern Iran) and northern Syria, and, as we will see, these regional powers were intimately involved with each other's histories for millennia—as they are to this day. While Hasan's family roots lay in southern Arabia, we will soon follow his wide-ranging travels in support of his missionary efforts throughout Mesopotamia and the land of his birth, the exotic realm of Persia.

Let's look first at the Near East (or Middle East) and the legacy of the world's cradle of civilization. (For clarity, "Near East" will here refer to the lands between the eastern Mediterranean and central Iran, and from the Black Sea to the Red Sea, excluding Egypt.)[2] By necessity, this survey will be quite limited, touching only on some of the main points of the millennia of history of the region, and only some of the cultures, city-states, kingdoms, and empires that shaped our common history. All dates in this chapter are BC unless otherwise noted.

---

1 William Wynn Westcott (trans. and ed.), *Collectanea Hermetica*, p. 23.

2 This lucid territorial description is given by Marc Van De Mieroop in *A History of the Ancient Near East: ca. 3000–323 BC*, p. 1.

Humankind emerged long before the keeping of written records. "Modern humans became established in the Near East by the Late Pleistocene, around 55,000 to 35,000 years ago."[1] "But, a continuous and persistent society was late in coming. It came into being first in the Near East, and thus the historical tradition of Babylon and Egypt became the fountainhead of our historical memory."[2] The uninterrupted roots of Near Eastern settlements and communities extend as far back as the year 10,000, with the final melting of the glaciers after the last Ice Age—the beginning of the current Holocene Epoch—and the evolution from the hunter-gatherer social organization to that of the herdsmen and farmers who cultivated and raised wheat, barley, goats, cattle, and sheep; and the urban dwellers who offered markets and facilitated trade and commerce in such items.

Mesopotamia (Greek for "between two rivers"—the land between the Tigris and Euphrates) is the birthplace of Western civilization. It was host to several empires and innumerable cultures. It is part of the region known as the Fertile Crescent, whose lands were periodically inundated by the Tigris, Euphrates, and Nile Rivers. Rising waters brought silt to nourish the soil, or were capable of being productively utilized, as is the case with the Jordan River. People learned to harness the powers of irrigation, levees, reservoirs, and dams so that the development of agricultural civilizations throughout the region commenced.

In the early seventh millennium, small irrigation systems appeared in the foothills of the Zagros Mountains in the region of Elam (see below), as well as the marshlands of southern Babylonia.[3] The need to manage water flow and crops was a great key to socializing people in a cooperative culture, to manage tasks which far exceeded the ability of a single individual. At the same time, the need to observe, calculate,

---

[1] Trevor Bryce and Jessie Birkett-Rees, *Atlas of the Ancient Near East: From Prehistoric Times to the Roman Imperial Period*, p. 21.

[2] John A. Garraty and Peter Gay (eds.), *The Columbia History of the World*, p. 49.

[3] I. M. Diakonoff, "Elam," in Ilya Gershevitch (ed.), *The Cambridge History of Iran, Volume 2: The Median and Achaemenian Periods*, p. 2.

and experiment was crucial to the ability to succeed. In the hunter/gatherer phase of human development, people foraged through wide areas and moved with the wildlife. If a place was "hunted out" or "foraged out," the community would trek on to the next target area. No permanent housing was part of such a nomadic lifestyle. All this changed with the development of agriculture, herding, and water management. Agriculture is the key to settled civilizations. The varying sources of sustenance in Mesopotamia would include herding, fishing, hunting, and growing crops, and would encourage specialization of tasks over time. Add to these the urban craftspeople who provided woven fabrics, pottery, jewelry, monumental art and statuary, in addition to writing and record-keeping services, and the traders who successfully moved all such goods and services along to others.

The history of Persia and Mesopotamia is that of the interaction between Semitic and non-Semitic peoples. According to historian Will Durant, the term "Aryan" is properly applied only to the eastern branch of the Indo-European people, "the Mitannians, Hittites, Medes, Persians, and Vedic Hindus."[1] Scholar Richard Foltz says that all languages within the Indo-European family extend to a common source located in the Eurasian steppes of the Ural Mountains and east to Siberia, at least to the fourth millennium. In time, the derivative language groups included Celtic, German, and Greek.[2] The Semitic languages developed in the eastern Mediterranean and Africa and included Hebrew, Arabic, Syrian, Aramaic, Assyrian, Amhamric, Tigrinya, Maltese, Phoenician, Ugaritic, and Akkadian.[3] The Aryans and Semites co-existed together and both language groups were long in simultaneous use. As noted by historian Paul Kriwaczek:

> The civilization that was born, flourished and died in the land between the rivers was not the achievement of any particular people, but the result of the coming together and persistence

---

1 Will Durant, *Our Oriental Heritage: The Story of Civilization*, vol. 1, p. 286. See also p. 356.

2 Richard Foltz, *Iran in World History*, pp. 1–2.

3 https://en.wikipedia.org/wiki/Semitic_languages [accessed May 4, 2019].

> through time of a unique combination of ideas, styles, beliefs, and behaviors. The Mesopotamian story is that of a single continuous cultural tradition, even though its human bearers and propagators were different at different times.[1]

Some of the accomplishments and innovations of our remarkable progenitors include the development of cities, agriculture, and irrigation; commerce and trade, including imports and exports; monotheism and monogamy; the wheel, and the use of the horse and wagon; coinage and letters of credit; crafts and industries, including the use of the potter's kiln, manufacture of fine furniture, cosmetics and jewelry, along with architecture, brick-making, and massive construction efforts; codes of law and evolving forms of government to include relative democracy, tyranny, central planning, and empire building; concepts such as private property, the divine right of kings, and the rights of the individual; myth, theology, and religion; income tax; mathematics, medicine, geometry, and astronomy; the use of weights and measures; the calendar, clock, and zodiac; writing, the alphabet, paper, ink, books, literature, libraries, and schools; indoor plumbing; music and sculpture; as well as games such as checkers, dice, and tenpins.[2] The concept of an intimate and personal relation with deity extends earlier in Mesopotamia than elsewhere, at least to the second or third millennium. It would reach Egypt during the Amarna period (beginning in the mid-fourteenth century) and Israel soon after, as exemplified in the Psalms of King David (ca. 1000).[3]

Discussing the evolution of government forms, particularly in the Mesopotamian region during the historical period, Marc Van De Mieroop summarizes:

---

[1] Paul Kriwaczek, *Babylon: Mesopotamia and the Birth of Civilization*, p. 12.

[2] Durant, *Our Oriental Heritage*, p. 116; Kriwaczek, *Babylon*, p. 11 ff; and Samuel Noah Kramer, *History Begins at Sumer: Thirty-Nine Firsts in Recorded History*, pp. 3 ff.

[3] Thorkild Jacobsen, *The Treasures of Darkness: A History of Mesopotamian Religion*, pp. 152 ff.

> The city-state was the primary political element from 3000 to approximately 1600, territorial states dominated the scene from that point on to the early first millennium, and empires characterized later history.[1]

The first identifiable temple building project in Mesopotamia dates to the mid-sixth millennium in the city of Eridu near the Persian Gulf. Subsequent building on the same site extended to the third millennium.[2] Later temple construction in Uruk would have involved a huge workforce with archaeologists estimating fifteen thousand workers laboring ten hours a day for five years.[3] Such figures are mirrored in Egypt in the construction of the Great Pyramid. Dr. Ogden Goelet estimates that the Great Pyramid's 2.5 million blocks, weighing 1.5 tons each, would have required fifty years of labor at ten hours per day to complete.[4] Such numbers in both civilizations speak to a massive planning and administrative apparatus, along with the likelihood of compulsion.

In addition to being places of worship, temples served as communal centers in the practical lives of the ancient Near East. Each city was identified as the home of a particular deity, protected by that deity, and the temple understood as His or Her domicile. Food and goods, collected as offerings to the gods, were distributed to the people in a process managed by administrators, who developed accounting methods and record-keeping to facilitate efficiency. Thus was developed the bureaucracy with its hierarchies of professionals. In time, laborers and other less-skilled workers became dependent on the temple administrators for distribution of rations.[5]

Active trading networks were also an essential part of the ancient Near East. People trafficked in raw materials such as lumber, tin, and

---

[1] Van De Mieroop, *A History of the Ancient Near East*, p. 3.

[2] Ibid., p. 17.

[3] Ibid., p. 24.

[4] Ogden Goelet, *The Egyptian Book of the Dead: The Book of Going Forth by Day* (third edition), p. 29.

[5] Van De Mieroop, *A History of the Ancient Near East*, pp. 28–30.

copper; luxury items such as gold, silver, semi-precious and precious stones; silks and other exotic fabrics, and dyes; incenses, herbs, and spices. There was a lively interaction with Arabia and India through the Persian Gulf; Europe across the land route of Anatolia[1] (Turkey) or via the Mediterranean Sea; and Egypt across the Red Sea or along the land route through southern Israel.

Elam / Susa

We continue this broad survey of our ancient historical roots among some dozen Mesopotamian peoples with Elam. Because of its location, Elam served as an essential transit point between Persia and Mesopotamia, a conduit between both lands and cultures. However, it was itself a significant actor in the saga of the Near East and the many other participants we will highlight in this chapter.

The ancient Persian city of Susa (modern Shush or Shushan) in Elam gives evidence of an advanced civilization as early as 5000–4500.[2] It is located some two hundred miles northeast of the Persian Gulf and about thirty-five miles east of the Tigris River, sitting just west of the foothills of the Zagros Mountains in the region of southwestern Iran now known as Khuzestan Province. Mountain ranges provided natural defensive barriers against invasion. It is mentioned in the biblical books of Esther, Nehemiah, and Daniel, and was Elam's capital.

Elamite civilization extended over two thousand years from the third to mid-first millennium, with military and commercial interests in Persia, Mesopotamia, and Syria. At its height (2100–1500), Elam reached all the way north to the Caspian Sea,[3] thus predating the Assassin community in that region by some three thousand years.

---

[1] The name Anatolia is derived from the Greek word for "sunrise" (i.e., to the east of Greece). Bryce and Birkett-Rees, *Atlas of the Ancient Near East*, p. 41.

[2] Durant, *Our Oriental Heritage*, p. 117

[3] Bryce and Birkett-Rees, *Atlas of the Ancient Near East*, p. 78.

Elam marks the first appearance of the wagon wheel and potter's wheel.[1] Susa, along with the Sumerian city-state of Uruk, was involved in developing pictographic representations of objects and quantity long before the development of writing.[2] Susa's hot, dry atmosphere encouraged the Elamites to develop skills in irrigation to allow for agriculture.

In the north of Susa, Elam's two primary deities were the mother goddess Pininkir and her husband Humban, heads of the pantheon since the Awan dynasty (ca. 2200). Humban's cult continued at least until the Achaemenid dynasty of Darius I (r. 522–486). Humban is identified with the Mesopotamian deity Enlil, head of the Sumerian pantheon. In the south of Susa was the cult of Napirisha and his consort Kiririsha, who seem over time to have ousted Humbam and Pininkir as the heads of the Elamite royal pantheon. Napirisha was identified with the Babylonian god Ea. The famed temple ziggurat of Choga Zanbil (originally called Al-Untash-Napirisha) was constructed by the Elamite king Untash-Napirisha (r. 1340–1300, or 1275–1240). The temple was apparently an attempt to combine and resolve the different pantheons of Elam.[3]

Elamite armies long battled the armies of ancient Sumer. The first Sumerian invasion took place around the year 2700.[4] But Elam was also a pivotal part of the Sumerian trade network, and Susa would serve as the route for Sumerian culture to extend into Persia. Some 250 miles to the southeast of Susa was the city of Anshan, which ruled

---

1 Durant, *Our Oriental Heritage*, p. 117

2 Van De Mieroop, *A History of the Ancient Near East*, p. 32.

3 Karel van der Toorn, Bob Becking, and Pieter W. van der Horst (eds.), *Dictionary of Deities and Demons in the Bible (DDD)*, pp. 432–434 and 489–490. The problem is complicated by earlier scholars (as late as the 1970s) concluding that Humban and Napirisha were different names for the same deity. This theory was abandoned only as recently as 1980. See also Van De Mieroop, *A History of the Ancient Near East*, p. 197. He writes that the massive ziggurat was dedicated to Napirisha, the patron deity of Elam, and Inshushinak, the patron deity of Susa.

4 Diakonoff, "Elam," in Gershevitch (ed.), *CHI*, vol. 2, p. 7.

over the highlands of the southern Zagros Mountains. In the mid- to late-second millennium, both cities were part of the greater territory of Elam. Kings of this period were known as the "King of Susa and Anshan."[1] Elam was finally conquered by the Assyrian emperor Ashurbanipal (r. 668–631) in 646, and later incorporated into the Persian Achaemenid Empire of Cyrus II, the Great, in the mid-sixth century. Its ancient culture would remain an important influence on Persia and the world that was to be inherited by our protagonist.

Sumer / Uruk

Sumer, located at the northern end of the Persian Gulf, was the southernmost and oldest civilization in Mesopotamia. The life of Sumer extended for over three thousand years and encompassed several different archaeological periods. It began in the prehistoric days of the fifth millennium and lasted until its conquest by Elam at the beginning of the second.[2] Uruk, Sumer's most important city, was founded ca. 4500–4000. It grew to become "the first true city in world history . . . a massive settlement . . . perhaps ten times the size of any of its contemporaries."[3] The culture of Uruk was so significant, its name is used to designate the prehistoric near-millennium that preceded the development of writing and extended to 3100.

During the Uruk Period, people streamed into cities, leaving behind the traditional lifestyles of their scattered rural villages. (At the same time, it should be noted that cities must be part of a more elaborate landscape that includes the smaller surrounding towns and villages which engage in agriculture and the pastoral activities that supply the urban centers with needed resources.) Temples were erected to local deities, and the terraced ziggurat designs towered over the landscape, impressing those who saw them in their travels. Uruk was ruled at one time by the legendary King Gilgamesh, immortal-

---

[1] Van De Mieroop, *A History of the Ancient Near East*, pp. 58 and 197.

[2] Samuel Noah Kramer, *The Sumerians: Their History, Culture, and Character*, p. vii.

[3] Van De Mieroop, *A History of the Ancient Near East*, p. 23.

ized in *The Epic of Gilgamesh.* He seems to have been a historical king reigning around 2600.[1]

The Epic of Gilgamesh anticipated the biblical story of Noah and popularized one of the earliest flood myths, in which humanity is drowned for its sins (the irritating clamor that disturbed the peace of the powerful deity Enlil). In one version, a righteous man, the Sumerian Ziusudra, and his family are warned by the god Enki to build an ark that can house pairs of all creatures in safety.[2] In another version, the pious king Utnapishtim (the Semitic name of Ziusudra) is instructed by the Sun god Utu to do the same. The flood is unleashed by Enlil, and Ziusudra/Utnapishtim and the paired creatures of earth survive. While the final form of the story was finished in the seventh century under the reign of the aforementioned Ashurbanipal, the myth was probably written down at the turn of the second millennium and was widely known throughout the ancient Near East from Anatolia to the Mediterranean.[3] A similar flood story is presented in the later Akkadian/Babylonian story of Atrahasis, another favorite of Enki, also saved by building an ark.[4]

Sumer included the ancient city of Ur, the biblical birthplace of the patriarch Abraham, some forty-five miles southeast of Uruk, along with the cities of Kish, Lagash, and Eridu, all in proximity to modern Basra. Sumerian civilization and the city of Uruk itself mark the first appearance of writing (cuneiform) sometime around the year 3300, although the use of seals for identification of either individuals or offices involved in certifying contents had been in use for some three thousand years by this time.[5] Sumer's use of cylinder seals spread to Egypt, which developed its hieroglyphic language about a

---

[1] Kramer, *The Sumerians*, pp. 49–50.

[2] Jacobsen, *The Treasures of Darkness*, p. 114.

[3] Samuel Noah Kramer, *History Begins at Sumer,* pp. 148–153 and 366. See also N. K. Sandars (trans. and ed.), *The Epic of Gilgamesh*, pp. 8 and 12.

[4] Stephanie Dalley (trans. and ed.), *Myths from Mesopotamia: Creation, The Flood, Gilgamesh, and Others*, pp. 1–39.

[5] Van De Mieroop, *A History of the Ancient Near East*, p. 31.

century later.[1] Sumerian civilization thus marks the transition from the pre-historic to historic ages.

Class distinctions are increasingly noted by archaeologists after the prehistoric period, as judged by the existing records of house size and graveyard goods. Such wealth disparities speak to the growing influence of an elite in the behavior and ordering of the community.[2] Within this class, the chief temple administrator, responsible for distributing offerings, gradually became less important than the effective military leader, who could protect agricultural land from rival city-states and, when possible, expand territory.

Thorkild Jacobsen points out that the fourth millennium and earlier ages were relatively peaceful times, with violence being sporadic; while during the third millennium, wars were a constant. He adds that the enormous walls ringing cities of the day—and the astounding costs and labor associated with their construction—were an indication of the danger.[3]

It is, therefore, not unusual that the concept of kingship developed during the third millennium. In the city of Kish, close to Babylon, "Lugalene" (Big Men) first protected their own people and wide holdings against the incursions of robbers and invading armies from the Iranian plateau or elsewhere.[4] From protecting his own property to serving the same role for his neighbors, the power of the "Big Man" grew. Competition among these powerful and wealthy individuals led to the strongest and most skilled being acknowledged at the top of the military hierarchy—the commander-in-chief. He was often seen as the representative of the local deity (later national deity), thus a warrior with a divine calling—conjoining the older role of temple chief with that of political military leader. One of the most significant

---

[1] While Kathryn A. Bard supports these dates, she writes, "the two writing systems are so different that it seems they are both the result of independent invention." Bard, "The Emergence of the Egyptian State (c. 3200–2686 BC)," in Ian Shaw (ed.), *The Oxford History of Ancient Egypt*, p. 78.

[2] Van De Mieroop, *A History of the Ancient Near East*, p. 24.

[3] Jacobsen, *The Treasures of Darkness*, pp. 77–78.

[4] Kriwaczek, *Babylon*, p. 87.

of the Lugalene was King Urukagina of Lagash (r. ca. 2350), who introduced the first legal code to protect the citizens of his realm. "[It] is in this document that we find the word 'freedom' used for the first time in man's recorded history."[1]

Sumer's rich religious tradition included gods and goddesses who founded and nurtured the towns and cities, and whose cults grew to become more widespread. They were later largely adopted by Babylon, Akkadia, and Assyria. A skeletal outline of the Sumerian pantheon includes the following eight archetypal deities as found in many cultures.

Sumer	**Babylon**	**Position**	**Keywords**[2]	**Egypt**[3]
An	Anu	Father of the Gods	Authority	Ptah
Enlil	Marduk/Elil	God of Air/Heaven	Force	Amun
Ninhursag	Aruru	Mother Goddess	Productivity	Isis
Enki	Ea	God of Wisdom	Cunning	Thoth
Nanna	Sin	The Moon	Princeliness	Shu
Ninurta	Ningirsu	God of Thunderstorm	Warlike Prowess	Horus
Inanna	Ishtar	Queen of Heaven, Goddess of Love & War	Infinite Variety	Hathor
Utu	Shamash	The Sun	Righteousness	Ra

By the second half of the third millennium, political leaders became identified with deities and ruled "in their names," thus further erasing the distinction between religious and secular identities. The property and land of the king and community became that of the god or goddess—who judiciously appointed the rulers to administer and control all their holdings. Disputes over territory between different city-states became quarrels between their patron deities. The

---

1 Kramer, *The Sumerians*, p. 79. See his pp. 79–83 for more discussion on this.

2 These keywords are given by Thorkild Jacobsen in *The Treasures of Darkness*, chapter four, to which the reader is referred for more on the Mesopotamian pantheon.

3 I include a column of suggested correspondences with the contemporary and nearby Egyptian pantheon. See Aleister Crowley, *777*, columns XIX and XX.

identification of the power of the ruler with the divine had the effect of elevating the concept of the human being.

It would remain for the Akkadian king Naram-Sin (r. 2211–2175) to take the identification between king and deity to its highest degree of development—presaging the entire Mesopotamian and Persian concept of the "god-man" archetype—ultimately influencing much of the subsequent history we will identify in the concept of the Imam. Naram-Sin first proclaimed himself "king of the four quarters of the universe."[1] After victories in Babylon, he declared himself a god and the beloved of Ishtar. He explained that he had the support of the deities Enlil, Dagan, Ninhursaga, Enki, Sin, Shamash, and Nergal, who wished him to be recognized as the god of Akkad, capital city of the Akkadian Empire (see below). A temple was built in his honor. While this was unprecedented, Naram-Sin would not be the last to make such claims.

Among the sacred mysteries of Sumer was the nuptial rite of the *hieros gamos* performed by the human king and the goddess Inanna. It brought fertility and well-being to the land.[2] The almost inconceivable levels of infant and child mortality, and the rapid spread of mortal disease within highly populated cities, determined the need for a high birth rate for civilization to survive. Discussing the varieties of sexual gnosis, Peter Levenda writes:

> The religions of Sumer, Babylon, Egypt, Greece, Rome, and so many others all expressed sexuality in religious or mystical terms. Perhaps the most interesting of these is the *hieros gamos:* the sacred wedding. In this scenario, either two divine partners marry, or a divine partner marries a human partner, or two humans marry under particularly sacred circumstances.[3]

The biblical Song of Songs, celebrating the union of heaven and earth through eros, is similar in literary form and bespeaks the likeli-

---

1 Van De Mieroop, *A History of the Ancient Near East*, p. 73.

2 Kramer, *History Begins at Sumer*, pp. 303–324.

3 Peter Levenda, *Tantric Temples: Eros and Magic in Java*, p. 245.

hood of Sumerian influence.[1] "The ability of humans to incarnate gods and powers is momentous, implying that they can act as these powers and so commit them."[2] Later, Sufism (esoteric Islam) would be infused with a tantric erotic component. The legend of the Old Man of the Mountain and the Garden of Delights hidden at Alamut may or may not hint at such a thread within the Assassin inner doctrine. According to the medieval tale, the young disciples (*fidais*) of the Master were initiated into the arts of love by women whom they believed were angelic beings or *houris*, reminding us of the archetypal theme of human intercourse with the Divine.[3]

Akkadia

The First Dynasty of Ur was conquered around 2334 by the Akkadian king Sargon the Great (r. ca. 2334–2279, or 2288–2235),[4] who successfully campaigned throughout Sumer.[5] He arose in Kish as the world's first empire-builder. A Semitic-speaking king, he relocated his capital from Kish to his nearby, newly-created capital city of Akkad (Agade). The name Akkad would ultimately describe a people, an empire, and a language.

Sargon was said to have been hidden by his mother in a basket of rushes and cast upon the water for protection, whereby he was discovered and raised by a kind man—a story that arose almost a thousand years before that of Moses.

---

1 Kramer, *History Begins at Sumer*, p. 316.

2 Jacobsen, *The Treasures of Darkness*, p. 39.

3 See appendix one.

4 Dating these over-four-thousand-year-old reigns and battles is complex. I have made extensive use of the two most recent and reputable sources I could find (both published in 2016), and here they disagree with each other by fifty years. Bryce gives the older dates on his page 73. Van De Mieroop gives the later date on page 348. Bryce is consistent with Sargon's conquest of Ur in 2334, while Van De Mieroop does not give a date for that victory.

5 Kramer, *The Sumerians*, p. 324; Bryce and Birkett-Rees, *Atlas*, p. 68.

Sargon fielded a large standing army. His reign integrated independent city-states into a more unified whole. Former city-state kings became governors and their fealty now belonged to Akkad. While this was undoubtedly an intelligent management strategy—one we will see being employed again and again in the Near East—lingering attachments to independence among this class may have contributed to the short life of the empire. It is further believed that, in time, Akkadian kings confiscated the lands of previous city-rulers—or purchased them at forced low prices—thereby amalgamating larger agricultural estates which they gave to their own loyal supporters. This became another source of resentment among the indigenous nobility.[1]

To the east, Sargon invaded Elam for the first time around 2300, a behavior repeated by several of his successors.[2] Akkadia's other territorial conquests reached as far south as the Persian Gulf, west to Syria and Lebanon, and north to Anatolia. They took the prominent cities of Mari along the Euphrates and Ebla even further west, and destroyed both. Mari had long functioned as the Mesopotamian gateway to Syria.[3] Ebla was home to a vast archive of administrative documents dating back to the latter half of the third millennium. Both cities were also important religious centers.

Sargon appointed his daughter Enheduana as priestess of the Sumerian/Babylonian Moon god Nanna, thus indicating the Akkadian desire to unite the pantheon of the south with the royal family. Enheduana is the author of the first signed writing in history, a series of liturgical prayers and hymns, including one to the Venusian goddess Inanna.[4]

---

[1] Van De Mieroop, *A History of the Ancient Near East*, p. 68 and 70.

[2] Diakonoff, "Elam," in Gershevitch (ed.), *CHI*, vol. 2, p. 8.

[3] Mari began a period of renewal in the mid-nineteenth century. It was a powerful city-state with varying diplomatic loyalties over the centuries, and briefly functioned as a center of Syrian Amorite influence (see below). Despite this history of alliance, Mari was again conquered by the Amorite king Hammurabi in 1765. See Van De Mieroop, *A History of the Ancient Near East*, pp. 109–110.

[4] Kriwaczek, *Babylon*, pp. 119–124.

Sargon used the Aryan Sumerian cuneiform script to record the Semitic Akkadian language. He thereby established this linguistic hybrid as the diplomatic language of the Near East—from Persia to the Mediterranean—for a thousand years.[1]

Despite its profound historical influence, the Akkadian Empire lasted for only about a century and a half. It was overthrown around 2150 by the barbarian Gutian tribe of the Zagros Mountains. That invasion may have been preceded by a period of changing climate and the ravages of drought and desertification.[2] The Gutians were soon defeated by the Sumerian king Ur-Namma around 2100.[3]

Ur III

Referring to the resurgent Sumerian empire, the Third Dynasty is also known as Ur III. Founded ca. 2110, its short-lived hegemony ended about a century later. It began in Sumer and soon extended its rule throughout all of Babylonia. After King Ur Namma (r. 2110–2093) defeated the Gutians, he continued on to conquer nearby Susa.[4]

Ur III's rulers introduced strict economic policies that will play out in the story before us, both with the socialist policies of Hamdan Qarmat[5] and in an aspect of the communal economic model adopted by the Nizaris under Hasan-i-Sabah.

The documentation from this period eclipses that of any other in the ancient Near East. It provides evidence of a massive bureaucracy composed of civilian and military functionaries who controlled almost every aspect of the life of the people. It should be no surprise that this state-centered culture included deification of the king, with temples both built and restored in his honor.[6] The state owned all land and resources. The people were fed and clothed by the state appara-

---

[1] Bryce and Birkett-Rees, *Atlas of the Ancient Near East*, p. 73.

[2] Kriwaczek, *Babylon*, pp. 131–132.

[3] Ibid., pp. 135–137.

[4] Van De Mieroop, *A History of the Ancient Near East*, pp. 79 and 349.

[5] See chapter three.

[6] Van De Mieroop, *A History of the Ancient Near East*, pp. 79–88.

tus. The vast administrative bureaucracy was necessarily ruthless in extracting taxes to support such a model—creating an environment of debt slavery, punishment, and corruption that has parallels in contemporary failed states.[1] (Such bureaucratic excesses were completely absent from the later Alamut model of shared resources.)

Massive construction projects were undertaken requiring a large labor force, paid primarily with rations. Irrigation was a priority to sustain and feed the increasingly large urban population. Colonial territories between the Tigris River and Zagros Mountains were exploited by military governors to supply cattle, sheep, and goats.[2]

The royal court of Ur sponsored the creation of literary works, many of which were hymns of praise to the king. It is likely that the timeless *Epic of Gilgamesh* was composed in Ur III.[3]

This dynasty was overrun by a new Elamite invasion in 2003.

The Amorites

The biblical Amorites (Amurru) were a Semitic tribe of uncertain derivation. They spread through Syria and Israel. Many came to appreciate and flourish in the urban environments they found there, but others remained committed to their traditional nomadic lifestyles and moved east to Mesopotamia."[4] They threatened Mesopotamia—first through peaceful immigration and later in military raids. "By the end of M3 [third millennium BC], they had overrun much of this region."[5]

The great Syrian desert provided a natural barrier to travel between Mesopotamia and the Levant, except through the Tigris and Euphrates river valleys and across the northern Syrian steppes. Semi-nomadic pastoralists, the Amorites sought grazing lands in these areas, tending to remain in their villages during the summer

1 Kriwaczek, *Babylon*, pp. 140–143.

2 Van De Mieroop, *A History of the Ancient Near East*, pp. 82–83.

3 Ibid., p. 87.

4 Bryce and Birkett-Rees, *Atlas of the Ancient Near East*, p. 81.

5 Ibid., p. 81.

and traveling with their herds during the winter months in search of viable pasture land. Their partially-settled/partially-nomadic lifestyle was complicated by the fact that their sedentary neighbors who practiced agriculture had to be protected against damage to their crops from grazing herds. Such tensions increasingly subjected the pastoralists to rule-making and social obligations.[1]

In time, wealthy herders began to settle in areas where they could better protect and manage their livestock and grow their own feed. Poorer Amorites would hire themselves out to the landed gentry class and thus be available as military resources when necessary. With the end of centralized power in Babylonia after the fall of Ur III, this growing aristocracy seized the thrones of various city-states and territories.[2]

It has been suggested that the patriarch Abraham was descended from Amorite tribes in Ur.[3] While Abraham and his family ultimately left the region, their kinsmen who remained behind founded the state whose capital was Babylon, ca. 1894.

The period between 2000 and 1600 in Mesopotamia was characterized by constant warfare between military leaders in various city-states who were growing in territory and influence, and who sought to unify their territories through both battle and diplomacy. Despite such disunity, the various warlords subscribed to a common religious tradition centered in Nippur. Its priesthood could bestow the title "King of Sumer and Akkad" upon he who controlled the city.[4] Furthermore, the tradition of identifying the royal family with the priesthood as instituted by Sargon in appointing his daughter Enheduana as priestess of Nanna, continued with later rulers.[5] Religious unity tended to reduce the chaos of the region.

---

1 Van De Mieroop, *A History of the Ancient Near East*, p. 93.

2 Ibid., pp. 94–95.

3 Kriwaczek, *Babylon*, pp. 163–165.

4 Van De Mieroop, *A History of the Ancient Near East*, pp. 95–96.

5 Ibid., p. 96.

Babylon

The ancient Mesopotamian creation epic *Enuma Elish* states that before the creation of man, Marduk saved the gods from destruction by slaying the elder goddess Tiamat. He then fashioned man from the blood of her husband Kingu so that the gods could have a convenient slave class to perform manual toil, freeing them to engage in the more desirable administrative roles of the cosmos and in the management of earthly affairs. In appreciation, the gods built Babylon as a permanent capital for the reign of Marduk, king of the gods, and the city was designated as the meeting place of the assembly of gods for all time.[1]

Famed beyond all other Mesopotamian cities in the West because of its importance in the Bible, Babylon was a cosmopolitan center that lay some 185 miles northwest of Ur. "Historically and ethnically Babylonia was a product of the union of the Akkadians and Sumerians . . . in which the Akkadian Semitic strain proved dominant."[2] Babylon's praises have been sung, and curses have been flung against it, for three thousand years.

Around the beginning of the second millennia, Mesopotamia was divided into two states. Babylonia was the name of the southern state. It extended from modern Baghdad to the Persian Gulf with the city of Babylon as its capital. The northern Mesopotamian state was Assyria (see below), whose capital was Ashur, and whose domain extended through northern Iraq, northeastern Syria, southeastern Anatolia, and northwestern Iran.

The people of Babylon and Assyria spoke and wrote in the Akkadian language. Babylonian was considered the southern dialect, Assyrian the northern. Thus, the older Sumerian language was largely replaced by the Semitic-Akkadian tongue, as the Aryan-Sumerian cultural dominance of Mesopotamia reached its end in Babylon.[3] The

---

1 Jacobsen, *The Treasures of Darkness*, pp. 174–186.

2 Durant, *Our Oriental Heritage*, p. 219.

3 Kriwaczek, *Babylon*, pp. 185–186.

Ur III model of a centralized economy also gave way to increased privatization in Babylon.[1]

Archaeologists refer to three distinct periods of Babylonian civilization.[2] The first is the Old Babylonian Amorite dynasty (1894–1595). The most well-known of the Amorites was King Hammurabi (r. ca. 1792–1750), who called himself "King of the Amorites." A skilled military strategist and ambitious conqueror, he established dominance in southern Mesopotamia. In a five-year campaign, he defeated first Elam, then Larsa, Eshnunna, and Mari.[3] Northern Mesopotamia would, however, elude his efforts at conquest.

Hammurabi was, of course, the author of the most famous law code of antiquity. (Ironically, the original stone column on which this code was inscribed was found in Susa in Elam, looted during a twelfth century invasion. Other copies have been found closer to Babylon.)[4] Though often severe, the Code of Hammurabi may be considered the basis of what would become our common law system. The establishment of a national legal code bespoke the end of the multitude of independent city-states, which had long characterized Mesopotamia, and the beginning of a more centralized and widespread imperial state.

The Amorite dynasty of the first period of Babylonian history was defeated by the northern Hittite (see below) invasion ca. 1595. The archeological evidence of Old Babylonian history has been submerged under the rising water-table in the area and has thus been rendered inaccessible to excavation.[5]

The second Babylonian period is that of the Kassite dynasty. It was founded by eastern immigrants whose homeland may have been the Persian Zagros Mountains. They took power soon after the Hittite conquest and expanded their control to southern Babylonia around 1475. Their political reach extended as far as Dilmun (mod-

---

[1] Van De Mieroop, *A History of the Ancient Near East*, p. 98.

[2] Ibid., p. 36.

[3] Van De Mieroop, *A History of the Ancient Near East*, p. 119.

[4] Kriwaczek, *Babylon*, p. 178.

[5] Ibid., p. 173.

ern Bahrain).[1] They were avid breeders of horses and proponents of the use of the light chariot.[2] The Kassites were defeated by Elam, ca. 1155, after having been weakened by decades of Assyrian aggression.

During the second Babylonian period, the god Marduk overtook the Sumerian Enlil as king of the gods. When the Kassite dynasty was defeated, the famed Babylonian cult statue of Marduk was taken to Susa. Half a century later, King Nebuchadnezzar I (r. ca. 1125–1104) returned the statue to Babylon and Marduk's importance grew dramatically—in part, because of the government's role as the literary patron for scribes and writers of the Akkadian language. Many hymns were written in Marduk's honor and stories celebrated his return to Babylon.[3]

Another long interval of multiple rulers and continual conflicts followed for the next half millennium in Babylon. These unstable times included periods of subjugation by Assyria, alliances between Elam and Babylon against Assyria, and battles with Elam itself. In addition to the indigenous military and political chaos of the region, a new technological development would influence Mesopotamia that will have direct relevance to our story. During the last years of the second millennium, Arabs learned to domesticate the camel. This allowed them to begin cross-desert travel and trade, and introduced a whole new people to the Mesopotamian region.[4]

The third dynastic period of Babylon is that of the Chaldean dynasty (which ruled from 626 to 538). Properly speaking, the name Chaldea refers to the kingdom in the marshlands of southern Mesopotamia at the head of the Persian Gulf, which lasted from the late tenth to mid-sixth century. The Chaldeans were a Semitic-speaking people who had migrated from the west. They engaged in constant military conflicts with the Assyrians. By 850, they had estab-

---

1 Van De Mieroop, *A History of the Ancient Near East*, pp. 185–186.

2 Diakonoff, "Elam," in Gershevitch (ed.), *CHI*, vol. 2, p. 40.

3 Van De Mieroop, *A History of the Ancient Near East*, pp. 187–188.

4 Ibid., p. 219.

lished themselves in fortified cities along the Euphrates in southern Babylonia.[1]

The first historical reference to Chaldea occurs in the writings of the Assyrian king Shalmanessar III (r. 858–824). In 852, he described his victorious military campaign through southern Mesopotamia,[2] proclaiming himself victorious at the Battle of Qarqar (853) against an anti-Assyrian coalition of twelve Mesopotamian rulers,[3] who had together fielded some fifty thousand men.[4]

The Chaldean dynasty (also known as the Neo-Babylonian dynasty) was technically founded in 626 by King Nabopolassar (r. 626–605) after the weakening of Assyria following the death of King Ashurbanipal in 631.[5] Chaldea achieved power over Mesopotamia as the result of a successful alliance with the Medes (see below). Together they defeated Assyria in 612.[6]

Among the kings of the Chaldean dynasty was Nebuchadnezzar II (r. 605–562), who would do battle with Egypt in 605 and 601. He later invaded Israel, destroyed the Temple of Solomon in 586, and brought large numbers of Jews to Babylon in what became known as the Babylonian Captivity. Nebuchadnezzar rebuilt Babylon in an effort to establish it as the center of the ancient world. The ziggurat of Marduk was so large and impressive it is said to have inspired the biblical story of the Tower of Babel,[7] as would Babylon's multilingual, multicultural heritage. The Chaldean kings devoted a great deal of attention to building, repairing, and expanding the irrigation system of the region that would result in agricultural prosperity long after the empire ceased to exist.

---

[1] Ibid., p. 226.

[2] A. Kirk Grayson, *Assyrian Rulers of the Early First Millennium* BC, vol. 2, 858–745 BC, quoted at https://en.wikipedia.org/wiki/Chaldea [accessed January 29, 2019].

[3] Bryce and Birkett-Rees, *Atlas of the Ancient Near East*, p. 171.

[4] Van De Mieroop, *A History of the Ancient Near East*, p. 247.

[5] Ibid., pp. 294–295.

[6] Bryce and Birkett-Rees, *Atlas of the Ancient Near East*, p. 215.

[7] Van De Mieroop, *A History of the Ancient Near East*, p. 297.

In 538, Babylon fell to King Cyrus II, the Great, of Persia, whom we shall soon discuss.

It is worth acknowledging that the term "Chaldea" can be confusing. It has long been in widespread use as a generalized name for all or most of Mesopotamia. For example, it is referenced in the Bible as the birthplace of the patriarch Abraham. "Ur of the Chaldees" refers to a period well before the actual Chaldeans entered the region. The Bible was compiled in Babylon in the sixth century when the word "Chaldea" was current among the Jewish scribes and authors. Before the early twentieth century, many Western scholars substituted the name "Chaldea" for "Mesopotamia." Such writers often had strong biblical backgrounds.

"Chaldea" is also considered to be an ancient mystical and legendary center of astrological and magical activity. *On the Mysteries of the Egyptians, Chaldeans, and Assyrians,* written by the Greek Neoplatonist Iamblichus and translated by Thomas Taylor, is an invaluable reference to the Gnostic mysteries of "Chaldea." *The Chaldean Oracles of Zoroaster,* quoted in the opening of this chapter, is another essential component of Western esotericism. Translated by W. Wynn Westcott, it was popularized through the Hermetic Order of the Golden Dawn and later in the works of Aleister Crowley.[1] In its more catholic usage, the term "Chaldea" is, thus, a primary conceptual link between ancient and modern schools of initiation.

Assyria

The northern Mesopotamian empire of Assyria had its capital in the city of Ashur, some 230 miles to the northeast of Babylon. Assyria was probably originally settled by travelers from Babylonia—thus the two lands had much in common. For example, Nineveh, the largest city of Assyria, was already home to a temple dedicated to Ishtar

[1] Needless to say, in popular parlance, other "Chaldean" derivatives include Tarot, Numerology, Magic, and Witchcraft.

originally built by the Akkadian king Manishtushu (r. 2226–2212).[1] It was generously restored by the Assyrian ruler Shamshi-Adad (r. 1807–1775).

Economic competition and military adventurism were a large part of the relationship between Babylon and Ashur as they evolved from city-states to nation-states. In the case of Assyria, this transition occurred from the fourteenth to the eleventh centuries and included a series of military campaigns and diplomatic activities. Both nations had independent, sometimes conflicting, diplomatic interactions with Egypt.

Ashur and Nineveh, were both located on well-traveled trade routes lacking natural protection. The Assyrian state thus demanded a series of strategic fortifications and a competent military to survive and prosper. Assyria was critical to the spread of the Iron Age in Mesopotamia. The superiority of iron weapons over the bronze and stone used by others gave them a great advantage. Assyria had learned the arts of smelting iron from the Hittites of Anatolia.[2] The Hurrian tribes of the Caucasus (who founded the empire of Mitanni, see below) taught them the arts of horsemanship, and the use of the quick and light chariots with spoked wheels as a tool of war.[3] It is estimated by historians that horses had been domesticated as part of the civilization of the Eurasian steppes since 3500.[4] Assyrian archers also used the more deadly and long-range compound bow.[5] Assyrian development of the knee-high leather infantry boot allowed soldiers to fight in any terrain or weather.[6] Such cutting-edge technology aided their quest for conquest and empire.

At the same time, Assyrian civilization did much in the fields of art, literature (including magical spells, hymns, astrological and

---

1 Van De Mieroop, *A History of the Ancient Near East*, p. 73.

2 Kriwaczek, *Babylon*, p. 212.

3 Ibid., p. 212.

4 Foltz, *Iran in World History*, p. 3.

5 For more on this weapon, see the discussion in chapter two, pp. 86–87.

6 Kriwaczek, *Babylon*, p. 236.

divinatory writings), science, and mathematics.[1] Assyrian military and trade interaction with the Hittites and Hurrians led to the spread of literacy among both groups.[2]

Assyrian agricultural resources were limited. The country lacked wide areas of fertile farmlands, which encouraged them toward sheep and goat raising. On the other hand, they enjoyed sufficient natural rainfall to be able to grow food on the limited land available. Assyria was, thus, not forced to rely on the extensive irrigation efforts necessary for the people of southern Mesopotamia. Yet, as we noted earlier, the social structure needed to anticipate and manage a limited water supply encouraged cooperation and the building of a strong sense of community. Assyrian civilization, by contrast, tended to be composed of more independent individual farmers and herders.[3]

In order to supplement its lack of agricultural resources, Assyria developed a vast trading network, becoming a thriving center of international exchange. In time, its merchants ranged as far and wide as Greece, making use of Phoenician ships and sailors. International traders were supported at home by a sophisticated economic system which included banking, investment, and contract law.

The state gave land to families who served either in the military or in the large building projects it sponsored. These grants were almost the equivalent of private property. They were subject to inheritance, and could even be sold, as long as the landholder was in the good graces of the state.[4] This anticipated what later became European feudalism.

Assyria's wealth grew to legendary proportions during its various centuries-long periods of conquest. It would seize vast amounts of spoils in addition to the tributes that later flowed from peace treaties. Huge construction projects and renovations were made possible with these resources.

---

[1] Van De Mieroop, *A History of the Ancient Near East*, pp. 281–283.

[2] Kriwaczek, *Babylon*, p. 212.

[3] Ibid., p. 212.

[4] Van De Mieroop, *A History of the Ancient Near East*, p. 194.

Assyria is well-known to the West through the Bible stories of the conquest of southern Israel, or Judah, by Tiglath-Pileser III in 736. Not long after, in 722, the Assyrian Shalmanessar V conquered northern Israel, or Samaria. In 700, King Sennacherib invaded Judah again, but this time the Assyrians were defeated by King Hezekiah.[1]

After gaining control of much of the Levant, Assyria under King Esarhaddon (r. 680–669) invaded Egypt in 671. He took Memphis. His successor, Ashurbanipal (r. 668–631), took Thebes in 664. But in 656, the Egyptian Psamtek, who had been educated in Assyria and was a son of the Assyrian vassal king Nekau, declared himself the independent sole ruler of Egypt. As the end of the Assyrian Empire was near, they were unable to prevail against him.[2]

The Assyrians tended to be tolerant of the religious and administrative cultures of the lands they conquered, seeking to employ existing social and bureaucratic structures to their own interests. On the other hand, Assyria used deportation and massive population movements to its own strategic ends. Whether to fill in gaps created by enlisting people in the military, to accomplish building or other large projects, or to disrupt specific groups of troublesome populations and political agitators, estimates range as high as 4.5 million people being displaced in the first three centuries of the first millennium.[3] In 722, the more than twenty-seven thousand deportees from Samaria—mentioned in the biblical story (2 Kings 17:3–6) of the invasion Shalmanessar V—were forced to walk 750 miles from Northern Israel to their new homes in the Zagros Mountains.[4]

One important cultural innovation that grew in Assyria over time was the idea of national identity—that all people in its land were citizens. No matter their language or previous status, they were entitled to the rights, and bound by the duties, of citizenship.[5] Similarly,

---

[1] 2 Chronicles, 1–22.

[2] Van De Mieroop, *A History of the Ancient Near East*, pp. 264, 274, 276.

[3] Bustenay Oded, *Mass Deportations and Deportees in the Neo-Assyrian Empire*, Wiesbaden, 1979, sourced by Van De Mieroop, p. 249.

[4] Van De Mieroop, *A History of the Ancient Near East*, pp. 250 and 268.

[5] Kriwaczek, *Babylon*, p. 241.

the concept of kingship was regarded with that respect accorded the divine representative of the heavens on Earth. The individual ruler was expected to be of the highest moral character.[1] Assyrian worship of their national deity Ashur had strong characteristics of monotheism. The idea that the national deity was responsible for order and the right functioning of society—and that it was the Assyrian king's duty as Ashur's agent on earth to present His truth to the world—is one we will find again when we meet the Ismaili Imam some fourteen hundred years later.[2]

The Assyrian Empire, at its height in the Late Period (745–612), held a vast territory stretching from western Persia to Syria, from the Black Sea to Israel and Egypt. Its progressive internal degradation took place almost simultaneously with the military campaigns of expansion waged by a very few strong kings of the Late Period. An invasion by the Persian Medes in the late seventh century took advantage of a long period of internal weakness and dissension. Assyria was finally conquered when Babylon and Media took Nineveh not long after in 612.

Aramaea

In time, the large movement of the western, desert-dwelling, pastoral Aramaeans from Syria challenged both Assyria and Babylonia. At the turn of the first millennium, mass movements of people from the steppe-lands and desert edges of the west sought to escape famine. They poured into Mesopotamia at the same time as they expanded their presence throughout western and southern Syria. They may have been driven by changes in climate that had been going on since 1200, which included decreasing rainfall and a temperature rise estimated at two to three degrees.[3] This period coincides with the Exodus of the Jews from Egypt to the Promised Land.

---

[1] Ibid., pp. 241–242.

[2] And, of course, in early medieval Europe as the divine right of kings, although this important concept is not to be confused with the idea of the Imam.

[3] Kriwaczek, *Babylon*, p. 233.

The Aramaeans brought with them their language. Aramaic was one of the first languages in history to work with a written alphabet composed of a manageable number of letters rather than the endless number of images used in the hieroglyphic and cuneiform scripts. (Ancient Uruk, for instance, made use of some seven hundred pictographic signs.)[1] Such languages required many years to learn, and were virtually the exclusive provenance of highly-trained professional scribes. Prior to this innovation in alphabetic language, rare indeed was the "normal" person who was able to read or write, even among the highest nobility. The earliest Aramaic inscription dates as far back as the tenth through ninth centuries in Syria.[2] The importance and widespread use of Aramaic has been contextualized by Andrew Robinson:

> Aramaic, which grew out of the Phoenician script, was immensely influential for well over 1000 years. The official script of the later Babylonian, Assyrian, and Persian empires (thus displacing cuneiform), it was also the vernacular language of Jesus Christ and the Apostles, and probably the original language of the Gospels (the Dead Sea Scrolls are written in Aramaic). It was also the principal language of traders from Egypt and Asia Minor to India. Its extinction came only with the unifying force of Arabic (whose script descended from Aramaic script) and Islam during the seventh century AD.[3]

Mitanni/Hurrians

The important Mesopotamian kingdom of Mitanni was established by Hurrian tribes around the sixteenth century. The Hurrians were a northern people of unknown origin who date to the late third mil-

---

[1] Bryce and Birkett-Rees, *Atlas of the Ancient Near East*, p. 47.

[2] J. C. Greenfield, "Aramaic in the Achaemenian Empire," in Gershevitch (ed.), *CHI*, vol. 2, p. 698.

[3] Andrew Robinson, *The Story of Writing: Alphabets, Hieroglyphs, and Pictograms*, p. 172.

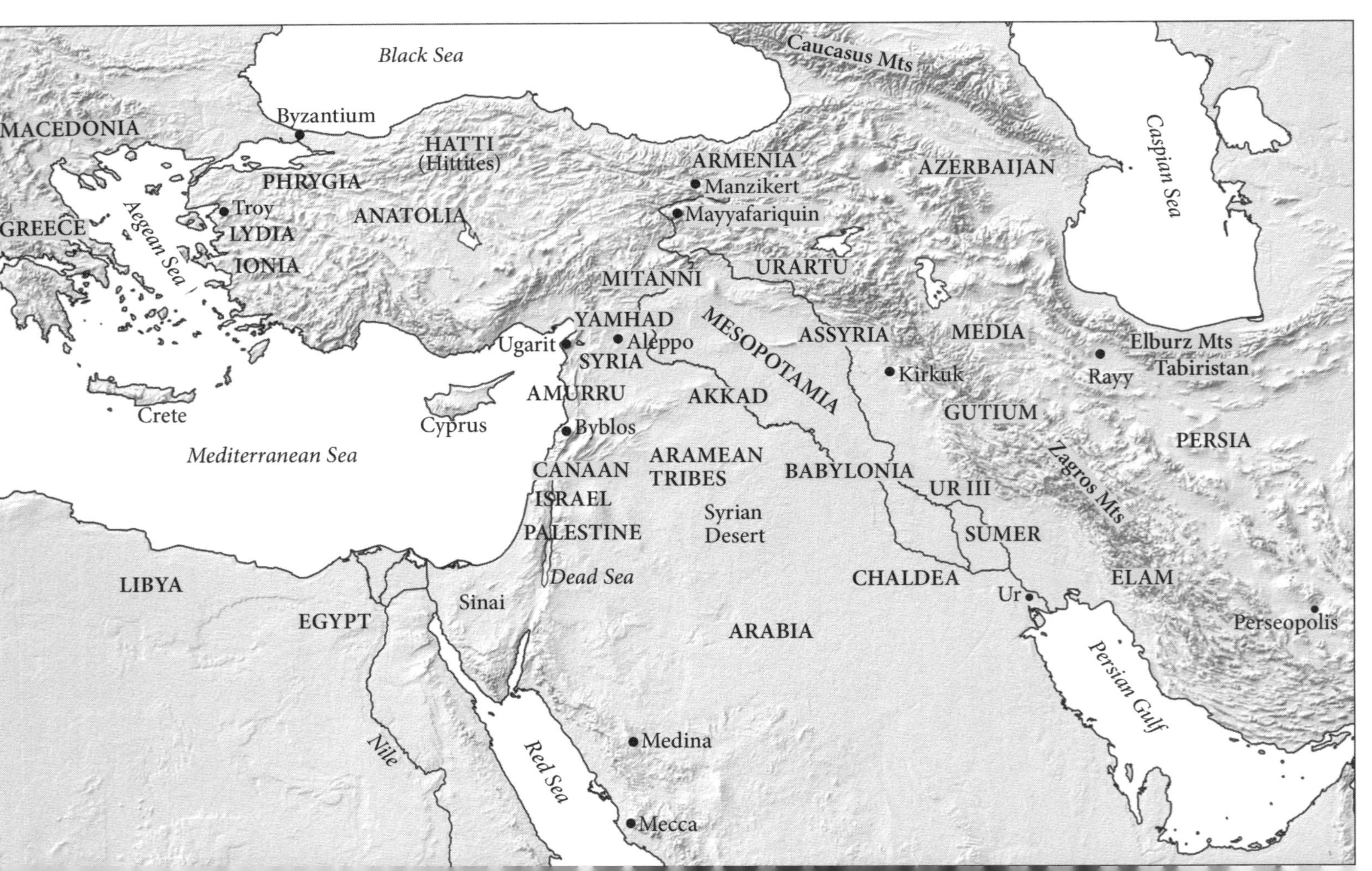

Black Sea
Caucasus Mts
Caspian Sea
Byzantium
MACEDONIA
HATTI
(Hittites)
ARMENIA
AZERBAIJAN
Manzikert
PHRYGIA
Troy
Mayyafariquin
ANATOLIA
GREECE
Aegean Sea
LYDIA
IONIA
URARTU
MITANNI
YAMHAD
MESOPOTAMIA
ASSYRIA
MEDIA
Ugarit
Aleppo
Elburz Mts
SYRIA
Kirkuk
Tabiristan
Rayy
AMURRU
AKKAD
Crete
Cyprus
GUTIUM
Byblos
PERSIA
Mediterranean Sea
ARAMEAN
TRIBES
CANAAN
BABYLONIA
Zagros Mts
UR III
ISRAEL
Syrian
Desert
PALESTINE
SUMER
LIBYA
Dead Sea
CHALDEA
ELAM
Ur
Sinai
EGYPT
ARABIA
Perseopolis
Persian Gulf
Medina
Nile
Red Sea
Mecca

lennia. They worshipped the Indian gods Mithra, Varuna, and the twin Vedic healing brothers Nasatya and Dasra.[1] Mitanni at its greatest extent controlled territory all the way from the Mediterranean, through eastern Anatolia, northern Syria, and northern Mesopotamia to modern Kirkuk. The Hurrians were an aggressive military people who are credited, as noted earlier, with introducing the horse and chariot to Mesopotamian warfare in the early sixteenth century, an innovation which spread rapidly. In time, the skilled warrior class of charioteers evolved into a privileged aristocracy because of their ability to meet the investment expense and training requirements of their craft, and for the efficiency they brought to the art of warfare.[2]

Mitannians were, for a time, at odds with Egypt over Syria, but reached an agreement in the early fourteenth century that divided the territory between them. Aleppo was at one time their capital. However, in 1327, Mittanian conflict with the Hittites over control of northern Syria and eastern Anatolia ended in their defeat. But much of the Mitannian/Hurrian legacy was preserved as their Hittite conquerors embraced Hurrian myths, religious practices, and culture. In the thirteenth century, a Hittite king married a Hurrian queen and their son succeeded to the throne.[3]

Hittites

An Indo-European people, the Hittites are believed to have entered Anatolia during the second to third millennium. They founded their kingdom probably in the early seventeenth century and called it Hattusa, also known as Hatti in Akkadian. It gradually grew in territory.[4] In 1595, the Hittites conquered both the Yamhad Kingdom in Aleppo (the precursors of the kingdom of Mitanni) and Babylon. During the fourteenth century they rose to their greatest territorial power, ruling from the Aegean Sea (and perhaps as far as Greece)

---

1 Van De Mieroop, *A History of the Ancient Near East*, p. 132.

2 Ibid., pp. 132–133, 152, and 164.

3 Bryce and Birkett-Rees, *Atlas of the Ancient Near East*, p. 124.

4 Ibid., p. 115.

in the west, to the Euphrates in the east. They controlled Syria as far south as Damascus. It was at the height of their power that they conquered the kingdom of Mitanni in 1327. Later, they battled the Egyptians in Syria at the battle of Qadesh in 1274. This ended in the first known international peace treaty, signed in 1259 between King Hattusili III and Pharaoh Rameses II.[1]

The Hittites had a sophisticated knowledge of metallurgy, with iron mines in Armenia. They shared a knowledge of iron-working with the Assyrians.[2] The use of iron, in preference to bronze, spread throughout the Near East beginning in the year 1200, marking the centuries-long transition between the Late Bronze Age to the Iron Age. Far stronger than bronze (bronze swords would break when striking iron weapons), iron was also available in the region, while the tin and copper that constituted bronze both needed to be imported.[3] Like several of the empires herein mentioned, the Hittites tended to respect local cultures and utilized the administrative apparatus of the territories they conquered.

The Hittite empire collapsed in the early twelfth century when its last king abandoned his capital to enemy forces.[4] A resurgence, known as the Neo-Hittite period, took place later in the twelfth century. States in southern Anatolia and northwestern Syria preserved a number of Hittite traditions in religion, architecture, iconography, and language. The Neo-Hittite states included Carchemich along the northwestern Euphrates River in eastern Syria and a number of smaller regional kingdoms.[5] Their wealth came from the control of trade routes and mining areas. Ultimately Assyria incorporated

---

1 Stephen Quirke and Jeffrey Spencer (eds.), *The British Museum Book of Ancient Egypt*, p. 45.

2 Durant, *Our Oriental Heritage*, pp. 286–287 and 274. We have no idea if this was a willing collaboration, forced technology transfer, or theft.

3 Van De Mieroop, *A History of the Ancient Near East*, p. 216.

4 Bryce and Birkett-Rees, *Atlas of the Ancient Near East*, p. 120.

5 Ibid., pp. 160–162.

these areas into its domain in the ninth century, sharing control with Urartu (see below) during periods of Assyrian weakness.[1]

The Levant

The term Levant is one that sometimes includes territory as far to the east as Iraq, but in this context we will use it to refer primarily to the coastal lands west of the Jordan River. In addition to Syria, Israel, and Palestine, we should note Canaan, Phoenicia, Philistia, Ugarit, and Amarru. The area was home to two of the oldest civilizations on earth: Abu Hureyra in Syria and Jericho in Israel, both dating to around 10,000 BC.[2] The earliest remains that have been found in Mesopotamian civilization date to some thirty-five hundred years later.[3]

The Mediterranean populations of the Levant exhibited different political tendencies than their Mesopotamian neighbors. They remained separate kingdoms, speaking different languages, and resisted the territorial unity evidenced during several periods by Babylon, Assyria, and Elam. In fact, the Levant more often served as a buffer zone between Egypt and Babylon, Assyria, Mitanni, and Hatti. To complicate matters even further, there was never any lack of military conflict among the territories which composed the region itself. Based on a reading of the Bible, the Levant seems to have been as much a hornet's nest then as it remains to this day.

Around 1500, a lively maritime trade developed between the Near East and the West. Cyprus, Crete, and the Aegean Islands, along with Egypt, became regular seafaring destinations and highlighted the importance of the eastern Mediterranean coast.[4] Those city-states with coastal access routes—such as Jerusalem, Damascus, Ugarit, Aleppo, and Amurru—grew in importance as merchant powers. Phoenicia's seafaring trade—with its harbors at Tyre, Sidon,

---

1 Van De Mieroop, *A History of the Ancient Near East*, p. 234.

2 Bryce and Birkett-Rees, *Atlas of the Ancient Near East*, pp. 23 and 25.

3 Ibid., p. 34.

4 Van De Mieroop, *A History of the Ancient Near East*, p. 133.

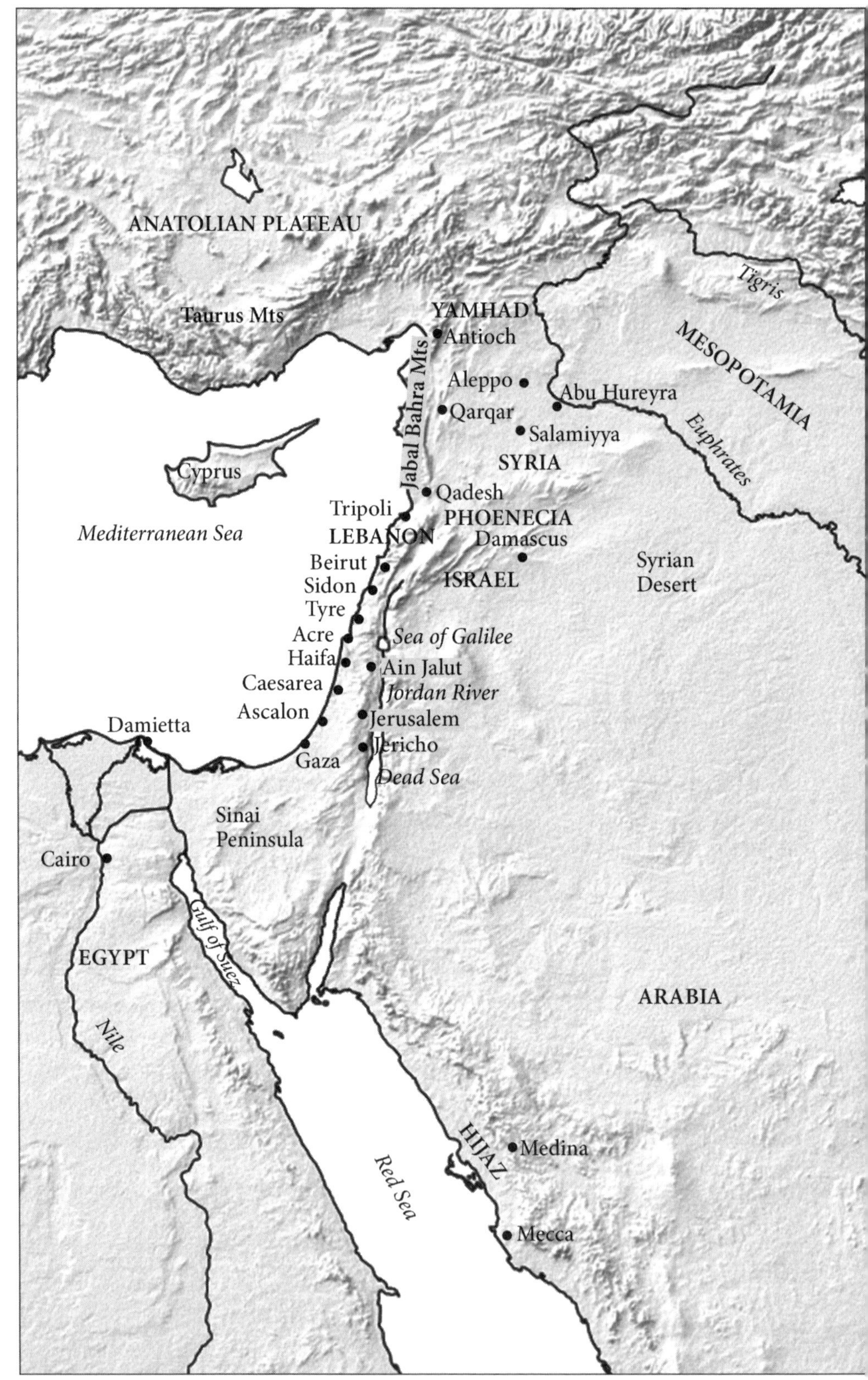

ANATOLIAN PLATEAU
Taurus Mts
YAMHAD
Antioch
Jabal Bahra Mts
Aleppo
Abu Hureyra
Qarqar
Salamiyya
Tigris
MESOPOTAMIA
Euphrates
Cyprus
SYRIA
Qadesh
Tripoli
PHOENECIA
Mediterranean Sea
LEBANON
Damascus
Beirut
Sidon
ISRAEL
Syrian
Desert
Tyre
Acre
Sea of Galilee
Haifa
Ain Jalut
Caesarea
Jordan River
Ascalon
Jerusalem
Damietta
Jericho
Gaza
Dead Sea
Sinai
Peninsula
Cairo
Gulf of Suez
EGYPT
ARABIA
Nile
HIJAZ
Medina
Red Sea
Mecca

and Byblos—extended as far as southern Spain and Morocco. The Spanish city of Cadiz had three temples to the Phoenician deities Astarte, Baal-Hammon, and Melgart. Phoenicia was instrumental in preseving and spreading the alphabetic systems of Hebrew, Aramaic, and Greek.[1]

Palestine (land of strangers) or Philistia (the land of the Philistines, from the Greek *Philistinoi*) is a broad term for the Holy Land, the whole country of Israel, or the land of the Jews.[2] The Philistines appear to have been descendants of a mysterious group known as the Sea People, who arrived toward the end of the second millennium. Before the coming of the Sea People, the entire region of Palestine or Israel was known as Canaan, and the indigenes as Canaanites.[3] According to scripture, the Hebrew God formed a covenant with Abraham of Ur giving him and his progeny their claim to the land. The Jews may have been of the Amurru or Aramean tribes, as mentioned.

While the tribes in the Levant always seemed to function as either independent city-states or vassal states to larger kingdoms, there was one exception. The Israelis/Canaanites took control of Egypt as the Hyksos dynasty in the mid-seventeenth century. Tribes from Israel entered Egypt toward the end of its Twelfth Dynasty (ca. 1985–1773). Nomadic herders, they traveled over the land route, and in time built political and military power.[4] Hyksos is a Greek term for the Egyptian *heqa-khasut*, "rulers of the hill countries."[5] A fierce warlike people, they became Egypt's Fifteenth Dynasty (ca. 1650–1550). They introduced the horse and chariot to Egyptian warfare, along with bronze swords and the compound bow. The Egyptians

---

1 Ibid., pp. 236 and 238.

2 William Smith, *Bible Dictionary*, p. 474.

3 Ian Barnes, *The Historical Atlas of the Bible*, p. 19.

4 The biblical story of Joseph and his rise to power in Egypt may be a reference to the coming of the Hyksos. See James H. Cumming, *Torah and Nondualism: Diversity, Conflict, and Synthesis*, pp. 25–34.

5 Quirke and Spencer (eds.), *The British Museum Book of Ancient Egypt*, p. 40.

would later successfully turn these weapons against their foreign occupiers.[1]

The Hyksos worshipped the Semitic/Asiatic storm god Baal, who has also been identified with Yahweh,[2] and whom they later identified with the Egyptian god Seth. The Old Testament records a huge and ongoing conflict between the pagan worship of the Canaanites (and their chief deities El and Asherah, and Baal and Anath) and the more puritanical Jews who were so often tempted by the rites of their neighbors. Religious scholars and mythographers have long suggested a more natural identity of El and Baal with the Hebrew Yahweh, and the likelihood that the supreme lord of the Israelites had a wife or divine consort who was edited out of the Bible a thousand years later. Despite their best efforts to conceal her, she has survived in spiritualized form as the Shekinah and in the contextually ironic Song of Solomon. While such speculation is well beyond the scope of this book, it suggests a more comprehensible identity between the Jewish deity and those of Mesopotamia, Egypt, and many other lands.[3]

Egypt aggressively campaigned against the Levant and Mesopotamia under the Eighteenth Dynasty warrior pharaoh Thutmose I (r. ca. 1504–1492). He battled as far as the Euphrates River. His grandson Thutmose III (1473–1458) launched at least eight campaigns

---

[1] Steindorff and Steele, *When Egypt Ruled the East,* pp. 27–28.

[2] This complex subject has been well explored in E. O. James, *The Ancient Gods: The History and Diffusion of Religion in the Ancient Near East and the Eastern Mediterranean*, among other places. Though Baal and Yahweh are depicted as fierce opponents, their roles seem to have morphed into one another over time and proximity. See also Cumming, *Torah and Nondualism*, pp. 64–75.

[3] See among many others: Robert Graves and Raphael Patai, *Hebrew Myths: The Book of Genesis*, p. 27; Toorn, Becking, and Horst (eds.) *Dictionary of Deities and Demons in the Bible (DDD)*, pp. 104 and 918; Raphael Patai, *The Hebrew Goddess*; and James, *The Ancient Gods*. Let us keep in mind, however, the unabashed monotheism that inspired Muhammad to write, "Lo! Allah pardoneth not that partners should be ascribed unto him." (surah 4:116, and elsewhere.)

against Israel and Syria. Nineteenth Dynasty kings like Sety I (r. ca. 1294–1279) also fought in Israel, erecting a temple in Galilee. His successor Rameses II (r. ca. 1279–1213) battled Syrians and Hittites at the Battle of Qadesh. After some sixteen years of warfare, Rameses II and the Hittites concluded their peace treaty, as mentioned, in 1259. Included in the agreement were the boundaries of the respective territories of each nation. Egypt lost control of southern Syria and northern Israel. The treaty was solemnized by the marriage of Rameses II with the daughter of the Hittite king.[1]

The story of Exodus, the departure of the remaining Jews from Egypt under Rameses II, begins in the mid-thirteenth century. By around 1200, Joshua crossed the Jordan River and entered the land of Israel after the decades-long desert wandering of the Hebrew tribes. Joshua battled the Canaanites and was victorious in a series of military campaigns. King David conquered Jerusalem about 1000, and established it as the capital of the United Monarchy of Israel. David's son and successor King Solomon completed his famed Temple in 957. The civil war that resulted in the Divided Monarchy of Judah and Israel (or Samaria) occurred around 928. The weakening of the Hebrew state opened Jerusalem to a new invasion in 925 from the Egyptian Pharaoh Shishak I (r. 945–924), who carried off treasure from the Temple of Solomon. Later, the Temple would be destroyed by Nebuchadnezzar II, as mentioned, in 586.[2]

The Levant remained an area of many cultures, languages, and religions. Its geographical position on the Mediterranean coast and the trading routes from the east meant that it increasingly interacted with Greece and Arabia through the ninth century and beyond. It thus spread the civilization of Mesopotamia even more widely through peaceful cultural and commercial means.

---

1 Van De Mieroop, *A History of the Ancient Near East*, pp. 152, 172, and 175.

2 These dates are given in the Suggestive Chronology in my *Temple of Solomon: From Ancient Israel to Secret Societies*, p. 364

Urartu

Urartu arose as a political power in eastern Anatolia in the ninth century. It was situated in the area between the Black Sea and the Caspian Sea. During its period of greatest territorial reach, it included all of modern Armenia. As important as it was, it remains an enigmatic state, known almost exclusively through the writings of its Assyrian enemies. Established by Sarduri I (r. ca. 832–825), Urartu grew to be the equal and bitter enemy of Assyria.[1] An aggressive people, they were able to expand as they did because of the periodic weakness of Assyria during the ninth and eighth centuries.

Urartu took strategic advantage of their numerous and decentralized mountain fortresses, a tactical approach later employed by the followers of Hasan-i-Sabah in Persia and Syria.

King Minua (r. 805–788) began construction of an extensive irrigation system which was continued by later rulers and resulted in great agricultural abundance. With access to mines and trade routes, Urartu was able to finance infrastructure spending, military exploits, and challenges to Assyria.[2] Under King Rusa (r. ca. 678–654), they engaged in an ambitious building program which included strategically-located, fortified cities. These cities were later violently destroyed by fire at the end of the seventh century, but the identity of the aggressors is not yet known.[3]

Media

The Medes were another historically important Indo-European people whose homeland was in western Persia in the northern Zagros Mountains. While the Medes also did not have written records, the Assyrians reported numerous military campaigns against Media between the ninth and seventh centuries. Media included the Khurasan Road portion of the ancient Silk Road. Assyria's inter-

---

[1] Bryce and Birkett-Rees, *Atlas of the Ancient Near East*, p. 189.

[2] Van De Mieroop, *A History of the Ancient Near East*, pp. 230–232.

[3] Bryce and Birkett-Rees, *Atlas of the Ancient Near East*, p. 192.

est was probably, in part, to control this lucrative trade route.[1] The Medians were horse breeders, which made them an important part of the Mesopotamian economy, as well as fearsome foes. They perfected the techniques of archery by sending their sons to be trained by the Scythians.[2]

Around 612, the Median king Cyaxares (r. 625–585) formed an alliance with the Babylonian king Nabopolassar (r. 626–605), the father of Nebuchadnezzar II. Together they launched the successful campaign that defeated the Assyrians.[3] This led to a brief period of conjoined Median/Babylonian ascendency over Mesopotamia.

Cyaxares was succeeded by his son Astyages (r. 585–550), who ruled as a tyrant. He was defeated by Cyrus II (who may or may not have been his grandson). This was an extremely consequential transfer of power. Cyrus, after conquering Media, took Babylon and then founded the first Persian monarchy, the Achaemenid dynasty. As Cyrus II, the Great, he would be responsible for the establishment of the Persian Empire.

The Persian conquest of Babylon in 539 by Cyrus put an end to the long-lived independent Mesopotamian civilization which had flourished for some twenty-five hundred years as a literate culture. Yet the end of the Babylonian political hegemony of Mesopotamia did not curtail its cultural importance, as is well explained by Paul Kriwaczek:

> Though Mesopotamia was reduced to the status of a mere province—albeit retaining the still prestigious name of Assyria—in an empire that now extended over four million square miles, the Persians never made any attempt to substitute their own traditions for those of their provincial subjects. How could they,

[1] Van De Mieroop, *A History of the Ancient Near East*, p. 291.

[2] Herodotus, *The History* (trans. David Grene), I:73; Diakonoff, "Elam," in Gershevitch (ed.), *CHI*, vol. 2, p. 118.

[3] Diakonoff, "Media," in Gershevitch (ed.), *CHI*, vol. 2, p. 123.

> when their own culture was by comparison so meager, and their own history so short? In fact the traffic was mostly the other way.[1]

And this outsized influence of Mesopotamia on Persian culture would become an important factor in the shaping of the life of Hasan-i-Sabah and the spiritual teachings of the Nizari Ismailis some fifteen hundred years later. We will come back to these multi-layered themes again and again when trying to understand the complexity of the cultural and religious influences that shaped Islam—as it moved so far away from its tribal roots in Arabia to the Neoplatonic sophistication we will find among the Assassins.

---

[1] Kriwaczek, *Babylon*, p. 277.

CHAPTER TWO

A Brief History of Persia

> They train their sons from their fifth to their twentieth year in three things only: horsemanship, archery, and truth-telling.
>
> —Herodotus[1]

WHAT WERE the roots of the culture into which Hasan-i-Sabah was born? Persia had a very rich religious and political history long before the Semitic Islamic conquest of the seventh century; its national memories were never far below the surface. Although Hasan is best known for his impact on Islam, and particularly his founding of the Nizari Ismailis, I think he can only be understood with reference to his fierce identification with his native land and its long and honorable heritage.

The Persians were an Aryan people, a pastoral-nomadic culture, descended from tribes who migrated to Iran (ca. 1000 BC).[2] They came from the regions north of the Caspian and Black Seas and the Caucasus Mountains of modern southern Russia, Ukraine, and Kazakhstan, anciently known as Scythia. They had migrated there from as far north and east as Siberia and the Ural Mountains. They scattered throughout Persia and lived alongside the indigenous Elamite populations in the southwest and the Medes in the northwest. "What would come to be the Iranian heartland in historic times was already inhabited by a wide range of peoples, including settled agricultural societies that predated the arrival of Iran-speakers on the plateau by almost seven thousand years."[3] The Persians called themselves *Irani* and their land *Iran,* the land of the Aryans, or, in Sanskrit,

---

1 Herodotus, *The History* (trans. David Grene), Book I:136. In the words of the immortal Colonel Jeff Cooper, "To ride, shoot straight, and speak the truth."

2 Maria Brosius, *The Persians: An Introduction*, p. 1.

3 Richard Foltz, *Iran in World History*, p. 4.

Arya.[1] Today their descendants inhabit Iran, Tajikistan, Uzbekistan, and Afghanistan: all Persian-speaking nations (*Farsi*), although Arabic has been a native language in Iran for well over a millennium.

The Pre-Islamic Persian Empires (559 BC–651 AD)

There were three indigenous dynasties that ruled in Iran during the eleven-hundred-year period from the Persian conquest of Babylon in 539 BC until the Arab-Muslim conquest of Persia in 651 AD. Eight decades of Greek rule, from 330–247 BC, were also part of this equation and, in my opinion, add further weight to the argument for a multidimensional esoteric current running through this realm. Wars between Persia and the West dated back to the Persian invasion of Greece in 490 BC. Extensive interactions also occurred between Persia and Egypt, Rome, and Byzantium. As such, the Persians were influential in and influenced by the West in such fields as literature, religion, philosophy, astrology, and medicine, as well as in sports, games like chess (imported from India), and the use of cosmetic creams.[2] "The Persians were one of the most highly developed civilizations of the ancient world . . . the first monarchy to create a world empire which included most territories of the known ancient world, from Egypt to India, and from southern Russia to the Indian Ocean."[3]

---

[1] Edward G. Browne, *A Literary History of Persia*, vol. 1, p. 4. On the other hand, the official name of the country today, Iran, was not adopted by the Persians until 1935, when their efforts to form an alliance with Nazi Germany encouraged them to abandon the ancient national name Persia in an effort to curry the favor of European Aryan admirers. Richard Foltz, *Iran in World History*, p. 98.

[2] Foltz, *Iran in World History*, p. 40; Durant, *Our Oriental Heritage*, p. 356.

[3] Brosius, *The Persians*, p. 1.

Achaemenid Dynasty (559 BC–330 BC)

The first Persian Empire was founded by Cyrus II, the Great (r. ca. 559–530 BC). It lasted almost 230 years until it was conquered by Alexander the Great. Cyrus' great-grandfather Teispes is said to have been the son of one Achaemenes. Teispes was a nobleman living in Persis (modern Fars) in southwest Iran along the Persian Gulf. Persis had been a part of the kingdom of Elam before its defeat by Assurbanipal in 646 BC. Teispes rose to become "King of Anshan."[1]

One reason for the success of the Achaemenid dynasty was Cyrus' policy of religious, linguistic, and cultural tolerance—respecting the inherent differences among the far-flung peoples of his vast territories.[2] As we have seen in Ancient Mesopotamia, this can be a more successful strategy than seeking to impose a dominant foreign ideology by force. When possible, the Achaemenids also tended to appoint local rulers, *satraps* ("protectors of the realm"), who were often experienced indigenous administrators willing to pledge loyalty to their new masters. This made for efficiency and continuity. There were also a series of minor rulers appointed as kings of their cities. Like the satraps, they were bound to provide tax revenue, meet military levees, and obey administrative policy directives.

The Achaemenids were especially active in establishing and maintaining an extensive network of roads, which featured way stations offering food and shelter. All this led to open and effective communication among outlying regions, and included the world's first postal system.[3] Cyrus extended his conquests all the way west to Lydia on the Aegean Sea, where he defeated the famed King Croesus—whose legendary wealth was ascribed to him, in part, because he was one of the first rulers in antiquity to mint coins.[4] Cyrus' conquest of Phoenicia added a navy to his military assets.

---

1 J. Hansman, "Anshan in the Median and Achaemenian Periods," in Gershevitch (ed.), *CHI*, vol. 2, p. 33.

2 Durant, *Our Oriental Heritage*, p. 353.

3 Foltz, *Iran in World History*, p. 19.

4 Brosius, *The Persians*, p. 9.

Babylonia surrendered to Cyrus without resistance in 539 BC. He went next to the east, as far as the Jaxartes River, adding Parthia, Bactria, Sogdia, and other territories. His son and successor Cambyses II (r. 530–522 BC) took Cyprus in the west. In 525 BC, he also conquered Egypt, where he was proclaimed as Pharaoh Mesuti-Ra, "Son of Ra,"[1] and instituted the First Persian Period, the Twenty-Seventh Dynasty of Egypt (525–404 BC).[2] Libya offered allegiance to Persia as Cambyses campaigned all the way south to Elephantine and Nubia. Under Darius I (r. 522–486 BC), the Achaemenid Empire expanded east to India and then north to Scythia along the northern coast of the Black Sea. Darius also completed a canal connecting the Red Sea with the Nile, increasing Persian naval reach for both military and trade purposes.[3]

The remaining Achaemenid kings were forced to fight to maintain their empire. Breakaway movements with varying degrees of success took place over the last 150 years of the dynasty, beginning in 499 BC with a revolt in Ionia. In 490 BC, the Battle of Marathon took place when Darius I invaded Greece because of their support for Ionia and was defeated.[4] His successor, Xerxes I (r. 486–465 BC), invaded Greece again in 480 BC and was victorious in the famous battle of Thermopylae against King Leonidas—who led Sparta and an alliance of Greek city-states in a heroic stand against the vastly more numerous forces of Xerxes.[5]

---

[1] Ibid., p. 13.

[2] Ian Shaw (ed.), *The Oxford History of Ancient Egypt*, p. 482. The Second Persian Period was a short-lived affair lasting from 343–332 BC.

[3] J. M. Cook, "The Rise of the Achaemenids and Establishment of the Empire," in Gershevitch (ed.), *CHI*, vol. 2, pp. 220–222.

[4] The modern word "marathon" is a reference to the runner Pheidippides (or Philippides) who was either sent to Sparta to appeal for help, or sent to Athens to announce the Greek victory over the Persians. In 1896, the modern Olympics in Athens celebrated the twenty-six mile run (Marathon to Athens) for the first time, a distance and terminology since embraced by many modern cities for their annual marathons. https://en.wikipedia.org/wiki/Marathon [accessed March 23, 2018].

[5] Introduced into pop culture in 2006 with the marvelous film *300*, an adapta-

By the time the Achaemenids, under Artaxerxes III (r. 359–338 BC), faced the Macedonian invasion of King Philip II around 340 BC, the end was close. Alexander succeeded his father in 336 BC after the latter was killed in battle in Asia Minor. Darius III ascended to the Persian throne the same year. His death in 330 BC would spell the end of Persian resistance to the young Macedonian conqueror. Alexander the Great's conquest of Persia was the first successful invasion from an outside power against the Achaemenids in over two centuries. Alexander would bring with him the legacy of Hellenism, as will be discussed shortly.

THE PERSIANS WERE A POLYTHEISTIC SOCIETY with a broad-based appreciation for the forces of Nature. Persian religious ceremonies included animal sacrifice, and they cultivated sacred fires for the protection of the ruler and their own homes and families. They were fascinated with the sky, and included astrology and astronomy in their myth cycles.[1] As mentioned earlier, they were tolerant of other religions which were widespread among their populations. Still more, however, Achaemenid kings worshipped at foreign altars and rebuilt damaged temples.[2] In Babylon, Cyrus paid homage to Marduk and declared that he had been chosen by the deity as His righteous and legitimate representative to restore the rule of order in the land. Cyrus' generosity in allowing the Jews to return to Israel after the Babylonian Captivity to rebuild the Temple (and his contributing to the cost) is familiar to readers of the Bible.[3] Cyrus was called "God's anointed" (literally, a "Messiah") by Isaiah.[4] Many Jews remained in

---

tion of the 1998 graphic novel of the same name by Frank Miller.

1 Richard Foltz, *Religions of Iran*, pp. 15–17.

2 Brosius, *The Persians*, pp. 33–34; Durant, *Our Oriental Heritage*, p. 353.

3 Among whom was American President Harry S. Truman, who identified his support of the creation of the modern state of Israel with the legacy of Cyrus helping the Jews to rebuild their Temple. Norman Podhoretz, *Why Are Jews Liberals?*, p. 134.

4 See Isaiah 45:1, "Thus saith the Lord to his anointed, to Cyrus . . ." (as noted by Foltz, *Iran in World History*, p. 15).

Babylon rather than return to Jerusalem. Babylon was becoming a vibrant center of Jewish culture. Here the text of the *Tanakh*, the Old Testament, was compiled and later, Talmudic scholarship was actively pursued. Other Jews moved east to Persia where they long thrived.

The Achaemenid king ruled as the representative of Ahuramazda, the "Wise Lord," the supreme deity of the Persian royalty.[1] The king was the bearer of Good and Truth against Evil and the Lie. He was expected to lead a moral life and so be worthy of his task. Warrior skills were important for a good king, but so was honor and the ability to reign over a peaceful land. The king and his entourage traveled widely to various regional centers so that he was able to survey his realm and be available to, and in touch with, the people.[2]

Darius I seems to have been the first ruler to bring the worship of Ahuramazda as the principal deity of the regime and the pantheon to prominence. He enthusiastically praised his patron in these words: "Ahuramazda is a great god, who created this earth, who created the sky, who created man, who created happiness for men, who made Darius king, one king among many, one lord among many."[3] At a later time, the royal worship of Ahuramazda expanded to include the Persian deities Mithra as god of the Sun and warfare, and Anahita, the Persian Isis, Venus, goddess of water and fertility.[4] The Persian New Year holiday, *Noruz*, is celebrated at the spring equinox and was widely observed at Persepolis, the capital city whose construction was begun by Darius in 515 BC. Richard Foltz points out that the roots of the importance of the spring equinox may be attributed to the earlier Mesopotamian myth of Ishtar and Tammuz, whose annual death and resurrection were later adapted in the Christian Easter resurrection rite.[5]

Darius established Aramaic as the language of administration throughout the empire. Its use demonstrates the importance of

---

1 Durant, *Our Oriental Heritage*, p. 361.

2 Brosius, *The Persians*, p. 37.

3 Ibid., p. 66, quoting an inscription of Darius I found at Susa.

4 Browne, *A Literary History of Persia*, vol. 1, p. 95.

5 Foltz, *Iran in World History*, p. 20.

Semitic Mesopotamia to the Achaemenids. At the same time, Darius developed the first written version of the Persian language, using a modified cuneiform script composed of thirty-six basic signs. This was initially used primarily for monumental inscriptions.[1] His linguistic accomplishment was demonstrated in the famous Behistun inscription, which featured a tri-lingual text of about thirty-six hundred words carved in Old Persian, with Babylonian and Elamite versions of the same.[2]

Zoroastrianism is the most well-known Persian religion (and is practiced to this day). Its adherents are followers of the prophet Zoroaster (Zarathustra) author of the *Avesta*, "a compilation of liturgy, dogmas, spells, mythological lore, and prescriptions."[3] Zoroastrianism is based on Dualism, the idea of a competition between Light and Darkness, Good and Evil, Truth and Falsehood. Ahuramazda is identified with the positive principle while Ahriman represents the negative. This is the primal spiritual struggle of all humankind, the battle between God and the Devil. Dualism would continue to have major repercussions in the Near East, as will be discussed. It was arguably the most important of the medieval European religious heresies contemporaneous with the Crusades and beyond.[4] Although there is much dispute as to the lifetime of Zoroaster,[5] elements of Zoroastrian doctrine developed among the Achaemenian royal family as the *Avesta* was first being compiled in written form during the

---

1 Van de Mieroop, *A History of the Ancient Near East*, p. 323.

2 Cook, "The Rise of the Achaemenids," in Gershevitch (ed.), *CHI*, vol. 2, pp. 208–209.

3 M. Schwartz, "The Religion of Achaemenian Iran," in Gershevitch (ed.), *CHI*, vol. 2, p. 664.

4 I discuss the progress of Dualism from Persia to Europe in *The Templars and the Assassins*. Norman Cohn's *The Pursuit of the Millennium* is a superb resource for a closer look at medieval heresies.

5 Ca. 1000 BC being one of the most reasonable. See Albert De Jong, "Zoroaster," in Wouter J. Hanegraaff (ed.), *Dictionary of Gnosis & Western Esotericism*, pp. 1182–1183.

fifth century BC. The Avestan canon was formalized during the later Sasanian period (AD 224–651) when Zoroastrianism became the Persian state religion.[1] The use of the term "Magi" for the Zoroastrian priesthood has forever associated Persia with magic, astrology, divination, and ritual, as has Zoroaster's reputed authorship of *The Chaldean Oracles*.[2] The three Magi who visited the infant Christ were said to have traveled from Persia, alerted by celestial signs to a significant cosmological event.[3]

Seleucid Dynasty (330 BC–247 BC) and the Spread of Hellenism

Will Durant, in discussing Alexander the Great (356–323 BC), best describes the overreaching concept of Hellenism when he writes:

> Amid all the excitement and chaos of his campaigns he kept clearly at the center of his thoughts the great purpose that even his death would not defeat: the unification of all the eastern Mediterranean world into one cultural whole, dominated and elevated by the expanding civilization of Greece.[4]

Hellenism is characterized by its embrace of Greek aesthetic principles in art, sculpture, architecture, classical philosophy, individualism, education, myth, and the celebration of physical prowess. These ideals were spread by the cultural self-confidence of Greek civilization and the interconnected web of commerce and communication throughout the Mediterranean and the Near East.

---

1 Schwartz, "The Religion of Achaemenian Iran," in Gershevitch (ed.), *CHI*, vol. 2, p. 664.

2 A hugely influential text in esoteric philosophy as noted in chapter one. Zoroaster has been further immortalized in Western philosophy through the efforts of Friedrich Nietzche and his classic work *Thus Spake Zarathustra*.

3 An excellent astronomical analysis of the celestial events that accompanied the Bible story of the birth of Christ may be found in Don Cerow's book *The 8th Seal*. See his appendix one, "The Star of Bethlehem," pp. 340–354.

4 Will Durant, *The Life of Greece: The Story of Civilization*, vol. 2, p. 542.

Alexander's eleven-year conquest of the vast reaches of the east began with his battle against Darius III (r. 336–330 BC) at the River Granicus, near the site of Troy in Anatolia in 334 BC. He went on to Damascus, Sidon, Tyre, Jerusalem, and Gaza. He crossed the Sinai into Egypt, where he was greeted as a liberator from the rule of the Second Persian Period, and was crowned pharaoh.[1] He approved the idea of building the new capital of Alexandria and marked out sites for temples dedicated to both Greek and Egyptian gods. Continuing back to Asia, he defeated Darius III again near Arbela in northern Iraq, after which Darius' generals assassinated their king for his cowardice. Quoting the first century historian Plutarch, Durant tells us that Alexander spent the night before the battle "performing magic ceremonies with the magician Aristander and offering sacrifices."[2]

Alexander marched on to Babylon where he made obeisance to their gods[3] and was greeted again as a liberator from growing Persian arrogance.[4] He then continued on to Persepolis (Parsa, the "city of the Persians"), which he totally destroyed in 330 BC.[5] A contributing motivation for this devastation may have been that his army is said to have met several hundred (or thousand) Greek prisoners on the outskirts of Persepolis. The prisoners had been mutilated by the Persians, enraging Alexander's men.[6] The young king participated in a drunken orgy of destruction, as described by first century BC Greek historian Diodorus Siculus:

> One day when the Companions were feasting ... a violent madness took hold of these drunken men..... One of the women present, Thais, the Athenian lover of the Macedonian

---

[1] Ibid., p. 544.

[2] Ibid., p. 540.

[3] Ibid., p. 545.

[4] E. Badian, "Alexander in Iran," in Gershevitch (ed.), *CHI*, vol. 2, p. 437.

[5] Built in 518 BC by Darius the Great, the destruction of the renowned capital of Persia was likely Alexander's retribution for the damage done to Athens by Xerxes in 480 BC, according to Foltz, *Iran in World History*, p. 21.

[6] Badian, "Alexander in Iran," in Gershevitch (ed.), *CHI*, vol. 2, p. 443.

> commander Ptolemy, declared that it would be Alexander's greatest achievement in Asia to join in their procession and set fire to the royal palace, allowing women's hands to destroy in an instant what had been the pride of the Persians. . . . . A quantity of torches was quickly collected, and . . . it was to the sound of singing and flutes and pipes that the king led them to the revel, with Thais the courtesan conducting the ceremony. She was the first after the king to throw her blazing torch into the palace. As the others followed their example the whole area of the royal palace was quickly engulfed in flames.[1]

After the sack of Persepolis and the looting of the royal treasury to finance his further efforts, Alexander continued east to Sogdia, Ariana, and Bactria. After the death of Darius III, Alexander also conducted a brief invasion into the Elburz Mountains, future home of Hasan-i-Sabah.[2] In 327 BC, he crossed the Himalayas and entered India. Here his tired army refused to continue and Alexander relented. When they reached the Indian Ocean, some of the army sailed by sea and the rest marched back with Alexander across the fierce Pakistani desert of Baluchistan. When they finally reached Susa, some ten thousand of his men had been lost.[3]

As Alexander slowed his years-long frenetic campaign and finally rested in Susa, he began to study the behavior and customs of the Persian nobles he had conquered. In a departure from the Greek tradition regarding all non-Greeks as "barbarians," he developed respect for their sophistication, refinement of manners, administrative management, and overall culture. He dreamed of uniting Europe and Asia with himself as the Greco-Persian conqueror, leavening the best of each into a vast cosmopolitan amalgam of creativity and civi-

---

[1] Quoting Diodorus Siculus (90–21 BC), https://www.ancient.eu/article/214/alexander-the-great--the-burning-of-persepolis/ [accessed October 13, 2018].

[2] Badian, "Alexander in Iran," in Gershevitch (ed.), *CHI*, vol. 2, p. 450.

[3] Durant, *The Life of Greece*, p. 547.

lization. He married the daughters of Darius III and Artaxerxes III, and encouraged his troops to take Persian wives. Some ten thousand marriages resulted.[1] He opened Mesopotamia and Persia to an influx of Greek colonists and drafted thirty thousand Persian youths into his army. He then had them educated along Greek lines and taught them Greek military tactics.[2]

Alexander's subsequent adaptation of the Near Eastern custom of the deification of kings and emperors may have made for an efficient ruling strategy in the East,[3] however, many of his troops were mortified by this behavior. Dissension grew within the ranks of an army once fiercely loyal to their beloved and charismatic commander. Increasingly isolated, Alexander retreated into drink and depression. He died at age thirty-three in 323 BC, eleven days after having consumed some six quarts of wine in a drinking contest.[4]

Alexander the Great brought the ideals of Hellenism to the ancient Near East through his vast territorial conquests and generally tolerant administrative attitude. Richard Burton remarks:

> [W]hen the conquests of the Macedonian Alexander . . . mingled the manifold families of mankind by joining the eastern to the western world, the Orient became formally Hellenized. Under the Seleucidae and during the life of the independent Bactrian Kingdom (BC 255–125), Grecian art and science, lit-

---

1 Badian, "Alexander in Iran," in Gershevitch (ed.), *CHI*, vol. 2, p. 480. Because of rising tensions caused by Alexander's embrace of the trappings of Persian monarchy, there followed a mutiny of his Greek troops. After forgiving them in a lavish ceremony, he sent them home. But he kept their wives and children in Persia, promising to care for them. Badian concludes that Alexander's real goal in arranging such large numbers of interracial marriages was to create a group of children who embodied his goal of a unified polity of Greco-Persian citizens, loyal to him alone. See pp. 483–484.

2 Durant, *The Life of Greece*, p. 548.

3 Known as *proskynesis*. Badian, "Alexander in Iran," in Gershevitch (ed.), *CHI*, vol. 2, p. 457.

4 Durant, *The Life of Greece*, p. 551.

> erature and even language overran the old Iranic reign and extended eastwards through northern India.[1]

The Greeks learned as well as taught. The effect of Alexander's contact with the Near East included the lessening of the importance of the Greek city-state as a model of organization, and an embrace of the more centralized administrative apparatus they found in Mesopotamia.[2]

After his death, Alexander's two leading generals, Seleucus and Ptolemy, established regional dynasties: the Seleucids in Syria and the Ptolemies in Egypt. Conflicts between them led to constant military confrontations which weakened both. Bitter rivalries also took place among the Seleucids themselves and frequently led to civil wars, eventually paving the way for their defeat.[3]

Despite the chaos and wars of his reign, among the accomplishments of Seleucus I was the founding of the city of Dura-Europus, ca. 300 BC, along the trade route passing across the Euphrates River in northeast Syria. It became an important international center, embodying the Hellenic ideal, and facilitated relations between the Greeks, Romans, and later Persian Parthians. Its archaeological finds include inscriptions in Greek, Latin, Hebrew, Aramaic, Persian, and other languages. A multi-ethnic city, it was home to a temple dedicated to the Persian-Greek-Roman god Mithra, a Jewish synagogue, and a Christian church and baptistery.[4]

The Seleucids retained the satrapal administrative apparatus of the Achaemenids, but because of Seleucid disunity, local Persian satraps were frustrated and rebelled. Incursions in the north from the Gauls and Scythians further weakened Seleucid stability, while

---

[1] Richard Burton, *The Book of the Thousand Nights and a Night*, vol. 10, Terminal Essay, p. 106.

[2] Durant, *The Life of Greece*, p. 552.

[3] Brosius, *The Persians*, p. 81.

[4] Farhad Daftary and Zulfikar Hirji, *Islam: An Illustrated Journey*, p. 16.

Roman campaigns in Asia Minor added to their problems.[1] Eastern Persia was ruled by the Indian Mauryan Empire (322–187 BC), which included the Bactrians and Parthians.

While the convulsions of conflict rocked the tenuous hegemony of the Selucids, the constant interaction between Persian and Greek cultures opened them both to social, political, and intellectual exchange, including mutually beneficial alliances. The Persians made extensive use of Greek mercenaries.[2] Encouraged by Alexander's example, or perhaps gifted by Alexander, Seleucus I took a Persian bride, a Sogdian noblewoman named Apama who became the mother of his successor, Antiochus I Soter.[3] At their height, the Seleucids ruled all of Syria, Asia Minor, and western Persia.

The rule of Hellenism was thus the primary native cultural influence in the region for about a century. However, the effects of Hellenism continued long after its political demise. Hellenism set the stage for the survival and vigor of the Mystery Traditions in later Islamic culture—as we will note in the widespread promulgation of Hermeticism and Neoplatonism within Islamic esotericism, particularly among the Sufis, Shia, and Ismailis. "While the pious hailed an almost monkish asceticism or fanatically exalted the new traditional code, intellectuals would accept nothing short of the full apparatus of Greek philosophy and Persian lore."[4]

Parthian Dynasty (247 BC–224 AD)

The initial success of the Parthian efforts to achieve political power in Persia was due, in large part, to the weakening of Seleucid control after the death of Antiochus II in 246 BC. The Ptolemies invaded

---

1 Brosius, *The Persians*, pp. 81–82.

2 Foltz, *Iran in World History*, p. 22. This had long been a practice of the Persians and Alexander's invasion found him battling Greek mercenaries on several occasions. See Badian, "Alexander in Iran," in Gershevitch (ed.), *CHI*, vol. 2, pp. 426 and 435.

3 https://en.wikipedia.org/wiki/Antiochus_I_Soter [accessed May 4, 2018].

4 Hodgson, *The Order of Assassins*, p. 5.

Mesopotamia under Ptolemy III in a campaign against Seleucus II, the successor of Antiochus II.[1] The five-year war which resulted consumed the resources and attention of the Seleucids in the western provinces of Syria and Mesopotamia, thus providing an opportunity for the ambitions of the Parthians in the east.

Founded by Arsaces (r. ca. 250–211 BC), the Parthian dynasty would rise over time to become an equal and powerful rival of Rome, thwarting Roman efforts to extend its conquest of the Near East. King Mithridates I (171–139/8 BC) fully established the Parthians as a significant political and military empire. He subjected all of Iran to Parthian rule and continued on to Mesopotamia in 144 BC.[2] Mithridates I is considered "the real author of Parthian expansion to the rank of world-empire."[3]

During this period, China became united under the Han dynasty (206 BC–220 AD). (We will see the effects of the Mongol conquest of both China and the Near East in the thirteenth century AD.) Formal contact between the Far East and the Parthians began during the reign of Emperor Wu-Ti (140–87 BC). A diplomatic envoy named Chang Chien was sent to Persia. He opened relations with King Mithridates II (124/3–88/7 BC), who had by then strengthened Parthian control of Mesopotamia and subjected Armenia.[4] China became an important political force in the life of the Near East for the first time.[5]

Meanwhile, Rome and Persia would remain locked in struggle from the early first century BC to the beginning of the third century AD. This began during the reign of the Parthian king Phraates III (r.

---

[1] Brosius, *The Persians*, p. 85.

[2] Wilhelm Eiler, "Iran and Mesopotamia," in Ehsan Yarshater (ed.), *The Cambridge History of Iran, Volume III(1): The Seleucid, Parthian, and Sasanian Periods*, p. 483.

[3] A. D. H. Birar, "The Political History of Iran Under the Arsacids," in Yarshater (ed.), *CHI*, vol. 3(1), p. 31.

[4] Ibid., pp. 39 and 73.

[5] Ehson Yarshater, "Introduction," in Yarshater (ed.), *CHI*, vol. 3(1), p. lvii.

ca. 70–58/7 BC).[1] In 53 BC, Mithradates III destroyed the Roman army under Crassus at the Battle of Carrhae.[2] Rome and Persia concluded a treaty in 20 BC deeming the Euphrates River as their border.[3] However, the alliance between Caesar Augustus and King Phraates IV caused resentments to fester among the Parthian nobility because of the "Romanizing" of their king. Phraates went so far as to choose as his successor one of his sons whose mother had been a gift from Augustus.[4]

This led to open revolt, and a weakening of the Persian monarchy that would yield long-lived consequences. The rising influence of the Persian nobility would open the Parthian Empire to factionalism as never before. The Parthian aristocracy took on the power to approve or reject the royal succession. Rome was fully able to take advantage of this Persian disunity. The next two centuries were filled with political conflict. The Parthian dynasty would ultimately fall to an internal rebellion in 224 AD.

DESPITE THE POLITICAL AND MILITARY turbulence of their reign, the Parthians continued to improve the infrastructure of the region. They built upon the earlier efforts of the extensive Assyrian road construction and the improvements made by the Achaemenids. The famed Silk Road was enhanced—the distribution network along the important caravan trade route from Central Asia and China to Persia, Mesopotamia, and all the way to Rome.[5] While the visit of Chinese envoy Chang Chien to Mithradates II officially opened the route to expanded trade, it is known through evidence of similarities in pot-

---

1 Birar, "The Political History of Iran Under the Arsacids," in Yarshater (ed.), *CHI*, vol. 3(1), p. 45.

2 Ibid., p. 49.

3 Brosius, *The Persians*, p. 96.

4 Ibid., pp. 96–99.

5 Although this is said to be a Parthian development, the well-trodden route between east and west reached far back into prehistory. Foltz, *Iran in World History*, p. 5.

tery and kiln design, that contacts with China and Persia dated back as far as the fourth millennium BC.[1]

Parthian trade was also conducted by sea. Ships sailed down the Euphrates River to the Persian Gulf and then to the Arabian Peninsula, or east to India via the Arabian Sea to the Indus River. Persia, thus, served as the primary meeting ground between East and West. It offered protection and profited from the free flow of luxury goods. Trade included silks and pearls from China, while Persia supplied horses and those who could train and sustain them to China. Steel and the secrets of smelting were part of this exchange, as were a variety of Persian fruits and incenses.[2]

THE PARTHIANS HAD LONG BEEN equestrian masters. Rome would learn firsthand of the deadly "Parthian shot," a devastating battle technique, perhaps learned from the Scythians (Sakas).[3] It consisted of the Parthian cavalry appearing to flee in retreat, leading their enemies to follow. The Parthians would then turn their bodies around while seated on their horses and deliver well-aimed arrows at their pursuers. This tactical battlefield maneuver could only be performed by highly-skilled horsemen and archers. The Parthians, like the Scythians, used the compound bow, making them a more deadly foe than those armed with simple traditional wooden arms. "We have evidence that the Persians derived the bow, which they afterwards brought to such perfection, from the Scythians."[4]

The composite bow was quite a technological marvel. Scholar An De Waele dates its development to the fourth millennium BC in regions where there had been a long tradition of archery: either the Turkmenian Steppe, Iran, the Arabian Peninsula, the Levant, or Anatolia. He writes:

---

[1] William Watson, "Iran and China," in Yarshater (ed.), *CHI*, vol. 3(1), p. 537.

[2] Brosius, *The Persians*, pp. 83, 91, 123–125.

[3] And possibly the origin of the mythic centaur, a man and horse joined together in perfect balance (female = "centaurides").

[4] Henry Balfour, "On the Structure and Affinities of the Composite Bow," *Journal of the Anthropological Institute of Great Britain and Ireland*, 1890, p. 227.

> The composite bow was manufactured from different kinds of pliable materials: over a wooden core, horn was glued on the inside—the belly—to resist compression, and sinew was fixed onto the outside—the back—to resist tension. Finally, parts of the bow or the whole weapon could have been covered with a sheath made of bark, leather or tendon. Because of the complexity of the manufacturing process (e.g. the drying of the glue), it took several months—sometimes even years—to complete a composite bow.[1]

LIKE THE ACHAEMENIDS, Parthian royalty traveled through their realm on a seasonal basis. Ctesiphon, on the eastern bank of the Tigris River some twenty miles southeast of modern Baghdad, became their primary capital. Mithradatkert ("built by Mithridates [I]"), or Nisa, lay east of the Caspian Sea, northeast of Alamut. It was the original capital of the Parthian homeland and the traditional burial grounds of Parthian royalty.[2]

Like both the Achaemenids and Seleucids, the Parthians governed through local administrators. The empire was divided into eighteen kingdoms as reported in the first century AD.[3] The rulers were called "kings," who recognized the Parthian king as the "King of Kings" (*Shahanshah*). Their territories were composed of ethnically, culturally, and religiously diverse populations. While each had considerable autonomy, they understood that they were not large enough to defend themselves in case of attack, so they relied on the military power of the Parthian king. These minor kings benefitted as well from the commercial and infrastructure advantages of being part of a larger whole. Smaller regions had local satraps. All local leaders contributed troops, and the funds to maintain them, to the King of Kings. All parties were rewarded by their association. This was a war-

---

1 An De Waele, "Composite bows at ed-Dur (Umm al-Qaiwain, U.A.E.)," *Arabian Archaeology and Epigraphy*, 2005, p. 154.

2 Brosius, *The Persians*, p. 103.

3 Ibid., p. 113.

like period with continual invasions from the Romans, Seleucids, and assorted nomadic tribes.

⊰⊱

Commercial routes were equally a path of ideas. Religious beliefs traveled freely and were communicated across vast territorial expanses. Such cross-fertilization allowed for an amalgam of spiritual concepts and practices to develop. The multi-ethnic Parthian Persian territories included indigenous Iranian paganism, Zoroastrianism, Dualism, the rich strains of Greek Gnosticism, and the multiplicity of the Roman gods themselves. Mithra, the older Achaemenid warrior god, became especially prominent during the Parthian dynasty. He was the all-seeing deity of celestial light, and, therefore, of truth, integrity, and the proper fulfillment of treaties and contracts.[1] Extensive contact with Rome led to Mithra being embraced by the Roman soldiers.[2]

Interactions along the Silk Road with Chinese and Indian mystical strains brought shamanism to Persia. In addition to this already vibrant mix, Mesopotamian spiritual ideals—derived from its widespread pagan traditions, the longtime Jewish presence, and the early years of Christianity—all became part of Persia's religious potpourri. The long-held Persian practice of the sacred fires continued among the Parthians as well.

This is the psychic spiritual cauldron from which Hasan-i-Sabah would emerge after Muslim beliefs were added to the mix some four-and-a-half centuries later.

---

1 Franz Cumont, *The Mysteries of Mithra*, pp. 2–3.

2 It is notable that the Western Roman Mithra, who evolved from this cross-cultural fertilization, is quite different than his Persian original. For example, the most characteristic iconography of the European deity is the slaying of the bull, the tauroctony, which is not part of Persian worship. For more on this, see David Ulansey, *The Origins of the Mithraic Mysteries: Cosmology and Salvation in the Ancient World*, pp. 8–9, *et passim.*

Sasanian Dynasty (224 AD–651)

Ardashir, king of Persis, would become the first king of the Sasanian dynasty (r. 224–239/40 AD) by defeating the last Parthian ruler Artabanus IV (r. 213–224).[1] The Sasanians would rule Persia as the last polytheistic dynasty before the coming of Islam. Ardashir was the son of a lesser king who had served under Parthian rule. He first established his dynastic capital in Istakhr in southwestern Persia near Persepolis in Fars Province. He later relocated the seat of government back to Ctesiphon.

The dynastic name comes from Sasan, the high priest of Anahita in Istakhr. Sasan may have been either the paternal or maternal grandfather of Ardashir. As later Persian kings of the Sasanian dynasty were proclaimed to be godlike appointees, this early identification of the royal line with the national goddess is significant. Stone reliefs over the span of the Sasanian dynasty show King Ardashir consecrated at his investiture by Ahuramazda. Khosrow II, one of the last kings, was depicted with Ahuramazda and Anahita flanking him.[2] The holy fires continued to be lit on the accession of the king and extinguished at his death.

Ardashir I spent several years subduing the remaining Parthian minor kings. The transfer of loyalty and support of the seven major Parthian noble clans was essential to the success of the Sasanian Empire. Ardashir ultimately ruled a territory that extended from the traditional Persian northern border east and west of the Caspian Sea, to the Oxus River in the east, the Indus River and Persian Gulf in the south, and the Euphrates in the west. The Mediterranean coast and Armenia were the goals for western expansion, accounting for endless battles with Rome, and the sad fate of Armenia as the land route buffer zone between east and west. Ardashir's son and successor Shapur I (r. 240–270) won a decisive victory over the Roman army in 244.[3]

---

[1] Brosius, *The Persians*, p. 139.

[2] Ibid., pp. 162 and 176–177.

[3] Foltz, *Iran in World History*, p. 33

KAZAKHSTAN
SCYTHIANS
KHAZARS
HUNS
OGHUZ
Mithradatkert (Nisa)
Aral Sea
KHWARAZM
Caspian Sea
PARTHIA
TURKMENISTAN
Marv
AZERBAIJAN
ARMENIA
KHURASAN
Tabriz
SAFFARIDS
Lake Van
Nishapur
Alamut
Lake Urmia
Girdkuh
Tigris
MAZANDARAN
DAYLAM
KURDISTAN
Qazvin
Rayy
Elburz Mts
Damghan
Qum
ZIYARIDS
BUWAYIDS
SELJUKS
Tabas
Baghdad
Zagros Mts
Euphrates
Ctesiphon
Anjudan
Herat
Isfahan
Kufa
KUHISTAN
KHUZESTAN
Yazd
Basra
Arrajan
Kirman
Shiraz
Istakhr
FARS (PERSIS)
Perseopolis
SISTAN
Persian Gulf

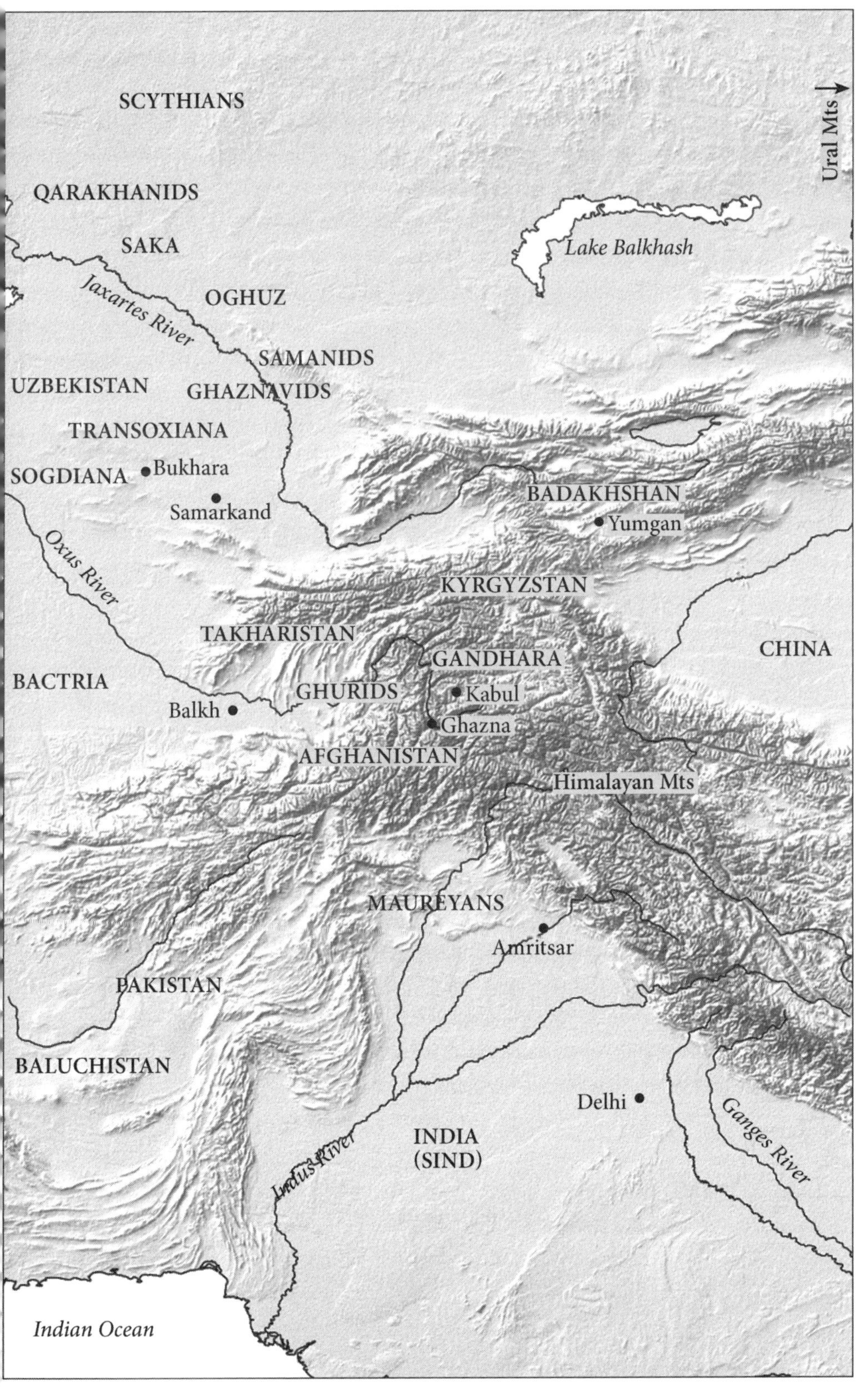
SCYTHIANS
Ural Mts
QARAKHANIDS
Lake Balkhash
SAKA
Jaxartes River
OGHUZ
SAMANIDS
UZBEKISTAN
GHAZNAVIDS
TRANSOXIANA
SOGDIANA
Bukhara
Samarkand
BADAKHSHAN
Yumgan
Oxus River
KYRGYZSTAN
TAKHARISTAN
CHINA
GANDHARA
BACTRIA
GHURIDS
Kabul
Balkh
Ghazna
AFGHANISTAN
Himalayan Mts
MAUREYANS
Amritsar
PAKISTAN
BALUCHISTAN
Delhi
Ganges River
INDIA
(SIND)
Indus River
Indian Ocean

THE SASANIANS CONTINUED THE policy of religious tolerance long characteristic of Persia.[1] In the mid-third century, a new faith arose preached by Mani (216–276), a Parthian raised in Mesopotamia and a member of a Gnostic and anti-materialistic sect. He drew additional inspiration from local Christians, Jews, and Zoroastrians. "Mani was of the opinion that his Wisdom was both the sum and perfection of all previous religious Wisdom," and that he was the continuation of the teachers Buddha, Zoroaster, and Jesus.[2] Mani received a series of visions between 228 and 240 in which the ideal of Truth was central.[3] The opposing forces of Good and Evil (Ahuramazda and Ahriman, Spirit and Matter) maintain a constant battle, although God (Good) is the stronger.[4] The Light must be freed from the Darkness by a graded ascent through ever-finer celestial realms.[5] This is a continuation of the dualist Zoroastrian dynamic.

Setting out on his travels to India, Mani encountered Buddhist and other beliefs which he freely added to his own developing system. He received the protection of King Shapur I and continued his proselytizing efforts, at first, within the Sasanian court and in Persia generally. He would also conduct widespread and extremely successful missionary efforts, sending disciples to eastern Iran and Central Asia, and later to Egypt, Syria, Palestine, north Africa, Europe, and as far away as China.[6] However, upon the death of Shapur in 270,

---

[1] Commenting on the religious policy of the founder of the Persian Empire, Cyrus II, the Great, Will Durant writes: "The first principle of his policy was that the various peoples of his empire should be left free in their religious worship and beliefs, for he fully understood the first principle of statesmanship—that religion is stronger than the state." *Our Oriental Heritage*, p. 353.

[2] G. Widengren, "Manichaeism and its Iranian Background," in Ehsan Yarshater (ed.), *The Cambridge History of Iran, Volume III(2): The Seleucid, Parthian, and Sasanian Periods*, p. 983.

[3] Ibid., p. 967.

[4] Ibid., p. 973.

[5] Ibid., pp. 974–982, in which more details of this complex cosmology may be found.

[6] Ibid., pp. 970 and 986. Many years later, Saint Augustine became a member of a Manichean sect before converting to Christianity in 386.

Kirdir, the chief priest of the Zoroastrian Magi, implored a successor of Shapur, King Bahram I (r. 273–276), to arrest the prophet and acknowledge Zoroastrianism as the official faith of Persia. Mani was subsequently imprisoned and tortured to death.[1] Though his followers were persecuted in Persia and later in Rome, Mani's faith spread far and wide and would become a significant force in medieval Europe via Bulgaria. Manichaeism was the root faith of several heretic movements, the most prominent among them being the Cathars of southern France.[2]

When the Roman emperor Constantine the Great gave his public support to the new faith of Christianity in 312, tensions again arose with Persia. Armenia was particularly affected as it was divided between those loyal to the Christian west and Pagan east. The identification of Christianity with the Roman/Byzantine enemy undermined the Christian community in Persia, leaving it vulnerable to charges of treason, or at least to sympathy for Rome.

Shapur II (309–379) managed to negotiate a truce with Constantine. This helped free Persian resources to defend their southern borders from invasion by pre-Muslim Arab tribes. After the death of Constantine in 337, the truce was abrogated and hostilities started again,[3] as did the ruthless persecutions of Christians in Persian territories which lasted some forty years.[4] Meanwhile, the Chionite tribe of Huns invaded in the north and east around 350, and Shapur was forced to defend his territories in an eight-year campaign.[5] In 360, the invasion by the Roman emperor Julian "the Apostate" ended in Julian's unfortunate early death. Another short-lived truce was declared with Rome/Byzantium.

The situation for Persian Christians would improve briefly during the reign of King Yazdgird (r. 399–421). In 410, he extended recogni-

1 Foltz, *Religions of Iran*, p. 49.

2 See my *The Templars and the Assassins* for more on medieval Cathar beliefs and history.

3 Brosius, *The Persians*, p. 149.

4 J. P. Asmussen, "Christians in Iran," in Yarshater (ed.), *CHI*, vol. 3(2), p. 936.

5 Brosius, *The Persians*, p. 150.

tion to them as a community distinct from the Roman Christians. He decreed that the head of the Persian Christian church was to be appointed by the Sasanian ruler. However, some of the more radical Christians rejected this solution. They burned down Zoroastrian temples and the persecutions resumed.[1]

As had been the case with their Parthian predecessors, the royal succession of the Sasanian dynasty became increasingly dependent on the assent of the aristocracy for the next century and a half. The support of the nobility was essential for the almost constant military efforts to either defend or expand the territory of the empire. Again, the monarchy's reliance on the nobility weakened it. The Persian aristocracy throned, dethroned, assassinated, and controlled succeeding kings. Yet the line of descent always came through the Sasanian royal family, and many of the regional kings of the empire who served under the King of Kings were also appointed from within the Sasanian family.

Toward the end of the fourth century, Hunnic tribes invaded Persia through the Caspian region, advancing as far as Mesopotamia.[2] During the fifth century, the barbarian tribes of the northern and eastern steppes launched more and more invasions against Iran, Rome, China, and India.[3]

A GNOSTIC RELIGIOUS MOVEMENT called Mazdakism grew in Persia at the end of the fifth century.[4] It seems to have been a reformist offshoot of both Zoroastrianism and Manichaeism.[5] The Mazdakites were also dualists. They believed the Supreme Lord rules Creation through the power of numbers and letters. Three elements gave rise to four powers, seven ministers, and twelve forces, and from these

---

[1] Ibid., p. 152.

[2] Ibid., p. 151.

[3] Bivar, "The History of Eastern Iran," in Yarshater (ed.), *CHI*, vol. 3(1), pp. 211–215.

[4] Foltz, *Religions of Iran*, p.153; Ehsan Yarshater, "Mazdakism," in Yarsharter (ed.), *CHI*, vol. 3(2), p. 991.

[5] Yarshater, "Mazdakism," in Yarsharter (ed.), *CHI*, vol. 3(2), pp. 995–998.

derive humankind.[1] Those who are wise in this doctrine are freed by their understanding.

With implications that would ultimately reach our protagonist, Mazdakism was also a social justice movement, a radical form of religious and cultural communism which included the equal sharing of food, property, and women. The hoarding of food supplies by some of the aristocracy during a period of famine had enflamed popular resentment. The lower classes were also angered by the nobility's ability to acquire and support a large number of wives and concubines. Mazdak "therefore called for the opening of both grain silos and harems to the general public."[2] "It is absolutely necessary that one takes from the rich for giving to the poor, so that all become equal in wealth."[3]

Mazdakism was initially tolerated by King Kavad I (r. 488–496 and 499–531). He is believed to have reasoned that the Sasanian embrace of Mazdakism would weaken the aristocracy by enflaming the hostility of the lower classes against them, while others claimed his interest was more sincerely religious and humanitarian.[4] Nobles reacted with anger to this challenge and temporarily imprisoned the king. Kavad was able to flee to the protection of his recent Hunnic allies, the Hephtalites, with whom the Sasanians had signed a peace treaty a decade earlier. The Hephtalites helped return Kavad to the throne several years later. His successor, King Khosrow I (r. 531–579), recognized the threat the Mazdakites presented to the stability of the realm and aggressively worked to eradicate their heresy. Mazdak, along with thousands of his followers, were executed. Despite the persecutions, some Mazdakites survived into the early centuries of Islam where they became a profound influence on the Shia and especially the Qarmatians under Hamdan Qarmat (see chapter three).[5] Khosrow also went after some of the more extreme Manichaean sects.

---

1 Ibid., pp. 1006–1008.

2 Foltz, *Iran in World History*, p. 39.

3 Yarshater, "Mazdakism," in Yarsharter (ed.), *CHI*, vol. 3(2), p. 998.

4 Ibid., p. 992.

5 Ibid., p. 1001.

DURING KHOSROW I'S REIGN, an alliance was made with the Turks against the northeastern invaders around 560. The Sasanian and Turks mutually established the Oxus River as their border.[1] The Turkish tribes had come from eastern Siberia and been known as raiders—from China to Iran—since several centuries before Christ. Related to the Huns, Mongols, and other tribes from the steppes of Central Asia, the Turks' interactions with the various cultures of the day were facilitated by commerce along the Silk Road. Serving as both warriors and merchants, they would become an increasingly powerful influence in Persia. By the time of Hasan-i-Sabah, the Seljuk Turks were the ruling dynasty of the land.

King Khosrow extended Persian hegemony as far as Yemen in southern Arabia. He expelled the Roman-backed Ethiopians in favor of the kingship of a member of the Himyar tribe, the ancestral tribe of Hasan-i-Sabah. Yemen remained a Sasanian outpost for decades after.[2]

Infrastructure improvement was also a key part of Sasanian policy. They worked on critical state needs such as irrigation and water storage, as well as fortifications along trade routes for protection. Khosrow was able to create a new class of small landowners (*dehkanan*) to balance the power of the land-owning aristocracy.[3] Khosrow was also active in social welfare policies designed to protect citizens, especially women and children. He instituted more fair taxation, which did much to improve life in Persia. He actively promoted science and the arts in his court, as well as medicine, music, philosophy, astrology, and the recitation and recording of the legends and history of the Persian people.[4]

---

1 Brosius, *The Persians*, p. 154.

2 G. W. Bowersock, *The Throne of Adulis: Red Sea Wars on the Eve of Islam*, pp. 120–121.

3 Brosius, *The Persians*, p. 156.

4 Ibid., pp. 155–157; Foltz, *Iran in World History*, pp. 39–42.

We have seen the religious melting pot that Persian tolerance had allowed. The extent of religious freedom in ancient Persia was unparalleled.[1] The Sasanians became the successors of the widespread religious fervor and creativity that had existed for millennia in Mesopotamia—despite the few persecutions we have noted. Persia's rich religious tradition would play a decisive role in the vibrant blend that would achieve its apotheosis at Alamut in the *Qiyama* proclamation of Hasan II in 1164.

A significant milestone in the spiritual ascent of humankind took place under the enlightened reign of Khosrow I. A new element was welcomed into Persia that, I believe, would have profound repercussions within the Sufi/Shia/Ismaili/Nizari sects of Islam, and extend through to the later European Renaissance. Richard Foltz well summarizes this development:

> After the Byzantine emperor Justinian closed the neo-Platonist academy at Athens in 529, a number of Greek academics took refuge in the Sasanian lands, praising Khosrow as the very incarnation of Plato's Philosopher King. Some found employment at Gondeshapur, where the curriculum included philosophy, astronomy, physics, literature, and medicine. Education at Gondeshapur drew on Greek, Indian, Persian, and Mesopotamian scholarly traditions, and in some ways laid a foundation for modern universities. After the Arab conquests in the seventh century, the school retained its prestige, and many sons of the Muslim nouveaux riches received their education from Christian, Jewish, or pagan professors.[2]

These academic and monastic refugees from the increasingly restrictive Christian hegemony of the Roman Empire brought with them the manuscripts and initiated wisdom of the Hermetic schools. Such teachings had flourished for centuries in Egypt, Israel, Greece, and Rome. Hermeticists taught a mystical doctrine

---

1 In sorry contrast to modern Iran.

2 Foltz, *Iran in World History*, p. 40.

of progressive emanations from Eternity to physical manifestation, and the reciprocal ascent of the soul from gross matter through ever-finer realms of Light. This had been the curriculum of the Egyptian priesthood and the school of Pythagoras. It had been passed on through the Qabalistic mysteries of the Gnostics and Essenes. Greek Neoplatonists like Plotinus, Porphyry, Iamblichus, and Proclus developed these doctrines, and they characterized the priestly inner mysteries of Eleusis and Mithra. The teaching of spiritual ascent through the hierarchy of Being would be a central theme of the teachings we will encounter among the Assassins. Gnostic wisdom fueled the esoteric revival that grew from the interaction of Europe and the Near East during the two-hundred year period of the Crusades.

Khosrow I's successors faced battles with the Turks, Khazars, and Byzantine Romans. The Sasanian army under Khosrow II (r. 590–628) took Egypt and went as far south as Nubia.[1] In 610, Emperor Heraclius ascended the Byzantine throne. Thus, ended an interlude of peace with Persia. In 611, Khosrow II took Antioch, Damascus, and Tarsus. In 614, he conquered Jerusalem and removed the fragment of the True Cross from the Church of the Holy Sepulcher.[2] In 623, Heraclius led his armies against Khosrow II, beginning in eastern Anatolia. By 627, they battled near Nineveh. When Heraclius caused Khosrow II to flee with his wife for safety, the Persian king was killed in a palace coup. This marked the beginning of the end of the Sasanian dynasty.

Interestingly, two of his daughters served very brief periods on the throne between 630 and 631. One of them returned the fragment of the True Cross to Jerusalem.[3] According to a *hadith* (sayings of the Prophet) narrated by Abu Bakra: "When Allah's Messenger

---

1 Brosius, *The Persians*, p. 156.

2 Ibid., p. 158. The Church had been built by Saint Helena, the mother of Constantine. It had been consecrated in 335 to commemorate the discovery of the fragment of the True Cross on which Jesus had been crucified.

3 Ibid., p. 174.

was informed that the Persians had crowned the daughter of Khosrau as their ruler, he said, 'Such people as ruled by a lady will never be successful.'"[1] Soon the Persian Empire would fall to the forces of Islam and be no more.

The Sogdians

Before discussing the arrival of the Arab Muslim conquerors to Persia, the Sogdian culture is worth a quick mention. Although never a reigning dynasty of Persia, the ancient Sogdians fulfilled a key role along the Silk Road between China and Persia. Located in Samarkand in eastern modern Uzbekistan, they shared in the cultures of both the Near and Far East. They spoke an eastern Persian dialect which was, for a time, the language of commerce along that trade route. Sogdia was originally a province of the Achaemenid Empire; however, its isolation from later Sasanian administration centers allowed the Sogdians far greater independence than was customary.[2]

They were a society of traders. Yet, because they were poised at the easternmost outpost of the Persian Empire, they were vulnerable to raids by the Turks and other barbarian troops traveling west. Sogdian ability to trade and persuade served them well with potential enemies. They provided the goods and services of advanced urban fashioning to nomadic tribes, receiving animal products in return, and often acted as a resting place for weary soldiers. They seem to have originally been Zoroastrians and are mentioned in the *Avesta*.[3] But religion for the Sogdians was often a means of facilitating trade, whether with Buddhists, Nestorian Christians, Manichaeans,

[1] Hadith *Sahih al-Bukhari* 4425 is quoted from https://sunnah.com/bukhari/64 [accessed May 23, 2018]. Noted by Foltz, *Iran in World History*, p. 43.

[2] See Foltz, *Iran in World History*, pp. 43–44.

[3] Azarpay Guitty, *Sogdian Painting: the Pictorial Epic in Oriental Art*, Berkeley, Los Angeles, London: University of California Press, 1981, pp. 2–3, referenced at https://en.wikipedia.org/wiki/Sogdia [accessed May 6, 2019].

or Muslims. They were adept at identifying with their clients and suppliers. After the fall of the Samanid dynasty in 999 (see below), the Sogdian language was replaced by Persian and Turkic tongues, and the Sogdian conversion to Islam was virtually complete.

The Islamic Persian Empires (From 651)

At the time of Muhammad's birth in Mecca (ca. 570), southern Arabia was under the political control of Persia. Arabia was a desert culture whose inhabitants thrived on raids of caravans, stealing the herds of neighbors, and engaging in continuous tribal warfare. The basic unit of political organization was the tribe, to whom intense loyalty and devotion were accorded. I offered this summation of sixth century Arabia:

> Nearly eighty percent of the population were Bedouins, nomadic herdsmen who traveled with their flocks seeking ever-changing seasonal pasture land. They also engaged in the cultivation of orchards: growing dates, peaches, apricots, and other fruits; and produced frankincense and myrrh—commodities as valuable in the ancient world as oil is in the modern. . . . The religion of these pre-Islamic desert warriors was polytheistic and pantheistic.[1]

When Muhammad united the various clans, Muslims were forbidden to steal from fellow Muslims. They began to look beyond their own territory for conquest. The early Arab Muslims were an enthusiastic force, united, young, lean, and committed to expansion—in contrast with the passivity of the Christians, and the dissension and weariness of the Syrians, Mesopotamians, and Persians, all of whom they would conquer. Muslim fighting skills had been well-honed. The moment of their ascendancy was at hand according to Hodgson:

---

[1] Wasserman, *The Templars and the Assassins*, p. 68.

> At the time of the Muslim conquests . . . , the hoary Roman Empire and its Persian Sassanid rival shared between them the vast intellectual and material heritage which had accumulated from earliest times in the Middle East. But the ventures of the classical Hellenistic culture had everywhere spent much of their force. Men had turned to building a new life . . . It was at this point that Islam appeared, in the most cultivated nations west of the Indus, offering a more perfect way to salvation.[1]

The Umayyad Dynasty (651–750)

Muhammad died in 632. He was succeeded first by his elderly father-in-law Abu Bakr, who passed the torch two years later to Omar (Umar, r. 634–644), a skilled warrior chieftain who completed the takeover of the entire Arabian peninsula. Seeking new lands to conquer, convert, and plunder, in 636 Omar set his eyes northward to Syria, Babylon, and Persia. His successors established their dynastic capital in Damascus. The Arabs mounted a fifteen-year campaign throughout the Persian Empire until the last Sasanian ruler, King Yazdgird III (r. 633–651), fell to assassination.

According to historian De Lacy O'Leary, Yazdgird's daughter Shahr-banu was married to Husayn, the son of Ali ibn Abu Talib, thus uniting the Islamic and Persian lineages. O'Leary writes, "Historically the evidence for this marriage seems to be questionable, but it is commonly accepted as an article of faith by the Persian Shiites."[2] Whether it is true or not, we will see that Shiism was far more successful in Persia than Sunnism ever was.[3]

The Sunni Umayyads were an alien nomadic force in a most established, urbanized, and civilized culture. However, in Syria and Mesopotamia, the Umayyads encountered fellow Semites—many of whom were only too happy to free themselves from the disdain of

---

[1] Hodgson, *The Order of Assassins*, p. 2.

[2] De Lacy O'Leary, *A Short History of the Fatimid Khalifate*, pp. 3–4.

[3] For more on the Sunni/Shia divisions in Islam, please see chapter three where this subject is extensively discussed.

their Persian Aryan overlords. Arab taxes were lower than Persian taxes, and, at first, the Arabs did not demand cultural or religious adherence from the defeated beyond acknowledging their political supremacy.

The Arab conquerors were cognizant of the advantages they could reap by cooperation with their Persian subjects, as well as by exploiting the economic opportunities available to them from the long-established commercial infrastructure of Persia. Thus the Arab "takeover" of Persia went two ways—establishing Arabic suzerainty and opening them to ancient Persian religious, economic, political, artistic, and literary achievements. At the same time, the newly-subservient Persians sought after the numerous advantages that sponsorship, membership, and alliance with their Arab masters could offer. This was especially true in the urban areas that were the initial targets of the Arab invasion. "Syrian and Persian officials could hold onto their jobs by finding Arab patrons, with whom they cemented ties by marrying each other's daughters, attending the mosque together, and entering into business partnerships."[1] By the eighth century, Persian Muslims outnumbered Arab Muslims.[2]

Abbasid Dynasty (750–1258)

We will discuss the wide-ranging cultural conflicts between the Sunni Arabs and their Persian *mawali* (clients) in chapter three. For now, it is sufficient to note that in the provincial regions especially, people were used to being more independent than their urban cousins; and the traditional values of Persian culture and national identity were more widely cherished. When such people converted to the religion of their conquerors, they expected to be treated with respect. The Umayyad Arabs, however, tended to look down on those who had fallen to their swords and treated them as subjects even after

---

1 Foltz, *Iran in World History*, p. 48.

2 O'Leary, *A Short History of the Fatimid Khalifate*, p. 2.

they converted to Islam—"the convert to Al-Islam being theoretically respected and practically 101-102."[1]

By exploiting the frustration and resentment of these dispossessed Muslim converts in Syria, Mesopotamia, and Persia, the Abbasids gained strength as a rival political movement. At first, the Abbasids defined themselves as Shiites, claiming descent from Muhammad's tribal clan. Abbasid popularity grew as the arrogance and lack of integration of the Umayyad Arabs chafed more and more on the population of Persia. Even the Zoroastrians embraced the Abbasid cause, as did the Mazdakites. They all supported Behzadan, a leading Abbasid Persian general, also known as Abu Muslim.[2] In 750, Abu Muslim defeated the Umayyads and the first Abbasid caliph Abu al-Abbas was enthroned. Almost at once, the Abbasids turned and rejected Shiism in favor of the more established Sunnis. Fearing Abu Muslim's popularity and power, the Abbasids executed him as a dissident troublemaker.[3] The Mazdakites considered Abu Muslim a religious Imam and his betrayal inflamed several anti-Abbasid movements, among them the Qarmatis.[4]

Arabic was the language of state and scholarship in Persia under the Abbasids. Thus, later researchers often confused non-Arab scholars as having been Arabs.[5] Non-Arabs, in fact, did much to regularize and expand the Arabic language, writing grammars and dictionaries to help themselves learn the language. They would also expand the range of Arabic as a tool for the communication of philosophic, scientific, and religious ideas.[6] Persian scholars translated texts written

---

[1] Burton (trans. and ed.), *The Book of the Thousand Nights and a Night*, vol. 7, p. 43, note 1.

[2] Foltz, *Iran in World History*, p. 49; Yarshater, "Mazdakism," in Yarsharter (ed.), *CHI*, vol. 3(2), p. 1006.

[3] Foltz, *Iran in World History*, p. 50.

[4] Yarshater, "Mazdakism," in Yarsharter (ed.), *CHI*, vol. 3(2), pp. 1003 and 1006. See also chapter three for more on the Qarmatis.

[5] Foltz, *Iran in World History*, pp. 55–56.

[6] G. Lazard, "The Rise of the New Persian Language," in Richard N. Frye (ed.),

in Middle Persian into Arabic to ensure wider dissemination. This included *The Thousand and One Nights.*[1]

Abbasid leaders increasingly took Persian wives, and their children were a blend of both races. The first Abbasid capital was established in Kufa in Iraq after they abandoned the Umayyad capital of Damascus in Syria. The move to Mesopotamia brought the Abbasid rulers closer to the administrative apparatus of the Sasanians. In 762, they went on to build their capital city of Baghdad, some twenty-two miles northwest of the old Parthian and Sasanian capital of Ctesiphon.

Over time, the Abbasid rulers fell to a cultural malaise. Like the Umayyads before them, they degenerated into corruption and arrogance:

> Wine, lechery, pederasty, and love of luxury so weakened the Abbasid dynasty that the empire dwindled, as region after region seceded from their authority. Oppression became common as renegade leaders usurped the power of appointed Abbasid administrators. So severe was Abbasid neglect, that the elaborate irrigation systems throughout the Near East—the life-blood of its food supply—ceased to be maintained.[2]

Despite their excesses, the Abbasids remained the titular heads of Islam—while plunging deeper into irrelevancy—over the next five hundred years. By the tenth century, the weakness of the Abbasid Caliphate was clear to all. Shiites had taken an increasingly powerful role in Baghdad through both the Persian Buwayhids and Egyptian Fatimids. Peasant revolts, Shiite organizing, and the power of various warlords and their followers replaced any remaining sense of order or

---

The Cambridge History of Iran, Volume IV: The Period from the Arab Invasion to the Seljuqs, p. 604.

[1] Foltz, *Iran in World History*, p. 56.

[2] Wasserman, *The Templars and the Assassins*, p. 82. See also Jawad al-Muscati, *Hasan bin Sabbah*, p. 5, for more on the chaos and suffering under Abbasid mismanagement.

coherence. Widespread famine was common. Buildings and libraries were destroyed. Anarchy and civil war reigned. Confusion and chaos were the coin of the realm. Such a disrupted environment would later become the fertile soil in which Hasan-i-Sabah and his Nizari Ismailis were able to cultivate and sustain their movement.

The Abbasids were finally put out of their misery in 1258 by the Mongol forces which had taken Alamut two years earlier.

Let us now take a brief tour of some of the more prominent dynasties that ruled in various parts of Persia, keeping in mind that all of the ruling Sunni dynasties served, at least nominally, under the Abbasid umbrella.

Samanid Dynasty (819–999)

Located in the region of Uzbekistan, the Samanid dynasty established its capital in the ancient city of Bukhara. The Samanids were originally Sunnis who ruled under the Abbasids until 892, when they became independent. The Samanids had converted to Islam from Zoroastrianism and later went on to embrace the Ismaili faith of the Fatimids, the rivals of the Abbasids, under Nasr II ibn Ahmad (r. 913–943).[1] The Samanid period saw the revival of the Persian language—after nearly two centuries of it having been ignored in favor of Arabic.[2] They supported the efforts of Abolqasem Ferdowsi, the creator of the magnificent Persian national epic, the *Shahnameh: The Persian Book of Kings*, which celebrated the ancient roots of their land. The Samanids are credited with saving "the legacy of ancient Iran from extinction."[3]

---

1 Al-Muscati, *Hasan bin Sabbah*, p. 8; R. N. Frye. "The Saminids," in Frye (ed.), *CHI*, vol 4, pp. 142 and 161.

2 Daftary, "Hasan-i Sabbah and the Origins of the Nizari Ismaili Movement," in Daftary (ed.), *Mediaeval Ismaili History and Thought*, p. 182.

3 R. N. Frye. "The Saminids," in Frye (ed.), *CHI*, vol 4, p. 160.

The Samanids were also traders who found trafficking in white Turkish slave troops (Mamelukes) to be particularly profitable. Beginning in the ninth century, Muslim rulers became increasingly reliant on the mercenary services of Turkish warriors.[1]

At its greatest extent, the Samanid Empire included large parts of Persia, Turkmenistan, Uzbekistan, Tajikistan, Kyrgyzstan, and Pakistan. Bukhara had long been an important cultural center and a stop along the Silk Road. The Samanids were defeated by Ghaznavid Turkish nomads (Turkomans) and Qarakhanids.

Qarakhanid Dynasty (840–1212)

This was a Turkish dynasty that ruled in Central Asia in the area of Transoxiana near the Oxus River, south of the Aral Sea and east of the Caspian Sea. They originated from the Qarluq and other Turkish tribes along the steppes that stretch from the Jaxartes River to the Tien Shan Mountains. In the tenth century the Qarluq tribe became Muslim. Among their capitals was Samarkand. They became vassals of the Seljuks and were ultimately defeated by the Khwarizmians.[2]

Saffarid Dynasty (861–1003)

A Muslim dynasty, they took advantage of the overall Abbasid decline and established themselves in eastern Persia, Afghanistan, Khurasan, parts of Tajikistan, Pakistan, and Uzbekistan. Founded by a regional warlord, the Saffarid expansion through Central Asia at first pitted them against various Buddhist tribes, whom they defeated before turning their attention west. They reached almost as far as Baghdad before they were stopped by the Abbasids, eventually becoming vassals of the Samanids.[3] They were supportive of Persian culture and

---

[1] C. E. Bosworth, "The Political and Dynastic History of the Iranian World (A.D. 1000–1217)," in J. A. Boyle (ed.), *The Cambridge History of Iran, Volume V: The Saljuq and Mongol Periods*, p. 10.

[2] Ibid., p. 3.

[3] Al-Muscati, *Hasan bin Sabbah*, p. 7.

the New Persian language, and were great patrons of literature and poetry.[1]

The Shuubiyyah Period (ninth and tenth centuries)

This term refers to the nationalist movement for the retention and celebration of Persian identity after the Arab Muslim conquest. Persians saw their culture being lost to foreign conquerors and resisted this trend, particularly by clinging to and sustaining the Persian language during Abbasid rule. They also supported the preservation of the Persian New Year celebration of *Noruz* at the spring equinox. The Samanid dynasty was an important part of the Shuubiyyah movement, as they were the first fully Persian Muslim ruling dynasty since the seventh century Arab Muslim conquest.[2] There was an overt hostility expressed toward the Arabs as unsophisticated savages, especially when compared to the richness of the Persian heritage.[3]

Ziyarid Dynasty (930–1090)

This empire, at its height, included all of northern and much of western Persia. But it is especially important to us because it was centered in the precise area of the Elburz Mountains in which Hasan-i-Sabah would later establish his community.

The Ziyarids were descendants of Ziyar b. Vardanshah, who claimed descent from the Sasanian royal family.[4] Their capital city was, at first, Isfahan, which would later become an important Nizari stronghold as well as a capital city of the Seljuk dynasty. Ziyar's

---

1 Daftary, "Hasan-i Sabbah and the Origins of the Nizari Ismaili Movement," in Daftary (ed.), *Mediaeval Ismaili History and Thought*, p. 182. New Persian succeeded the Sasanian Middle Persian and is written in a modified Arabic alphabet with many Arabic terms included.

2 https://en.wikipedia.org/wiki/Islamization_of_Iran [accessed June 1, 2018].

3 O'Leary, *A Short History of the Fatimid Khalifate*, p. 7.

4 W. Madelung, "The Minor Dynasties of Northern Iran," in Frye (ed.), *CHI*, vol. 4, p. 212.

son Mardavij (r. 930–935) had ambitions to restore the glories of the Pre-Islamic Persian Empire, intending to be crowned at ancient Ctesiphon; but his murder at the hands of his Turkish troops prevented this.[1] Under Mardavij's brother and successor Vushimgir (r. 935–967), they converted from Zoroastrianism to Sunni Islam and moved to Rayy, which served as their dynastic capital between 935 and 943. The Ziyarid political situation was chaotic and fluid. They allied and disputed with the Samanids and Buwayhids, reached out to the Ghaznavids, but were ultimately to acknowledge the authority of the Seljuk Turks.

The final king of this line, Gilanshah (r. 1087–1090), reigned for three years before he was conquered by the Nizari Ismailis under Hasan-i-Sabah.[2]

Bavandid Ispahbadhs (665–1210)

This group also originated among the pre-Islamic Sasanians. They ruled in Tabaristan (later Mazandaran Province) along the southern bank of the Caspian Sea and into the Elburz Mountains—where the Buwayhids, Ziyarids, and Ismailis also held power. Vassals for a time under the Seljuks, they retained enough independence for their king Husam al-Daula Shahriyar to refuse the summons of Sultan Muhammad Tapar to join an expedition around 1107 against the Assassins of Alamut. The Ispahbadh line of the Bavandids was defeated by the Khwarazmians in 1210.[3]

Ghaznavid Dynasty (977–1186)

The Ghaznavids were a Persian Sunni Muslim dynasty of Turkish Mameluke origin, who had served the Samanid Empire before declaring their independence. They were the first of the Turkish pow-

---

[1] Ibid., p. 213.

[2] Bosworth, "The Political and Dynastic History," in Boyle (ed.), *CHI*, vol. 5, pp. 25–27.

[3] Ibid., pp. 28–29.

ers to successfully rule in Persia.[1] At their greatest extent, they dominated large parts of Persia, Afghanistan, much of Transoxiana, and northern India. However, their territories were divided among several family members, and leadership was diffused among a number of different people including a Great Khan, Co-Khan, and subordinate under-khans.[2] During the leadership of their greatest chief, Sultan Mahmud (r. 998–1030), they campaigned in Daylam against the Buwayhid Shiites. The sultan's announced goal was the liberation of the Abbasid caliph in Baghdad from Shia control. In 1029, Mahmud deposed the Buwayhid ruler in Rayy. He also defeated the Samanids.[3] The Ghaznavids made extensive use of armor-plated elephants in battle, adding a level of terror and power to their military.[4] They were defeated in 1040 by the Seljuk Turks, with whom they later made an alliance. Their power was finally terminated by the Ghurids.[5]

Ghurid Sultanate (879–1215)

An eastern Persian dynasty of uncertain origin, possibly Tajik, they ruled in central Afghanistan. They claimed descent from an ancient family of heroes. Under the influence of the Ghaznavid sultan Mahmud, they converted to Sunni Islam ca. 1011, although paganism remained a strong cultural force until the twelfth century.[6] Under the Ghurids, Persian became the spoken and written language of government.[7] So intent did they become in their devotion to Sunnism in the latter third of the twelfth century that Sultan Ghiyath al-Din

---

1 C. E. Bosworth, "The Early Ghaznavids," in Frye (ed.), *CHI*, vol. 4, p. 162.

2 Bosworth, "The Political and Dynastic History," in Boyle (ed.), *CHI*, vol. 5, p. 11.

3 Al-Muscati, *Hasan bin Sabbah*, p. 10.

4 Bosworth, "The Early Ghaznavids," in Frye (ed.), *CHI*, vol. 4, p. 171.

5 Bosworth, "The Political and Dynastic History," in Boyle (ed.), *CHI*, vol. 5, p. 160.

6 Ibid., p. 160.

7 http://www.richardfrye.org/files/History_of_the_Persian_Language_in_the_East.pdf, p. 12 [accessed August 21, 2019].

(r. 1163–1202/3) applied to become a member of the *Futuwwa* chivalric order of the Abbasid caliph al-Nasir (r. 1180–1225). The Ghurids were especially hostile to the Ismailis, who were forced to humble themselves in a peace treaty around 1200.[1] The Nizaris later claimed a role in the assassination of the brother of the Ghurid sultan. This may or may not have been true, but it has been suggested they did it (or, at least, made the claim) to gain favor with the Khwarazmians.[2] After supplanting the Ghaznavids in Afghanistan, the Ghurids became rivals of the Khwarazmians, who later defeated them.[3]

Buwayhid Dynasty (934–1062)

The Buwayhid dynasty was a Persian Shiite state originating in the mountainous Daylam region, the future Assassin headquarters and home to much of the Nizari organizing efforts. At its greatest extent, the Buwayhid Empire included most of Persia, along with Syria, Iraq, Turkey, Arabia, Afghanistan, and Pakistan. The Sunni Abbasid caliph al-Mustakfi in Baghdad fell under their authority in 945, but he was treated as a figurehead and not harmed. The Abbasid Caliphate would remain under Buwayhid control until Caliph al-Qaim was freed by the Seljuk ruler Toghril Beg's conquest of Baghdad in 1055.[4]

The Buwayids were the descendants of Ali b. Buya (Imad al-Daula), who converted to Islam and was reputed to be of the lineage of the Sasanian king Ardashir.[5] Imad al-Daula's successors employed the symbols and titles of the Sasanian period. They also developed

---

[1] However, soon after, Hasan III, Jalal al-Din Hasan *Naw-Musulman* (the New Muslim) of Alamut (r. 1210–1221) would also become a member of the *Futuwwa* order under Caliph al-Nasir during the period of *Satr* (see chapter sixteen).

[2] M. G. S. Hodgson, "The Ismaili State," in Boyle (ed.), *CHI*, vol. 5, p. 468.

[3] Hodgson, *The Order of Assassins*, p. 213; Bosworth, "The Political and Dynastic History," in Boyle (ed.), *CHI*, vol. 5, p. 166.

[4] Bosworth, "The Political and Dynastic History," in Boyle (ed.), *CHI*, vol. 5, p. 46.

[5] Heribert Busse, "Iran Under the Buyids," in Frye (ed.), *CHI*, vol. 4, p. 274. The genealogy is described by Busse as fictitious.

and made extensive use of the *iqta* system of land-ownership for compensating the military.[1] The *iqta* system would play an important role in the foundation of Alamut, as will be discussed in chapter eight. The Buwayids subscribed to a decentralized model of governance in which each member of the dynasty held a share of territory and power.[2] This led again to the type of fragmentation and disunity we have seen before. In the eleventh century, they were forced to recruit Sunni Turkish mercenaries and were ultimately defeated by the Seljuk Turks.

Seljuk Dynasty (1037–1194)

At last we come to the dynasty that ruled Persia throughout the lifetime of Hasan-i-Sabah and the entire first century of the Alamut period. As mentioned earlier, these Turkish rulers were a Central Asian people who originally came from eastern Siberia. They were a nomadic and illiterate steppe tribe who shared much in common with the Huns and Mongols. Called Ghuzz, or Oghuz Turks, they were descended from a leader named Duqaq and his son Saljuq. "Certain sources state that Duqaq and Saljuq served the king of the Khazars, whose kingdom embraced the lower Volga and southern Russia, but this seems to be merely a memory of earlier Oghuz-Khazar connexions."[3]

The Seljuks traveled between Central Asia and the ancient lands of the Near East through the transition zones of the Oxus and Jaxartes river basins, arriving in the rich pasture lands of Khurasan. The regional disunity and confusion of goals represented by the many competing contemporary dynasties—as highlighted above—contributed to the Seljuk ability to seize power. At their height, they would rule from Uzbekistan to Syria. After they defeated the Byzantine army at the Battle of Manzikert in 1071, they poured into Anatolia

---

[1] Ibid., p. 260.

[2] Ibid., pp. 259–260.

[3] Bosworth, "The Political and Dynastic History," in Boyle (ed.), *CHI*, vol. 5, pp. 17–18.

creating the ethnic blend of people who now form the modern nation of Turkey.[1]

Originally the Seljuks hired themselves out as soldiers in service to the Samanids until that dynasty fell to the Ghaznavids in 999. The Seljuks moved on to Bukhara and Samarkand. They served for a time as paid troops of both the Qarakhanids and the Ghaznavids. They then fought their way south and west to Khurasan from around 1037 to 1040. Here they defeated their former Ghaznavid masters. When they reached further west to the urban civilization of Persia, they entered an altogether different world. As Professor C. E. Bosworth writes:

> For nearly a thousand years . . . Iran has generally been ruled by non-Persian dynasties, usually Turkish . . . [who] have lacked the administrative expertise necessary for ruling a land of ancient settlement and civilization. Whether consciously or unconsciously, they have adopted Iranian culture at their courts, and they have been compelled to employ Iranian officials to administer the country and collect the taxes. The first such alien rulers were the Saljuq Turks. . . . For them, as well as their successors, the process of assimilation to the indigenous culture and practice of Persia was not uncongenial, because they were able to draw on the country's ancient tradition of exalted monarchic power and submissiveness by the people.[2]

The Seljuks adopted Sunni Islam and fought against Shia domination. With the zealousness of the convert, they became almost fanatical supporters of the Abbasid caliph in Baghdad, seeking to protect and enforce his authority, to unite Islam and revive its former glory. The Abbasid caliph al-Qaim (r. 1031–1075) recognized the Seljuk Toghril Beg (r. 1038–1063) as Sultan. Toghril Beg freed the Abbasids from the domination of the Shia Buwayhids in 1055 and

[1] Ibid., pp. 3–4.

[2] Ibid., p. 1.

the Ismaili Fatimids in 1060. The Seljuks were extremely effective as the caliph's allies and enforcers, becoming the virtual rulers of Islam, in fact if not in name.

But the Seljuks became increasingly disillusioned. "The germs of religious disorders and widespread political chaos in those times . . . affected them. After they established themselves, their zeal for religion was replaced by their lust for power ."[1]

The Selkuk rulers contemporaneous with Hasan-i-Sabah included Toghril Beg, who established the Seljuk capital first in Rayy and then in Isfahan. He was succeeded, after some dispute, by Alp Arslan (r. 1063–1073), the first Seljuk ruler to lead as the sole Sultan. He hired the famed Nizam al-Mulk (r. 1064–1092) as his wazir or prime minister. Nizam would be retained by Alp Arslan's son and successor Sultan Malikshah (r. 1072–1092). As will be discussed in more detail in chapters six, ten, and fourteen, Nizam was assassinated by Hasan-i-Sabah because of his anti-Ismaili policies. Malikshah was succeeded by his son Barkiyaruq (r. 1092–1105), then by another son Muhammad Tapar (r. 1105–1118), and finally by a third son Sanjar (r. 1118–1157) who would conclude various agreements with Hasan.[2]

The Seljuks became great patrons of the Persian language, culture, and religion. "The importance of the Saljuk period lies especially in the fact that religious learning was organized in great teaching institutions, which might be considered to be amongst the first universities of the civilized world."[3] Nizam al-Mulk was particularly active in spreading religious schools (*madrassas*) called *Nizamiyya*.[4] In his youth, Nizam had also been a pupil of a Sufi teacher named Abu

---

1 Al-Muscati, *Hasan bin Sabbah*, p. 13.

2 See chapter twelve.

3 A. Bausani, "Religion in the Saljuq Empire," in Boyle (ed.), *CHI*, vol. 5, p. 289.

4 Bosworth, "The Political and Dynastic History," in Boyle (ed.) *CHI*, vol. 5, p. 70.

Said b. Abil Khair, for whom he retained a lifelong gratitude. Nizam was thereafter a generous supporter of the Iranian Sufi movement.[1]

The Seljuks supported a number of talented people including the mathematician/poet/astronomer Omar Khayyam, who will be discussed in chapter six. Another luminary was the philosopher and theologian al-Ghazali (d. 1111), the head of the *Nizamiyya* school of Baghdad, who later taught at the *Nizamiyya* in Nishapur.

Al-Ghazali propagated the theory that the Seljuk Sultan was the "Shadow of God upon Earth,"[2] a concept with a long tradition. According to Burton, the Persian king spoke of himself in the third person, swore oaths by his own blood, and one of his titles was the "Shadow of Allah," expressing his quasi-divine status.[3] The same title had been used by the Abbasid caliph in 977.[4] Al-Ghazali's applying this concept to the foreign-born Seljuk ruler may have been as much an encouragement to moral behavior as an acknowledgement of the reality of the Persian state of his time. Who else but the sultan could maintain the civil order, and thus allow for the greatest well-being and religious adherence of the people, and the good fortune of the Abbasid caliph? These are examples of the ancient concept of the divine right of kings with so long a tradition in the Near East, and of one with the concept of the Imam.[5]

The Seljuks ultimately fell to dissension and fragmentation. Added to their internal problems were the military pressures of the Crusaders, as well as attacks from tribes in the east. Sultan Toghril III (r. 1176–1194), the last of the Seljuk rulers, was defeated and killed by the Khwarazmians in a final battle at Rayy in 1194. The sultan's

---

1 Bausani, "Religion in the Saljuq Empire," in Boyle (ed.), *CHI*, vol. 5, p. 301.

2 A. K. S. Lambston, "The Internal Structure of the Saljuq Empire," in Boyle (ed.), *CHI*, vol. 5, p. 208.

3 Burton, *Supplemental Nights to The Book of the Thousand and One Nights*, vol. 3, notes 3 and 4, p. 346.

4 Busse, "Iran Under the Buyids," in Frye (ed.), *CHI*, vol. 4, p. 276.

5 Chapter three explores the meaning and importance of the Imam.

head was sent to Baghdad.[1] In total, fourteen sultans had sat on the Seljuk throne.

Khwarazmian Dynasty (as independent rulers, 1194–1231)

Another Turkish Mameluke dynasty, they had served as vassals of the Seljuk Turks in the eleventh century. Mamelukes were highly valued for their ferocity and fighting skills, yet they often rose to overthrow their masters and create their own dynasties.[2]

The Khwarazmians were also known to be travelers and merchants whose activities extended as far to the east as the Eurasian steppes and southern Russia, and as far west as the Danube basin. The prosperity of their walled cities and fortified villages during the early thirteenth century—before the Mongol invasions—was noteworthy.[3] The Khwarazmians were finally defeated by the Mongols.

Ilkhanate Dynasty (1260–1335)

Huelgu, the grandson of Genghis Khan, established his capital in Tabriz in modern Azerbaijan, southwest of the Caspian Sea. He did so after he learned of the death of his brother, supreme leader Magu Khan. Some three-quarters of his Mongolian army stayed on in Persia, presenting another demographic and environmental challenge. Shamanism was the religion of the Mongols, and they favored both Tibetan Buddhism and Nestorian Christianity over the Muslim majority. In 1295, the Ilkhanate sultan Ghazan Khan converted from

[1] Kenneth Allin Luther (trans.) and C. E. Bosworth (ed.) *The History of the Seljuk Turks*, p. 153.

[2] A later Mameluke dynasty in Egypt overthrew Saladin's Ayyubid dynasty and ruled that land from 1250 to 1517. They defeated both the Mongols and the Crusaders during the thirteenth century, as well as the Syrian Assassins.

[3] Bosworth, "The Political and Dynastic History," in Boyle (ed.) *CHI*, vol. 5, p. 142.

Christianity to Islam after receiving Muslim political support for his bid to the throne.[1]

Trade along the Silk Road was enhanced under the Ilkhanates, while scientists from China worked with their fellows in Persia. The Ilkhanate dynasty ultimately fell to the ravages of the Black Death of the mid-fourteenth century, one of history's most lethal plagues. The armies of the Turko-Mongol conqueror Tamerlane completed the devastation.

Our story of the region in which Hasan-i-Sabah and the Assassins were born and flourished draws to its close as we note that Hasan's biographer, Rashid al-Din Tabib, was employed as a historian by the Ilkhanates and served for a time as prime minister of that dynasty.

[1] Richard Foltz, *Iran in World History*, p. 67.

CHAPTER THREE

A Brief History of the Development of Islam

There is no god but God, and Muhammad is His Prophet.
—*Shahada*

HASAN REPORTS that his father was a Twelver Shiite (*Ithna ashariyya*).[1] To understand the meaning of *Ithna ashariyya* and the impact of his childhood faith on Hasan's later belief and eventual religious mission, we must explore the history of Islam during the four centuries between Muhammad's death and Hasan's birth. Islam had experienced a complex series of doctrinal expansions, evolutions, schisms, and developments that had resulted in a religio-philosophic world that was far different for Hasan-i-Sabah in northern Persia than it had been for the Prophet Muhammad in Arabia.

Muhammad

Muhammad was born in Mecca, ca. 570. Poised between the Persian and Roman empires, Mecca was an active commercial hub as well as a lively pagan center of the Bedouin population. Descended from the Meccan nobility of the Quraysh tribe, Muhammad's family had fallen on hard times due to the death of his father Abd Allah during the pregnancy of his mother Amina. She died when the Prophet was six. He was then raised by his maternal grandfather, who died two years later. He was next passed to the care of his paternal uncle Abu Talib, a highly respected elder of the Banu Hanifa tribe and the father of Muhammad's cousin Ali. Muhammad eventually became a successful merchant and married Khadijah in 595, his first wife, the mother of Fatima, and his business partner.[2]

---

[1] Juvaini, *Genghis Khan*, p. 667; Rashid al-Din, appendix two, p. 301.

[2] Daftary and Hirji, *Islam: An Illustrated Journey*, pp. 51–53. The significance of Ali and Fatima will shortly be made clear.

About the year 610, Muhammad began to experience what he called "true visions," during which he sought the solitude of a cave and where he began to receive verses of the Muslim holy book known as the Quran from the archangel Gabriel. It is believed by most Muslims that Muhammad was unable to read or write, so he received and memorized the verses, then recited them to his growing number of disciples. Scribes recorded the *surahs* (verses), which continued to be received until Muhammad's death.[1]

In about 613, Muhammad began to preach his message of submission to Allah. He was enthusiastically received by many of the pagan Arabs, but his teachings were rejected by many more. In 622, Muhammad and his Meccan followers, *Muhajirun* ("The Emigrants"), were forced to flee about 185 miles northeast to the city of Yathrib (later renamed Medina). The year of their flight (the *Hijrah*) marks the first year of the Muslim calendar.[2] In Medina, he won the support of those who became known as the *Ansar* ("The Helpers"), while facing problems with other Arabs who were less than sincere in their professed support, the *Munafiqun* ("The Hypocrites"), as well as the skepticism, and sometimes animus of the substantial Jewish community. In 627, at the Battle of Badr, Muhammad defeated an overwhelming attack against the Muslims of Medina from the Meccan Quraysh tribe.[3]

Muhammad's Islam was the third of the monotheistic faiths sprung of Abrahamic roots, which also included Judaism and Christianity.[4] Islam, too, teaches the unique and total power and presence of the Creator God—who offers a universal answer to all questions

---

[1] William Montgomery Watt, Introduction to Pickthall, *The Meaning of the Glorious Koran*, p. xvii.

[2] Because the Islamic calendar is based on the lunar year, it is not easily converted to the solar Gregorian calendar of the West. One useful converter may be found at https://www.searchtruth.com/hijri/ [accessed March 17, 2018].

[3] Pickthall (trans. and ed.), *The Meaning of the Glorious Koran*, Introduction, pp. 9–10.

[4] Islam means "submission" and a Muslim is "one who submits to God." Daftary and Hirji, *Islam*, pp. 51 and 54.

and all peoples. Islam has been the most successful in its outreach. Richard Burton notes that it "covered more ground in eighty years than Rome had gained in eight hundred."[1]

The Lord of Heaven is one in the three faiths. His judgments extend to all human beings, and in Him is salvation possible to those who follow His prescriptions. This Law, for Muslims, includes first and foremost an adherence to the *Shahada*, whose words open this chapter. It is a declaration of faith in the unity of Allah and the belief that Muhammad is the Prophet of Allah. The *hadith* (statements of the Prophet) and *sunnah* (reports of the behavior of the Prophet) were collected during Muhammad's life by his contemporaries. They became codified during the ninth century and are considered the traditional guides for the living of one's life based on the Prophet's advice and the example he set.[2] Finally, the *sharia* is accepted by Muslims as the proper rule of conduct for all. Regularized as well in the ninth century, this set of behaviors includes the Five Pillars of Islam. These are: 1) Faith: the belief in Allah and acceptance of the prophethood of Muhammad. 2) Prayer: the Muslim prays five times per day at set times facing Mecca. 3) Almsgiving: the acceptance of a tax for the benefit of the poor and the overall duty of generosity. 4) Fasting: observance of the annual month-long Ramadan daylight fast to celebrate the reception of the Quran. Islamic dietary law forbids the consumption of pork and wine amongst other prohibitions. 5) Pilgrimage: once during the life of each Muslim who is physically able, he or she is to visit Mecca and the Kaaba. A sixth duty is often added called *Jihad*: the obligation to battle against spiritual error.[3]

Muhammad was an able general and the new religion was spread by the sword—first throughout the Arabian peninsula among those who resisted during the Prophet's lifetime. He brought a sense of

---

[1] Burton, *The Book of the Thousand Nights and a Night*, vol. 10, Terminal Essay, p. 163. He also points out that those who would identify Islam with "the arid and barren" Wahhabism are making the same mistake as those who would judge Christianity by its "sourest" model of Calvinism, p. 165.

[2] Younis Tawfik, *Islam*, pp. 106–107.

[3] Ibid., pp. 108–119.

national and racial unity that had been absent from the widely scattered independent tribes that preceded him. He was also a social reformer against some of the more barbarous pagan Arab customs. Chief among these was the practice of burying girl children at birth, especially in times of want. He included verses in the Quran specifically calling out this practice and forbidding it. He also showed women a level of respect and legal protection that had previously been lacking in Arab culture.[1]

Muhammad abjured the concept of a professional clergy. He made each head of family the high priest of his own home. Yet, in time, the councils of *ulema*, Islamic elders, naturally developed, even before the Prophet's death. Their main redeeming principle may be that they must ("or ought to," to quote Burton)[2] earn their living separately from the pursuance of their religious duties.

The Kaaba

The Quraysh had been the traditional rulers of Mecca since about 400 AD and were charged with responsibility for the Kaaba.[3] This sacred space was said to have originally been erected by Allah as a shrine for the angels before the creation of mankind, or erected by Adam and Eve as their shrine in the Garden of Eden. After being lost during the Flood, it was rebuilt by Abraham and his son Ishmael, the progenitor of the Arab races. There remained Abrahamic monotheists among the pre-Muslim Arabs who looked at the Kaaba as the shrine of the One God, rejected the worship of idols, and welcomed Muhammad.[4]

The Bible discusses the flight of Hagar and Ishmael in Genesis: 16 and 21:13–21. Mother and child were saved by a spring of water that

---

[1] For girl children, see among others surahs 6:141; 6:152; 16:57–60; 81:8–9. For women, see e.g. 2:221–237; 4:15–25.

[2] Burton, *The Book of the Thousand Nights and a Night*, vol. 5, note 1, p. 183.

[3] Martin Lings, *Muhammad: His Life Based on the Earliest Sources*, p. 6.

[4] Ibid., p. 16.

flowed from the desert sands (Genesis 21:19). Known as the Wells of Zamzam, here Abraham was instructed to build the Kaaba. As the purity of the monotheistic faith of Abraham was eclipsed by Arab paganism, the wells were covered with sand until they were rediscovered by Muhammad's paternal grandfather, Abd al-Muttalib.[1]

The Meccan shrine had long been an annual pilgrimage point for the Arab Bedouin. The Kaaba was first a pagan temple filled with 360 deity images, the chief of whom was Hubal, the main deity of the Quraysh, depicted in human form as a warrior and rain god.[2] He could be approached for true answers in divination conducted with arrows.[3] When the Quraysh were finally defeated and converted en masse in 630, Muhammad cleansed the Kaaba of its idols. "And (remember) when We prepared for Abraham the place of the (holy) House, saying: Ascribe thou no thing as partner unto Me, and purify My House for those who make the round (thereof) and those who stand and those who bow and make prostration."[4]

The Kaaba has remained the central shrine of Islam ever since. Pilgrims make a series of seven circuits or circumambulations, walking in a widdershins direction (counter-clockwise) with their left shoulder turned toward the sanctuary.[5] Inside the shrine is an object known as the Black Stone. This holy rock, some seven inches in diameter, was built into the east wall of the Kaaba. It was said to have been cast into the Garden of Eden to show Adam and Eve where to build their shrine, or to have been given to Abraham by an angel. Muhammad taught that it had been pure white when it came to earth but that the sins of mankind turned it black.

---

1 Tawfik, *Islam*, pp. 21–23.

2 The idol of Hubal had been a gift from the Moabites of Syria. Lings, *Muhammad*, p. 5.

3 Ibid., p. 11.

4 Pickthall (trans. and ed.), *The Meaning of the Glorious Koran*, 22:26.

5 Lings, *Muhammad*, p. 11.

Sunnis

Upon Muhammad's death, the Muslim community was faced with its first doctrinal challenge. Seeds of division arose in the social cohesion that Islam had almost miraculously wrought among the formerly disparate Arab tribes. Muhammad had, by this time, forged a separate community of the faithful with its own set of beliefs and social values, offset from those of the local and national pagan tribes. He had separated Islam from what he regarded as the superstitions and errors of the older monotheistic faiths: particularly the idea of the identity of Jesus with God in Christianity; and the Jewish preference for Abraham's younger son Isaac, the half-brother of Ishmael, ancestor of the Arabs. Muhammad had also shifted the direction of Muslim prayer from the older center of Jerusalem to the cleansed Kaaba of Mecca.

When he became ill in 632, Muhammad asked his father-in-law Abu Bakr to lead the daily prayers in his stead. Abu Bakr had been his first convert among the nobility of Mecca, and he had brought a number of high-placed friends to the new faith. He was talented, well-respected, and had been part of the *Muhajirun* who had accompanied the Prophet to Medina. He was the father of Aisha, Muhammad's favorite wife. The majority of Meccans assumed that Abu Bakr was Muhammad's chosen successor and elected him as the *caliph* (prince of the faithful). This office indicates the political and religious leader of the Islamic community, whose task is to ensure proper adherence to the teachings of the Prophet and to hold the reins of a well-ordered state. Those who accepted Abu Bakr as Muhammad's successor were called *Al as-Sunnah* (People of the *sunnah*, i.e. those who followed the model of behavior set by the Prophet) or *Sunnis*. Sunnis were the party of community and consensus, seeking the largest and most inclusive body of the faithful.

Shiites

Another group of Muslims, however, believed that the proper succession to the office of caliph must be passed only to those who shared the Prophet's genetic bloodline, the *Ahl al-Bayt* or People of the

House. They believed that the caliph was charged with the spiritual—as well as the political and religious—leadership of Islam; that he must be designated by Allah with the insights necessary to guide the community through all the uncertainties that were bound to confront it over time, and to act as an inspiration to the faithful to strengthen and practice their religion through the centuries to come. According to the Shiites, the true leader would be guided by *ilm*, the special inspiration received directly from Allah. The caliph was certainly not regarded as a new Prophet—Muhammad is regarded as the Seal of the Prophets. His predecessors were Adam, Noah, Abraham, Moses, and Jesus.[1]

Those who believed in the importance of the Prophet's bloodline held that only Ali, Muhammad's cousin and son-in-law, the husband of the Prophet's daughter Fatima, his only surviving child, was worthy to hold the office of caliph.[2] Ali's successor would ideally be the eldest of Ali and Fatima's two sons, Hasan and Husayn. Ali's followers were known as the *Shiiatu Ali* (the party of Ali) or *Shiites*. They pointed to the fact that Ali had been raised with Muhammad since he was five years old, and that at the age of ten, Ali had become the second Muslim following Khadijah. Muhammad spoke fondly of the boy throughout the earliest years, referring to him publicly as "my brother, mine executor, and my successor among you. Hearken unto him and obey him."[3] In the Prophet's last year, he had proclaimed Ali his successor in 632 at Ghadir Khumm, an ancient town in western Arabia on the Red Sea. He had taken Ali's hand and said to the assembled

---

1 Hodgson, *The Order of Assassins*, p. 230.

2 Modern Western preferences aside, the leader of Islam was always a male. I wrote in *The Templars and the Assassins* that had Fatima been a man, or Islam willing to accept a female leader, the religion would have been a unified force with even greater world power (as noted by my wife during the writing of that book). Certainly there is no doubt that if Muhammad had a surviving son, the child would have been universally acknowledged as caliph and the high price of dissension might never have needed to be exacted from Islam. This is actually briefly addressed in the Quran in surah 108.

3 Lings, *Muhammad*, p. 57.

faithful, "He of whom I am the patron, of him Ali is also the patron."[1] After the investiture, a tent was set up where Ali received allegiance from the thousands of Muslims present. This event and designation is still celebrated by the Shia annually at the festival of *Eid al-Ghadeer*.

The division between Sunni and Shiite is more complex than that between, for example, Orthodox and Reformed in Judaism, Catholic and Protestant in Christianity, Republicans and Democrats in the US, or Conservatives and Labour parties in the UK. As a theocracy, differences in religion in Islam are essentially both blasphemous and treasonous. The world's headlines to this day are filled with reports of conflicts and slaughter between Sunnis and Shiites whose roots lie nearly fourteen hundred years in the past. The bitter statement below, written in 1866 by Chief Justice Joseph Arnould, could be found today inscribed in blood anywhere from a market in Baghdad to one in Damascus:

> In a world agreeing in reverencing Mahomet as the Apostle and the Quran as the word of God, the Sunis and Shias agree in little else except hating each other with the most cordial and bitter hatred. The quarrel of Ayesha and Fatima is an undying one, and Islam is still divided by the fierce enmities of the respective partizans of the favourite wife, and of the only daughter of the Apostle of God.[2]

The division between Sunni and Shia was to be a decisive factor in the career of Hasan-i-Sabah.

---

[1] Farhad Daftary, *The Ismailis: Their History and Doctrines*, p. 37.

[2] A. S. Picklay, *History of the Ismailis*, quoting Chief Justice Arnould in the Khoja case decision, p. 126. (For more on this case, see chapter seventeen of this book.) According to Arnould, Aisha hated Fatima and lobbied ceaselessly to have her father Abu Bakr acknowledged as caliph instead of Ali, p. 121.

The Early Years of Islam

The elderly Abu Bakr reigned for only two years after Muhammad's death. But he was charged to fight the Ridda Wars of 632–633 against the Banu Hanifa, a subtribe of the Quraysh, many of whom fought against the Prophet at the Battle of Badr in 627. In 632, the Banu Hanifa finally pledged their full allegiance to Muhammad shortly before his death. But unrest followed soon after and it remained for Abu Bakr to suppress any remaining dissent among the holdouts.

Abu Bakr would be progressively succeeded by three other "Companions of the Prophet," the designation for the earliest Muslim loyalists (*as-Sahabah*), who had been converted by Muhammad and had died in the faith. There are fifty or sixty of these men and women usually named, but the list can be expanded to as many as seventy thousand and well more when Muhammad's troops and the citizenry of various towns and cities who saw or heard him preach are considered.[1]

The first four caliphs after Muhammad are known as *Rashidun*, the Rightly Guided Caliphs. The Islamic armies under Abu Bakr's successor Omar (or Umar) brought all of Arabia under their rule and ultimately expanded their military conquests through Syria, Israel, Iraq, and Iran. They took Damascus in 635, Antioch in 636, and Jerusalem in 638. By 641 they controlled much of Syria, Persia, and Egypt. Caliph Omar was murdered in 644 and was succeeded by Othman. During Othman's reign, political and tribal rivalries predominated and there was much dissension. Those who supported Ali were active in their recruiting efforts to have him elected as caliph. In 656, Othman, too, was assassinated.

In 656, Ali was finally elected as the fourth of the Righteous Caliphs. But he walked into what would become a civil war. The Prophet's widow, Aisha, allied herself with two other companions

---

1 https://www.britannica.com/topic/Companions-of-the-Prophet. Also see https://en.wikipedia.org/wiki/Companions_of_the_Prophet [accessed September 5, 2019].

and began a full-scale revolt.[1] Although they were defeated, Ali was weakened.

Shiites believed the Islamic community had taken a wrong turn by focusing its efforts on building an empire. They preached the need to return to the true teachings of the Prophet. They reiterated that the only way to accomplish this was to maintain the succession of leadership within the Prophet's bloodline so that the spiritual mission of Islam could succeed and be recognized as the most important part of the religion. They accused the first three caliphs of being guilty of apostasy. They argued that the evidence of the two decades since the Prophet's death offered bleak testimony in support of their assertion that a formal link to divine wisdom and religious authority was essential.

Next, in 657, a cousin of Caliph Othman named Muawiya claimed the right of succession directly from Othman, and the civil war expanded. Ali and his diplomats attempted to negotiate a settlement but were outwitted by Muawiya. Ali was tricked into temporarily abdicating as caliph so that the issues of the rightful caliph could be resolved by a new election. Muawiya then proclaimed himself caliph and Islam was now split between two caliphs. The Sunni/Shiite split was inexorably hardening.

Ali fled from Medina to Kufa in Iraq where he established his new capital. He was murdered in 661. Muawiya established a rival capital in Damascus which would be the home of the Sunni Umayyad dynasty until 744.

The Crisis in Shiism

Hasan and Husayn were the two sons of Ali and Fatima. The Prophet was their maternal grandfather. Hasan, the eldest, succeeded his father as caliph of the Shiite party. A man of low character, he was bribed

---

[1] In addition to her hostility to Fatima, Aisha, had a longstanding grudge against Ali. She had once been publicly accused of adultery and believed (probably in error) that Ali was among those who had slandered her. See Lings, *Muhammad*, pp. 240–246. This is also mentioned in the Quran 24:11–17.

into abdicating by Muawiya.[1] His brother Husayn was approached to lead the Shiites, but he felt himself bound by Hasan's agreement to abdicate during the lifetime of Muawiya. Thus, when Muawiya died in 680, Husayn came to reclaim the caliphate as Ali's successor. Muawiya had been succeeded as the Sunni Umayyad caliph by his son Yazid. Yazid and his army of four thousand men attacked Husayn and his traveling party of seventy people at Karbala in Iraq. Among the very few survivors of this massacre were a number of women and children—including Husayn's young son Ali ibn Husayn (also known as Zayn al-Abid ["the adornment of the worshippers"]), the Prophet's great-grandson, who had been lying ill in his tent during the attack.[2] He was taken to Medina where he, the sole lineal descendant of Muhammad, remained quiescent. His piety and renown earned him the title of "Ornament of the Pious."[3]

The Karbala massacre was the event that gave birth to Shiism as a formally separate faith from that of the Sunnis. Today, approximately ten to thirteen percent of Muslims are Shiites.[4]

The death of the Prophet's grandson Husayn at the hands of the reigning religious and political leaders of the Muslim community caused a great deal of soul-searching, anger, betrayal, and shame among Muslims. Husayn's followers were especially disturbed by their inability to save him, adding the potent religious and psychological themes of expiation, suffering, and martyrdom to their understanding of Allah's will. "The story of Mohammed's grandson Husayn, who was betrayed and killed in an abortive attempt at the Caliphate, has won oceans of tears through the generations."[5] Husayn's martyrdom

---

[1] Although, in his opinion in the Khoja case regarding the proper Ismaili succession, Chief Justice Arnould wrote in 1866 that while Hasan did sell his birthright, he was "a saint and a recluse," and spent the money he received from Muawiya, "in works of charity and religion at Medina." A. S. Picklay, *History of the Ismailis*, p. 121.

[2] Daftary, *The Ismailis*, p. 50.

[3] Ibid., p. 69.

[4] https://en.wikipedia.org/wiki/Shia_Islam [accessed October 13, 2018].

[5] Hodgson, *The Order of Assassins*, p. 9.

has since been commemorated annually as the *Ashura* Mourning on the tenth day of the month of *Muharrum* by Shia worldwide.

Emotional attachment is a characteristic of the Shia, who incorporate a powerful sense of personal mission and earnestness in their beliefs. Their individual experience of the faith, as described by Marshall Hodgson, is composed of "a rich dramatic piety."[1]

A new Shiite leader arose named Muktar. He formed an Army of Penitents who defeated Yazid in 686. Although Muktar was a short-lived leader, he imbued Shiism with two of its most critical concepts, the power of the Imam and the advent of the Mahdi. As I wrote previously:

> These two figures are unique to Shiism. The Imams are viewed as the spiritual guides of mankind and temporal rulers of Islam, direct representatives of Allah. The Mahdi is the rightly-guided one, the messianic Imam chosen by Allah who will emerge from hiding at the proper time, triumph over his enemies, make the inner doctrine public, and usher in the age of truth, justice, and equality.[2]

Muktar also introduced a rather significant wrinkle into the Shiite understanding of leadership. He proclaimed one of Ali's sons (who was not Fatima's child) to be the Imam and Mahdi. Ali had married a woman named Khawla after Fatima's death. Khawla was also a member of the Banu Hanifa, the Prophet's tribe. She gave birth to a son with Ali named Muhammad ibn al-Hanifiyya. Muhammad ibn al-Hanifiyya was, thus, not a lineal descendant of Muhammad but of Ali. He died or disappeared in the mountains near Medina in the year 700. A small sect of Shiites believed that he had not died but he will reappear at the end of time as the Mahdi.[3]

---

1 Ibid., p. 8.

2 Wasserman, *The Templars and the Assassins*, p. 75.

3 Bernard Lewis, *The Assassins: A Radical Sect in Islam*, p. 23.

The Spread of Shiism

Shiism was widely embraced in Persia and Iraq. Muktar had capitalized on the frustration of the non-Arab Muslims who felt they were being treated as second-class citizens and were frustrated by the arrogance of the Sunni Arabs.[1] He tailored his outreach to these *mawali* (clients) and thus stimulated the growth of Shiism. "The discontent and grievances of the *mawali,* the non-Arab converts to Islam, provided a fertile recruiting ground for any revolutionary movement."[2] At the same time as these internal rebellions were occurring in Persia and Iraq, the Sunni Umayyads were extending their conquests abroad as far west as the Pyrenees, India to the south, and China to the east.[3]

The preaching mission of the Shia, and later the Ismailis and Nizari Ismailis, was a crucial and carefully-developed aspect of their efforts. They felt a great spiritual and religious hunger which they tried to answer through their missionary efforts. They also celebrated a vitality and diversity among the non-Arabs of the Middle East. Under the Fatimids, at the beginning of the eleventh century, the Ismailis would go so far as to create the *Dar al-Hikma* (House of Wisdom), a university designed specifically to teach the requisite skills and behavior for its students to serve as effective missionaries. Rashid al-Din in his *Jami al-Tawarikh* describes the Shiite *dai*:

> For every region and every district they appointed propagandists, men of pleasant speech, goodly eloquence, and sweet lucidity, as well as of sagacious and alert intelligence. To them the terms of their compacts and the benefits promised for their association were set forth in detail, and they were ordered to rule their lives in spiritual immaculateness, bodily purity, and unblemished conduct; they were, moreover, to be good-natured, pleasant spoken, and hail-fellow with all men; [in short] they were to be worthy of the "white hand of Moses and the breath

---

[1] See chapter two.

[2] Lewis, *The Origins of Ismailism*, p. 24.

[3] Franzius, *History of the Order of Assassins*, p. 11.

> of Christ." And with every man they were bidden to put forward their reasoning and conduct their arguments in fashion suited to his character and desires in life.[1]

The Imam was a concept that was familiar to the Persians. As we have noted earlier, Mesopotamian and Persian god men and women had been a characteristic archetype for millennia, as was the idea of revealed religion. It was part of

> the cult of the holy men—Imams and dais—who were believed to possess miraculous powers, and whose doctrines reflect mystical and illuminationist ideas derived from Gnosticism, Manichaeism, and various Iranian and Judaeo-Christian heresies.[2]

The Imams were the human representatives, the links between the impersonal vastness of Allah and His community of believers. The Imams offered personal contact and an emotional connection to the devotee. "[T]he imam is the full revelation of God."[3] Muhammad had fulfilled that role during his life.

The Political Nature of Schismatic Proselytizing

It cannot be stated often enough that Shiism, Ismailism, and Nizari Ismailism are political as well as religious movements. Their organizing outreach to the dispossessed non-Arabs included the promise of the betterment of the living conditions of the faithful by adherence to the proper modes of worship, and their alignment of social goals and principles with the will of Allah.

Among the Arabs themselves, many were unhappy about the loss of spiritual concerns in the face of politics and materiality that seemed

---

1 Rashid al-Din, *Jami al-Tawarikh*, translated by Reuben Levy, "The Account of the Ismaili Doctrines in the *Jami al-Tawarikh* of Rashid al-Din Fadallah," in *Journal of the Royal Asiatic Society*, 1930, p. 518.

2 Lewis, *The Assassins*, p. 24.

3 Hodgson, *The Order of Assassins*, p. 163.

to infect Islam. The poor resented the arrogant display of wealth by the Arab nobility, while the nomadic classes despised the control of property and the restrictions on travel and grazing rights that were being instituted by their rulers.[1] The murder of the Prophet's grandson—within half a century of Muhammad's death—plagued the conscience of all good Muslims, whether Sunni or Shiite.

The Abbasid Betrayal

The next stunning insult to the Shia would come from the establishment of the Abbasid Caliphate in 750. This dynasty would rule Islam for five hundred years and would remain a sworn enemy and target of Hasan-i-Sabah throughout his life. Powerful, corrupt, cynical, weak, bloodthirsty, and intriguing are all words that apply. However, the violence of the destruction of the last Abbasid caliph in Baghdad at the hands of Huelgu and his Mongol hordes in 1258 was a stiff price to pay. Some eight hundred thousand Muslims were slain over forty days.[2]

The Abbasid family was descended, as mentioned, from a paternal uncle of the Prophet named Abbas ibn Abdul-Muttalib. While a nominal supporter of Muhammad in Mecca, he did not emigrate to Medina, and later joined the polytheists of Mecca and fought against the Prophet at the Battle of Badr in 627. He became a convert to Islam after being captured. His later descendants claimed to subscribe to the Shia cause and announced their support for the passing of the Imamate from Muktar's chosen Muhammad ibn al-Hanifiyya, to his son Abu Hashim, and then to a distant cousin named Muhammad ibn Ali, the great-grandson of the Prophet's uncle.[3] In 716, a

---

1 Lewis, *The Assassins*, p. 22.

2 I. P. Petrushevsky, "The Socio-Economic Condition of Iran under the Il-Khans," in Boyle (ed.), *CHI*, vol. 5, p. 485. He is quoting the contemporary Persian historian Hamd Allah Qazvini (1281–1344) writing in his *Tarikh-i Guzida*. See also Burton, *The Book of the Thousand Nights and a Night*, vol. 10, Terminal Essay, p. 153 for the citation of forty days.

3 Daftary, *The Ismailis*, p. 62.

significant number of Shiites backed the Abbasid claim that they were legitimate holders of the Prophet's bloodline—through their common tribal roots and extended family ties—and were thus fit to lead Islam. Shiites enlisted in the Abbasid campaign to supplant the Umayyad caliphate, and they succeeded in 750, recognizing the son of Muhammad ibn Ali, Abu al-Abbas, as the first Abbasid caliph. On his accession to the throne, Caliph al-Abbas immediately turned around and betrayed his Shiite supporters, as mentioned in chapter two, ordering violent reprisals to curry favor with the majority Sunni Muslims. They then declared themselves a Sunni dynasty and established their capital in Baghdad.[1]

The Abbasid military victories and growing support encouraged the Sunni majority to embrace Abbasid leadership. Sunnis did not expect the same level of spiritual perfection among its leaders as the Shia sought in theirs. However, it should be noted that the initial Abbasid victory is witness to the growing strength of the Shia movement at this time. For with Shia support, claiming at first the mantle of Shiite leadership, the Abbasids managed to seize control of all of Islam (other than in Umayyad outposts like Spain and Morocco).

The Shia Turn Within

The Shia themselves were devastated. Their thirty-year-plus campaign for recognition, equality, and power had ended in betrayal and outrage. How could they have fallen for these lies? Perhaps there was a fundamental error in their doctrinal understanding. Perhaps there was a need for higher standards than they had applied to the Abbasid pretenders. Did not their entire program depend on their initial understanding that membership in the *Ahl al-Bayt*—the bloodline of the Prophet shared by Ali and Fatima—constitute the sole qualification for leadership of the Muslim community? Fatima was the key

---

[1] "Baghdad" in Persian means the Garden (*bagh*) of Justice (*dad*). Hardly how the Shiites must have felt about it after the Abbasids turned their backs on them. Burton (trans. and ed.), *The Book of the Thousand Nights and a Night,* vol. 3, note 1, p. 100.

despite the fact that early Islam entertained no provision for a female leader. At this point in time, the caliph was as much a warrior and a general as he was a religious guide and a political administrator. Ali, as the husband of the Prophet's daughter and a family member with deep spiritual ties to the Prophet, was the perfect choice for the role of caliph. But only because Fatima carried the precious DNA that she alone could pass to their descendants. How could some half-apostate uncle be the scion of a line of infallible Imams? Their error was palpable and the course forward was absolutely clear.

The Growth of the Concept of the Imam

Imams had been understood more broadly as applying to a variety of spiritual teachers following the Prophet's death. The idea, however, became far more restrictive after the Abbasid fiasco. No longer one of a broader group of wise teachers, the Imam developed into a more unique and messianic conception.[1] As the lineal descendent of Fatima, the Imam was the only one capable of guiding the community and defining the absolute values of Islamic practice. He was also the only one in a position to assess contrasting verses of the Quran, or discuss *hadith* that seemed ambiguous. He was in sole possession of the *ilm,* spiritual understanding. He chose his successor, usually his eldest son, and imbued him with *ilm* through a ceremony known as the Passing of the *Nass.* After receiving the *nass*, this designated successor was known as the *samit* or *hujja* during the lifetime of his father. There could only be one Imam at a time. The Imam's representatives, the *dais,* were those chosen, trained, and charged with the spreading of Truth (the *Dawa*), the summons to allegiance to the Imam.[2]

Fatima's husband Ali is universally recognized by Shia as the first Imam. Ali and Fatima's two sons, Hasan and Husayn, were respectively the second and third. Muktar's designation of Muhammad

---

1 Lewis, *The Assassins*, pp. 23–24.

2 Aziz Esmail and Azim Nanji, "The Ismailis in History," in Seyyed Hossein Nasr (ed.) *Ismaili Contributions to Islamic Culture*, pp. 232–233.

ibn al-Hanifiyya is considered a blind, a false path that resulted in the Abbasid charade. Such excursions in search of spiritual direction outside of the Prophet's immediate bloodline were to be shunned henceforth. The legitimate fourth Imam was Husayn's son Ali Zayin al-Abid, who had miraculously survived Yazid's slaughter at Karbala. He lived until 714. His son Muhammad al-Baqir was the proper fifth Imam as the great-great-grandson of the Prophet. He was the first of the Shiite Imams to openly fill the spiritual and political role of leader and Imam.[1]

Muhammad al-Baqir introduced the doctrine of *taqiyya*, caution or dissimulation. It allows the Shiite to conceal his true beliefs—to lie—without entering a state of sin, if it would prevent martyrdom, arrest, or shunning—primarily by the Sunnis—because one communicated Shia religious doctrine. It is a survival skill that allowed for preaching missions by *dais* and political organizing by the Shia throughout hostile territories and cities under Sunni control.

Upon his death in 732, al-Baqir was succeeded by his son Jafar al-Sadiq (d. 765), a learned and pious leader who is recognized by all Shiites as the sixth Imam. Jafar's Imamate coincided with the Abbasid rise, success, and betrayal—thus, making him especially conscious of the dangers the Shia faced.

Jafar enlarged upon his father's teaching of *taqiyya* by explaining that the Imam could not only exercise his spiritual authority in silence, but that the Imam was not bound to lead political opposition movements against the Sunni power structure. He could appear to retreat in the political realm and thus escape the persecution mounted against enemies of the state.[2]

The Ismaili Schism

The road leading us to Hasan-i-Sabah split again for Shiites in the choice of the seventh Imam. In the following discussion of the twists

---

[1] Daftary, *The Assassin Legends*, p. 13.

[2] Lewis, *The Assassins*, p. 25.

and turns of the Ismaili schism of 765 will be found significant roots of Hasan's Nizari Ismaili schism of 1094. Hasan-i-Sabah is first and foremost a religious leader, understood by all as the first outward voice and leader (*hujja*) of the Nizari Ismailis. To understand Hasan, one must understand the branching of Shiism that occurred at this point.

As is customary, Jafar al-Sadiq designated his eldest son Ismail his successor as the seventh Imam. The ceremony known as the Passing of the *Nass* is believed to have taken place. As mentioned above, this is the crucial moment when the reigning Imam passes on his inspiration and spiritual connection to his successor in anticipation of his own death. The chosen successor will become the Imam after his father's death.

It is believed that, for unknown reasons, Jafar later disinherited Ismail and "revoked" the *nass*. He is said to have passed it instead to another considerably younger son named Musa al-Kazim, his son by a slave girl.[1] The reasons for this are shrouded in obscurity.

Some say it was because Ismail was involved with a fervent political and spiritual revolutionary named Abul-Khattab.[2] Abul-Khattab was a close associate of Muhammad al-Baqir and later of Jafar al-Sadiq. He appears to have gone off the rails (according, at least, to Sunni heresiologists) with claims to being a prophet himself, that he was heir to Jafar's Imamate, preached libertinism, the extreme use of *taqiyya* beyond what is acceptable, taught doctrines of successive incarnations of Imams, and that he proclaimed the divinity of Jafar al-Sadiq. Abul-Khattab was publicly denied by Jafar in 755 and executed in 762 by order of the regional Abbasid governor. Ismaili sources on Abul-Khattab are very scarce. Maymun al-Qadah (see below) is said to have been one of his many disciples. The extremist strain of radical Shiite theology—which was not uncommon in these early years—is identified by the term *ghulat* (exaggerators).[3] Sunni

1 Juvaini, *Genghis Khan*, p. 643.

2 For reference to the discussion of Abul-Khattab in this paragraph, please see Lewis, *The Origins of Ismailism*, pp. 32–40.

3 Daftary, *The Assassin Legends*, p. 12.

heresiologists claim that after his death, Abul-Khattab's followers transferred their allegiance to Ismail's son Muhammad ibn Ismail.[1]

Other reasons have been advanced for Jafar's public abandonment of Ismail. It is said that Ismail had taken to strong drink. Some believe Ismail predeceased his father by five years, and that is the reason Jafar was forced to anoint Musa. Ismailis believe Ismail had passed the *nass* to his son Muhammad ibn Ismail before he died.[2] People say Jafar paraded Ismail's body before the notables and elders of Medina in the city cemetery and signed a document testifying to his death, while others believe that Jafar only pretended to appoint Musa as part of the doctrine of *taqiyya*.[3]

Musa al-Kazim is recognized as the seventh Imam by the majority of Shiites, then and now. His line continued through the twelfth Imam, Muhammad al-Mahdi, who disappeared about 873. The reappearance of the twelfth Imam at the End of Time, in triumph as the Mahdi, is still awaited by the majority of Shiites today. They are known as Twelver Shiites or *Ithna ashariyya*. This more moderate branch of Shiism has been the official religion of Iran since the sixteenth century.[4] It is estimated that some eighty-five percent of Shia today are Twelver Shiites.[5]

There is another possibility for the elevation of Musa al-Kazim. The Abbasids were actively hunting Shia. The Imam was, of course, their prime target. If Jafar was trying to protect Ismail by appointing Musa as a stand-in, events could be said to have borne out his

---

[1] An altogether different picture of Abul-Khattab is presented by Ismaili scholar Henri Corbin in "A Shiite Liturgy of the Grail." Khattab is here treated as an exalted spiritual figure, a founder of Ismailism, whose death was a tragedy, a willing self-sacrifice to honor his higher duties. It is an utterly fascinating document, brought to my attention by Peter Levenda. Initially published in 1974, it has been republished in *The Voyage and the Messenger: Iran and Philosophy*, see bibliography.

[2] Lewis, *The Origins of Ismailism*, p. 41.

[3] Juvaini, *Genghis Khan*, p. 643.

[4] Lewis, *The Assassins*, p. 26.

[5] https://en.wikipedia.org/wiki/Shia_Islam [accessed June 15, 2018].

intuition. Musa was later arrested by the Abbasids during the reign of Caliph Harun al-Rashid (r. 786–809), and imprisoned in Baghdad, where he is said to have been poisoned.[1] Rashid al-Din wrote that some Ismailis believed that Musa willingly gave his life for the sake of his elder brother Ismail.[2] Whatever actually happened and why, the consequences of the Shia split regarding the true identity of the seventh Imam have been enormous. Very little is known about Ismail in Ismaili sources. The majority of sources are Twelver and hostile to the conception of his Imamate.[3]

Ismailis are those who support the Imamate of Ismail as the true seventh Imam. They are known as Sevener Shiites or *Sabiyya*. Whether Ismail died before or after his father Jafar, Ismail was succeeded by his son Muhammad ibn Ismail (740–813). To complicate matters even further, some Ismailis believe that (if Ismail predeceased his father) Jafar secretly recognized Muhammad ibn Ismail as the seventh Imam.[4]

Little is known about the biography of Muhammad ibn Ismail. He was in his mid-twenties when his grandfather died.[5] After Jafar's recognition of Musa al-Kazim, Muhammad ibn Ismail left Medina and began a series of travels first to Iraq and later to Persia. He eventually settled in western Syria in Salamiyya, near Homs and Hama. Salamiyya was to be the center of the Ismaili *dawa* for the next century-and-a-half. Muhammad ibn Ismail was known as *al-Muktum* (the Hidden)—spared the wrath of the Abbasids that descended on Musa. "According to the later Ismailis, this emigration marks the beginning of the period of concealment (*dawr al-satr*) in

---

[1] Juvaini, *Genghis Khan*, p. 644.

[2] Rashid al-Din, *Jami al-Tawarikh*, translated by Levy, "The Account of the Ismaili Doctrines in the *Jami al-Tawarikh* of Rashid al-Din Fadallah," in *Journal of the Royal Asiatic Society*, 1930, p. 531.

[3] Daftary, *The Ismailis*, p. 97.

[4] Lewis, *The Origins of Ismailism*, p. 41.

[5] Daftary, *The Ismailis*, p. 102, from whom the biographical details of Muhammad ibn Ismail in this paragraph have been summarized.

early Ismailism, the concealment ending with the establishment of the Fatimid Caliphate."[1]

The Ismaili Period of Concealment

Muhammad ibn Ismail was succeeded by his son Wafi Ahmad Abdulla (d. 827), then by his grandson Taqi Muhammad (Ahmad ibn Abd Allah) (d. 843), and thereafter by his great-grandson Radi-u-din Abdulla (Husain) (d. 901).[2] The Ismaili Imams had entered a period of profound silence, *satr* or concealment, during which they kept the fact of their Imamate secret from all but a very small number of their most advanced chief *dais* in Salamiyya. Their time was devoted to quietly developing the Ismaili religious and philosophical doctrines that would sustain them for centuries to come. While they built upon their *Dawa* activities, their public teachings did not include the then-secret revelations about the continuing existence of the Imamate. Rather, making use of *taqiyya* for their own protection, they preached the Mahdiship of Muhammad ibn Ismail, the secret Imam who disappeared but did not die and who would return one day bringing salvation to all.

In 909, the Ismailis totally reversed this stance and proclaimed the establishment of the Fatimid Caliphate under the eleventh Imam known as Ubayd Allah.[3]

The Qarmatis

Hamdan Qarmat was an energetic preacher and political organizer who had been converted to Ismailism around 873. He and his brother-in-law Abdan worked in favor of the Imamate of Muham-

---

[1] Ibid., pp. 102–103.

[2] Esmail and Nanji, "The Ismailis in History," in Seyyed Hossein Nasr (ed.), *Ismaili Contributions to Islamic Culture*, p. 259.

[3] It is important to mention that different systems are used to number the Ismaili Imams. See Daftary, *The Ismailis*, pp. 104–105 and Rajput, *Hasan bin Sabbah*, p. 89.

mad ibn Ismail. Hamdan rose to become the chief *dai* of the Ismaili *Dawa* in Iraq, and responsible for appointing the district *dais*. His headquarters was located near Baghdad. While he worked under the authority of the Syrian *Dawa*, he was not aware of the identity of his superiors, nor apprised of their belief in the continuing Imamate. Hamdan was a successful organizer and his efforts spread through much of Iraq, Persia, Transoxiana, Sind, Syria, Bahrain, and Yemen.[1]

His followers were known as Qarmatis (or Carmatians) and the group attracted many people who were dissatisfied with the Abassid Caliphate and the lack of any highly organized resistance movement.

Hamdan organized a state in the area of Kufa in Iraq. His message of adherence to the Imam was heavily laced with the concept of social justice and economic equality. He and many others felt that the coming of the Mahdi would herald the end of poverty. Hamdan instituted numerous taxes on his people: the first was called *fitra*, a larger one called *hijra*, and an even greater one called *bulgha*.[2] He justified such taxes with reference to the duties of charity spelled out in the Quran. He distributed sweets as tokens of blessings among those who contributed. Ultimately, he arranged to value the belongings of everyone in his domain and collected one-fifth of that valuation from all, male and female.

After instituting these taxes, he arranged for his followers to gather their wealth together and contribute it to a common fund. This system began in 889 and was called the *ulfa*.[3] Such a practice is not uncommon in monastic communities. For example, Pythagoras instituted a similar discipline among his disciples in the sixth century BC. The primary difference in the Pythagorean community was that if a student chose to leave the academy, his goods would be returned.[4] Hamdan arranged for a trustworthy *dai* to be appointed in each village to oversee the distribution of all these goods. The poor and needy would be clothed and fed.

---

1 Daftary, *The Ismailis*, pp. 116–120.

2 Al-Muscati, *Hasan bin Sabbah*, p. 82.

3 Ibid., p. 83.

4 Thomas Stanley, *Pythagoras: His Life and Teachings*, p. 125.

The only personal property a person would retain was his sword. Professor Jawad al-Muscati speculates that since the appellation "Qirmat" was applied to Hamdan because of his red hair, the association of "red" with the socialist/communist movements of later times comes from the Qarmati.[1] Nizam al-Mulk wrote that the Ismailis/Qarmatis were a continuation of the Sasanian era religion of Mazdakism, discussed in chapter two.[2]

Hamdan Qarmat and his followers would become the first casualties of the *satr* policies of the nascent Ismaili Imams in Salamiyya. By 899, Hamdan had noted a subtle change in the message emanating from the Syrian Ismaili headquarters. He sent Abdan to investigate the claims of Ubayd Allah (Abd Allah). He was shocked to learn that Ubayd Allah considered himself an Imam, and more shocked to learn that he had declared himself a successor Imam within the lineage of Muhammad ibn Ismail.[3] Ubayd Allah stated that Muhammad ibn Ismail had died in 813 and was therefore not the Mahdi or *Qaim*, the redeemer of all at the end of time—as Hamdan and the Qarmatis believed and had preached for so long.

Hamdan and Abdan refused to acknowledge the Imamate of Ubayd Allah. The Qarmati schismed off. They were embraced by the ruler of Bahrain which became an important Qarmati center thereafter.[4] They continued to follow the silent Imam Muhammad ibn Ismail, whom they expected would return as the Mahdi in line with their earlier beliefs. They wrote to their *dais*, many of whom broke away from the Fatimids. Soon after, Hamdan traveled to Kalwadha in Iraq, a large town on the left bank of the Tigris just south of Baghdad. There is no further historical record of his doings. Abdan was murdered, possibly under orders from the Ismaili leadership.[5]

---

1 Al-Muscati, *Hasan bin Sabbah*, p. 93.

2 Lewis, *The Origins of Ismailism*, p. 96, referring to Nizam al-Mulk's book the *Siyasat-Name*.

3 Daftary, *The Ismailis*, pp. 125–126.

4 Daftary, *The Assassin Legends*, p. 19.

5 Daftary, *The Ismailis*, p. 126.

Another difference between the Fatimids and Qarmatis was political. The Fatimids sought for a more inclusive outreach to the most potential converts possible, while the Qarmatis intended to keep their government strictly limited to fellow Ismailis.[1] The Qarmatis became so radical that in 930, under the leadership of Abu Tahir al-Jannabi (r. 923–944), they attacked Mecca, massacred pilgrims, and stole the Black Stone from the Kaaba.[2] It was only returned in 950–951 after a significant ransom was paid by the Abbasid caliph.[3] During the reign of the fourth Fatimid caliph al-Muizz (r. 953–975)—who established Cairo as the Fatimid capital—the Qarmatis went to war against their former allies in a two-year campaign from 972 to 974. The Qarmatis went through a series of their own doctrinal and political developments, ultimately disappearing as a separate entity by 1077, and generally reintegrating back into the Fatimid fold.

The radicalism and antinomianism of the Qarmatis has long plagued the reputation of the Ismailis. They were often indiscriminately linked together, especially by Sunni heresiologists who pursued an ideological vendetta against the growing power of the Fatimid state.

The Slander of Maymun al-Qaddah and his son Abd Allah b. Maymun

More controversy swirls around Maymun al-Qaddah and his son Abd Allah b. Maymun al-Qaddah. An anti-Ismaili Sunni historian named Ibn Rizam in the early tenth century called Maymun al-Qaddah the founder of Ismailism, identified him as the progenitor of the Fatimid dynastic line, and stated that he led a sect called al-Maymuniyyan. Ibn Rizam further declared Maymun to be a non-Alid follower of the Syrian Christian Gnostic Bardesanes (154–222).[4] Others asserted that Maymun al-Qaddah was of the Zoroas-

---

1 Lewis, *The Origins of Ismailism*, pp. 85–86.

2 Daftary, *The Ismailis*, p. 162.

3 Ibid., p. 164.

4 Ibid., pp. 109–115

trian Dualist faith, a philosopher, whose mission was to corrupt Islam with atheism and similar evils.[1]

These are extraordinary charges if we consider all the beliefs about the bloodline of the Prophet that would be violated if they were true. Ibn Rizam's original work is lost but it was used extensively in 980 by another anti-Ismaili polemicist called Akhu Muhsin. Ibn Rizam and Akhu Muhsin's work became the basis of the "Baghdad Manifesto," an anti-Fatimid tract issued in 1011 under the Abbasid caliph al-Qadir (r. 991–1031).[2] This epistle was a public denunciation of the Fatimid claims to a proper Alid descent. Its charges became the standard historical fare by which the Ismailis were long attacked, and which served as an important source for nineteenth-century European orientalists.[3] A similar manifesto was released in Baghdad in 1052 under Caliph al-Qaim (r. 1031–1075), again seeking to discredit Fatimid claims to an Alid descent.[4]

The story goes on to state that Maymun's son, Abd Allah, claimed to be a prophet and to have instituted a clandestine degree system of seven stages that culminated in libertinism and atheism.[5] He preached on behalf of Muhammad ibn Ismail as the expected redeemer. After fleeing various religious opponents, he ended up in Salamiyya, from which he sent *dais* to neighboring areas. He died around 874 after his *dais* succeeded in converting Hamdan Qarmat in Iraq. Abd Allah is identified in this anti-Ismaili broadside as the ancestor of Ubayd Allah, the first of the Fatimid Imams.

Despite the name Maymun being an integral part of the anti-Ismaili propaganda for centuries, Farhad Daftary offers an interesting supposition. He states that the Ismaili Imams were forced to adopt various levels of concealment to protect themselves against persecution by both the reigning Sunni Abbasids and hostile Twelver Shiites. He posits that the name Maymun (the Fortunate One) may, in fact,

---

1 Hodgson, *The Order of Assassins*, p. 123.

2 Daftary, *The Assassin Legends*, pp. 25–26.

3 Daftary, *The Ismailis*, p. 109.

4 Daftary, *The Assassin Legends*, p. 24.

5 Daftary, *The Ismailis*, p. 110.

have been an alias of Muhammad ibn Ismail. If this is accurate, it makes complete sense that he would be considered the progenitor of the Fatimid dynasty.[1]

The Proclaiming of the Fatimid Dynasty

The Fatimid dynasty, by its choice of name, identified itself as composed of the lineal descendants of Fatima and Ali. The Fatimids ruled Egypt from 910 for some two-and-a-half centuries with eight functioning caliphs. The Nizari Ismail split in 1094 fractured the already waning political power of the Fatimid Caliphate, which survived through four progressively weaker leaders until Saladin returned Egypt to Sunni control in 1171.

The two-hundred-year period of the Fatimid state, before the Nizari Ismaili schism, is known as the Golden Age of Ismailism. At its greatest extent, the Fatimid Empire included Egypt, Syria, North Africa, Sicily, the Red Sea coast of Africa, Yemen, and the Hijaz in Arabia.[2] Arts and sciences were encouraged as was education. The Fatimids established the world's first university, the Al-Azhar. They founded the city of Cairo as their capital in 969, and it became a center of culture and commerce. Fatimid administrators were generally fair and competent, providing stable leadership that encouraged well-being and prosperity. There was a sense of religious tolerance in which Christians and Jews were welcomed. For example, al-Aziz (r. 975–996), the fifth Fatimid caliph, appointed both Christians and Jews to high position in his government. He was also married to a Christian woman who may have been the mother of his son and successor, al-Hakim.[3]

The exception to this overall Fatimid policy of religious tolerance was during the reign of Caliph al-Hakim (r. 996–1021). He proved to

---

[1] Ibid., p. 112.

[2] Lewis, *The Assassins*, p. 31. (The Hijaz is the most populous western region of Saudi Arabia bordering the Red Sea. It includes the holy cities of Mecca and Medina and the important port city of Jeddah.)

[3] Daftary, *The Ismailis*, p. 189.

be a particularly unstable and erratic leader who persecuted both Jews and Christians. His intolerance extended to Sunni Muslims as well, and he promoted the Shiite practice of cursing the first three caliphs as usurpers of the legitimate rights of Ali.[1] He did however found the *Dar al-Hikma,* or House of Wisdom in 1005, as a center for the training of *dais*. Hasan-i-Sabah would travel to Egypt to attend this prestigious institution in 1078. Al-Hakim ordered the destruction of the Church of the Holy Sepulcher in Jerusalem in 1009, which ended the Fatimid/Byzantine truce and would become a proximate cause of the Crusades decades later.

In the year 1017, a group of Ismailis loyal to al-Hakim began to splinter off from the more orthodox Fatimid fold and form a distinctly separate group, later known as the Druze. Several of his *dais* began to preach that the Imam was actually a deity.[2] This was in stark contrast to all the traditional views of the Imam. To the majority of Shiites and Ismailis, the Imam was the human representative of Allah. He was the leader of the Muslims, divinely appointed and inspired through his genetic link to the Prophet. His judgment was infallible and sinless. But he was human. The extremity of the doctrine of the Druze *dais* led to the wrath of the Ismaili establishment. Druze leader al-Akhram was assassinated in 1018.[3] The movement continued, however, and proclaimed Caliph al-Hakim as the *Qaim,* the final Imam, whose reign heralded the *Qiyama,* the end of Islam, the abrogation of *sharia*, and the beginning of Paradise on Earth. Caliph al-Hakim himself died or disappeared in 1021 and was succeeded by his son al-Zahir, who became the seventh Fatimid caliph. Al-Hakim's reappearance is still awaited by some three hundred thousand Druze living today mainly in Syria, Lebanon, and Egypt.[4]

Belief in the *Qiyama* would reappear in 1164 and will be discussed in chapter nineteen.

---

1 Ibid., p. 189.

2 Lewis, *The Assassins*, p. 33.

3 Daftary, *The Ismailis*, p. 195.

4 Ibid., p. 198.

The Brethren of Sincerity

Another notable group was centered in Basra and Baghdad during the tenth century. They called themselves the *Ikhwan al-Safa* (Brethren of Sincerity or Brethren of Purity). Their revolutionary Gnostic and Neoplatonic teachings were preserved in the anonymous and encyclopedic *Rasail Ikhwan al-Safa* ("Epistles of the Sincere Brethren"), a collection of fifty-one essays divided into four sections which discussed all known science of the time, including: astronomy, astrology, geometry, mathematics, acoustics, music, geography, and optics, in addition to philosophical and religious speculation on cosmology, theology, eschatology, and the transmigration and survival of souls. The goal of their teachings was to help the reader purify the soul and achieve salvation through a blending of Greek Neoplatonism, Christian ethics, Sufi mysticism, and Muslim law. It "is saturated with Ismaili thought, and exercised a profound influence on Muslim intellectual life from Persia to Spain."[1]

One of the best descriptions of the work is published on the website of the Institute of Ismaili Studies, a modern research organization under the direction of the Aga Khan:

> The Ikhwan were also implicitly influenced by Ancient Indian and Persian classics, and they were enthusiastically inspired by the Greek legacies of the likes of Pythagoras, Socrates, Plato, Aristotle, Plotinus, Euclid, Ptolemy, Porphyry, and Iamblichus. Finding "truth in every religion" and seeing knowledge as the pure "nourishment for the soul," the Ikhwan associated the pursuit of happiness and the hope of salvation with the scrupulous unfolding of rational and intellectual quests. They furthermore promoted a friendship of virtue among their companions and gave a venerable expression to the liberal spirit in Islam. Their syncretism . . . would prudently assist their co-religionists in overcoming the sectarian discords that plagued their era.[2]

---

1 Lewis, *The Assassins*, p. 30.

2 https://iis.ac.uk/encyclopaedia-articles/brethren-purity [accessed July 6, 2019].

The *Rasail* may also have been raised as an anti-Fatimid banner under which to unite non-Fatimid Ismaili dissidents, including the Qarmatis, because its teachings support Muhammad ibn Ismail. As it was written in Basra, when the Qarmatis controlled the region, it was likely done with their support.[1] The *Rasail* was known to have been studied by the charismatic Syrian Assassin leader Rashid al-Din Sinan,[2] who undoubtedly shared it with his friend and fellow student Hasan II, later the fourth Lord of Alamut.

Samuel M. Stern suggests that the Society of Sincere Brethren was meant to be the idealized Ismaili community itself.[3] He believed the anonymous authors of the *Rasail* were revealed in an account of a late-tenth-century author named Abu Hayyan al-Tawhidi. Stern wrote that a small group of friends in Basra connected with the Ismaili movement composed the *Rasail* "in order to propagate their ideas about the reconciliation of philosophical and religious truth."[4] He is contradicted by Abbas Hamdani, a modern scholar, who dates the work to a century earlier, between 873 and 909 (before the declaration of the Fatimid Imamate). Hamdani rejects Abu Hayyan's assertion by name.[5]

Stern presents an alternate theory that, following the death of Muhammad ibn Ismail, the authors were actually the secret Ismaili Imams and the *dais* working under them. Muhammad's son Abd Allah ibn Muhammad (Wafi Ahmad Abdulla), or his son and successor Ahmad ibn Abd Allah, in this version, is alternately credited with supervising the epistles, thus placing the *Rasail* at the highest level

---

[1] Daftary, *The Ismailis*, p. 248.

[2] Edward Burman, *The Assassins: Holy Killers of Islam*, p. 55 (citing Philip K. Hitti, *History of the Arabs*, London: Macmillan, 1979, p. 373). Daftary reports specifically that Sinan studied the *Rasail* at Alamut. *The Ismailis*, p. 397.

[3] Samuel M. Stern, "New Information About the Authors of the 'Epistles of the Sincere Brethren,'" in *Studies in Early Ismailism*, p. 176.

[4] Ibid., pp. 155–156.

[5] Abbas Hamdani, "A Critique of Paul Casanova's Dating of the *Rasail Ikhwan al-Safa*," in Daftary (ed.) *Mediaeval Ismaili History and Thought*, p. 146.

of Ismaili authority.[1] Yet another theory of authorship attributes the *Rasail* to a tenth/eleventh century Muslim mathematician in Spain named Maslama al-Majriti. His name was used by a forger who attributed to him the *Ghayat al-Hakim*, a pseudepigraphical work on magic and astrology later known in the West as the *Picatrix*.[2]

Edward Burman summarizes the ambitious and encyclopedic content of the *Rasail*. The fifty-one epistles include four categories: Epistles one to thirteen discuss mathematics and logic; fourteen to thirty cover natural sciences and anthropology; thirty-one to forty are concerned with psychology; and forty-one to fifty-one discuss theology, including the occult sciences.[3]

The words of John Donne seem particularly appropriate in closing this Part One.

> "No man is an island, entire of itself; every man is part of the continent."[4]

Having illumined some of the landscape of that continent, let us now move on to the man Hasan-i-Sabah.

---

[1] Stern, "New Information About the Authors of the 'Epistles of the Sincere Brethren,'" in *Studies in Early Ismailism*, pp. 168 and 171. Daftary mentions that "according to Ismaili tradition," Ahmad was the author of the *Rasail*. *The Ismailis*, p. 107.

[2] Stern, "New Information About the Authors of the 'Epistles of the Sincere Brethren,'" in *Studies in Early Ismailism*, pp. 173–174.

[3] Burman, *The Assassins*, p. 56.

[4] John Donne, *Devotions Upon Emergent Occasions*, 1624.

PART TWO

The Life of Hasan-i-Sabah

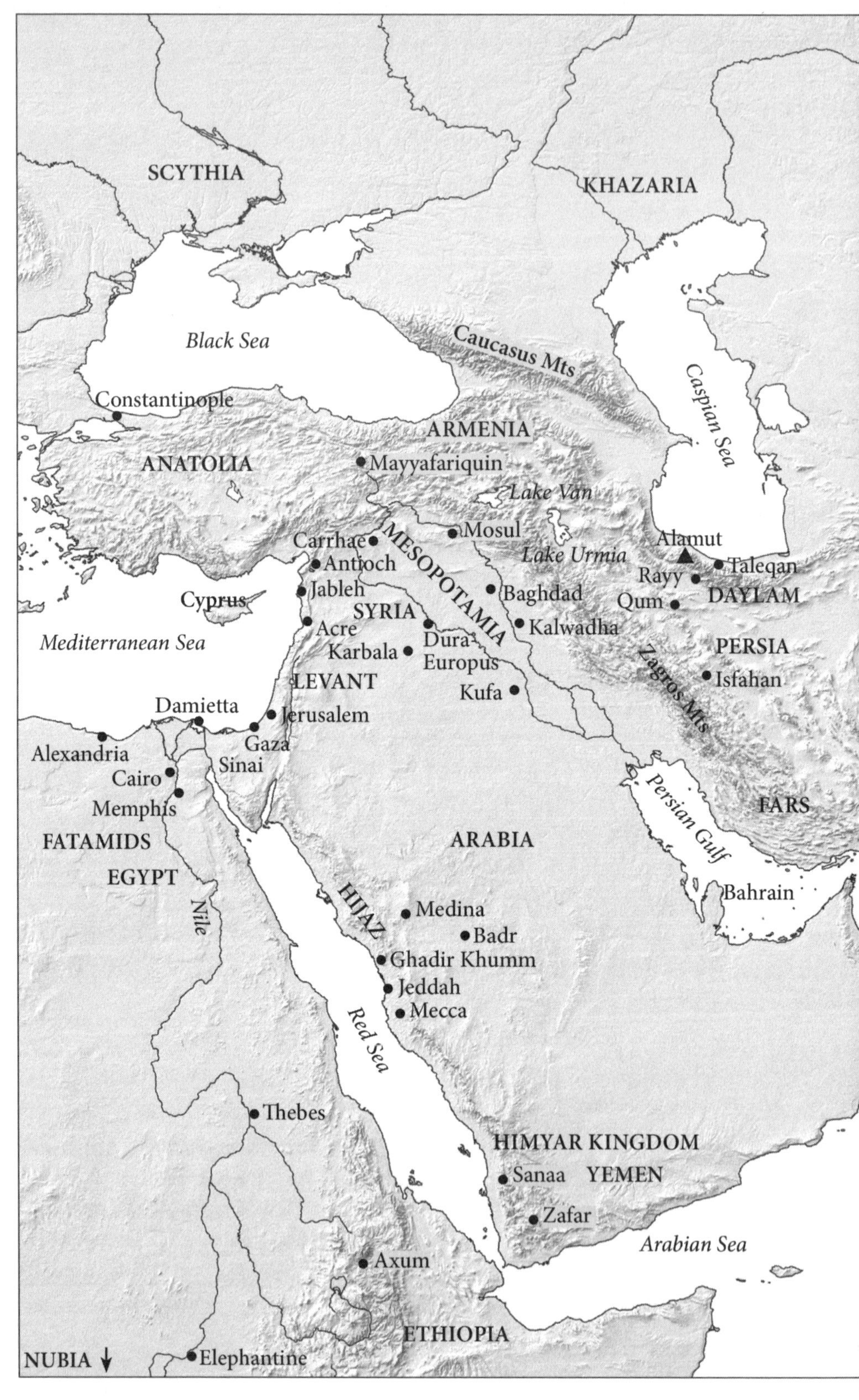
SCYTHIA
KHAZARIA
Black Sea
Caucasus Mts
Caspian Sea
Constantinople
ARMENIA
ANATOLIA
Mayyafariquin
Lake Van
Mosul
MESOPOTAMIA
Carrhae
Alamut
Lake Urmia
Antioch
Taleqan
Rayy
Jableh
Baghdad
Qum
DAYLAM
Cyprus
SYRIA
Acre
Kalwadha
Mediterranean Sea
Karbala
Dura
Europus
PERSIA
Zagros Mts
Isfahan
LEVANT
Kufa
Damietta
Jerusalem
Gaza
Alexandria
Sinai
Cairo
Persian Gulf
Memphis
FARS
FATAMIDS
ARABIA
EGYPT
HIJAZ
Bahrain
Nile
Medina
Badr
Ghadir Khumm
Jeddah
Mecca
Red Sea
Thebes
HIMYAR KINGDOM
Sanaa
YEMEN
Zafar
Arabian Sea
Axum
ETHIOPIA
NUBIA ↓
Elephantine

CHAPTER FOUR

Hasan's Roots and Youth

Hadra Baba Sayyid-na Hasan-i Sabbah (may his grave be hallowed and may we be blessed in him).
—*Haft Bab-i Baba Sayyid-na*[1]

HASAN-I-SABAH (ca. 1050–1124) was the founder of the Nizari Ismaili movement and of the state that embodied its *Dawa*. The oldest record of his story is the biography/autobiography that was preserved from the flames of the Mongol conquerors in 1256, and recounted by Ata-Malik Juvaini and Rashid al-Din Tabib not long after. Known as *The Biography of Our Master* (*Sar-Guzasht-i-Sayyidna*), it begins by stating that Hasan traced his descent to the ancient Himyar tribe.[2]

The Himyar Kingdom was located in Yemen at the south of the Arabian peninsula along the Red Sea. It was established in 115 BC and lasted until 525 AD.[3] Its capital was originally Zafar, but was moved north in the fourth century to the modern Yemeni city of Sanaa. The Himyarite Kingdom was an active trading society dealing in ivory, frankincense, and myrrh, which they shipped along the east African coast to customers in the Roman Empire. The Himyars first conquered the neighboring Saba (Sheba) tribe in 25 BC, although it was not until 280 AD that they were fully victorious over the Sabaean kingdom. Saba was, of course, the home of the biblical Queen of Sheba who had visited King Solomon in Jerusalem circa 950 BC.[4]

---

1 *Haft Bab-i Baba Sayyid-na*, ca. 1200, translated by Marshall Hodgson as appendix one of *The Order of Assassins*, p. 301.

2 Juvaini, *Genghis Khan*, p. 667; Rashid al-Din, appendix two, p. 301.

3 https://www.britannica.com/topic/Himyar [accessed May 5, 2018].

4 In Burton (trans and ed.), *The Book of the Thousand Night and a Night*, Solomon is called the "Sovereign of the land of Saba," vol. 7, p. 316.

The Himyarite kings abandoned their pagan beliefs and converted to Judaism in 380.[1] Surprising as this may sound, "We can now say that an entire nation of ethnic Arabs in southwestern Arabia had converted to Judaism and imposed it as the state religion."[2] They worshipped their sole deity under His name Rahmanan (the Merciful), referred to themselves as "the people of Israel," and invoked His blessing as "Lord of the Jews."[3]

Himyar was conquered by Christians from the Ethiopian kingdom of Axum in 525, after the Himyarites had launched a brutal campaign two years before against Arabian Christians refusing to convert to Judaism.[4] Himyar then became Christian before the Muslim hegemony was established throughout the region in the seventh century. The history of the Himyar Jewish kingdom and the Ethiopian Christian kingdom was intimately connected with the political rivalry between the Sasanian Persians (who supported Yemen) and Byzantine Christians (who supported Ethiopia). According to scholar G. W. Bowersock, "The tumultuous events in sixth-century Arabia may reasonably be called the crucible of Islam."[5]

The connection to Judaism is also intriguing because Hasan's domain was carved out of the Elburz Mountains along the southern end of the Caspian Sea. In the northwest Caspian territory, just above the Caucasus Mountains, was the kingdom of Khazaria. Sometime around the year 838, the Khazar king Bulan converted to Judaism.[6] After almost a century and a half as a Jewish

---

[1] Christian Julien Robin, "Arabia and Ethiopia," in Scott Johnson (ed.), *The Oxford Handbook of Late Antiquity*, p. 279.

[2] Bowersock, *The Throne of Adulis*, p. 4.

[3] Ibid., p. 81.

[4] According to Pickthall in *The Meaning of the Glorious Koran*, verses 4–7 of surah 85 refer to the massacre, p. 644.

[5] Bowersock, *The Throne of Adulis*, p. 87. In 1949–1950, surviving Yemeni Jews, about fifty thousand, were airlifted to Israel. See Ariel David, "Before Islam: When Saudi Arabia Was a Jewish Kingdom," *Haaretz*, 11/29/2107, https://www.haaretz.com/jewish/archaeology/1.709010 [accessed May 1, 2018].

[6] Kevin Alan Brook, *The Jews of Khazaria: Second Edition*, p. 113.

kingdom, the Khazars converted to Islam around 965 in return for military support against the Rus tribes to their north.[1] Prior to their ninth-century conversion, the Khazars had long welcomed displaced Jews traveling from the Mideast, as well as from Byzantium and elsewhere.

Hasan's Early Years

Juvaini and Rashid al-Din continue their quotes from the *The Biography of Our Master*, explaining that Hasan's father, Ali ibn-Muhammad, had emigrated from Yemen to modern Iraq, settling first in Kufa, Caliph Ali's short-lived capital on the Euphrates River. He continued on to Iran where he lived in Qum, now Iran's largest city, east of the Namak Lake on the banks of the Qum River. From there he traveled to Rayy, which would become the birthplace of Hasan-i-Sabah.[2]

Rayy flourished near modern Tehran and was one of the greatest cities of Iranian antiquity, dating as far back as the third millennium BC. It was at one time the capital of ancient Media. The northern route of the Silk Road passed through here, thus bringing exotic wares and travelers from lands east and west, near and far. Mentioned in the *Zend Avesta*, the apocryphal *Book of Tobit*, and throughout *The Shahnameh*, Rayy was captured by Arab Muslims in 641 and was reputed to be one of the most beautiful cities of its day. It later served as the birthplace of the famed Abbasid caliph Harun al-Rashid (b. ca. 765, r. 786–809).[3] It was the Seljuk capital between 1043 and 1051 during

---

1 Ibid., p. 153.

2 Bernard Lewis writes that Hasan was born in Qum, in *The Assassins*, p. 38. Modern Ismaili scholar Farhad Daftary agrees, writing this in several places. See, for example, http://iis.ac.uk/encyclopaedia-articles/hasan-sabbah [accessed March 20, 2018]. Both Juvaini, *Genghis Khan*, p. 667, and Rashid al-Din, appendix two, p. 301, specify Rayy as Hasan's birthplace. Lewis, in a note (see p. 149, note 1), ascribes the problem to a "careless abridgement by Juvayni." Qum is about eighty miles south of Rayy.

3 Burton, *The Book of a Thousand Nights and a Night*, vol. 4, p. 104, note 1.

the reign of Sultan Toghril Beg (r. 1037–1063). He later moved his administrative headquarters to Isfahan which remained the Seljuk capital until 1118, or most of the rest of Hasan's life. Rayy had been a center of activity for Ismaili *dais* since the ninth century. The city was destroyed by the Mongols in 1220.[1]

Hasan, thus, grew up in a sophisticated metropolitan hub of international trade, religious proselytizing, and political activity, with a long and diverse history.

---

[1] *Encyclopedia Britannica*, https://www.britannica.com/place/Rayy [accessed July 9, 2018].

CHAPTER FIVE

Conversion to Ismailism

> After the Ismaili system had been elaborately completed at Cairo under the Fatimite Caliphs, receiving there a superstructure of Egyptian Hierophantism upon the basis of Magian and Indian dogma, which it had derived from its Persian founders, it had the fortune, a little after the eleventh century of our era . . . to attract the attention of a very accomplished young Persian of Arabian descent and Shia faith, who had earlier given promise of a brilliant career. —Sir Joseph Arnould[1]

HASAN IDENTIFIED HIMSELF in his first-person portion of the *Sar-Guzasht-i-Sayyidna* as a Twelver Shiite. In the version of this story published by Rashid al-Din, Hasan explains, "In my childhood, and at the age of seven, I was interested in learning various sciences and I wanted to be a religious scholar. I was seeking this knowledge until I was seventeen years old. I was faithful to Shiism, *Ithna ashariyya,* the religion of my ancestors."[2]

Hasan then tells the story of meeting Amira Zarrab (the Coiner),[3] his first Ismaili contact, a *rafiq* or comrade, the first level of Ismaili instructor below a *dai.*

> We constantly disputed with each other and he tried to destroy my beliefs. I did not give in to him but his words took root in my heart. Meanwhile I was overwhelmed with a very dreadful illness and I thought to myself: "That is the true religion and because of my fanaticism I would not admit it. If, which Heaven forfend, my appointed hour should come, I shall have perished

1 Arnould, in Picklay, *History of the Ismailis*, p. 131.

2 Rashid al-Din, see appendix two, p. 301.

3 It was customary for Ismaili *dais* to take up a trade and adopt trade names as a form of disguise. Burman, *The Assassins*, p. 29.

without attaining the truth." It so happened that I recovered from that illness.[1]

In Rashid al-Din's longer presentation of the *Sar-Guzasht-i-Sayyidna,* Hasan mentions that before his time with Amira Zarrab, he had been introduced to the Ismaili doctrine by the *hujja*[2] of Khurasan, Nasir-i Khusraw (ca. 1004–ca 1088). Nasir-i Khusraw was an important figure in the Ismaili movement and the history of Persia. Considered one of the greatest Persian poets, he was a philosopher and traveler as well as a religious teacher. Born into a family of government officials in Balkh in Khurasan (about two hundred miles northwest of Kabul), he served in the Ghaznavid court until a religious experience at around age forty-two transformed his life.[3] Nasir-i Khusraw resigned from his position and set off on a pilgrimage to Mecca around 1045. His journeys lasted some seven years. He arrived in Cairo in 1047 where he met Caliph al-Mustansir. Nasir-i Khusraw stayed in Egypt for about three years and became certified as a high-ranking *dai.* He returned eventually to Balkh where he preached the Ismaili doctrine. Persecuted by Sunni forces, he traveled on and continued his proselytizing in the Caspian region around the time of Hasan's birth, before returning again to Balkh. After further persecution by the Sunni *ulema*, he traveled on to Yumgan in the Badakhshan Province of northern Afghanistan. Here Nasir-i Khusraw remained until his death under the protection of an independent emir. A shrine to his memory is located there today and the area is a prominent Nizari Ismaili center. We do not know when he met the

---

[1] Juvaini, *Genghis Khan*, p. 667.

[2] *Hujja* (proof) was a high-ranking teacher in the Fatimid hierarchy, generally charged with the administration of a territory (Hodgson, *The Order of Assassins*, p. 44) and supervising the *dais* or "summoners" in his region. Hasan would later become the *hujja* of Alamut, the outer representative of the Hidden Imam, as the Hidden Imam could be considered the outer representative of God. *Hujja,* as mentioned in chapter three, is a term also applied to the *samit,* or designated successor (who has received the *nass*) of the living Imam.

[3] The biographical details are summarized from Daftary, *The Ismailis,* pp. 215–219.

young Hasan-i-Sabah, but the latter reports that "he was not successful in this work" of converting him.[1]

Hasan considered the Ismaili faith a *philosophy,* a term of denigration when compared to the more pure concept of religion. Later, Amira Zarrab patiently and gently led him to an embrace of the Ismaili doctrine. "At night, when you reflect in your bed, you will know what I say is necessary for you."[2] Hasan and Amira were separated for a time and Hasan continued his studies in the Ismaili literature. Then the aforementioned illness took place and he realized he could die in a state of disbelief because of his anxiety about accepting the truth of the Imam.

Hasan next met a *dai* named Abu-Najam Sarraj (the Saddler) who took him even deeper into the Ismaili hidden secrets and doctrinal complexities.

Finally, a meeting with another Ismaili agent named Mumin resulted in Hasan taking the oath of allegiance to the Fatimid Ismaili Imam al-Mustansir. There is a humorous incident of wordplay recorded about their interaction. The meaning of the name Mumin in Arabic is "believer." The meaning of the name Hasan is "good." Hasan was also the name of the son of Ali who followed him as Imam. Mumin quipped that Hasan was, thus, more spiritually advanced than himself. How could Mumin deliver the covenant to Hasan?[3]

In 1071–1072, Abd al-Malik ibn Attash, the chief *dai* of Iraq who would be an important figure in Hasan's life, came to Rayy. Hasan writes, "I met with his approval, and he made me a deputy *dai* and indicated I should go to his Majesty in Egypt, who at the time was Mustansir."[4] It would be several years before Hasan made this journey. Abd al-Malik ibn Attash was headquartered at Isfahan and in charge of all western Persia from at least Kirmin to Azerbaijan. He was widely respected, even by Sunnis.[5]

---

1 Rashid al-Din, appendix two, p. 302.

2 Rashid al-Din, appendix two, p. 303.

3 Rashid al-Din, appendix two, p. 304.

4 Juvaini, *Genghis Khan*, p. 668; Rashid al-Din, appendix two, p. 304.

5 Hodgson, "The Ismaili State," in Boyle (ed.), *CHI*, vol. 5, p. 428.

In addition to their religious preaching, the Ismailis of the 1080s to 1090s (i.e., before Hasan established Alamut as an active military center) were fighting a series of diffuse rebellions against Seljuk domination. Widespread individual uprisings were the theme rather than a coordinated military campaign.[1]

The Fatimid caliph al-Mustansir would be intimately involved with the mission of Hasan-i-Sabah. Al-Mustansir began his long reign (1036–1094) at the age of seven. For one brief moment in 1058, and lasting about a year, the Fatimids took control of Baghdad and the Abbasid Caliphate. The Friday *khutba* prayer for the leader of Islam was, thus, spoken in the name of Caliph al-Mustansir, representing the height of the Fatimid power.[2]

The Ismaili Mysteries

Let us pause to ask what Mysteries, what hidden secrets, Hasan might have been exposed to by his several Ismaili instructors. We have earlier discussed some of the problems of the succession of the caliph and the identity of the Imam. But there is a great deal more. Part One of this book illustrates that Islam in Mesopotamia and Persia had absorbed a wide variety of indigenous ideologies as it pursued its seventh century conquests.

Shiism and Ismailism were spread by conversion. And conversion involves dialogue, a mutual sharing of ideas and beliefs. This theme of transformation is crucial to an understanding of the Nizaris and is here cogently expressed by the eminent scholar of Islam, Bernard Lewis:

> [T]he entry of large numbers of superficially Islamized Persians, Aramaeans, Syrians and others necessarily worked a fundamental change in Shiism as a doctrine and as a purpose. Soon a welter of strange beliefs, brought over from Christian, Iranian, and Old Babylonian heresies, found their way into Shia theol-

[1] Ibid., p. 428.

[2] Daftary, *The Ismailis*, pp. 205–206.

> ogy. The movement came to be dominated by the *mawali* and oppressed classes, and became the instrument of their social and religious revolt against the oppression of the orthodox state.[1]

Ideas totally foreign to either the Arab people or Islam itself become incorporated through contact with alien cultures. The Zoroastrian Persians had no problem with the concept of semi-divine higher beings like the Imam, any more than the Egyptians of old would have questioned the divine status of the pharaoh, or Jews be concerned with the elevated status of a prophet like Moses who spoke directly with God. Doctrines like the sacred blood of the Prophet, transferred through Ali and Fatima to their descendants, echoed similar ideas of the House of David among Christians and Jews. Jesus carried the messianic legacy of the bloodline of the poet-warrior king of Israel. All historians discuss the input of Greek ideas into Shiism and later Ismailism. The Mideast has always functioned as the crossroads of the world, and Hindu and Chinese merchants and philosophers traveled the Silk Road for centuries, undoubtedly introducing Buddhist, Hindu, and Taoist mysticism, as well as shamanism and other esoteric practices, into the creative mix of Shiism.

The concepts of the Neoplatonic hierarchy of celestial beings, the interplay between the Lord of the Universe and His creation through angelic and celestial intermediaries, was hardly foreign to anyone of this period. Muhammad himself took down the verses of the Quran from the archangel Gabriel. Gnostic and Sufi beliefs about the possibility of direct spiritual illumination were incorporated into Shiism and Ismailism, and would eventually manifest in the breakthrough revolutionary pronouncement at Alamut in 1164 by a successor of Hasan-i-Sabah. "[N]eo-Platonism and Gnosticism . . . found in Al-Islam a rich fallow and gained strength and luxuriance by the solid materialism and conservatism of its basis."[2]

As mentioned in chapter two, the third- through fifth-century writings of Greek Neoplatonic philosophers had been carried to Per-

---

[1] Lewis, *The Origins of Ismailism*, p. 24.

[2] Burton, *The Book of the Thousand Nights and a Night*, vol. 10, Terminal Essay, p. 167.

sia by fleeing monks after the sixth century campaigns of Justinian had closed the pagan monasteries and outlawed religions other than Christianity. The Sasanian king Khosrow I welcomed them. Zoroastrianism was not incompatible with the concepts of a supreme transcendent and incomprehensible Deity opening itself gradually through a refined descent through levels of Being of decreasing complexity, that its essence could be better communicated with mankind.

Neither were tales of miracle-working Imams and other holy men uncommon. Ismail himself was reported to be alive—even after his father had pronounced him dead, showed his body in the cemetery of Medina, and issued the proclamation of the death of his son. "The Ismailis say that Ismail was still alive five years after Jafar's death when he was seen in a market-place in Basra. A paralytic begged alms of him. Ismail took him by the hand and he was healed; and rising to his feet he departed in his company. Ismail also prayed for a blind person and he recovered his sight."[1]

Ismail came along after the Shiites had embraced the Alid line in response to the Abbasid betrayal. There had been numerous false claimants to the exalted status of Imam or even Mahdi by then. "During the formative period mentioned, the sects are too numerous to be counted. Again and again various pretenders of Alid descent rise in revolt, and, on their failure, pass into mythology. Again and again does some too zealous missionary forget his Alid master and begin to preach on his own account."[2] I enumerated some of the details of this interaction in my previous book on the Assassins:

> Illuminist doctrines from various earlier heresies so altered mainstream Islamic beliefs that the resulting cults were nearly independent. Transitions of membership between these different sects were frequent. The eclectic doctrines that grew among the various Shiite groups included: beliefs in reincarnation and metempsychosis; deification of Imams and sometimes *dais;* intense speculations on the nature of God; attention to divina-

---

[1] Juvaini, *Genghis Khan*, p. 644.

[2] Lewis, *The Origins of Ismailism*, p. 27.

> tion and prophesy; doctrines concerning the nature of the soul, death, the afterlife, and immortality; teachings on the cyclical nature of time and history; qabalistic investigations of the esoteric significance of letters and numbers; and occasionally, the overthrowing of traditional Islamic behavioral restrictions on sexuality, the use of intoxicants, and dietary matters.[1]

The Ismailis had spent the century and a half between the death of Ismail and the proclamation of the Fatimid Caliphate refining and perfecting their doctrines in secret and in silence. The absence of early Ismaili literature speaks more to a need for secrecy than a lack of production. Privately circulated clandestine manuscripts among trusted allies would have been the rule.

The Shia/Ismaili concept of the living Imam allowed for an emotional connection between the aspirant and his or her master that was absent from the more straitlaced Sunni milieu. The ability to direct the disciple's love of God through the spiritual master is an ancient practice. The teacher serves as the physical manifestation of the divine principle. Meanwhile, the anticipated redeemer or Mahdi awaits the divinely ordained moment for His appearance, silently guiding the Imam in his duty to shepherd humankind through the dark hours in which we must all spend our material existence. These hidden and speaking Imams are the personification of the metaphysical soul of the universe. They are wise enough to guide us all toward Truth. The Imam is sometimes referred to as the "speaking Quran,"[2] for he alone can be trusted to separate the outer, exoteric teachings, or *zahir*, of the written text from its inner esoteric meaning, or *batin*, at its essence. "[E]very literal meaning implied an inner hidden reality (*haqiqa*)."[3]

Hasan-i-Sabah would learn from his Ismaili instructors that they had carried this reverence and appreciation of the Imam to the highest level of any Shiite sect; that the Imam enjoys the greatest amount of *ilm* or gnosis, and that he can communicate this to the community.

---

1 Wasserman, *The Templars and the Assassins*, p. 78.

2 Daftary, *The Ismailis*, p. 233.

3 Daftary (ed.), *Mediaeval Ismaili History and Thought*, p. 2.

When Hasan II *ala dhikrhi al salam* later proclaimed the *Qiyama*, most of Alamut, as well as the scattered Nizari Ismaili community, accepted their Imam's radical proclamation of Truth because they believed in his spiritual power and insight.

Hasan would also have learned that the Ismailis analyzed creation in vast cycles composed of incomprehensibly mysterious and profound cosmological eras, and of the energies operative in each. Ismailis viewed seven prophets (*natiqs*) as being charged with the guidance of humanity. We have already mentioned the first six: Adam, Noah, Abraham, Moses, Jesus, and Muhammad. But Ismailis added a seventh, Ismail or his son Muhammad ibn Ismail, to this rarified group of world teachers. Hasan would have been smart enough to understand that accepting a prophet after Muhammad was an unforgivable blasphemy to orthodox Islam. His own capacity for independent thought must have been stimulated by this.

Each of the Prophets brought a code of behavior, the *sharia*, to rein in the harmful tendencies and mischief normally associated with mankind. *Sharia* was not an example of success. Rather it was an admission that the higher message of the Prophet had reached its limit and rules became necessary.[1] The Prophet is accompanied by a *wasi*, which means executor, as of a will: "He, the *Natiq*, then always raises a *Wasi* to remain after himself; the *Wasi* is the guardian of the inner meaning (*tawil*) of the prescriptions of the *shariat*."[2] Ali filled the role of *wasi* for Muhammad. The Imam is a successor to the Prophet and continues the work of the *wasi*. The Imam is charged with conveying the original message of the Prophet and with revealing the *batin* or *haqiqa*. While the Prophet appears only periodically, the Imam is always present, otherwise the world would collapse. The Prophets are accompanied in their missions by the *samit*, or silent

---

[1] Wladimir Ivanow (trans. and ed.), *Kalami Pir: A Treatise on Ismaili Doctrine*, pp. xxxiii–xxxiv. Ivanow describes this religious text: "The *Kalami Pir* is of outstanding importance to the student as it gives the fullest known account of the Nizari doctrine in its purely religious aspect." (p. vi.) It appeared in its written form in the fifteenth or mid-sixteenth century. (p. xxiv.)

[2] Ibid., p. 13.

one, who interprets the hidden doctrines (and is sometimes identified with the *wasi*). Seth accompanied Adam; Shem followed Noah; Ishmael was the *samit* of Abraham; Aaron filled that role for Moses; and Simon Peter was the *samit* or *wasi* of Jesus; Muhammad's *samit* was Ali. The *samit* is also called the *asas*, or Foundation.[1] As noted several times, there can only be one Imam at a time, but his successor (*samit*, *wasi*, or *asas*) may silently serve beside him until he passes.

Hasan would have been taught about the Final Judgment, when the unredeemed and the ignorant would be separated from those who had dared to perfect themselves and become the worthy companions of the Imam and his Truth. Hasan also understood that these teachings needed to be conducted in silence and accompanied by ritualized personal pledges. How else could the Ismaili *dais* have been protected? How else could they know who to trust? How else could Hasan be expected to reach out to others and spread a fundamental heresy without some kind of oath-taking?

I think Hasan must have been tantalized by the end-goal of that teaching, as described by Wladimir Ivanow:

> When the human soul thus attains its highest wisdom, it becomes assimilated with the Highest Wisdom of the Universe which is an eternal substance. Divine in its origin. Thus what was originally an individual human soul becomes entirely identified with and absorbed in God.[2]

---

1 See chapter twenty, where *asas* is discussed as a possible derivation of the term "Assassin." See Daftary, *The Ismailis*, pp. 86 and 139 for more on these multilayered, complex concepts. Ivanow in *Kalami Pir*, writes: "As they are essentially the same, the Imam, or *asas*, as he is called when he co-exists with a great Prophet, does not carry on his preaching when the Prophet is still alive." pp. xxxviii–xxxix.

2 Ivanow, *Kalami Pir*, p. xlviii.

CHAPTER SIX

Purported Service in the Seljuk Court

THE SELJUK Sultanate ruled Persia from 1037 to 1194, so this was the political environment in which Hasan spent his entire life. At the time of his birth, the Seljuks were extending their hegemony as far as the court of the caliph in Baghdad. It is possible that Hasan served for a time as an administrator in the Seljuk court. Rashid al-Din discusses this at some length in *The Biography of Our Master*, beginning with the "Tale of the Three Schoolfellows."[1]

The story states that Hasan, Nizam al-Mulk (the famed statesman whom we met in chapter two), and the future poet and mathematician Omar Khayyam were fellow students and friends. They studied together at the school of the Sunni Imam al-Muwaffaq in Nishapur. Knowing the fame of the Imam for preparing his students for future success, Hasan suggested the three make a pact, sealed by their blood. Whoever succeeded first in life would share the bounty of his success with the other two.

Nizam was the first to achieve worldly success as the wazir in the court of Sultan Alp Arslan (r. 1063–1072). Omar Khayyam presented himself to remind him of his pledge. Nizam proposed a government appointment but Omar declined such a post, and Nizam arranged an annual pension that allowed him to write, study mathematics, and meditate instead. Hasan later sought his share. Nizam offered to make Hasan a governor of a Seljuk province but Hasan declined and said he wanted a position within the Sultan's court. Nizam arranged for Hasan to be so employed.

Then Hasan was accused by enemies in the court of plotting ways to discredit Nizam and supplant him as wazir. Nizam plotted against him in return, and ultimately succeeded in disgracing him. Hasan was forced to flee the court. Rashid al-Din fills in the details.

Because of Hasan's intelligence, administrative abilities, work

---

[1] See Rashid al-Din, appendix two, pp. 316–317. The story is not included by Juvaini.

ethic, and facility for mathematics, he became a rising star within the administration of Alp Arslan's son and successor, Malikshah, and thus excited the jealousy and fear of Nizam al-Mulk. Sultan Malikshah's leadership style was the opposite of that of his father. Alp Arslan had been a hands-off ruler who left the daily details of political administration to Nizam. Malikshah, by contrast, plunged himself into the many aspects involved in governing.[1] At one point, Malikshah wished to reorganize his realm and make an accounting of each of the provinces of the empire. He asked Nizam how long it would take to prepare a full accounting. Nizam told the sultan he was looking at a massive effort that would take at least two years.

The sultan was frustrated by this estimate and asked Hasan-i-Sabah how long it would take him to accomplish the accounting. Rashid al-Din writes that Hasan said he could do it in two weeks.[2] Impressed, Sultan Malikshah assigned the work to him and gave him staff to help. Hasan worked diligently and was on time. His report began to take shape, each section with statistics of different provinces. Nizam al-Mulk was beside himself, aware of the dislike of the sultan toward himself and fearing the loss of his position to Hasan. He therefore plotted to discredit the young courtier. He assigned one of his assistants to befriend an assistant of Hasan and win his confidence.

Meanwhile Hasan was putting the finishing touches on his report of the revenues and expenditures of each of the districts, and had accumulated a substantial number of pages. As Hasan was soon due to present his findings to the sultan, Nizam arranged for Hasan's disloyal servant to ruin the sequence of the report by dropping the large stack of pages and reassembling them in a chaotic and confused order.

Hasan was sure of himself after his diligent and careful work and did not feel the need to check his presentation before entering the presence of the sultan. When asked to provide details on one province he turned to the appropriate section and was startled to find it missing and out of order. He stammered in embarrassment through

---

1 Al-Muscati, *Hasan bin Sabbah*, p. 56.

2 Rashid al-Din, appendix two, p. 317, writes two weeks. The estimate is given as forty days in al-Muscati, *Hasan bin Sabbah*, p. 56.

this ordeal and several other questions from the sultan. Malikshah was angry. Nizam al-Mulk counseled the sultan that Hasan was a pretender and a danger to the administration of the court, and should be ejected from employment and even executed. While the sultan's fondness for Hasan deterred him from execution, he was forced by the circumstances to banish Hasan from the court and he returned to Rayy and afterward fled to Isfahan.[1]

Bernard Lewis, however, cites medieval historian Ibn-al-Athir (1160–1233), who wrote instead that Hasan fled Rayy because the authorities accused him of harboring Fatimid agents and being a dangerous agitator.[2] That account is confirmed by the Egyptian historian al-Maqrizi, who identified the lord of Rayy as Abu Muslim, the son-in-law of Nizam al-Mulk.[3]

This story of ambition and betrayal might help to account for the bitter rivalry between Nizam and Hasan. Nizam relentlessly hunted Hasan after the latter's return to Persia as an agent of the Fatimid Imam; led a military attack against Alamut after Hasan had established it as his headquarters; and was felled as the first victim of the daggers of the Assassin *fidais*.

Why Hasan, a Shiite, might have been sent to a Sunni school can be explained by the religious persecutions and suspicions directed against the Shia by the reigning Sunni Seljuks. As we have discussed, political and religious differences are one and the same in Islam. A Shiite or an Ismaili could well have been regarded as a hostile agent of either the Buwayhids or the Fatimid caliph against the Seljuk sultan. Therefore, under the banner of *taqiyya,* or permissible use of dissimi-

---

[1] This account has been summarized from Rashid al-Din, appendix two, pp. 317–318.

[2] Lewis, *The Assassins*, p. 40.

[3] Carole Hillenbrand, "A Neglected Source on the Life of Hasan-i Sabbah, the Founder of the Nizari 'Assassin' Sect," in *Iran: Journal of the British Institute of Persian Studies*, 2017, p. 4.

lation for the protection of the devotee, it would be prudent to send one's children to a Sunni *madrassa*. Imam al-Muwaffaq was highly regarded by the Seljuks and had a record of successfully recommending students to positions in government. Silvestre de Sacy suggests that Hasan's father held ideas "of very doubtful orthodoxy," so that the choice of Imam al-Muwaffaq's academy was an intelligent one.[1]

Imam al-Muwaffaq an-Naysaburi was a well-known and highly-respected luminary of his day. He was a member of the *Shafii* school,[2] one of the four Sunni schools of Islamic jurisprudence—the others being the *Hanafi*, *Maliki* and *Hanbali*. Established in the early ninth century by Abu Abdullah Muhammad al-Shafii (767–820), this school relies for its understanding of the duties and boundaries of *sharia* first on the Quran and the *hadiths*, next on the consensus of Muhammad's companions, then on the individual opinion of any of these companions, and finally on interpretation by analogy. C. E. Bosworth writes that the Hanafi school was favored by the Seljuks, although Nizam favored the Shafii, as did the Abbasid caliphs.[3]

This story of the Three Schoolfellows was brought to prominence in the English-speaking world by Edward FitzGerald in his widely-read preface to his translation of the *Rubaiyat* of Omar Khayyam.[4] In addition to Rashid al-Din, this story appears in the *Wasiyat* or Testament, a guide to future statesmen of Nizam al-Mulk. Nizam's authorship of the *Wasiyat* is disputed. It appears to have been compiled after his death. The introduction says it was created partly from books and

---

1 Silvestre de Sacy, *Memoirs on the Dynasty of the Assassins*, translated in Daftary, *The Assassin Legends*, p. 142.

2 Rajput, *Hasan-i-Sabbah*, p. 35.

3 C. E. Bosworth, "The Political and Dynastic History," in J. A. Boyle (ed.), *CHI*, vol. 5, pp. 72–73.

4 Edward FitzGerald, *The Rubaiyat of Omar Khayyam*, first published in 1859, with a second edition in 1868, third in 1872, and a fourth in 1879. See bibliography.

partly from oral tradition handed down though his family, yet the text is written in the first person.[1]

Most historians reject the story of the Three Schoolfellows because of the disparity in age between Hasan (ca. 1050/1055–1124) and Nizam. Nizam (1020–1092) would be some thirty to thirty-five years older than Hasan, while Omar Khayyam (1048–1131) was a contemporary.[2]

One modern Ismaili scholar and author, Ali Mohammad Rajput, accepts the story as likely true and advances several arguments in its favor. He writes that people attended schools at different ages, and Nizam may have simply been an elder student and friend of the younger two students. He adds that there are three separate but roughly contemporaneous accounts of (at least) parts of the story.[3] On the other hand, Jawad al-Muscati believes the story was advanced by enemies of Hasan-i-Sabah to impugn his character and reputation.[4]

Harold Bowen wrote that it was possible the story of the Three Schoolfellows may have actually been derived from the relationship between Nizam and two other contemporaries: a poet by the name of al-Bakharzi and a Seljuk wazir named Abu Nasr Kunduri.[5] These three were closer in age to each other and all had contact with Imam al-Muwaffaq. Al-Kunduri was an officeholder in the court of Sultan Alp Arslan. He was dismissed from his position and later executed,

---

1 Rajput, *op. cit.*, p 219.

2 Birth data of Nizam and Omar according to J. A. Boyle, "Umar Khayyam: Astronomer, Mathematician, and Poet," in Frye (ed.), *CHI,* vol. 4, p. 659.

3 Rajput, *Hasan-i-Sabbah,* pp. 40–41. The third source is the *Tarikh-i-Guzeda* (1330) by Hamd Allah Mustawafi Qazini, which mentions an earlier relationship between Hasan and Nizam during the reign of Alp Arslan.

4 Al-Muscati, *Hasan bin Sabbah*, pp. 48–49.

5 Bowen, Harold, "The *sar-gudhashti-i sayyidna*, the 'Tale of the Three Schoolfellows' and the *wasaya* of the Nizam al-Mulk, *Journal of the Royal Asiatic Society*, 1931, pp. 781–782. Bowen notes that the *Tarikh-i-Guzeda*, which has an account of Hasan's service as a chamberlain in Alp-Arslan's court, does not discuss the story of the Three Schoolfellows, p. 775. Al-Kunduri is also mentioned by Hasan in the letter exchange with Malikshah, appendix three, pp. 347–348.

in part because of Nizam's actions against him. Nizam also arranged to patronize the works of the poet al-Bakharzi.

There are, of course, other explanations for Hasan being able to enter the Seljuk court (if he did) without Nizam's involvement. He may have exploited his wealthy father's contacts among fellow Shia nobles. Highly-placed Shiites in the Seljuk administration would be quiet about their religious faith, but such a network could have helped secure a position for the talented young man. And if he had studied with Imam al-Muwaffaq, that is another likely route to the court.

Al-Muscati asserts that Hasan served in the Seljuk court, despite his rejection of the Tale of the Three Schoolfellows. He writes:

> Therefore Hasan's entering the Saljuqid service and winning over the confidence of Malikshah were due to his own efforts and qualities and not to the benevolence and patronage of Nizam al-Mulk as it is generally made out. On the contrary Nizam al-Mulk was jealous of Hasan.[1]

If it is true that Hasan served in the Seljuk administration, we cannot be certain whether his time in the court preceded or followed his conversion to Ismailism. It may be that after his formal initiation, mentioned in chapter five, he became a highly-motivated practitioner. However, the idea that his full-hearted conversion may have came after his initial exposure to Ismailism and/or followed his time at the Seljuk court is buttressed by a reputed letter exchange with Sultan Malikshah, ca. 1091.[2] Hasan's reply to Malikshah is filled with autobiographical insights. He says that he was exposed to the Ismaili doctrine, temporarily abandoned his religious quest for worldly material concerns, then returned to his proper spiritual responsibilities. Again, as in so much else of this story, the authenticity of these two letters is disputed by some authorities and accepted by others.[3]

---

1 Al-Muscati, *Hasan bin Sabbah*, p. 48.

2 The two letters are given in appendix three.

3 We will return to the letter exchange in chapter nine.

NIZAM AL-MULK is said to have been a brilliant and capable administrator who served the Seljuks for thirty years, bringing many improvements to the land. He encouraged industry, trade, and finance; improved roads and bridges; and undertook educational, cultural, and architectural efforts. Historian C. E. Bosworth postulates that Nizam's extensive focus on continuing to build the Sunni *madrassa* education system throughout Iran and Iraq—that had begun in the second half of the tenth century—may have been, in part, a response to the Fatimid institutions for the training of *dais* such as the *Dar al-Hikma*, where Hasan studied.[1] Nizam was an advocate for the model of the centralized administrative power of the sultan, of which he had seen evidence during his tenure with the Ghaznavids at the beginning of his career in government.

OMAR KHAYYAM, known in the West chiefly for his poetry, was one of the greatest mathematicians of medieval times. Aside from his work in algebra and astronomy, he participated in the reform of the Persian calendar in service to Sultan Malikshah. "The new calendar, named Maliki or Jalali was more accurate than the Gregorian, although five hundred years earlier."[2] It was not, however, widely used in Islamic lands because it was based on solar calculations rather than the orthodox lunar calendar specified by Muhammad. Khayyam is also said to have invented clay scarecrows to protect crops.[3] He is reported to have been an Ismaili according to at least one source.[4]

---

[1] Bosworth, "The Political and Dynastic History," in Boyle (ed.), *CHI*, vol. 5, p. 70.

[2] J. A. Boyle, "Umar Khayyam: Astronomer, Mathematician, and Poet," in Frye (ed.), *CHI*, vol. IV, p. 659. The Gregorian calendar was introduced by Pope Gregory XIII in 1582.

[3] Browne, *A Literary History of Persia*, vol. 2, p. 252.

[4] Lewis, *The Origins of Ismailism*, p. 96, citing *Al-Falak ad-Dawwar* by the fourteenth to fifteenth century Persian historian Ibn al-Murtada.

CHAPTER SEVEN

Hasan Begins His Travels

After the chief *dai* Abd al-Malik ibn Attash appointed Hasan as his deputy, Hasan accompanied his teacher to Isfahan, the center of the Ismaili *dawa* in Persia, about 275 miles south of Rayy. Hasan would remain in Isfahan for some three years from approximately 1074–1077.[1] According to Rashid al-Din, Hasan continued on his way to Egypt by way of Azerbaijan, then to Mayyafariquin in eastern Turkey. Here he got involved in a theological debate regarding the exclusive right of the Imam to interpret religion, rather than relying on the consensus of the Sunni *ulema*.[2] Hasan challenged the ability of Sunni jurists to determine spiritual truth without the superior guidance of a proper Imam. The Prophet himself was quoted in a *hadith* discussing the possibility of error by such religious judges no matter how sincere they might be.[3] Hasan's arguments so outraged the jurist that he sought out a *qadi,* a judge or magistrate, who was concerned with the threat to public safety such ideas might kindle. He expelled Hasan from the city. Hasan continued on to Mosul, then Damascus, Beirut, and Israel, where he sailed from Caesarea to Egypt.[4]

Hasan in Egypt

Hasan arrived in Egypt in 1078. According to the account in Juvaini, he stayed in Egypt for a year and a half.[5] Rashid al-Din's account says

---

1 Dr. Farhad Daftary and Dr. Omar Ali-de-Unzaga, Hasan Sabbah, at http://iis.ac.uk/encyclopaedia-articles/hasan-sabbah [accessed January 12, 2018]. This timeline would have allowed for Hasan's diversion at the Seljuk court.

2 The *ulema* are the councils of scholars—educated and trained Sunni theologians charged with interpreting and transmitting religious knowledge and Islamic law.

3 *Sahih Muslim* 1716, for which see appendix two, note 1, p. 305.

4 See *The Biography of Our Master*, appendix two, pp. 305–306.

5 Juvaini, *Genghis Khan*, p. 668.

three years, a year and a half first in Cairo and then Alexandria.[1] In *The Biography of Our Master*, as reported by both Juvaini and Rashid al-Din, Hasan says that "I was not admitted before Mustansir, he knew of me and several times spoke in praise of me."[2] On the other hand, the medieval historian Ibn al-Athir (1160–1234), author of *al-Kamil fil Tarikh*, wrote that Hasan and the Imam met and discussed the Imam's plans for the succession of Nizar, the Imam's eldest son.[3] Another medieval Egyptian historian named al-Maqrizi (1364–1442), author of the *Kittab al-Muqaffa al-kabir*, also wrote that Hasan met al-Mustansir. Al-Maqrizi says that Hasan was traveling in the guise of a merchant, that the caliph was initially taken with him, but then heard some things about Hasan (not specified) which caused him to imprison him. Al-Mustansir then released him, bestowed favors on him, and personally confirmed to Hasan the intended succession of his son Nizar.[4]

Caliph al-Mustansir had become a very unsteady ruler by this time. The Fatimid kingdom had been weakened by a long-standing state of warfare which helped plunge the country into a series of economic crises. Several severe famines worsened conditions further. By 1062, open warfare had broken out in Cairo between dissident elements of the army. Availing himself of the services of his Turkish mercenaries to quell the rebellion, al-Mustansir became dominated by a corrupt commander named Nasir al-Dawla, who was assassinated in 1073. In 1074, al-Mustansir reached out to his Armenian military governor of Acre, Badr al-Jamali (1015–1094), to come to Egypt and restore order and discipline. Al-Jamali took control of all three branches of the traditional responsibilities of the caliph: the administration of civil government, the military, and the domain of

[1] Rashid al-Din, appendix two, p. 308.

[2] Juvaini, *Genghis Khan*, p. 668; Rashid al-Din, appendix two, p. 306.

[3] Reported by Rajput, *Hasan-i-Sabbah*, p. 62.

[4] Hillenbrand, "A Neglected Source on the Life of Hasan-i Sabbah, the Founder of the Nizari 'Assassin' Sect," in *Iran: Journal of the British Institute of Persian Studies*, 2017, pp. 4–5.

religious instruction and the training of Fatimid missionaries.[1] Caliph al-Mustansir, the Fatimid Imam, was reduced to a mere figurehead.

The most common explanation given for Hasan not meeting al-Mustansir is that Badr al-Jamali forbade such a meeting. I believe Juvaini and Rashid al-Din incorrectly attribute the conflict between Hasan and Badr al-Jamali to a dispute over the succession of the Imamate.[2] If Hasan was there from 1078 to 1080 (or even 1081 or 1082), we are over a decade away from the succession conflict that did engulf the Fatimid Caliphate. Is it possible that Juvaini sought to undermine Hasan's integrity by claiming he never met al-Mustansir? Since he had the only copy of the *Sar-Guzasht-i-Sayyidna* and presumably burned it, he could have said anything. Al-Muscati attributes Badr's animosity toward Hasan as jealousy when he realized Hasan's intelligence and organizational capacity.[3]

Hasan was briefly imprisoned by Badr in Damietta, a port city on the Mediterranean at the northernmost extremity of the Nile that would be the landing point for the Fifth Crusade. Rashid al-Din reports that friends of Hasan from Daylam offered to assassinate Badr al-Jamali rather than allow Hasan to be imprisoned. But he demurred. Later, when the walls of the prison collapsed, it was interpreted as a miracle and attributed to both Caliph al-Mustansir and Hasan. He was released by Badr and deported; Rashid al-Din reports he went to Alexandria in 1080 and later sailed to Syria with a party of Franks and other travelers. They encountered a severe storm which damaged and nearly sank the ship. Hasan remained calm during the general panic and his fellow passengers viewed him with astonishment. He informed them that the Imam al-Mustansir had warned him of the storm and assured him no harm would come because of the importance of his mission. A number of his fellow passengers became

---

1 It is perplexing and alarming to contemplate that a foreign military dictator (likely with Sunni roots) would be in command of the religious outreach efforts of the Fatimid *dawa*.

2 Juvaini, *Genghis Khan*, pp. 668–669; Rashid al-Din, appendix two, pp. 306–307.

3 Al-Muscati, *Hasan bin Sabbah*, p. 76.

his first converts to the *dawa* of the Fatimid Imam. They landed safely in Jableh, Syria (near Acre).[1]

Hasan's Mission Continues

Hasan went on from Acre to Aleppo, Baghdad, and Khuzistan in southwest Iran. He arrived back in Isfahan in 1081. His missionary activities then took him to Kirman in southeast Persia, and Yezd in central Persia, about 170 miles from Isfahan. He thereafter traveled back to Isfahan and made a second trip to Khuzistan. He proceeded on to the mountainous region of northern Persia near where he would eventually locate, first to Firrim along the south of the Caspian Sea (modern Eastern Mazandaran region, also known as Tabiristan) and then to Shahkouh (near the modern Hezar Jarib mountain range). *The Biography of Our Master* continues that Hasan spent three years in Damghan (about two hundred miles east and north of Tehran). From here he sent *dais* to the Rudbar region of the Elburz Mountains and "the other districts of Alamut to convert the people."[2] He continued on to Jurjan, Tarz, Sarhadd, and Chinashk in the same rough, mountainous, isolated region along the Caspian Sea.

It is possible that during his return to Isfahan, he stayed with his old friend and mentor, the Rais Abufasl, as cited by Juvaini, although Rashid al-Din places the story of this visit after Hasan fled from Rayy and before his travel to Egypt.[3] In either case, Hasan shocked Abufasl by stating that if he had just two devoted friends, he could overpower both the sultan and his wazir and turn the Seljuk Empire upside down. Rais Abufasl concluded that Hasan may have been suffering from a brain fever or a severe case of melancholia to make such an apparently irrational statement. He offered Hasan aromatic drinks and dishes to strengthen his body and "moisten" or cool his brain, a regimen which was common to those who suffered such a

---

1 Rashid al-Din, appendix two, p. 307.

2 Juvaini, *Genghis Khan*, p. 669.

3 Juvaini, *Genghis Khan*, p. 677; Rashid al-Din, appendix two, pp. 317–318.

condition. Hasan understood at once what Abufasl was thinking and departed on his continued travels.

The Biography of Our Master states that Nizam al-Mulk had sent orders for Hasan's arrest so that he was forced to avoid his hometown of Rayy. He wanted to be in the area of Daylam and the Elburz Mountains because, in the words of Bosworth, he knew that:

> Islam was late in coming here; the Dailami mountaineers were notorious for their depredations in the settled lands to the south of the Alburz, and Qazvin was long regarded as the *thaghr* [frontline fortress town] against these infidels. In the early part of the 3rd/9th century Dailam was a centre for Alid propaganda, and the local people were gradually won over to Shiism. Here then is why the majority of Dailami dynasties in the 4th/10th and 5th/11th centuries were Shii.[1]

What better group of people could Hasan have found among whom to conduct his revolutionary efforts? Brave, independent, and fierce, the inhabitants of the Daylami region were spiritually akin to their inspired preacher. He must have indeed realized he had arrived among the most perfect and receptive audience for his message. These hardy mountain people were set apart from their more genteel Iranian cousins of the plateau below, and had been for centuries. A free and autonomous group would be swift to resent the authoritarian behavior of their foreign Turkish masters—especially as the Seljuks had put an end to the Daylami Buwayhid dynasty, the Shiite power that had dominated the Abbasids of Baghdad. With no cultural or regional roots, the Seljuks were seen as usurpers. Hasan is said to have referred to the Turks as *jinn,* not men.[2]

Hasan would also have been acutely aware of the inability of the Egyptian Fatimid dynasty, in its weakened state, to provide mate-

---

[1] Bosworth, "The Political and Dynastic History," in Boyle (ed.), *CHI*, vol. 5, p. 30.

[2] Hodgson, "The Ismaili State," in Boyle (ed.), *CHI*, vol. 5, p. 427. *Jinn*, in this usage, would undoubtedly refer to the evil spirits.

rial or military support to his efforts. The revolutionary energy, creative fire of rebellion, and sense of divine mission had placed him and his Ismaili supporters at the forefront of the romantic excitement of change. Both the Abbasids and the Fatimids were well past the youthful, charismatic vigor that had contributed to their initial political ascendency.

To be able to continue his preaching and organizing, Hasan therefore avoided Rayy, but stopped at Sari in the Elburz Mountains and Qazvin (west of Rayy), Dunbavand (Damavand/Damghan, east of Rayy), and Khuvar, another area east of the city.[1] His time in Damghan was spent directing the efforts of his *dais* in their conversion among the indigenous Daylamis and avoiding the attention of the Seljuk wazir.[2]

By this time, Hasan had been on the road after leaving Egypt for nine or ten years. Serving the Imam as an itinerant *dai,* we have seen him traversing region after region, town and city after town and city. His wide travels gave him the opportunity to understand and observe the military readiness of the Seljuks and any other local forces. He was able to gather onsite intelligence and, thus, to plan and strategize his own future martial needs and the opportunities afforded by the situation and terrain of various potential centers throughout Persia.

Hasan undoubtedly moved by horse, donkey, camel, caravan, and by foot. Horses had long been known in Persia and the Caucasus region, as mentioned earlier, and reference to ancient Egyptian art depicts the use of the horse for transport and battle. The domestication of the camel extends back equally into antiquity. They were especially valuable along the Silk Road because of their ability to transport substantial loads (four to five hundred pounds), as well as their capacity for survival in desert regions with little water access. A donkey conveyed Jesus into Jerusalem two thousand years ago.

---

[1] Juvaini, *Genghis Khan*, p. 669.

[2] Rashid al-Din, appendix two, p. 308; Lewis, *The Assassins*, p. 42.

One wonders how Hasan supported himself for the decade of his preaching mission. Did Caliph al-Mustansir or the *Dar al-Hikma* provide funds, or was he sustained by a combination of wealthy donors, contributions from the laity, and any family funds or personal savings he may have accumulated before leaving Egypt? We learn that a wealthy donor named Dindan in the late ninth century handed the early Ismaili *dai,* Abdallah b. Maymun, two million dinars that he might further the *dawa* efforts to which Dindan had been converted.[1] Did the local *dawa* of Persia provide their missionaries with funds?

Hasan continued his travels in the region for a little while longer. Juvaini writes, "Because of his extreme asceticism many people fell victims to him and were converted by him."[2]

But it was time for Hasan to find a settled headquarters from which he could direct his mission without the constant insecurity of discovery by the Sunni enemy. A defensible fortress was needed where he could gather his followers, conduct and develop his preaching, and continue the ongoing struggle against the Seljuk state. The Ismailis would never rise to conquer all of Persia or be able to overthrow the Seljuks. Instead, they would establish their own independent centers of activity with Hasan as the primary leader of these far-flung, semi-autonomous command posts.

---

1 Lewis, *The Origins of Ismailism*, p. 69.

2 Juvaini, *Genghis Khan*, p. 670.

CHAPTER EIGHT

Alamut

"My name is Baba Sayyid-na, and I am appointed in this province to lead those who are lost in the desert of errors, out to recognition of the Imam of the day—exalted be his mention—making them see and hear the great proof, thus ultimately making them reach the eternal Paradise in future life."
—*Kalami Pir*[1]

The Biography of Our Master continues Hasan's story, introducing his future headquarters and capital of Alamut. The castle had been built in 860 by Wah Sudan ibn Marzuban, a Daylami king who was out hunting one day and watched an eagle alight on top of the rock. The ruler immediately realized the strategic advantage of the position and began construction. He named the castle "Alamut," *aluh-amut,* or the "Eagle's Teachings," in the Daylami dialect.[2] The castle was many years later assigned as a fief or *iqta* holding from the Seljuk sultan Malikshah to an Alid nobleman named Mahdi.

The *Iqta* System

The *iqta* system was a means of land management and tax farming that has been compared with European feudalism. In medieval Europe, as the savagery of northern invasions during and after the fall of the Roman Empire in the fifth through tenth centuries became increasingly more dangerous—and plagues spread through populated areas like wildfires—the nobility were encouraged to move from the cities to their great country estates. Local peasant farmers willingly attached themselves to the protection of these landowners, sacrificing

1 Ivanow (trans. and ed.), *Kalami Pir*, p. 10.

2 Daftary, *The Ismailis*, p. 340. The word "Alamut" has also been translated as "eagle's nest."

their independent status by selling their land and becoming essentially tenant farmers in the rural villages that grew around the castles. In return they were entitled to the security of the walled fortresses and military forces such nobles afforded the surrounding community, as were the bound serfs attached to the land. Feudalism grew in France, England, Italy, and Germany during the sixth through eleventh centuries as weak monarchs rewarded jealous aristocrats and efficient generals with greater land holdings in return for their services and support in administration and war. Ninety percent of the European medieval feudal economy was agricultural.[1]

Contrary to much modern opinion, Will Durant wrote of the European system: "In theory, feudalism was a magnificent system of moral reciprocity, binding the men of an endangered society to one another in a complex web of mutual obligation, protection, and fidelity."[2]

Iqta was introduced by the Buwayhid emir Muizz al-Dawla (r. 946–967) "for allocating revenue from land to his soldiers."[3] It was also used in diplomatic missions to secure the loyalty of those who integrated into the Buwayhid regime. The *iqta* system was primarily operative from the tenth through sixteenth centuries.[4] All property was owned by the ruler. Soldiers provided military service to the sultan in return for such land grants and were given the authority to tax the peasant farmers and townspeople in their domains. Non-military property grants were known as *qati*. Their owners provided tithe revenues, or *usher*, to the state in lieu of military service. Sato Tsugitaka explains its development:

---

[1] Steven A. Epstein, *An Economic and Social History of Later Medieval Europe, 1000–1500*, p. 40.

[2] Durant, *The Age of Faith*, p. 564.

[3] Sato Tsugitaka, *State and Rural Society in Medieval Islam: Sultans, Muqtas, and Fallahun*, p. vii.

[4] Its roots lay in the pre-Islamic Sasanian model of tax farming. Military leaders were allocated land in payment for their services to the empire, deriving their income from tenant farmers.

> Muizz al-Dawla assigned *iqta*s to his Turkish and Daylamite troops when he conquered Iraq, but the assignees (*muqta*) were still confined to Turkish and Daylamite officers (*qaid*) and Turkish cavalrymen, while Daylamite enlisted soldiers continued to receive the same salary as before from the government. Then, when the whole of Iraq came to be apportioned into *iqta*s, small *iqta*s were granted to Daylamite soldiers, too.[1]

Great tension between the native northern Persians and their conquerors resulted in widespread battles between the Daylamites and Turks.[2] As the Seljuks replaced the Buwayhid dynasty in the eleventh century, they largely maintained the *iqta* system. Nizam al-Mulk was particularly active in efforts to supervise and unify the *iqta* holders. He also sought to clarify the rights of *iqta* holders, while he instituted policies that forced them to change their holdings every two or three years. Such land ownership rotation would obviously not encourage the reciprocal relationship between peasant (*fallah*) and *iqta* holder (*muqta*) that existed in Europe between lord and serf, as it was more transitory, less permanent, and less grounded in mutual interest in the land. The Islamic system was not passed on by inheritance, as it most often was in Europe. And while the Seljuk system was similar in execution to its Buwayhid predecessors, "the grants of the administrative *iqta*s to emirs, which were limited during the Buwayhid period, were generalized as the Seluqid rule over Iran and Iraq came to be stable."[3] It would seem that this was the case with Mahdi, the holder of the Alamut *iqta,* whose behavior, recounted below, was not that of a military man.

Hasan Acquires Alamut

Hasan is said to have chosen Alamut as the site for his headquarters some time in 1088. The Alamut rock in the Elburz Mountains rises

---

[1] Tsugitaka, *State and Rural Society in Medieval Islam*, p. 5.

[2] Ibid., pp. 24–26.

[3] Ibid., p. 41.

some six hundred feet above the Rudbar Valley. Rudbar means "by the river" in Persian and the river is named Shahrud. Alamut is six thousand feet above sea level. Four hundred fifty feet long, the rock ranges from thirty to 125 feet wide.[1] The Elburz Mountain range is also home to Mount Damavand, the highest mountain in Persia.[2] Access to the Alamut castle was limited to one steep and narrow path. It was an impregnable fortress. The castle dominates the large fertile valley some thirty miles long and three miles across at its widest point. The valley contains several villages.[3]

Hasan first sent his trusted *dai*, Husayn Qaini, and two others to convert the inhabitants of the Rudbar Valley. Then, many residents and soldiers of Alamut itself were secretly converted to Ismailism. *The Biography of Our Master* explains that the conversion mission of the *dais* was quite successful, so much so that Mahdi himself pretended to have been converted. He attempted a ruse by sending the new Ismaili converts out of the castle, then closed the gates and proclaimed that Alamut belonged to Sultan Malikshah. He finally relented and readmitted them after much discussion, but they henceforth refused to leave the rock.

Meanwhile, Hasan came to the Alamut area and disguised himself as a school teacher to the children of the garrison, while continuing his clandestine efforts to take over the castle.[4] On September 4,

---

1 Franzius, *History of the Order of Assassins*, p. 39.

2 Foltz, *Religions of Iran*, p. 14.

3 Edward Burman gives a picturesque description of his modern visit to Alamut in *The Assassins: Holy Killers of Islam*, pp. 9–12. Freya Stark describes both Alamut and Lammasar at the end of the 1920s in *The Valley of the Assassins: and Other Persian Travels*. Peter Willey in *Eagle's Nest: Ismaili Castles in Iran and Syria* offers color photographs and addresses Hasan's construction, irrigation, and agricultural efforts. One of the best descriptions of Alamut and the surrounding area is that of Laurence Lockhart, who traveled there in the summer of 1928 and spoke with several locals who shared legends of Hasan and the Assassins. Lockhart, "Hasan-i-Sabbah and the Assassins." *Bulletin of the School of Oriental Studies*, 1930, pp. 689–696.

4 Daftary, "Hasan-i Sabbah and the Origins of the Nizari Ismaili Movement," in Daftary (ed.), *Mediaeval Ismaili History and Thought*, p. 187. The technique

1090, Hasan finally ascended the rock of Alamut and entered the castle in disguise, calling himself Dehkhoda (the literal meaning of the word is "headman of a village," but Hasan concealed its meaning by using it as his proper name).[1] He continued to act as a schoolteacher.

Hasan remained anonymous for a time in Alamut. According to Rashid al-Din, when the Alid Mahdi learned of the ruse, he had no choice but to accept the fact that Hasan had outwitted him and was now in control of Alamut. He was allowed to leave the castle, and Hasan gave him a paper addressed to Rais Muzaffar Mustafi, the governor of Girdkuh and Damghan. Hasan instructed Muzaffar to pay Mahdi three thousand gold dinars as the price of the castle.

Rais Muzaffar was an important deputy of one of the Seljuk emirs, Amirdad Habashi. Mahdi had little hope that this was anything but a false promise, but some time later he was in Damghan and in need of funds. He presented the note to Rais Muzaffar who, when he saw the signature, kissed the paper and paid out the sum.

A well-known variant of the story of how Hasan acquired Alamut alleges tantalizing humor and cunning. Hasan and Mahdi were said to be disputing about making an agreement. Hasan convinced the Alid to accept three thousand dinars for the amount of land able to be enclosed within a single ox-hide. Mahdi agreed, whereupon Hasan carefully cut the hide into fine strips that ultimately encircled the entire Alamut rock.[2]

Yet another amusing story is provided by traveler and scholar Laurence Lockhart. During his 1928 visit to Alamut, he met the headman of Shuturkhan, a village located a few miles from Alamut. The local told Lockhart (incorrectly) that there had been no fortification on the rock when Hasan first saw it. But Hasan was so impressed with the strategic location of Alamut, he determined to purchase it. He sought for its owner, who turned out to be an ignorant peasant.

---

of conversion while teaching children was used a decade later by Ahmad ibn Attash in the takeover of Shahdiz (see chapter twelve).

[1] Juvaini, *Genghis Khan*, p. 670; Rashid al-Din, appendix two, p. 309.

[2] Marshall Hodgson identifies the earliest source of this tale as the *Dabistan-i Madhahib*, written in 1645. See Hodgson, *The Order of Assassins*, p. 50.

Hasan noticed the peasant was carrying a heavy load on his back, which he did not set down during their entire conversation. Realizing the opportunity offered by the owner's lack of intelligence, Hasan proceeded with the ox-hide trick.[1]

A different version of the acquisition of the fortress comes from the Egyptian historian al-Maqrizi in the *Kittab al-Muqaffa al-kabir*. He states that Hasan prepared for the taking of Alamut in a military campaign. "He began to buy arms and weapons of war secretly." Hasan then appointed a date for his disciples to meet him, and they took the fortress.[2]

The *Sar-Guzasht-i-Sayyidna* mentions a kabbalistic correspondence between the spelling of Alamut and the date of Hasan's securing the castle as the Assassin headquarters in 483 AH (1090 AD). The *abjad* values of the twenty-eight letters of the alpha-numeric Arabic alphabet, as with the Hebrew and Greek alphabets, allow for such exegesis.[3] Translator J. A. Boyle helps to explain in a note. Taking the spelling of Alamut as Aluh-Amut (ALH AMWT), the values of the letters add to 483.[4]

Hasan worked diligently to fortify the castle and lay in a stock of provisions that would allow his community to withstand a siege. Ivanow estimated Alamut could accommodate a garrison of about two hundred warriors.[5] Hasan had large storerooms hollowed out of the rock to allow provisions to last longer in a cool and dark environment. He also arranged for the irrigation of the fields surrounding the rock

---

1 Lockhart, "Hasan-i-Sabbah and the Assassins," *Bulletin of the School of Oriental Studies*, 1930, p. 678.

2 Hillenbrand, "A Neglected Source on the Life of Hasan-i Sabbah, the Founder of the Nizari 'Assassin' Sect," *Iran: Journal of the British Institute of Persian Studies*, 2017, p. 4.

3 In all three languages, letters do double duty. They serve as numbers as well.

4 Juvaini, *Genghis Khan*, p. 670, see note 23 by J. A. Boyle. (A)1 + (L)30 + (H)5 + (A)1 + (M)40 + (W)6 + (T)400 = 483

5 W. Ivanow, "Alamut," *Geographical Journal*, vol. 7, no. 1, 1931, p. 42, cited by James Waterson, *The Ismaili Assassins: A History of Medieval Murder*, p. 75.

so they could be successfully cultivated at maximum productivity.[1] His agricultural efforts to produce fruits and crops to enhance long term survival were later followed by other commanders of Nizari fortresses. Such practices had the additional benefit of sweetening the air and adding an aesthetic loveliness to the Assassin fortresses. This behavior was said to lend credence to Marco Polo's legend of the Garden of Paradise.[2]

Hasan-i-Sabah had finally created a headquarters where he and his community could plan strategy, worship, study, and develop the doctrines which they would then spread through their trained *dais* in an attempt to universalize their faith. This was little different, although on a smaller scale, than the tenth- and eleventh-century efforts of the Fatimid dynasty in Egypt.

Hasan would not emerge from Alamut until his death in 1124. If he was born in 1050 or 1055, he would have been thirty-five or forty years of age when he secured the fortress.

---

1 Hodgson, "The Ismaili State," in Boyle (ed.), *CHI*, vol. 5, p. 431.

2 Silvestre de Sacy, *Memoirs on the Dynasty of the Assassins*, translated in Daftary, *The Assassin Legends*, pp. 144, 155. See appendix one of the present volume for Marco Polo's full account of the Garden.

CHAPTER NINE

Letter Exchange with Malikshah

> Whenever he saw injustice, or an area that was not flourishing, he tied the hands of evildoers as a king should, making the world an earthly paradise amd planting cypresses and roses in place of thorns and weeds. —*Shahnameh*[1]

AROUND 1091, there was a reputed letter exchange between the Malikshah and Hasan, as mentioned.[2] According to the text of the letters, the sultan wrote to Hasan accusing him of having invented a new faith and religion, enticing people to join him by devious arguments and encouraging them to kill. At the same time, he continued, Hasan was denying the legitimate authority of the Sunni Abbasid caliphs and the Seljuks as their representatives. He warned Hasan to rescind these beliefs and actions and become a good Muslim, otherwise the sultan would be forced to send troops against Alamut. He closed by saying, "Do not be proud of the strength of your castle. Be aware that if your castle of Alamut, was the castle of the fortress of heaven, we would destroy it by the grace of God."

Hasan made a detailed reply that included much useful biographical information (if it is legitimate). Hasan's tone was respectful as one might expect of a person writing to his king. He asked that his words not be shared with Nizam al-Mulk, whose hostility against him was well known. As one who speaks untruth, Nizam should be regarded as a slanderer.

Hasan wrote that his father belonged to the Shafii school of Islam (and was therefore a Sunni) and sent Hasan to a Sunni school that taught those doctrines when he was four years old. We have already

---

1 Abolqasem Ferdowsi (Dick Davis, trans and ed.), *Shahnameh: The Persian Book of Kings*, p. 29.

2 See appendix three for a translation of both letters. All quotations in this chapter will be found there.

mentioned that this lie may have been a case of *taqiyya*, the ability to protect oneself and one's spiritual integrity by telling untruth to powerful enemies. Hasan continues that he was a deep student of religion, the Quran, and scriptural exegesis. These studies led him to an appreciation for the superior qualities of the descendants of the Prophet, the Alid line of Imams, and he was motivated to seek the Imam of his day.

He then describes losing interest in religion and becoming attached to worldly affairs (suggesting this may have been the time when he served in the Seljuk court). He goes on to state that the forsaking of his duties to the Creator set up enemies who harmed him. He says that he then wandered in towns and deserts and was subject to many hardships. He refers to the sultan being aware of the persecutions conducted by Nizam al-Mulk against him.

He attributes such difficulties, however, as the cause of his reawakening to the spiritual quest and his need to serve religion. He says he traveled from Rayy to Baghdad, where he was exposed firsthand to the Abbasid corruption. "I found that the activities of the Abbasid Caliphs were far from the Islamic ideals of justice and truth. Also, I concluded that if the basis of Islam and its faith were those embodied by these Caliphs and Imams, atheism would be better than such a faith." Hasan traveled on to Egypt where he learned of the Fatimid caliph al-Mustansir and accepted his Imamate as superior to that of the Abbasids, recognizing him as the legitimate leader of Islam.

He continued that when the Abbasid caliph learned of Hasan's conversion, he sent troops after him, but that God saved him. The Abbasids continued their efforts to persecute him by bribing the Commander of the Armies, Badr al-Jamali, with much treasure. When Caliph al-Mustansir learned of all this, he took Hasan under his protection and gave him a document that he should take up the work of a *dai* among the Muslims, and was free to adopt any methods he chose to advance the *dawa* of the caliph, Imam, and divine nature of the Fatimid cause.

Hasan pleaded with Malikshah to consider his own religious duties to the Quran: "'Obey Allah and obey the Apostle and those in authority from among you,' then he should not deny my speeches."

Here was a path for the sultan that led to blessing and good fortune for his reign.

He next answered Malikshah's charge that he had invented a new religion. "May a curse fall upon Hasan if this be true." He wrote that he followed the true faith of the Prophet and, "The religion which I believe is the same religion that was prevalent among the Companions of the Prophet, and which will remain the true faith until the Day of Judgment." Further on this: "It is my belief that the children of the Prophet are more qualified for the Caliphate of their father than the children of Abbas." He implored the sultan to reconsider his allegiances for the good of his people, his family, and his soul. Hasan compared his own beliefs to those of the four Righteous Caliphs and the ten Blessed Companions of the Prophet.[1] In his mind, criticism of the Abbasids was a religious duty. They must be exposed to the whole world.

He denied encouraging his people to kill, and said the truth of that should be left to the judgment of fair and impartial people. He went on to accuse the officials and soldiers of Nizam al-Mulk of despoiling the people of Khurasan and surrounding areas, including the women and wives of good Muslims under their control. He pointed to Nizam again as unfair and lacking in the decency Malikshah should expect of those in his administration. He spoke of Nizam's financial crimes, oppression, and nepotism. He blamed Nizam for any political violence committed against the Seljuks and characterized it as self defense.

Hasan proclaimed himself a loyal subject and stated, "I, Hasan, could never be guilty of any act which would be opposed to the sultan's opinion." Instead, there was a clique in the sultan's court bent on smearing him. He pledged his military support when called to provide it, as well as the support of his people. "After I finish my works against my enemies, I will present myself in the court of the Sultan and serve the king like so many others in your court. I will devote myself to the best of my ability to the betterment of your worldly

---

1 The Ten Blessed Companions were those early Muslim stalwarts promised Paradise by the Prophet. The Four Righteous Caliphs were the first leaders after his death.

affairs and to the spiritual salvation of the sultan." He acknowledged the sultan as the legitimate political authority of his time.

He again explained his difficulty with Malikshah's allegiance to his mortal enemies the Abbasids who persecuted him in Egypt. He pointed out that he is the leader of the *dawa* of the Fatimid caliphs and Imams, and has many good friends and supporters, which made him a target of the Abbasids. They tried to poison the ears of the sultan against Hasan. Malikshah was faced with a difficult choice of doing the wrong or the right thing.

Hasan began to close his letter by saying that the sultan's threat to take Alamut even if it were a fortress of heaven, contradicts the complete faith of his people in the protection of their Imam. "The inhabitants of this fortress trust to speeches of truth from the Imam of our time."[1] Hasan prayed that the sultan would be led by God to make the correct choices: "If the sultan is destined to achieve salvation in his faith, and on the day of Judgment, and in his worldly affairs, he must arise against the Abbasids."

According to al-Muscati, after reading this letter, Malikshah was greatly impressed and turned his thoughts favorably to Hasan.[2] Unfortunately, that would not last for long.

If this letter is true, Hasan still represented an independent source of power that did not fit in with the political structure of their reign as envisioned by the Seljuks. This would have been particularly true of his arch-enemy Nizam al-Mulk, who held tremendous sway in the court.

---

1 A reference to Imam al-Mustansir.

2 Al-Muscati, *Hasan bin Sabbah*, p. 42.

CHAPTER TEN

Expansion of the *Dawa* and the Early Seljuk Military Campaign against Alamut

"The hunter returneth not but with quarry after the measure of his intention."—Kanmakan[1]

HASAN-I-SABAH's acquisition of Alamut would serve the Nizaris as a physical headquarters for their *dawa* activities until 1256. *Dais* were dispatched throughout the region and as far away as Syria. Juvaini gives, unsurprisingly, hostile interpretations of Hasan's teaching regarding the importance of the role of the Imam in interpreting the true meaning of the Quran. While we will be discussing doctrinal issues again later, the tone of Juvaini's summary of Hasan's teaching is worth noting: "Such then was the nonsense which he expounded; whereof the outward form were snares of deceit and the inner meaning the wiles of Iblis and the purpose of which was to prevent the use of reason and the acquisition of knowledge."[2]

Juvaini goes on to discuss Hasan's expansion of territory throughout the mountainous region of Daylam both by persuasion and conversion, or by war. The Shia were well established in both Daylam and Kuhistan. *Dais* in different locations, though independent of a central leadership, often cooperated with each other.[3]

Juvaini and Rashid al-Din relate the story of a fierce opponent in the earliest days of Alamut, a Seljuk emir named Turan-Tash, who held the district of Alamut as a fief from Malikshah. Turan-Tash's ferocious military assault against Alamut so demoralized the residents of the castle that they were prepared to surrender and depart. Hasan

1 Burton (trans and ed.), *The Book of the Thousand Nights and a Night*, vol. 3, p. 79.

2 Juvaini, *Genghis Khan*, p. 671. Iblis is the Islamic version of Lucifer, the Devil or Satan, also known as Shaytan or Shaitan.

3 Hodgson, "The Ismaili State," in Boyle (ed.), *CHI*, vol. 5, p. 439.

had not yet had the time to lay in the supplies or build the water systems that would eventually allow the garrison to be self-sustaining for long periods of siege. But he told his people that he had received direct assurances from Imam al-Mustansir that they should continue to hold out and that they would survive. They did, and subsequently named Alamut *Baladat-al-Iqbal* ("the Town of Good Fortune").[1] While both Juvaini and Rashid al-Din dismiss Hasan's message as "imposture," the facts of the history may more accurately bear out the truth of his claim to divine guidance.[2]

Hasan secured his second citadel, the nearby fortress of Sanamkuh near Abhar in the mountains west of Qazvin, in 1091.[3] The presence of the Ismailis would continue to be of concern to Sultan Malikshah and his court. In 1092, he sent another emir, Arslan-Tash, in command of an army against Hasan. At this early point in the Assassin history, there were still but sixty or seventy men at Alamut, and their food stores remained low. Hasan appealed for help to his *dai* Bu-Ali Dihdar in Qazvin. Bu-Ali Dihdar arrived to help defend Alamut with some three hundred troops, weapons, and supplies. Locals from Rudbar also came to Hasan's defense and attacked Arslan-Tash and his troops. After some three to four months, the Assassins and their allies were victorious and the attackers retreated, leaving behind precious supplies.

The year 1092 was not an auspicious one for the Seljuk sultanate. Nizam al-Mulk, the powerful chief wazir who was intimately involved with the planning for the military campaigns against the Assassins, fell victim to an Assassin dagger. His death marked their first high-level political assassination.[4] While traveling in his litter during Ramadan, Nizam was killed after having broken his fast and

---

1 Juvaini, *Genghis Khan*, p. 674, translation in note 34 by J. A. Boyle (ed.).

2 Ibid., p. 674; Rashid al-Din, appendix two, p. 313.

3 Hodgson, "The Ismaili State," in Boyle (ed.), *CHI*, vol. 5, p. 432.

4 See chapter fourteen for more on the use of assassination.

attending an audience with the sultan. Returning to his harem, he was stabbed by an Assassin *fidai* named Bu-Tahir Arrani who had disguised himself as a Sufi. Some weeks later, Sultan Malikshah himself died—most likely independently of any Ismaili involvement.

In chapters two and six we discussed some of the accomplishments of Nizam al-Mulk. However, there is another side to his legacy, as suggested by Hasan's letter to Malikshah in chapter nine. Stories circulate that point to his ruthlessness and corruption. For example, the Egyptian historian Abul-Mahasin ibn Taghri Birdi (1411–1470) accused Nizam of being a dishonest and petty tyrant, who used slander, imprisonment, and murder to cling to power.[1] While Nizam's implacable hostility to the Ismailis was particularly noteworthy, his intolerance extended to Christians, Jews, and Shiites as well. Some believe Nizam had become so odious to Malikshah that his assassination occurred at the hands of the sultan and his allies.[2]

Nizam al-Mulk was very aware of his key role in the reign of Malikshah, and his arrogance may have gotten the best of him. His prior service to both the Ghaznavid sultan Chaghri Beg and the Seljuk Alp Arslan involved mature men in positions of great authority. Malikshah was eighteen when he was handed the reins of leadership, and Nizam played a large role in tutoring and advising him. Nizam is quoted in a frank statement shortly before his death that cannot have sat well with anyone: "Tell the Sultan, 'If you have not already realized that I am your co-equal in the work of ruling, then know that you have only attained to this power through my statesmanship and judgment.'"[3] If this is accurate, it lends credibility to the accusation

---

1 Al-Muscati, *Hasan bin Sabbah,* p. 50, summarizing the Egyptian historian Abul-Mahasin ibn Taghri Birdi's *An-Nujum Az-Zahira.*

2 Al-Muscati writes that Malikshah arranged for the killing of Nizam al-Mulk in retribution for the wazir's participation in a plot to overthrow the sultan, and that Hasan-i-Sabah and the Assassins were publicly blamed for it. *Hasan bin Sabbah,* p. 52.

3 Bosworth, "The Political and Dynastic History," in Boyle (ed.), *CHI,* vol. 5, p. 68. Bosworth is quoting Ibn a-Athir in *al-Kamil.*

that Malikshah had either fired Nizam, or was about to, or was even complicit in his assassination.[1]

According to Rashid al-Din, Malikshah colluded with an enemy of Nizam al-Mulk. That enemy was said to have contacts among the Assassins or Deviationists.[2] As the sultan was traveling from Isfahan to Baghdad, the Assassins killed Nizam al-Mulk as the royal entourage reached Nahawand on October 22, 1092. Forty days later, Malikshah himself died in Baghdad (November 27, 1092). Rashid al-Din writes he may have been poisoned.[3]

Al-Muscati believes that the poisoning of the sultan may have occurred on orders from the Abbasid caliph al-Muqtadi (r. 1075–1094).[4] There is convincing evidence of motivation for this claim. Nizam helped negotiate a marriage alliance between one of Malikshah's daughters and the caliph. The conditions of the contract were that the caliph would take no concubines or other wives. This angered al-Muqtadi. The situation further deteriorated when Malikshah's daughter complained to her father of her husband's neglect. Malikshah demanded her return with her young son. In 1092, the sultan made a second visit to Baghdad and informed al-Muqtadi that he was about to be replaced by his son (Malikshah's grandson), who was then five years old. Al-Muqtadi was spared this indignity when Malikshah died in Baghdad very soon after.[5]

---

[1] Ibid., vol. 5, p. 102.

[2] Kenneth Allin Luther (trans.) and C. E. Bosworth (ed.) *The History of the Seljuk Turks*, p. 62.

[3] See Rashid al-Din, *The Biography of Our Master*, in appendix two, pp. 318–319, where he says Sultan Malikshah was poisoned and died forty days after Nizam al-Mulk. However, elsewhere in the *Jami al-Tawarikh*, Rashid al-Din wrote that it was eighteen days later. See Bosworth (ed.), *The History of the Seljuq Turks*, p. 62. The medieval historian Ibn al-Athir says it was fifty-three days after, as reported by Bosworth in "The Political and Dynastic History," in Boyle (ed.), *CHI*, vol. 5, p. 101. We do know that in the long history of the Assassin murders, they were never known to use poison.

[4] Al-Muscati, *Hasan bin Sabbah*, p. 53.

[5] Bosworth, "The Political and Dynastic History," in Boyle (ed.), *CHI*, vol. 5, pp. 100-101.

⊰⊱

The deaths of Nizam al-Mulk and Malikshah had immediate military repercussions for Hasan and his community. The Ismailis were involved in a major defensive operation in Kuhistan, in southeast Persia some 650 miles from Alamut, that would be favorably resolved by the sultan's death. Husayn Qaini's success in converting the garrison at Alamut undoubtedly inspired Hasan to send him to his native Kuhistan to further the mission in 1091–1092.[1] Conditions there were favorable for Nizari organizing.[2] The Seljuk governor of the region was abusing the Ismaili populace and their great resentment was a potent motive for rebellion. (Among other things, he was demanding the favors of the sister of a local noble who defected to the Ismailis in defiance.)[3] Sultan Malikshah had ordered his chief emir Ghizil-Sarigh to fight against Husayn Qaini, and ordered the Seljuk armies of Khurasan to assist in the campaign. The Seljuks laid siege to the castle of Dara, but a natural spring flowing within its precincts helped the Ismailis to withstand the siege.[4] While eventual Seljuk victory seemed assured, news of the death of Malikshah caused the army to be dispersed. The Ismaili success in Kuhistan established a second fortified regional center and greatly aided morale. It was a significant marker of the Ismaili revolt against Seljuk domination.

Another mountainous regional base was established in southwest Persia in the Zagros Mountains, some four hundred miles from Alamut between the provinces of Khuzistan and Fars. This area, too, had enjoyed a strong tradition of Shiite and Ismaili influence and independent thought. With the development of this fortress, a triangle-shaped zone of Assassin influence was built across Persia. A *dai* named Abu Hamza (the Shoemaker) had also studied in Egypt. He successfully seized two castles near his hometown of Arrajan.[5]

---

1 Lewis, *The Assassins*, p. 45.

2 Hodgson, *The Order of Assassins*, p. 74.

3 Lewis, *The Assassins*, p. 45.

4 Juvaini, *Genghis Khan*, p. 676, note 40 by J. A. Boyle (ed.).

5 Lewis, *The Assassins*, p. 45. While this territory did grow for a time, most of

⁂

The passing of Sultan Malikshah and Nizam al-Mulk meant that any further plans against Alamut or Kuhistan were suspended during the inevitable internecine succession battles that would rack the Seljuk Empire for years to come. Hasan grew stronger.

Hasan's old friend, teacher, and ally Rais Abufasl came to Alamut at this time and enlisted himself as one of Hasan's devoted disciples. Hasan is said to have teased him one day for his suspicion that Hasan had been experiencing madness when he mentioned a decade before that with just two strong friends, he could make use of the levers of power and upend the Seljuks. "Rais, which of us two was out of his senses . . . and which would the aromatic drinks and dishes dressed with saffron . . . have best suited, thee or me?"[1]

⁂

As Hasan worked to fortify Alamut, he continued to send *dais* to the neighboring regions. He would establish the role of the Chief *Dai* of Alamut as one-part military commander and one-part religious leader. Bosworth helps us to understand the milieu in which Hasan and the Ismailis were operating: "We have to conceive of the Saljuq empire as a series of political groupings rather than a unitary state."[2] This would not only allow for the rise of the Ismailis (and later Nizari Ismailis) at Alamut, it would help explain the network of power bases established by Hasan, and his relative freedom of movement in extending the Nizari state. The key was the semi-autonomous nature of the Ismaili fortresses that allowed for a free flow of warriors in times of need or opportunity.

---

the southern Zagros castles would be lost during the reign of Malikshah's son Muhammad Tapar. The Nizaris would, however, with the support of local Jewish clans, acquire several fortresses in the northern Zagros Mountains near Luristan. See Hodgson, "The Ismaili State," in Boyle (ed.), *CHI*, vol. 5, p. 448.

[1] Hammer-Purgstall, *The History of the Assassins*, p. 46.

[2] Bosworth, "The Political and Dynastic History," in Boyle (ed.) *CHI*, vol. 5, p. 78.

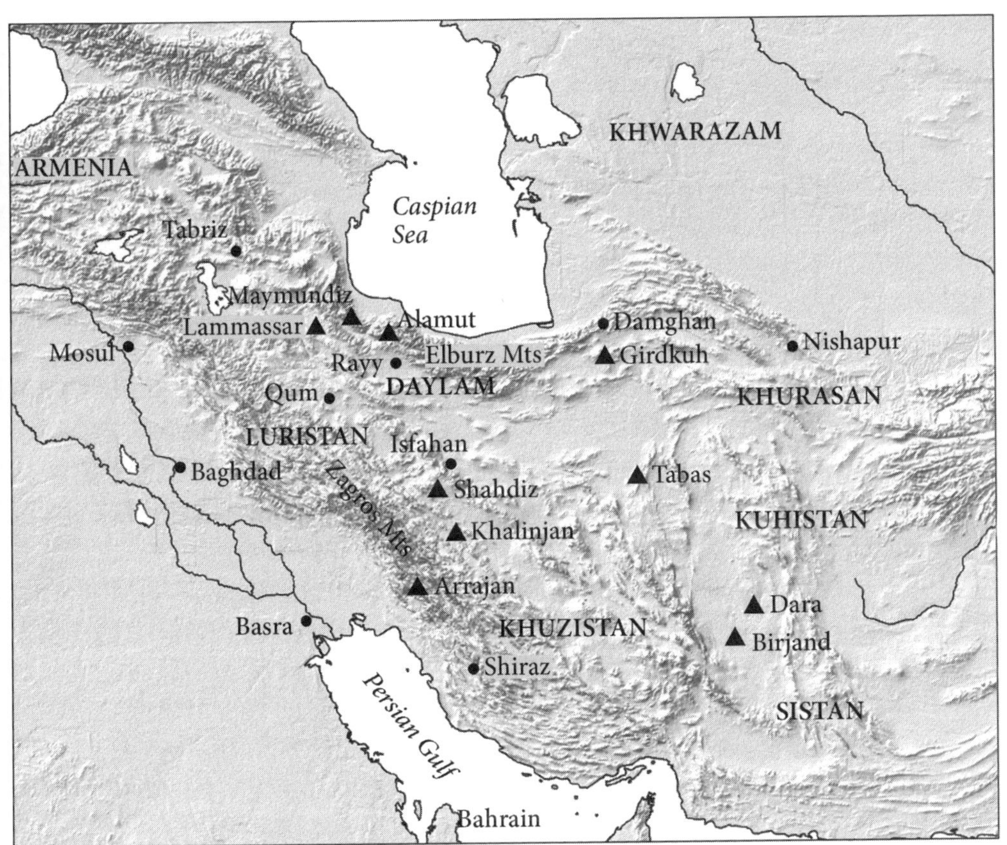

It must be stated again that with all their military organizing, political outreach, and religious proselytizing, the Assassins would always remain a small group within a much larger and more chaotic region. However, their use of assassination and the fervor of their intransigence gave them a romantic and outsized patina, both in their own time and today. While their survival and success were long a thorn in the side of the Sunni establishment, in reality they were a phenomenon limited in scope.[1] (This is not to say that they did not make earth-shattering changes to the political dynamics of Persia through their policy of assassination, as will be further illustrated in chapter fourteen.)

We should keep in mind that, in addition to the challenges presented by Alamut and the Ismailis, the Seljuks during the Alamut period were facing imminent threats to their survival from both the Egyptian Fatimids and the European Crusaders.

---

[1] Ibid., p. 71.

CHAPTER ELEVEN

The Founding of the Nizari Ismaili Faith

> As a wise and reverent man once remarked, "If you are a king, be as a slave toward God; the heart of any man who is ungrateful to God will be filled with countless fears." —*Shahnameh*[1]

In 1094, Caliph al-Mustansir, the eighth Fatimid Imam, died. And we now come to the seminal event that would place Hasan-i-Sabah firmly in the pages of religious history (as opposed to legend) for all time. Here was the decisive schism from which the Nizari Ismailis emerged and became a faith, headquartered at Alamut and other outposts established by Hasan. That faith continues its vibrancy to this day.

We discussed Hasan-i-Sabah having been born into the majority Twelver Shiite religion and being very skeptical of any other doctrine. And we explored his conversion to the Sevener beliefs of the Ismailis, for whom he became a powerful *dai* and organizer, rising in the hierarchy and being given ever-expanding responsibilities and areas of operation. When Hasan took Alamut, he did so in service to the *dawa* of Caliph al-Mustansir. Hasan's position as an important Persian proselytizer was not at all unusual in and of itself. Many *dais* in service to the Fatimid Imam were Persian. When they retired from the dangerous missions in their home areas, they often traveled to the peace, safety, and respect afforded them by residence in Egypt. "Indeed, the intellectual leadership of Cairo was largely of Iranian origin."[2]

Finally, we intimated that an Imamate succession struggle was (I believe) incorrectly blamed for the difficulty between Hasan and Badr al-Jamali while the former was in Egypt. Badr al-Jamali was the de facto ruler of Egypt. This alone would have surely incited

---

1 Ferdowsi (Davis, trans and ed.), *Shahnameh*, p. 8.

2 Hodgson, "The Ismaili State," in Boyle (ed.), *CHI*, vol. 5, p. 426.

Hasan's concerns. Badr was a scheming and power-hungry politician who played a zero-sum game in the court of Caliph al-Mustansir. As Badr's power increased, that of the Imam decreased. Hasan, with his fine discernment of the levers of power, would have been acutely aware of this and, thus, represented a threat to Badr.

It is conceptually important to understand that from 1090 to 1094, despite the weakening of the Egyptian state and Hasan's quarrel with Badr al-Jamali, Alamut functioned as a pro-Fatimid center of Ismaili religious proselytizing and anti-Seljuk revolutionary military activity. In 1094, this changed dramatically. While it is clear that Hasan had been a foe of the Fatimid bureaucratic administration—to the extent of his having been arrested, imprisoned, threatened with death, and expelled from Egypt—his true rebellion began only on the death of the Imam and Caliph al-Mustansir and the usurpation of Nizar's Imamate by the military dictatorship of Egypt.

Badr al-Jamali had also died in 1094 some months before al-Mustansir. The wazirate and post of Commander of the Armies was passed to Badr's son al-Malik al-Afdal. Al-Afdal had earlier arranged a marriage between his daughter and Caliph al-Mustansir's younger son al-Mustali, the twenty-one-year-old brother of his eldest son, Nizar. Nizar, on the other hand, was fifty years old, a mature and able leader who had been prepared for the responsibilities that awaited him on his father's death. He had long been designated as al-Mustansir's successor as the nineteenth Ismaili Imam, and the ceremony of the Passing of the *Nass* had already taken place.[1] But al-Afdal had other plans. He unilaterally declared his son-in-law al-Mustali as the nineteenth Imam and appointed him caliph. Al-Mustali's youth and inexperience would make him a perfect tool in the hands of the Commander of the Armies. He did this on the morning after al-Mustansir's death in what has been called a *coup d'état*.[2]

---

1 Daftary, *The Ismailis*, p. 261.

2 Samuel Stern, "The Epistle of the Fatimid Caliph al-Amir (al-Hidaya al-Amiriyya)—Its Date and Its Purpose," *Journal of the Royal Asiatic Society*, 1950, p. 20. Stern says Bernard Lewis shares his use of the word *coup*, as does Daftary, *The Ismailis*, p. 261.

Egypt had been terribly weakened by this time. The territorial holding of the Fatimid Caliphate had been reduced to Egypt alone. Many Ismailis were disgusted by what they saw and refused to acknowledge al-Mustali. The Druze movement, as small as it was, provided some haven for dissent, while the Qarmatis were long gone. Other minor opposition movements provided some relief from this cynical travesty against religious doctrine. The strength of the Ismaili movement in Persia, particularly the growing success of Hasan-i-Sabah's efforts, stood in stark contrast to the anemic and corrupt skeleton of the once-vibrant Fatimid Caliphate.

After his father's death and the treachery of his younger brother, Nizar fled to Alexandria. Here he attempted to organize a revolt to reclaim his birthright with the help of an anti-Afdal military faction and the Ismaili governor of Alexandria, Nasir al-Din Aftekin. In Alexandria, Nizar was proclaimed Imam and caliph.[1] Still, he was outnumbered by al-Afdal's armies and defeated near Cairo. Nizar was captured. Most people believe he was killed by the Fatimid army, or imprisoned in Cairo and executed. The majority of Ismailis in Egypt, Yemen, and Oman then accepted the claims of the Imamate of al-Mustali. But many in Syria and Persia refused to acknowledge al-Mustali even after they learned of the death of Nizar.[2]

The Hidden Nizari Imam at Alamut

Some people believe that Nizar was not killed, but escaped from his prison in Alexandria or Cairo and secretly reached the safety of Alamut. Marshall Hodgson notes that a historian named Abu Muhammad al-Iraqi, writing soon after Hasan acquired Alamut, acknowledged that an Imam was living there under his protection.[3]

---

[1] Daftary, "Hasan-i Sabbah and the Origins of the Nizari Ismaili Movement," in Daftary (ed.), *Mediaeval Ismaili History and Thought*, p. 194. Daftary supports the assertion that Nizar was declared caliph by citing numismatic evidence unearthed in 1994.

[2] Hodgson, "The Ismaili State," in Boyle (ed.), *CHI*, vol. 5, p. 437.

[3] Hodgson, *The Order of Assassins*, p. 66.

There is so much speculation about this because it is such a crucial issue.[1] The living Imam passing the *nass* to his son is a condition of the Nizari belief. The unbroken chain of Imam to Imam extends from the Prophet and then through his daughter Fatima to the first Imam Ali. Caliph al-Mustansir passed the Imamate to his son Nizar by the time of his death in 1094. Political machinations aside, it was critical that either Nizar, or his son or grandson, survive and continue the Alid Imamate (assuming, as the Nizaris do, that the succession of al-Mustali is illegitimate).

The question is, who was the Imam when Hasan-i-Sabah established the Nizari Ismailis? Hasan—and his two successors Buzurgumid and Muhammad I—were the *hujja* or proof of the Hidden Imam. The *hujja* is one rank below the Imam and is considered the messenger of the Imam, the one through whom the Imam could be accessible to his followers especially during periods of concealment.[2] We have already noted in chapter three the long period of concealed Imams (*dawr al-satr*) from the death of Muhammad ibn Ismail in 813 to the proclamation of the Fatimid Imam Ubayd Allah in 909. Hasan-i-Sabah never claimed to be the Imam. But his integrity is such that he stands as the most important witness (*hujja*-proof) to the continuity of the Ismaili succession. "Hasan was the custodian of the Ismaili mission until the imam should reappear, at which time he would point out the imam to the faithful."[3]

People believed that the hidden Imam—concealed and protected in the safety of Alamut—contributed to the development of Hasan's

---

[1] See chapter nineteen for a discussion of the proclamation of the Alamut Imamate in 1164 and the various theories and statements on the continuation of the bloodline of Nizar, and consequently of the Prophet through Fatima and Ali.

[2] Daftary, *The Ismailis*, p. 127.

[3] Hodgson, "The Ismaili State," in Boyle (ed.), *CHI*, vol. 5, p. 438. See also Ivanow, *Kalami Pir*, p. xlv, where he writes, "In the Nizari system there is only one *hujjat*. He is a kind of diminutive copy of the Imam, and stands in relation to the latter the same as that of the Imam to God. . . . It is only through him that one can know the Imam, just as it is through the Imam that one can know God."

al-dawa al-jadida or "New Preaching." In fact, Rashid al-Din quotes a statement that Hasan sent out from the castle to a group of religious scholars in the service of Sultan Muhammad Tapar during his campaign against Alamut in 1107. Hasan wrote, "Also, in our congregation, there is an Imam who is one of the descendants of Mustafa, peace be upon him and his progeny. The followers ask him about various issues and learn from him the facts."[1] Mustapha (chosen man) is a reference to the Prophet, so if Rashid al-Din is accurate here, this is an extraordinary piece of evidence.

When Hasan-i-Sabah died in 1124 and Buzurgumid became his successor, the Nizari Imam still remained in occlusion. Then Buzurgumid was succeeded by his son Muhammad I in 1138. Muhammad reigned as the head of Alamut until 1162, when he died and his son Hasan II became the fourth Lord of Alamut. The Imam had remained hidden for sixty-eight years.

The Revealed Nizari Imam

It was Hasan II who embodied the Alamut Imamate (although it is doubtful that he ever *publicly* announced himself as such). The open declaration of Hasan II's Imamate remained the teaching of his son and successor as the fifth Lord of Alamut, Muhammad II. Their genetic line continues to this day to the Aga Khan IV, the forty-ninth Nizari Imam and legally-recognized descendant of Hasan II. It was Hasan II who proclaimed the *Qiyama*, the Resurrection, on August 8, 1164. This will be discussed in more detail in chapter nineteen.

When Hasan II was killed in 1166, Muhammad II began his long reign as Lord of Alamut (r. 1166–1210). He devoted his life to developing the doctrine of the Alamut Imamate and regularizing what had been the revolutionary *Qiyama* proclamation of his father. He officially announced his father as the Imam and, therefore, the blood

---

[1] Rashid al-Din, appendix two, pp. 335–336. Hasan's statement to the theologians does not appear in Juvaini. It is a bold affirmation of the presence of an Imam at Alamut over a decade after the death of al-Mustansir. (See chapter nineteen.)

descendant of Nizar—rather than being the grandson of Buzurgumid and son of Muhammad I. Thus, Muhammad II acknowledged himself and his father as of the same bloodline as the Prophet and Fatima. As we shall discover in chapter seventeen, this assertion was legally codified in 1866 by the British High Court of Bombay, a ruling that remains in place to this day.

The Rival Mustalian Succession

In Egypt, following the deaths of Caliph al-Mustansir and Badr al-Jamali, the Fatimid Caliphate under al-Mustali grew increasingly weaker and more isolated, continuing the downward trend observed during the reign of his father. In 1121, Hasan's *fidais* traveled to Cairo to execute the Commander of the Armies al-Afdal for usurping Nizar's rights. In 1130, the son and successor of al-Mustali, Caliph al-Amir, was also murdered by Assassin *fidais* sent by Hasan's successor Buzurgumid. While technically the Fatimid dynasty lasted through four more caliphs, these political leaders were not considered Imams.[1]

The Mustalian Ismailis endured schisms of their own. While the circumstances are unclear, a cousin of al-Amir, named al-Hafiz, took power after the latter's assassination—rather than al-Amir's son al-Tayyib, as would have been expected. Still, al-Hafiz was recognized as the Fatimid caliph and twentieth-first Ismaili Imam by the majority of Egyptian Ismailis, who became known as Hafizi Ismailis. Their line disappeared after the dissolution of the Fatimid dynasty by Saladin.[2] Another unusual schism occurred in the fifteenth century when a small number of Bohras (Mustalian Ismailis) became Sunnis under the leadership of Syed Jafar Ahmad Shirazi. They may be found today primarily in India and Pakistan.[3]

---

[1] Lewis, *The Assassins*, p. 35.

[2] https://en.wikipedia.org/wiki/Isma%27ilism#Musta%27ali. See also http://iis.ac.uk/encyclopaedia-articles/modern-ismaili-communities [accessed September 29, 2018].

[3] https://en.wikipedia.org/wiki/Sunni_Bohra [accessed May 3, 2019].

The Fatimid Caliphate ended in 1171 when Saladin established his own Ayyubid dynasty and returned Egypt to the Sunni faith after two centuries of Ismaili rule. He burned the books of the Ismailis in bonfires.[1]

Today, the majority of Ismailis who follow the line of al-Mustali live in India and Yemen, with smaller pockets in Pakistan, Saudi Arabia, the United States, and Canada. They believe that al-Amir's infant son al-Tayyib was given the *nass* by his father and that he was the true Imam. His descendants constitute their current line of Imams. This community is known as the *Tayyibiyya* (Tayyibi Ismailis) and *Bohras* (traders), and number approximately one million souls.[2]

---

1 Lewis, *The Assassins*, p. 35.

2 https://en.wikipedia.org/wiki/Dawoodi_Bohra [accessed July 14, 2019].

CHAPTER TWELVE

Military Campaigns and Territorial Acquisitions after the Death of Malikshah

Civil War in Persia

The death of Sultan Malikshah ended several decades of a unified Seljuk government that had been made possible by his rule and that of his father, Alp Arslan. "The lands of the Great Saljuqs were never more extensive than during Malik-Shah's reign."[1] But the state of Seljuk power and unity began to fall apart on the death of the sultan and his chief wazir. Difficulties in financing the army began to arise from the decline in state revenues.[2]

The disunity in the realm and subsequent diversion of attention left opportunities for Hasan to spread the Alamut mission. The decentralization of the Seljuk realm resembled that of the Ismailis in a certain sense, although the latter remained ideologically unified while the former were in a civil war. Battles could be fought fortress by fortress, town by town. Assassination was a very useful tool because when local leaders and strongmen were removed, incapacitation was the general result.[3]

Rashid al-Din explained that Sultan Malikshah had a son through one of his wives, an ambitious, beautiful, and highborn woman named Tarkan Khatun. She had her own wazir named Taj al-Mulk, a learned man known for his magnanimity.[4] Tarkan Khatun wanted Taj al-Mulk to replace Nizam al-Mulk and lobbied ceaselessly against Nizam. Her relentless efforts gradually succeeded in turning

---

1 Bosworth, "The Political and Dynastic History," in Boyle (ed.), *CHI*, vol. 5, p. 66.

2 Ibid., p. 231.

3 Hodgson, "The Ismaili State," in Boyle (ed.), *CHI*, vol. 5, pp. 440–441.

4 Rashid al-Din, *The History of the Seljuq Turks: From the Jami al-Tawarikh*, Edmund C. Bosworth (ed.), Kenneth Allin Luther (trans.). p. 61.

Malikshah against his wazir. At this time, Malikshah and Tarkan Khatun's son, Mahmud, was six years old. If Malikshah appointed the young child his successor, Tarkan Khatun and Taj al-Mulk would be de facto rulers of the empire until his maturity. Nizam al-Mulk, on the other hand, favored the succession of Malikshah's eldest son, Barkiyaruq, who was thirteen when his father died in 1092, and had been designated as the crown prince.

After Malikshah's death, Tartun Khatun persuaded the Abbasid caliph al-Muqtadi to appoint Mahmud to the sultanate. However, supporters of Barkiyaruq had him crowned in Rayy at the same time.[1] They had also seized the weapons that had been stored in Isfahan by Nizam al-Mulk.[2] The problems between the two groups of supporters of the rival sons of Malikshah was resolved when Mahmud suddenly died of smallpox in 1094.

That same year, Muayyid al-Mulk, the son of Nizam al-Mulk, gained his father's position of wazir under Barkiyaruq (r. 1094–1105). Yet his brother Fakhr al-Mulk supplanted him in that role through gifts and wealth distributed among the sultan's court. Muayyid al-Mulk went on to inflame dissension among the Seljuks—later convincing another son of Malikshah, Muhammad Tapar, to do battle for Khurasan. After capturing Barkiyaruq's mother in Rayy around 1099–1100, Muayyid al-Mulk strangled her. Barkiyaruq ultimately killed Muayyid al-Mulk in revenge by his own hand in 1101.[3]

Barkiyaruq had earlier been attacked by his uncle Tutush, a brother of Malikshah who served as the Syrian Seljuk governor of Damascus. Tutush had traveled up to Baghdad in 1093 and proclaimed himself sultan. He was killed in battle in 1095 in Rayy, giving Barkiyaruq a brief respite after a series of other complex uprisings and attempts to dethrone him.

Then came Muhammad Tapar in 1097, enflamed by Muayyid al-Mulk, to challenge his half-brother for the leadership of the realm.

---

[1] Ibid., pp. 65–66.

[2] Bosworth, "The Political and Dynastic History," in Boyle (ed.), *CHI*, vol. 5, p. 103.

[3] Ibid., pp. 109–110.

Barkiyaruq had given Muhammad Tapar the governorship of Ganja in Azerbaijan. But Muhammad Tapar rose in revolt, killing his *atabeg* (appointed political mentor) and seizing the entire region of Arran west of the Caspian Sea.[1] Barkiyaruq was forced to defend himself against Muhammad Tapar in a multi-year campaign.

Another son of Malikshah was named Sanjar. He was the half-brother of Barkiyaruq and full brother of Muhammad Tapar. Sanjar was governor of eastern Khurasan and Tukharistan under Barkiyaruq, and he successfully held these eastern territories against Ghaznavid ambitions to take advantage of the Seljuk divisions.[2]

Hasan and his Nizari Ismailis were obviously affected by all this chaos and did what was strategically necessary to hold their own. Barkiyaruq had frequently been accused of being either an Ismaili sympathizer or even a secret Ismaili. Rashid al-Din writes, "Sultan Barkiyaruq was a lover and a believer of the Nizaris."[3] Edmund G. Browne says that Barkiyaruq was taunted by enemy troops as "*Ya Batiniyya* [i.e., Ismaili]."[4] At one point in 1100, the Ismailis sent a force of five thousand troops to Barkiyaruq's defense against Sanjar, who was then supporting the efforts of Muhammad Tapar.[5]

Various Ismaili fortresses might contribute soldiers to various Seljuk factions. Ismaili leaders might offer submission to a Seljuk emir, send their troops to aid him, share their tax revenues with him, and thus avoid direct conflict. In the towns, Ismaili cells flourished (most often in secret), frequently among the artisan class. These men were armed and available. Secrecy was an integral part of their survival.

---

[1] Ibid., p. 107.

[2] Ibid., p. 103.

[3] Rashid al-Din, appendix two, p. 325. However, according to Rashid al-Din's *History of the Seljuk Turks*—another portion of the *Jami al-Tavarikh*, Bosworth (ed.) and Luther (trans.)—Barkiyaruq was described as a Shiite rather than an Ismaili (see note 62, p. 171).

[4] Browne, *A Literary History of Persia*, vol. 2, p. 312.

[5] Hodgson, *The Order of Assassins*, pp. 86–87.

Generally, the only known Ismailis were the leaders: preachers and public figures.[1]

Bernard Lewis reports that during the Seljuk civil war, a significant number of Hasan's assassinations were directed against supporters of Muhammad Tapar—enemies of Barkiyaruq.[2] Yet, it was said that Barkiyaruq himself had been stabbed by the Assassins in a conflict over his choice of an anti-Ismaili wazir.[3] It seems that either the Ismaili influence had grown so strong they became arrogant, or that Barkiyaruq realized the danger he faced from being perceived as an Ismaili sympathizer.

In 1101, Barkiyaruq joined with Sanjar in a campaign against the Ismaili fortress of Tabas in Kuhistan.[4] But the Seljuk siege is believed to have been lifted because the Ismailis bribed the commanding emir to suspend it. The emir returned three years later—after the Ismailis had been able to reinforce the castle. While this second Seljuk campaign against Tabas was also victorious, it, too, was resolved by a withdrawal of Seljuk forces and a weakly negotiated settlement. In short, the Nizaris were allowed to reestablish themselves in Kuhistan.[5]

Barkiyaruq then launched a series of massacres against Ismailis in Isfahan, Baghdad, and elsewhere.[6] Yet his efforts here do not display the definitive passion of ruthless destruction that they might have. While widespread attacks most definitely occurred, the victims were urban Ismailis or their sympathizers. There were no efforts to take fortified Nizari strongholds.[7] Nizari leaders in Kuhistan and Isfahan began to levy taxes on residents of these Seljuk domains.

Attacks against the Assassin community were countered with assassinations against their instigators. Barkiyaruq's court and army were infiltrated by Ismaili agents, as well as converts. Anti-Nizari

---

1 Hodgson, "The Ismaili State," in Boyle (ed.), *CHI*, vol. 5, p. 440.

2 Lewis, *The Assassins*, p. 52.

3 Hodgson, *The Order of Assassins*, p. 88.

4 Ibid., p. 88.

5 Lewis, *The Assassins*, p. 52.

6 Hodgson, *The Order of Assassins*, pp. 88–89.

7 Lewis, *The Assassins*, pp. 52–53.

officials in the Seljuk court wore chain mail armor to protect against the daggers of the Assassins.[1]

There were five battles between Barkiyaruq and Muhammad Tapar, in four of which Barkiyaruq was victorious. (The second battle was when Barkiyaruq captured and killed Muayyid al-Mulk.) Sanjar joined Muhammad Tapar against Barkiyaruq in 1101–1102. However, in 1105, despite his victories and attempts to negotiate a peace, Barkiyaruq died of illness at the age of twenty-five.

The sultanate passed to Muhammad Tapar (r. 1105–1118). The thirteen-year Seljuk civil war was resolved. On the death of Muhammad Tapar, the Seljuk leadership would pass to Sanjar, whose reign extended from 1118 to 1157.

Originally confined to the Rudbar region and the Elburz Mountains, Hasan had expanded his territory to Kuhistan in the southeast and Khuzistan in the southwest, as mentioned. Malikshah's death and the resulting chaos, and the progress in fortifying Alamut and the Rudbar Valley, opened more options to Hasan. In 1093, the Nizaris attempted military actions due south in Isfahan, then capital of the Seljuk Empire, some 320 miles from Alamut.

The castle of Shahdiz had earlier been an important Seljuk stronghold. Ahmad ibn Attash was the son of the head of the Persian *dawa* Abd al-Malik ibn Attash, who had helped to train the young Hasan-i-Sabah. Ahmad succeeded his father as the *dai* of Isfahan. He quietly began conversion activities among the children of the Seljuk garrison of Shahdiz. A diligent organizer, he was said to have converted some thirty thousand people in the area. By 1100, he had seized the fortress of Shahdiz.[2] The Nizari presence in Isfahan

[1] Ibid., pp. 51–52, quoting Ibn al-Athir writing in 1100; also Daftary, *The Ismailis*, p. 355.

[2] Hodgson, *The Order of Assassins*, p. 85.

represented a major inroad into the heart of Seljuk power. Other fortresses followed, including nearby Khalinjan.[1]

The acquisition of Girdkuh in the eastern Elburz region in 1096 or 1099 bore the classic Assassin signature. Located just south of Damghan, where Hasan had worked for three years before taking Alamut, it was another receptive area for Nizari expansion. The Seljuk governor of the region was Rais Muzaffar, a secret Ismaili.[2] He had originally been converted by Hasan's teacher, Abd al-Malik ibn Attash.[3] Concluding that the castle was strategically ideal for the Nizaris, he persuaded the Seljuk emir Amirdad Habashi to request that Sultan Barkiyaruq appoint him commander. Muzaffar conducted extensive repairs and renovations, and stocked and fortified Girdkuh at Seljuk expense. Then he declared himself a disciple of Hasan-i-Sabah. He continued to rule the castle for forty years. He dug a well through the solid rock over 1100 feet deep but was unable to reach water. Not long after his death, an earthquake sent water gushing up through the well.

In 1096 (or 1102), Kiya Buzurgumid, one of Hasan's most loyal commanders, was sent to acquire the nearby Lammasar castle, situated some twenty-five miles to the west of Alamut overlooking the Ninehrud River.[4] Unable to convert the occupants, he took it by a military assault.[5] He remained there for twenty years until summoned by Hasan to succeed him as the chief *hujja* and second Lord of Alamut.

Author/explorer Peter Willey made a forty-year study of Assassin castles in Persia and Syria. He identified their extensive fortifications

---

[1] Hodgson, "The Ismaili State," in Boyle (ed.), *CHI*, vol. 5, p. 444.

[2] We recall in chapter eight that the *rais* had paid out the three-thousand dinar draft from Hasan to the Alid Mahdi for the acquisition of Alamut.

[3] Lewis, *The Assassins*, p. 50.

[4] See Willey, *Eagle's Nest*, in which he says the year was 1096, p. 30; Rashid al-Din also gives 1096, appendix two, p. 321; Juvaini, *Genghis Khan*, says it occurred in 1102, p. 679.

[5] Juvaini, *Genghis Khan*, p. 679.

as numbering some 250 castles, fortresses, and watchtowers. He was impressed with what he found and wrote the following:

> In contrast to the malevolent view of the Ismailis held by their opponents, we can now positively assert that they were a people of exceptional intelligence and determination with a sophisticated knowledge of military architecture, administration and logistics, as well as being highly successful agriculturalist and water engineers in a mostly arid and mountainous terrain.[1]

When Muhammad Tapar succeeded Barkiyaruq in 1105, he proved himself a Sunni leader with no sympathies toward his Ismaili neighbors. He personally led an attack against Shahdiz near Isfahan in 1107. The attack was delayed by appeals from the Nizaris led by Ahmad ibn Attash to the *ulema* council of Isfahan. Ahmad argued that the Nizaris were fellow Muslims who accepted *sharia*; their only difference was their acceptance of the Imam. Thus, it was forbidden for Muslims to conduct war against them. They said they accepted Sultan Muhammad Tapar as their legitimate political ruler while maintaining their religious allegiance to the Imam. At first, most of the Sunni judges were inclined to accept the Ismaili position until an argument from one staunch clerical enemy, Abul-Hasan Ali, convinced the council that the Ismailis were outside the pale of Islam.[2] He argued that the Nizari allegiance was first to the Imam and second to *sharia*. If the Imam permitted something *sharia* forbade, those who supported his authority were legitimate blood targets.[3] Several

1 Willey, *Eagle's Nest*, p. xxiv. See appendix two of his book for a listing of the Ismaili castles and fortifications he visited, pp. 270–276.

2 Hodgson, *The Order of Assassins*, p. 96; Daftary, *The Ismailis*, p. 362.

3 Summarized from Lewis, *The Assassins*, p. 54. This is precisely what happened during the reign of Hasan *ala dhikrhi al salam*, and does, in fact, perfectly elucidate the problem of the Nizari Ismaili heresy.

of the legists who ruled against the Ismailis were later assassinated.[1] This would become a significant doctrinal challenge for the Sunni community thenceforth. What constitutes a "true" Muslim? How far does tolerance extend to those who proclaim the *Shahada*?[2]

After several more delaying tactics—which included the safe release and relocation of a number of his troops to Arrajan and Tabas—Ahmad ibn Attash broke his truce with Muhammad Tapar and the sultan attacked. Ibn Attash held out gallantly with a force of eighty men until they were betrayed by a traitor within. Then Ahmad's wife bedecked herself in jewels and leapt to her death from the castle wall. Ahmad was captured and paraded through the streets of Isfahan, and then crucified in the public square. He had been known for his skills in astrology. As he hung in the square, a bystander asked if he had not been able to foresee his doom by the stars. Ibn Attash replied, "I perceived from my horoscope that I should traverse the streets of Isfahan with pomp and parade more than royal, but I did not know that it would be in such fashion."[3] He was then flayed alive and his skin stuffed with straw and sent, along with his head and that of his son, to Caliph al-Mustazhir in Baghdad. This all earned much prestige for Muhammad Tapar.[4] Upon Ahmad's death, if not earlier, Hasan-i-Sabah was acknowledged as the supreme head of the Nizari Ismaili movement.[5]

Sultan Muhammad Tapar launched a new assault against Alamut in 1107. It was led by Ahmad ibn Nizam al-Mulk, another son of the slain wazir who had succeeded his father in the Seljuk court. His

---

[1] Hodgson, *The Order of Assassins*, p. 96.

[2] James Waterson points to the real-world consequences of describing the Nizaris as *malahida*. The rules of Islamic law regarding combat would not apply to them, so that their women and children would be fair game to Seljuk soldiers. *The Ismaili Assassins*, p. 90.

[3] Browne, *A Literary History of Persia*, vol. 2, pp. 315–316.

[4] Lewis, *The Assassins*, p. 55.

[5] Hodgson, "The Ismaili State," in Boyle (ed.), *CHI*, vol. 5, p. 446. This makes sense if we recall that Ahmad's father was the supreme *dai* of Persia and the teacher of Hasan-i-Sabah himself. Thus, his son would be considered by many to be his successor until his own death.

hatred of the Assassins was magnified when his brother, Fakhr al-Mulk, had been seriously injured by *fidais* in Nishapur a year earlier.[1] His was a scorched-earth campaign in which the goal was to starve out the garrison at Alamut by destroying crops throughout the valley.

The Seljuk armies continued this sustained assault under different commanders for eight long years. So severe was the food shortage, it is said the Assassins lived on grass. Hasan's *fidais* would stab Ahmad in Baghdad and leave him paralyzed. As mentioned in chapter two, the Bavandid Ispahbadhs of the Daylami region refused to join Muhammad Tapar's campaign. True to his warrior pride, their leader Shahriyar was offended by what he considered the arrogance of the sultan's demand for his participation.[2]

During this campaign and resulting famine, Hasan sent his wife and two daughters to the safety of Rais Muzaffar in Girdkuh. He wrote to the *rais* that they should henceforth earn their living by the work of the spindle. They never returned to Alamut and future chiefs never allowed their women to remain at the fortress during military attacks.

Sultan Muhammad was determined to make an end of the Nizari Ismailis. He appointed his *atabeg*, Anushtagin Shirgir, to lay siege to the castles of Alamut and Lammasar in 1117–1118. The Turks fought with determination and were almost to the point of winning when the news came that Sultan Muhammad had died in Isfahan. The invaders departed en masse, leaving their weapons and stores of food behind. The Assassins reclaimed these with much relief.

There is evidence that an Ismaili sympathizer in the court of Muhammad Tapar's initial successor, his son Mahmud, may have influenced the young sultan to cease the campaign against Alamut. Anushtagin Shirgir was imprisoned and executed.[3]

The Assassins again regained their strength as Sultan Muhammad was ultimately succeeded by his half-brother, Sultan Sanjar

---

1 Rashid al-Din, appendix two, p. 319.

2 Bosworth, "The Political and Dynastic History," in Boyle (ed.), *CHI*, vol. 5, p. 28.

3 Lewis, *The Assassins*, p. 57.

(r. 1118–1157), after another brief Seljuk internecine rivalry for the throne. Sanjar made his nephew Mahmud his ally. When established, Sanjar focused his attention on Kuhistan, sending his army to take that Assassin stronghold. Hasan tried fruitlessly to open negotiations with Sanjar for several years but his ambassadors were refused an audience at the court. According to Juvaini and Rashid al-Din, Hasan bribed certain courtiers to plead his case with Sanjar.[1] He then paid one to stick a dagger into the ground beside the sultan's bed while he slept. When Sanjar awoke, he saw the dagger and ordered complete secrecy from any servants who knew of the threat.

Hasan sent a messenger to the sultan saying, "Did I not wish the Sultan well that dagger which was struck into the hard ground would have been planted in his soft breast."[2] Sanjar was from then inclined to peace and coexistence with the Assassins. This allowed for a period of growth and prosperity for the Nizari community. Sanjar gave them an annual pension of three thousand dinars collected from taxes on lands they owned, and even allowed them to charge tolls to travelers passing near Girdkuh. Juvaini reports seeing records of gifts, grants, and licenses from Sanjar in the library at Alamut.[3]

For the next several decades, a basic cease fire and even an alliance between the Nizaris and the Seljuks ensued. At one critical moment of a Seljuk civil war, Sanjar's army battled that of his nephew Mahmud with a force that included Nizari soldiers. Ismaili troops also served under Sanjar in 1126 in Kuhistan.[4] The Assassins became an established and stable political force in their numerous far-flung centers of power, and remained in a relatively comfortable relationship with the Sunni majority. While occasionally there would arise the need for activities against one or another individual or group, the period of Nizari open revolt against the Seljuks was over.

---

1 Juvaini, *Genghis Khan*, pp. 681–682; Rashid al-Din, appendix two, p. 329.

2 Juvaini, *Genghis Khan*, p. 682; Rashid al-Din, appendix two, p. 329.

3 Juvaini, *Genghis Khan*, p. 682; Rashid al-Din, appendix two, p. 329.

4 Bosworth, "The Political and Dynastic History," in Boyle (ed.), *CHI*, vol. 5, p. 151.

CHAPTER THIRTEEN

The Mission to Syria

AROUND THE year 1100, Hasan sent some *dais* to Syria in an effort to spread the Nizari Ismaili teachings to a region he knew well from his earlier travels. After the travesty of 1094, people reacted as may have been expected to the competing claims of Nizar and al-Mustali. Al-Mustali was spiritually discredited. Despite Nizar's reputed death, Hasan's mission to Syria succeeded in establishing Nizari Ismailism as the primary form of Ismailism. By 1130, when the Assassins had killed Fatimid caliph al-Amir, Syrian Ismailis were virtually exclusively Nizari.[1]

Interestingly enough, Malikshah's ambitions had also extended to Syria. Hasan's *dais* would thus find themselves interacting with Seljuk rulers and notables in Damascus, Aleppo, Mosul, Harran, Antioch, Edessa, and Jerusalem.[2] The other significant force in Syria was, of course, the newly-arrived European Crusaders.

We recall that the First Crusade was launched in 1095. The Crusaders conquered Jerusalem in 1099, achieving their most important and sacred goal. The Holy City in Christian control had been the original ideal that inspired the European campaign. They had also taken Antioch and Edessa by this point.

The success of the Crusader campaigns was aided by the political disunity among their Muslim enemies. The Fatimids in Egypt and the Abbasids in Mesopotamia were the two most pronounced divisions. But we have seen much evidence of other disputes, such as between the Qarmatis, Druze, and Mustalians. The rise of the Turkish Seljuk power over the Abbasids was confused by the Seljuk civil war following the death of Malikshah. Add to all this the Nizari assertion of power in Persia and Syria and we have a recipe for instability.

---

1 Hodgson, *The Order of Assassins*, pp. 69–71.

2 Bosworth, "The Political and Dynastic History," in Boyle (ed.), *CHI*, vol. 5, p. 98.

Hasan's Syrian *dawa* was responsible for the spread of the Nizari story to the West—although the early Western myths of the Nizaris were loaded with slander and inaccuracy. One of the first reports of the Syrian Assassins to reach Europe from the Holy Land was crafted probably by Burchard of Strassburg, an envoy of Emperor Frederick Barbarosa, in 1175.[1] Its author referred to the Ismailis as *Heyssessini,* describing them as living in inaccessible mountain fortresses and following a master who inspired terror in all Christian lords. He wrote that the group lived outside the bounds of Muslim law, ate pork, shared their women, and even indulged in incest. He continued that the master trained his young recruits in various languages and absolute obedience. They regarded him as having unlimited power over even the living gods. His disciples had been taught to worship him since earliest childhood. Growing up in absolute isolation from all competing instruction, they became his willing tools, ready to kill on command as he handed them a golden dagger and identified their target. A similar storyline was offered in *The Travels of Marco Polo* over a century later, except it reflected the Persian Assassins and added drugs and tantric sex to the mix.[2]

Soon after Burchard's report, William, the Archbishop of Tyre, estimated in his *Historia*[3] that there were some sixty thousand Nizaris living in ten castles in the Jabal Bahra mountains of Syria. His account described their reverence for the Old Man of the Mountain, minus the sinister hyperbolic accusations of Burchard:

> If for example there be a prince who is hated or mistrusted by this people, the Chief gives a dagger to one or more of his followers. At once whoever receives the command sets out on his mission, without considering the consequences of the deed nor

---

[1] Lewis, *The Assassins*, pp. 2–3.

[2] See appendix one.

[3] His history of the Kingdom of Jerusalem (in twenty-three volumes) was written between 1170 and 1184 according to Peter W. Edbury and John G. Rowe, *William of Tyre: Historian of the Latin East* (Cambridge University Press, 1988), p. 26 (https://en.wikipedia.org/wiki/William_of_Tyre [accessed January 12, 2019]).

> the possibility of escape. Zealous to complete his task, he toils and labours as long as may be needful, until chance gives him the opportunity to carry out his chief's orders. Both our people and the Saracens call them, Assissini; we do not know the origin of the name.[1]

⁂

The Syrian Assassins struggled for decades to find their balance in the region. They endured great hardships in their urban organizing efforts in Aleppo and Damascus, both governed by the Seljuk sons of Tutush—Ridwan in Aleppo and Duqaq in Damascus.

After Barkiyaruq's death in 1105 heralded the end of the Seljuk civil war, Muhammad Tapar became the undisputed sultan of the Persian Seljuks. The newfound security of his station encouraged him to support his nephew Ridwan's efforts against the Frankish Crusaders in Syria.[2]

Ridwan tended to look with favor upon the Nizaris, relying on them as military and strategic allies despite any other other differences they may have had.[3] Their cooperation worked to the benefit of both. Ridwan gave them a headquarters in the city. The Assassins aided him against his brother and rival Duqaq in Damascus, other Sunni rivals, and, of course, the Crusaders. However, on Ridwan's death and the ascension of his son Alp Arslan (named after his great-grandfather), Nizari fortunes were reversed. They faced a series of murders, executions, property seizures, and finally expulsion from Aleppo in 1124.

The Assassins tried one more time to establish themselves in an urban center. They went to Damascus, ruled by its then-current governor Tughitigin. They provided him with critical military support

---

1 Quoted by Lewis, *The Assassins*, pp. 3–4.

2 Bosworth, "The Political and Dynastic History," in Boyle (ed.), *CHI*, vol. 5, p. 116.

3 The following brief recap of events in Aleppo and Damascus is summarized from Wasserman, *The Templars and the Assassins*, pp. 130–132.

against the Crusaders and were given a headquarters in the city, as well as possession of the castle of Baniyas to the southwest. However, with the death of Tughitigin in 1128, their fortunes again plummeted on the ascension of his son and successor Buri. Some six thousand Ismailis were massacred. Buri was later assassinated in revenge by *fidais* sent from Alamut.

In 1133, the Assassins purchased the castle of Qadmus in the Jabal Bahra mountain range of western Syria. Soon they acquired several more castles, including Masyaf in 1140. They had finally found the key to be able to survive and establish stable roots in Syria.[1] The fact that their leaders were always appointed by Alamut introduced some tension to their efforts as they were perceived as outsiders. But in 1162, Alamut leader Hasan II sent his friend Rashid al-Din Sinan to study the local situation and then take over the Syrian mission. His community flourished under the headship of a truly enlightened, stable, and qualified ruler. He reigned until his death in 1193 and was universally loved and respected by his people.

The Crusader presence in the Holy Land extended for two hundred years. Many of the details of the rising and falling fortunes of the Crusaders are discussed in *The Templars and the Assassins,* as they are in other reputable studies. The important point is that we know beyond doubt that there were numerous recorded historical instances of contact and association between the Assassins and the Crusaders. This was particularly true of the interactions between Assassins and the military orders of the Knights Templar and the Knights Hospitaller.

The theme of *The Templars and the Assassins* is that the two orders shared a great deal in common because of their embrace of the religious ideal of the holy warrior. Their mutual allegiance to this archetype, I suggest, was often more important than their being on opposite sides of the conflicts—more important than the differences

[1] Daftary, *The Assassin Legends*, p. 67.

between Islam and Christianity. Like numerous warrior orders in a variety of cultures from Japan to India to Scandinavia, they shared common values of honor, courage, self-sacrifice, and a faith in the overarching righteousness of their cause. While they certainly fought against each other at certain times, it is also known that they allied themselves against common enemies at other times.

Some examples of the contact between the Syrian Nizaris and the Crusaders during the twelfth century include the following:[1]

In 1106, Tancred, Prince of Antioch, conquered the Assassin chieftain Abu Tahir (the Goldsmith) at Apamea, the Syrian Assassin headquarters near Aleppo, and forced the Assassins to ransom themselves. In 1110, Tancred seized a second Assassin fortress. In 1125, the Syrian Nizari leader Bahram fought against the Franks alongside Tughitigin, the Seljuk lord of Damascus. But after the death of Bahram in 1128, and Tughitigin soon after, Tughitigin's son and successor Buri mounted a fierce campaign against the Nizaris, as noted. Bahram's successor Ismail al-Aljami reached out to the Crusader king Baldwin II of Jerusalem for asylum.

In 1142, the Hospitallers received the castle of Krak des Chevaliers at the southern end of the Jabal Bahra mountain range—becoming neighbors of the Assassins, who had recently established this area as their Syrian headquarters. In 1149, Prince Raymond of Antioch perished alongside the Assassin chief Ali ibn Wafa in a battle against the Sunni Zangids. In 1152, the Nizaris assassinated Count Raymond II of Tripoli, their first Crusader victim (see chapter fourteen). This caused the Templars to invade in retaliation and extract an annual tribute of two thousand gold pieces.

The ascension of Sinan as the Assassin leader in 1162, and the entry of the Sunni leader Saladin into the region, created a new situation for all. Sinan attempted peace negotiations with the Christian king Amalric in 1173. He sent an ambassador who was favorably received by Amalric. Sinan sought a relaxation of the Templar tribute and an alliance against Saladin. Amalric agreed. Sinan also expressed

---

1 These contacts are summarized from the account in Daftary, *The Assassins Legends*, pp. 64–69, 72–74.

interest in learning more about Christianity, and his envoy asked for teachers to be sent to educate the Ismailis, even, apparently, suggesting a willingness to convert.[1] But the Templars killed Sinan's ambassador on his return journey to the Nizari court. Though Amalric arrested and imprisoned the offending knight, and apologized to Sinan, chances for an alliance were dashed by Amalric's death in 1174.

Saladin took Jerusalem in 1187. When Sinan and Saladin later forged an alliance (see chapter fourteen), Saladin was accused, along with King Richard the Lionhearted, of having arranged the assassination in 1192 of Conrad of Montferrat, King of Jerusalem. A peace treaty between Richard and Saladin included terms favorable to Sinan at Saladin's request. When Richard's nephew Henry of Champagne, the new King of Jerusalem, visited the Assassin fortress of Kaph in 1194 (where Sinan had died in 1193), the famous death leap of the *fidais* was said to have taken place (see chapter fifteen).

During the thirteenth century, contacts between Assassins and Crusaders continued.[2] In 1213, Raymond, son of Prince Bohemond IV of Antioch, was assassinated. This led to reprisal raids by Bohemond, in which the Assassins were aided by the Ayyubid rulers of Aleppo and Damascus. In 1227, the Assassins received diplomatic gifts from Holy Roman Emperor Frederick II the Great. In 1228, they battled the Hospitallers, were defeated, and forced to pay tribute. But in 1230, they joined with the Hospitallers in a new campaign against Bohemond IV. During this period, Bohemond V, Bohemond's son, wrote to Pope Gregory IX complaining that both the Hospitallers and Templars were entirely too cordial with the Assassins. The

---

[1] Archbishop William of Tyre mentioned this in his writing, as did Walter of Map writing in 1182. The story is recounted in Hodgson, *The Order of Assassins*, p. 204, as it is in many other places. Hodgson points out the similarity between the *Qiyama* and Christianity. Hasan II overturned *sharia* as Jesus overturned Mosaic Law. While numerous authors suggest that Sinan's interest in Christianity was either manipulative—i.e., to curry favor with Amalric—or that his scholarly/spiritual quest of new knowledge was simply misinterpreted by early Christian historians as a desire to convert—no one can possibly know what was in his mind.

[2] Summarized from Daftary, *The Assassins Legends*, pp. 60, 74–76, 79–82.

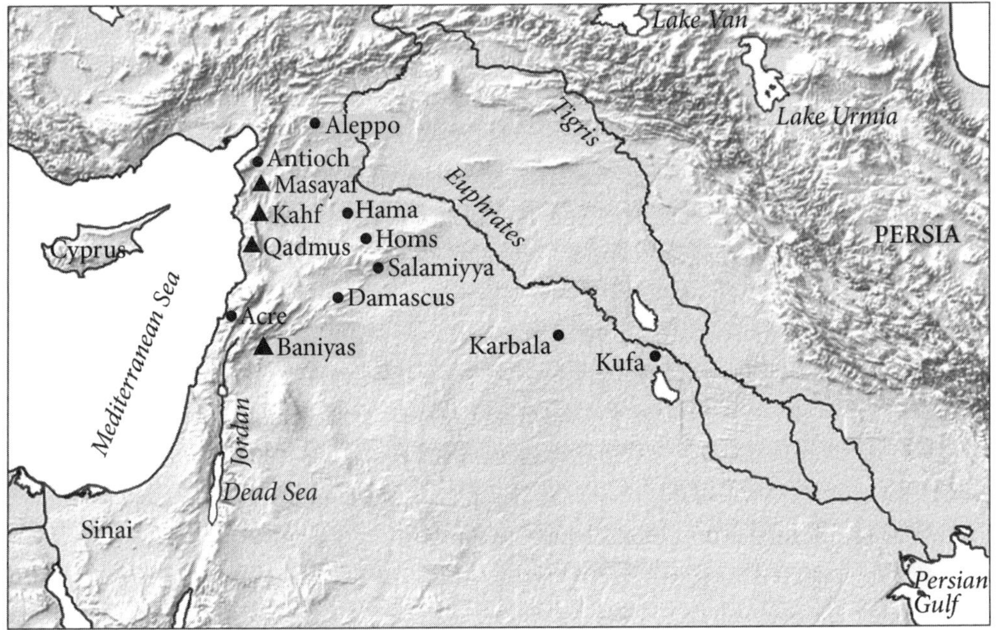

pope replied in anger, forbidding contact between the military orders and the Nizaris. Around 1250, King Louis IX had an exchange of diplomats and shared gifts with the Assassins. His emissary, Yves the Breton, found the Assassin chief highly educated, quite familiar with Christian books, and they held long discussions of Ismaili and Christian doctrines.

How well would the Assassins have been known to the West without their Syrian mission? While the popularity of Marco Polo's fourteenth-century tales of his travels—with his famous cameo of the Assassins—would have made them a curiosity, I do not believe we in the West would be speaking about the Assassins today unless Hasan's vision had been realized by the success of his Syrian mission. European Crusaders, diplomats, historians, and religious missionaries were fascinated by this eclectic group and spread their tales far and wide.

CHAPTER FOURTEEN

The Technique of Assassination

> Brothers, when the time comes, with good fortune from both worlds as our companion, then by one single warrior on foot a king may be in terror, though he own more than a hundred thousand horsemen. —Ismaili poem[1]

Brocardus, a German priest, warned King Philip VI of France in 1332 about the dangers of the Assassins should the king embark on the Crusade he was then contemplating:

> I name the Assassins, who are to be cursed and fled. They sell themselves, are thirsty for human blood, kill the innocent for a price, and care nothing for either life or salvation. Like the devil, they transfigure themselves into angels of light, by imitating the gestures, garments, languages, customs and acts of various nations and peoples; thus, hidden in sheep's clothing, they suffer death as soon as they are recognized.[2]

The word "Assassin" had entered widespread use in Europe by the fourteenth century to describe a professional hired killer.[3] As was noted in the previous chapter, the contact between the Crusaders and the Syrian Nizaris brought the Assassins into popular European culture beginning in the late twelfth century. At first, the devotion of the *fidai* to his master was that which enflamed the poetic imagination

---

[1] W. Ivanow, "An Ismaili Poem in Praise of the Fidawis," *Journal of the Bombay Branch of the Royal Asisatic Society*, 1938, p. 71. Quoted by Waterson, *The Ismaili Assassins*, p. 53.

[2] Brocardus went on: "Since indeed I have not seen them, but know this of them only by repute or by true writing, I cannot reveal more, nor give fuller information." Quoted in Lewis, *The Assassins*, p. 1.

[3] Ibid., p. 9.

rather than their acts of murder. Troubadours hymned their fealty to the beloved, pledging absolute obedience. "I am your Assassin, who hopes to win paradise by doing your commands."[1]

On a more practical level, however, for Hasan, selective political murder was an extremely effective technique. The continuity of Seljuk policy was greatly dependent on the skills of the individual ruler. The Muslim leaders were unlike the Christian military orders of the day, the Templars and the Hospitallers. A fallen leader among these groups would simply be replaced by a competent successor who shared the goals and training of his predecessor. In the case of the Muslims, when a leader died, his work stopped.[2]

Assassination within Islam is said to date to the Prophet.[3] He complained about certain enemies who, he proclaimed, did not deserve to live, and he expressed gratitude when they were killed. One of the first Companions to answer such a call was Abd Allah ibn Unays, who saved the early Muslim community of Medina from a ruthless enemy.[4] By murdering the chief of a hostile tribe, these early Muslims were able to avoid a full-scale military engagement.

As I have pointed out in earlier writings, assassination may be considered a more humane method of conducting political war then the sending of vast armies with their multiple casualties, including especially civilians who have neither power nor vested interests in such conflicts. During the thirteenth-century Mongol invasion of Kuhistan, some *eighty thousand* Ismailis were said to have been killed in one day.[5] The numbers of civilians slaughtered during the Mongol invasions of 1220–1258 are likely to bring tears to the eyes of anyone

---

1 F. M. Chambers, "The Troubadours and the Assassins," in *Modern Language Notes*, lxiv (1949), pp. 245–251, quoted by Lewis, *The Assassins*, p. 5.

2 Hodgson, *The Order of Assassins*, p. 81, note 3, commenting on observations of Jean de Joinville (1225–1317), historian of the Crusades and biographer of King Louis IX.

3 Hodgson, *The Order of Assassins*, p. 82.

4 Lings, *Muhammad*, p. 199.

5 Hodgson, *The Order of Assassins*, p. 270; Wasserman, *The Templars and the Assassins*, p. 129; Wasserman, *Templar Heresy*, p. 15.

paying attention. While the body counts are certainly exaggerated by medieval Muslim historians, they are astronomical, pointing to incomprehensible levels of destruction. For example: the casualties at the conquest of Nishapur in 1220 are given as some 1.7 million by Saifi in his *Tarikh Nama-yi Harat*; Ibn al-Athir gives a figure of seven hundred thousand killed in the taking of Marv, while Juvaini expands that casualty count to 1.3 million; at the capture of Herat in 1222, a number of 1.6 million people killed is given by Saifi. Lesser statistics of casualties resulted from the taking of smaller towns, such as Nasa, where the historian Nasawi reports seventy thousand slain; Sabzavar, where another seventy thousand were killed according to Juvaini; and Tun, where twelve thousand were killed according to the *Nuzhat- al-qulub*. Let us not forget the eight hundred thousand people slaughtered in Baghdad in 1258, as documented in chapter three.[1]

Hasan turned assassination into an art form. His *fidais* did not expect to survive their missions. They went after political leaders protected by heavily-armed men who most often killed the assassin immediately after his attack. They sought to commit their murders in large crowds to create maximum intimidation. They were often insinuated into royal courts as courtiers, guards, or other insiders, or into the households of powerful men as servants.[2] They might wait years for the signal to act, if and when the behavior of their targets became a threat to the Assassins. They were adept at surveillance and intelligence-gathering, so were able to anticipate the moves of their quarry.

Scholars, teachers, religious leaders, military commanders, and politicians all walked in fear of the invisible threats they faced from nameless agents. We recall from chapter twelve that anti-Nizari officials in the Seljuk court of Barkiyaruq wore chain mail to protect

[1] All these figures and the citations from medieval sources are given by I. P. Petrushevsky, "The Socio-Economic Condition of Iran under the Il-Khans," in Boyle (ed.), *CHI*, vol. 5, p. 485.

[2] Hodgson, "The Ismaili State," in Boyle (ed.), *CHI*, vol. 5, p. 442.

themselves against the daggers of the Assassins. They also appealed for permission to carry arms in the sultan's presence.[1]

Both Muslims and Europeans searched for an understanding of the reasons for the self-sacrifice of the *fidais*. Sunni heresiologists slandered them as mindless acolytes without judgment. Their behavior was likened to that of drunkards or drug addicts. Marco Polo told a tale of a secret Garden of Paradise at Alamut, ascribing their behavior to a sophisticated form of brain washing, aided by the use of drugs and sexual intimacy that rendered them the willing tools of their devious master.

Hasan, on the other hand, has been adopted as a mythic hero in bohemian literature, hip culture, and art as a mystic icon of drug use, rebellion, free-thinking, and libertinism. This extends as far back as the fourteenth century, when the Italian raconteur Giovanni Boccaccio wrote in the *Decameron* of an amorous abbot who made use of a concoction that "was wont to be used by the Old Man of the Mountain" to accomplish a seduction.[2] In more modern times, the reclusive musician Turner, Mick Jagger's character in the film *Performance*, reads Polo's description of the Garden of Delights in a tantalizing scene.[3] William S. Burroughs has embraced this aspect of Hasan-i-Sabah throughout his writings.

Though Hasan-i-Sabah is often slandered as a mass murderer, Bernard Lewis cites the Roll of Honor at Alamut as containing the names of fifty assassinations performed during the thirty-five-year reign of Hasan.[4] Rashid al-Din stated that, in total, seventy-five people were assassinated by Hasan and his two successors, Buzurgumid and Muhammad I.[5] Hodgson points out that most assassinations took place within these first decades of the Nizari struggle and

---

1 Lewis, *The Assassins*, p. 52.

2 Giovanni Boccaccio, *Decameron*, The Third Day, The Eighth Story.

3 *Performance*, written by Donald Cammell and co-directed by Donald Cammell and Nicholas Roeg, 1970.

4 Lewis, *The Assassins*, p. 51.

5 Burman, *The Assassins*, p. 37.

became less frequent thereafter. The practice of assassination caused an unprecedented hatred to be directed at the Nizaris, with retaliatory massacres following hard on the heels of assassinations. As assassinations declined, so did these indiscriminate massacres.[1]

With that said, some assassinations changed the balance of power in dynasties throughout Islam. The first instance of this was, of course, the murder of Nizam al-Mulk in 1092. As the powerful Seljuk prime minister, he was in charge of virtually all operations of the sultanate. From education to taxation, foreign policy, construction, agriculture, record-keeping, the military, there was nothing in the Seljuk kingdom that did not reflect his influence. He is also considered one of the most widely read and intelligent of the medieval Sunni political class, and is celebrated as a philosopher and political administrative theorist.

One possible reason for the assassination of Nizam al-Mulk is given by the medieval historian Ibn al-Athir. He wrote that it was in retaliation for a local Ismaili carpenter's death. As discussed by Lewis, the first blood to be shed by Ismailis in their war with the Sunnis would take place in Sava, a small town between Rayy and Qum, perhaps even before the acquisition of Alamut. Some eighteen Ismailis were arrested for conducting a separate prayer meeting. After questioning by the town sheriff, they were released. But they had tried to convert the *muezzin* (he who issues the call to prayer five times per day from the town minaret). The *muezzin* refused their efforts. Fearing exposure, they killed him. When Nizam al-Mulk learned of the crime, he ordered the execution of the ringleader, a carpenter named Tahir, the son of a local religious teacher who had earlier been lynched as a suspected Ismaili.[2]

The next assassination that rocked a kingdom was launched in 1121. Hasan's *fidais* traveled from Syria to Egypt to kill the Fatimid wazir and Commander of the Armies al-Afdal, the son and successor of Hasan's nemesis Badr al-Jamali, the virtual ruler of Egypt during the weakened reign of Caliph al-Mustansir. Al-Afdal had deprived

---

1 Hodgson, *The Order of Assassins*, p. 115.

2 Lewis, *The Assassins*, pp. 45–46.

Nizar of the Imamate. Rashid al-Din writes about the assassination, "Sayyidna [our Master] ordered a great celebration at Alamut and entertained the comrades for seven nights."[1]

After the assassination of al-Afdal, Caliph al-Amir (r. 1101–1130), the son and successor of Caliph al-Mustali (r. 1094–1101), wanted to reach out to Hasan-i-Sabah and implore him to renounce his Nizari beliefs—offering peace between Alamut and Egypt.[2] He was said to be relieved by the killing of al-Afdal, having resented the usurpation of the caliphate by this clan of Turkish military warlords, and rapidly seized al-Afdal's property upon his death.[3] He encouraged his new wazir, al-Mamun, to write Hasan. This "letter of pardon, inviting the Nizari leaders by name to return to the fold without fear of punishment, was apparently never sent."[4]

Al-Mamun, a Twelver Shiite in the Sevener Fatimid court, was suspicious of any alliance with Alamut. Fearing further Ismaili assassinations, he instituted strict border controls, citizen registration, elaborate use of domestic spies and "snitch patrols" to inform on fellow citizens, travel restrictions, citizen identification documents, and mass arrests of suspected Nizaris and their supporters. He also voiced suspicions that members of the court and the family of the Imam might hold pro-Nizar views. Chief among those suspected was the caliph's aunt, Nizar's full sister. In 1122, in a star-chamber-like setting, al-Mamun presided over an assembly of high officials of state and supporters of the Mustalian succession. From behind a veil, Nizar's sister proclaimed her allegiance to al-Mustali, testifying that Nizar had no right to the Imamate, that there had been no transfer of *nass* to him, and that her father had designated al-Mustali as his successor. Nizar was then temporarily placed in custody by al-Amir.[5]

---

1 Rashid al-Din, appendix two, p. 339.

2 Lewis, *The Assassins*, p. 59.

3 Daftary, *The Ismailis*, p. 264. Daftary even suggests al-Amir may have had a hand in the assassination of al-Afdal.

4 Lewis, *The Assassins*, p. 61.

5 Stern, "The Epistle of the Fatimid Caliph al-Amir (al-Hidaya al-Amiriyya)—Its Date and Its Purpose," *Journal of the Royal Asiatic Society*, 1950, pp. 22–26.

Al-Mamun then arranged to draft a statement refuting Nizar's claims, which included points raised in the testimony of the princess. This 1122 letter, *al-Hidaya al-Amiriyya*, a pastoral epistle from Caliph al-Amir, was widely disseminated in Syria and Egypt, souring relations even more between the Mustalians and Nizaris.[1] In 1128, al-Amir arranged for the execution by crucifixion of al-Mamun.[2]

In 1130, Caliph al-Amir himself would be the victim of an assassination of consequence conducted under the reign of Hasan's successor, Kiya Buzurgumid. Al-Amir's death was acclaimed with a new seven-day-and-night celebration at Alamut.

Another significant religious murder was conducted by Buzurgumid in 1135. Twenty-four Assassins managed to kill the Abbasid caliph al-Mustarshid (r. 1118–1135). As the official leader of all Sunni Muslims, this was a breathtaking symbolic event. He had been captured in battle and imprisoned by Sultan Masud (r. 1133–1152), the regional Seljuk sultan of Isfahan and nephew of Supreme Sultan Sanjar. While treated with respect during his confinement, rumors persisted that the Assassins had acted with the approval of both Masud and Sanjar.[3] Another seven days of feasting were celebrated at Alamut.

The Assassins would next be responsible for the death of al-Mustarshid's son and successor, Caliph al-Rashid, in 1138. He had served as caliph for only one year and was then deposed. According to Rashid al-Din, he next marched to Isfahan with an army to take revenge for the killing of his father (presumably against Sultan Masud), where Buzurgumid's *fidais* stabbed him.[4]

Under the reign of Buzurgumid's son and sucessor Muhammad I, the Nizaris created another vicious enemy in the person of Shah Ghazi Rustam (r. 1140–1163), the Bavandid king of Mazandaran

---

1 Lewis, *The Assassins*, pp. 60–61.

2 Daftary, *The Ismailis*, p. 264.

3 Bosworth, "The Political and Dynastic History," in Boyle (ed.), *CHI*, vol. 5, p. 128.

4 Rashid al-Din, *The History of the Seljuq Turks: From the Jami al-Tawarikh*, Bosworth (ed.) and Luther (trans.), pp. 106–107.

and Gilah. They assassinated his son and designated successor, Girdbazu, in 1142. The shah thereafter mounted annual attacks against the Ismailis.[1] He is known to have built several towers of Ismaili heads gathered in his campaigns against the Rudbar.[2] Ghazi Rustam led during a period of Seljuk decline which allowed the Bavandid king to become a prominent regional power. Although unsuccessful against Alamut, he was allied with the Seljuks in other efforts, which earned him the reward of the suzerainty of Rayy and nearby Saveh.[3]

Soon after the assassination of Girdbazu, the Assassins killed the grandson of Sultan Muhammad Tapar, Sultan Daud b. Mahmud, in 1143.[4] The Seljuk ruler of Azerbaijan, he had persecuted Nizaris. Another motivation for his death was attributed to the instigation of Zangi, the powerful Sunni Kurdish ruler (r. 1127–1146) and founder of the Zangid dynasty.[5] Zangi was a fearsome warrior who battled ceaselessly against the Franks and succeeded in taking the Crusader state of Edessa in 1144.[6]

Not long after, the Seljuk governor of Rayy, Abbas, conducted a massacre against the Ismailis, again building towers of their heads from the slaughter. In 1146 or 1147, Abbas was killed in Baghdad by Seljuk Sultan Masud with the support of Supreme Sultan Sanjar. His head was sent to the Assassins in Khurasan.[7]

The Syrian Assassins would create relentless opponents when they killed their first European Crusader. In 1152, they assassinated Count Raymond II of Tripoli (1116–1152), along with Ralph of

---

1 Bosworth, "The Political and Dynastic History," in Boyle (ed.), *CHI*, vol. 5, pp. 28–29.

2 Hodgson, "The Ismaili State," in Boyle (ed.), *CHI*, vol. 5, p. 450.

3 Bosworth, "The Political and Dynastic History," in Boyle (ed.), *CHI*, vol. 5, pp. 28–29.

4 Daftary, *The Ismailis*, p. 384.

5 Bosworth, "The Political and Dynastic History," in Boyle (ed.), *CHI*, vol. 5, p. 125.

6 Lewis, *The Assassins*, p. 68.

7 Ibid., p. 70.

Merle and another knight outside the gates of Tripoli.[1] This shocked the Crusaders, with whom the Assassins had previously found themselves allied in the shifting sea of political arrangements of the Holy Land. For example, they had joined the campaign of Count Raymond of Antioch against the Sunni Zangids in 1149. However, after the murder of Count Raymond II of Tripoli, the Knights Templar attacked the Nizari enemy and imposed an annual tribute, as mentioned. A century later, this tribute would become a negotiating point between the Assassins and King Louis IX.

Later still, in 1192, another royal assassination of a European took place—that of the Frankish king of Jerusalem, Conrad of Montferrat. It has been suggested that this was carried out because of an alliance between Sinan (r. 1162–1192) and Saladin (r. 1174–1193).[2] Two *fidais,* disguised as Christian monks, were responsible for Conrad's murder. Other motives have been suggested for this most crucial assassination, including that it was done at the behest of King Richard I the Lionhearted as "confessed" by the *fidais* under torture.[3] The simplest explanation may be that there had been problems between the Assassins and the Franks during the last several years. Conrad's having pillaged and put to death an Assassin who was shipwrecked, and then refusing to pay compensation to Sinan, may have been sufficient motivation for vengeance.[4]

The murder of Conrad of Montferrat splashed the Assassins onto the front pages of the historians of the Third Crusade and cemented their legacy in the West for all time. Their fearsome reputation spread far and wide, reaching to the courts of Europe—sparking fears, rumors, and confusion of suspected alliances with the unholy sect against royal rivals. While anyone could enlist the services of a mur-

---

[1] Steven Runciman, *A History of the Crusades*, vol. 2, p. 271. On page 322, he refers to the "the arbitrary murder of Raymond II."

[2] Hodgson, *The Order of Assassins*, p. 189. He refers to the accounts of two medieval historians: Abu Firas and Ibn al-Athir.

[3] Lewis, *The Assassins*, pp. 117–118. Also see Lockhart, "Hasan-i-Sabbah and the Assassins," *Bulletin of the School of Oriental Studies*, 1930, p. 686.

[4] Hammer-Purgstall, *The History of the Assassins*, p. 131.

derer for hire, the exotic identity of the Assassins added a level of sheer hysteria to the popular imagination. Assassins were accused of threatening Frederick of Barbarosa in Milan in 1158, and Richard the Lionhearted at Chinon in 1195.[1] While the Nizari leaders of Persia and Syria were not murderers for hire, some European leaders paid tribute in hopes of avoiding their displeasure. This was explained to King Louis IX about 1250 during the Seventh Crusade by a delegation of Ismailis from Masyaf who tried to frighten the king with a pantomime performance. The Assassin ambassador entered followed by two young men, one holding a knife of three blades, walking in front of another bearing a burial shroud.[2] They explained that the emperor of Germany and the king of Hungary paid them tribute for safety, as did the sultan at Cairo.[3]

Their infamy spread far to the east as well. In 1254, Mangu Khan (r. 1251–1259), the grandson of Genghis Khan, received a European delegation in China from King Louis IX of France, led by the Franciscan friar and ambassador William of Rubruck. They were seeking an alliance with the Mongols against the Muslims during the Seventh Crusade. William learned that even the great Khan feared for his life. Rumors swirled around the Mongol court that as many as forty Assassins in various disguises had been sent in retaliation for the Mongol campaign against the Ismaili lands of Persia.[4] The Nizaris themselves had sent a peace delegation in 1248, but they had been turned away.

---

[1] Lewis, *The Assassins*, p. 9.

[2] Robert Payne, *The Dream and the Tomb: A History of the Crusades*, p. 354.

[3] The Grand Masters of the Knights Templar and the Hospitallers warned the ambassadors that such threats against the king were not welcome. See *The Templars and the Assassins*, p. 208.

[4] Lewis, *The Assassins*, p. 6, citing *The Journey of William of Rubruck to the Eastern Parts of the World, 1253–1255*, translated and edited by W. W. Rockhill, London, 1900.

Not all of the activities of the Assassins resulted in fatalities. In chapter twelve we described Hasan-i-Sabah's successful threat against the Seljuk sultan Sanjar and the peace that was established between them as a result.

A later Alamut chief, Muhammad II (r. 1166-1210), the son of Hasan II *ala dhikrhi al salam*, wielded the fearsome reputation of Alamut to encourage a change of behavior from a Sunni scholar. Fakhr ad-Din al-Razi (d. 1209) had begun a vigorous lecture campaign against the Nizari doctrine.[1] Learning of this, Muhammad sent a disciple to attend the scholar's lectures in Rayy. After some months, the *fidai* threatened the scholar at dagger point, and extracted an oath from him to cease his teachings against the Assassins. He then conveyed Muhammad's invitation to visit Alamut and passed along the Imam's gifts of gold and beautiful garments. When another student asked al-Razi why he no longer railed against the Assassins in class, he responded that their arguments were both too pointed and too weighty.[2]

Hasan's missionary efforts in Syria were highlighted in chapter eleven. The Syrian Assassin chief Sinan faced the implacable might of the equally legendary Sunni chieftain Saladin. Bad blood had arisen between Sinan and Saladin because in 1174–1175, local Sunni vigilantes called Nubuwwiyya had raided two Nizari fortresses, killing some thirteen thousand Ismailis. When Saladin learned of this while passing through the Jabal Bahra Mountains, he attacked several other Nizari targets of opportunity.[3] Sinan had since made two unsuccessful assassination attempts against Saladin in 1175 and 1176. In August

---

1 According to one story, he did so because he had been falsely accused of being a secret Ismaili. Lockhart, "Hasan-i-Sabbah and the Assassins," *Bulletin of the School of Oriental Studies*, p. 684.

2 Hodgson, *The Order of Assassins*, p. 183. His fate was far different than that of Abu l-Mahasin Ruyani, a famed Sunni teacher who was assassinated in 1108. The vehemence of his anti-Nizari preaching marked him as a more stubborn enemy. He claimed that the Nizaris were so far afield of Islam they should be killed as non-Muslims. Hodgson, pp. 123–124.

3 Lewis, *The Assassins*, pp. 114–115.

of 1176, Saladin attacked Masyaf and laid siege to this central Nizari fortress. Without warning, he ended the siege and departed.

Various explanations have been given, including the following reliable account from Sinan's biographer, Kamal al-Din. One day a messenger from Sinan approached Saladin. He stated that the message was personal and must be delivered in privacy. Saladin progressively emptied his court until only two Mameluke attendants were left. Sinan's messenger then asked Saladin why he would not order the Mamelukes to depart so he could deliver his message in private. Saladin replied, "I regard these two as my own sons. They and I are one." The messenger then turned to the Mamelukes and said, "If I ordered you in the name of my master to kill this Sultan, would you do so?" They drew their swords together and replied, "Command us as you wish."[1]

I would like to close this discussion of assassination with a comment on what I consider the ethical difference between the modern terrorist and the medieval Assassin. The victim of the *fidai* was chosen by the master for a specific purpose, and his death would be of benefit to the community. If it were a ruler, a high-ranking advisor, or a general, the assassination would serve a military goal of either ending or preventing a war. If it were an educator or religious preacher who was chosen for death, the purpose was to prevent harm coming to the people from a rabble-rousing jihad promoted by people who purposely twisted the religious doctrines of the Nizaris to their own ends. Even if these orthodox Muslims were not necessarily wrong about the Nizaris being "heretics," their viewpoint was the opposite of "live and let live." Their goal was death for the people they despised. Yes, the murder of some people mentioned here was revenge or doctrinal rigor—as was the case of the Fatimid Commander of the Armies and the caliph. In contrast to these, we have seen several well-directed "staged" threats, designed to change minds without violence.

---

[1] Ibid., pp. 116–117.

Nowhere do we find the indiscriminate mass casualty violence that marks the suicide bombers of today who slaughter innocents—men, women, children, fellow Muslims, Christians, and Jews—with no concern for the active individual accountability or responsibility of their victims. They show no respect for the sanctity of life. They may be said to worship death. Having personally viewed the full-color printed, Hollywood-style *shahid* (martyrdom) posters on display in the markets of the Palestinian territories of Israel, I can attest that there is an ill-wind blowing from that quarter that I do not detect among the medieval Assassins.[1]

Western law recognizes different levels of culpability in killing. We interpret bringing death in self-defense as different than purposeful murder. We acknowledge motivation in judging a person guilty of killing—whether their act falls into the category of first or second degree murder, manslaughter, or accidental homicide. As a culture, we allow both abortion and the death penalty, in addition to physician-assisted suicide in a growing number of states and countries.

I believe that a certain subtlety of perception and knowledge of their history may allow the Assassins to be judged by contemporary people with both intelligence and compassion.

---

[1] *The Templars and the Assassins* was released almost four months to the day before the 9/11 attacks of 2001. I was mortified to consider that my enthusiasm for Hasan and the medieval Assassins might be misinterpreted. Failing in my attempt to add an appendix to that book, I self-published *The Slaves Shall Serve* in 2004, which included an essay on the indiscriminate use of mass murder by Sunni terrorists entitled "September 11, 2001 Remembered," along with a translation of, and commentary upon, the infamous "Letter to the Terrorists" that had been found at the airport.

CHAPTER FIFTEEN

Life Among the Medieval Ismailis

> That this handful of villagers and small townsmen, hopelessly outnumbered, should again and again reaffirm their passionate sense of grand destiny, reformulating it in every new historical circumstance with unfailing imaginative power and persistent courage—that they should be able to keep alive not only their own hopes but the answering fears and covert dreams of all the Islamic world for a century and a half—this in itself is an astonishing achievement. —Marshall Hodgson[1]

There are several anecdotes, stories, and legends of the Assassin community and Hasan, in particular, that will be of interest to the reader.

Perhaps the most troubling is that Hasan-i-Sabah was responsible for the death of his two sons. He is said to have proclaimed that his execution of both sons was proof that he had not conducted his mission in order to carve out a personal dynastic legacy.[2]

Hasan killed his first son because of a traitor at Alamut named Zaid Hasani, who clandestinely proclaimed himself Imam, conducted teachings in his own name, and plotted to overthrow and kill Hasan. Zaid Hasani was responsible for the murder of Hasan's respected *dai*, Husayn Qaini of Kuhistan, at the hands of one of his henchman named Ahmad of Dunbavand. But Hasan's son Ustad Husain was falsely accused of the murder and Hasan ordered his execution. A year later, he learned the truth of the matter and executed both Zaid Hasani and Zaid's son.[3] Hasan's second son was named Muhammad. He put this young man to death because he was drinking wine.

---

1 Hodgson, "The Ismaili State," in Boyle (ed.), *CHI*, vol. 5, pp. 423–424.

2 Juvaini, *Genghis Khan*, p. 680; Rashid al-Din, appendix two, p. 330.

3 Juvaini, *Genghis Khan*, p. 679; Rashid al-Din, appendix two, p. 330.

Hasan was following the strictest prohibitions against wine in the Quran and *hadith* (outlined in chapter twenty of this book).[1]

When Juvaini accompanied Huelgu to witness the destruction of Alamut in 1256, they discovered vats of wine in underground chambers. These had obviously been filled after the death of Hasan-i-Sabah. The amount of wine-drinking and overt intoxication (including with hashish) that is depicted throughout the tales of *The Arabian Nights,* for example, makes clear that the prohibitions against alcohol were the province of only the strictest Muslims. Most of the stories of *The Arabian Nights* are set in the early centuries of the Abbasid Caliphate. The examples they offer of the lack of concern for the moral teachings of the Prophet add even more weight to an understanding of Hasan's drive to root out cultural and religious corruption among the Sunni rulers of Islam.

Various snapshots of Hasan and the Nizari community are offered throughout the literature. *The Biography of Our Master* states that Hasan was once presented with a genealogy of his family compiled by his students at Alamut. He at once destroyed the pages by throwing them into the water.[2] Juvaini attributes his motive to a desire to deceive.[3] A more favorable interpretation of his action may suggest that Hasan was instead acting with humility, refusing to countenance a cult of personality being built in his name.

Another story demonstrating Hasan's well-known monastic asceticism and personal rigidity was that he had a musician expelled from Alamut for playing the flute.[4] Such behavior on his part, I believe, further militates against accepting the legendary use of hashish by his *fidais* or their sexual initiation in the Garden of Delights. Drug use will be discussed in more detail in chapter twenty.

---

[1] Juvaini, *Genghis Khan*, p. 680; Rashid al-Din, appendix two, p. 330.

[2] Rashid al-Din, appendix two, p. 301.

[3] Juvaini, *Genghis Khan*, p. 667.

[4] A position not at odds with that of the Prophet, according to Sir Richard Burton. "Mohammed having objected to music and indeed to the arts in general." Burton, *The Book of the Thousand Nights and a Night,* vol. 9, p. 245, note 2.

Hasan is profiled in the *Kittab al-Muqaffa al-kabir* (an enormous biographical history in eighty volumes of the rulers and prominent visitors to the Fatimid kingdom) by the Mameluke-era Egyptian historian al-Maqrizi. He states that Hasan was "an astute, capable man knowledgeable in geometry, arithmetic, the stars, magic and other matters."[1]

Al-Maqrizi goes on to tell a romantic story of Hasan answering doubting disciples when they learned of the death of the Imam Nizar. They remonstrated with him, reminding him that he had said Nizar would come to them:

> He said to them: "The sign of that is that the moon will appear (but) not at its (usual) time of rising." Then he went to an extremely high mountain beside them, and he performed one of his miraculous tricks and it began to look as if the moon had risen behind the mountain. Thereupon some of them began announcing to others the good news about the Imam Nizar.[2]

Despite the vagueness of this description, there is a sense of deep mystery and magic in Hasan's behavior. Hasan continued that the Imam Nizar was surrounded by many enemies and in a country far away. Thus "he decided to hide in the belly of a woman and to be born again in order to arrive in safety."[3] After introducing the young pregnant woman to them, his followers accepted his words and protected her until she gave birth to a son.

Historian Enno Franzius writes that the Patriarch of Constantinople sent envoys to Alamut who were favorably impressed by Hasan:

---

1 Hillenbrand, "A Neglected Source on the Life of Hasan-i Sabbah, the Founder of the Nizari 'Assassin' Sect," *Iran: Journal of the British Institute of Persian Studies*, 2017, p. 4.

2 Ibid., p. 5.

3 Ibid., p. 5. See chapter nineteen of this book for more on the continuation of the Nizari Imamate.

> His natural dignity, his distinguished manner, his smile, which is always courteous and pleasant but never familiar or casual, the grace of his attitudes, the striking firmness of his movements, all combine to produce an undeniable superiority. This is fundamentally the result of his great personality, which is magnetic in its domination. There is no pride or arrogance; he emanates calm and good will.[1]

The uniquely self-sufficient, isolated, and rebellious Assassins presented a perfect opportunity for the dark underbelly of the Muslim unconscious to fabricate imaginative complaints against them. Nizam al-Mulk accused the Alamut community of sharing their women in common, as the Mazdakites had during the Sassanian dynasty.[2] Marshall Hodgson explains that "the Ismailis put fewer restrictions on the life of women than the Sunnis had come to do, and that may have been taken for license."[3] Hodgson later relates the story, first told by the poet, writer, and traveler Ibn Jubayr (1145–1217), who wrote that the master of Alamut commanded forbidden orgies with indiscriminate coupling under cover of darkness.[4]

Every legitimate account of Hasan presents a totally antithetical picture to these characterizations. If Hasan must be criticized by a behavioral label, I think the word "Puritan" might be more appropriate. Juvaini was the first to report the since often-told tale that, from the time Hasan entered Alamut until his death thirty-four years later, he only twice emerged from his house. On both these occasions he went up to the roof. Juvaini also states that the rest of his time Hasan

---

1 Franzius, *History of the Order of Assassins*, p. 60. Franzius sources this report to a document obtained from the Ecumenical Patriarch of Constantinople, note 11, p. 231.

2 See chapter two.

3 Hodgson, *The Order of Assassins*, note 4, p. 122. Nizam al-Mulk's accusation is cited in the text.

4 Ibid., p. 139 and note 49. See the same charges made against the medieval Cathars in *The Templars and the Assassins*, pp. 193–194.

spent in prayer, fasting, meditation, study, doctrinal writing, and planning and administering the affairs of his kingdom.[1]

As mentioned here several times, in addition to Hasan's role as a religious innovator and spiritual leader, he was a Persian nationalist and patriot with an abiding resentment of the Turkish domination of his homeland. Thus, he substituted the Persian language for Arabic in the religious writings of the Persian Nizaris. They became the first significant religious community to so craft their doctrinal literature.[2]

The stability of the Alamut leadership and the overall unity of the Nizari community are also worthy of mention. We recall that three of the four Righteous Caliphs were murdered in office. We have also seen countless examples of civil war, murder, division, conspiracy, and usurpation among the Seljuks and Abbasids, let alone in the earlier regional histories of Mesopotamia and Persia. Despite periods of extreme tension within Alamut, there were orderly transitions of leadership—with two exceptions—for the entire life of the Nizari state. While Hasan II and Aladdin were murdered in office, they were both succeeded by their sons without incident. The same consistency applies to leadership in Nizari centers of Syria and the various far flung territories of Persia.

The Assassins themselves demonstrated an extraordinary amount of courage and dedication to their fellows and their master. *The Biography of Our Master* notes the loyalty, fortitude, and self-abnegation of the Nizari warriors during the eight-year campaign of Malikshah's army. The famine at Alamut was so hideous the soldiers lived on seeds and little pieces of wood.[3] He was held in such high regard by his community that Rashid al-Din writes, "Anyone who had argued or threatened him would have been killed by the devotees. It was said

---

1 Juvaini, *Genghis Khan*, p. 683; Rashid al-Din, appendix two, p. 340.

2 Daftary, "Hasan-i Sabbah and the Origins of the Nizari Ismaili Movement," in Daftary (ed.), *Mediaeval Ismaili History and Thought*, p. 189.

3 Juvaini, *Genghis Khan*, pp. 680–681; Rashid al-Din, appendix two, pp. 337–338.

that those who had bad feelings toward him would be destroyed by destiny."[1]

The incredible image of the wife of Ahmad ibn Attash at Shahdiz—dressing herself in her finest apparel, bedecking herself with jewels, and then flinging herself to death is worth noting again. Her personal flare and style displayed an utter contempt for secular attachment and a profound inner faith in the midst of mortal peril.

One story that illustrates the shared values of the Persian and Syrian branches of the Order is that of the mother of a Syrian *fidai.* Upon learning of the death of her son during a successful mission of political murder, she rejoiced and adorned herself in celebratory garb. However, upon the unexpected safe return of the young man, she entered into a state of mourning.[2] One can see unfortunate echoes of this mindset today in the well-publicized pride of certain parents of young suicide bombers.

The famous death leap of the *fidais,* as told in William of Tyre's history, has been dramatically adapted in film by John Milius in *Conan the Barbarian* and in fiction in my *Templar Heresy.* Count Henry of Champagne, nephew of King Richard the Lionhearted and later King of Jerusalem, made a diplomatic visit in 1194 to the Syrian Assassins and the Old Man of the Mountain. The two leaders were out walking one day. When the latter stated that Henry's Christian soldiers were not as loyal to their leaders as his disciples were to him, Henry was about to disagree. The Old Man signaled to two youths high above in the watchtowers. Both immediately leapt to their deaths on the rocks below.[3]

---

1 Rashid al-Din, appendix two, p. 331.

2 Lewis, *The Assassins*, p. 105.

3 The death leap is sometimes attributed to Hasan-i-Sabah at Alamut. See citation of the medieval historian Ibn al-Jawzi by Hillenbrand in "A Neglected Source on the Life of Hasan-i Sabbah, the Founder of the Nizari 'Assassin' Sect," *Iran: Journal of the British Institute of Persian Studies*, 2017, p. 9. Daftary, *The Assassin Legends*, mentions Georgius Elmacin, an Arabic-speaking Coptic historian of the thirteenth century, writing of a visit by an ambassador from Sultan Malikshah to Alamut, p. 106. Hasan is also mentioned in the context of

Hodgson reminds his readers of another significant and unique aspect of the Assassin communal culture. That is the tremendous respect accorded to intellectual pursuits. We discussed the Mongol destruction of the famed library of Alamut. It is known that many of the other Nizari fortresses had their own libraries. Visiting scholars of all religions were welcomed at their centers and the Ismaili tolerance for different points of view stands in almost complete contrast with Muslim norms. They extended patronage and afforded access to their extensive libraries, which, in addition to the many volumes of a religious nature, included historical, scientific, and mathematical treatises as well.[1]

---

the death leap motif by Franzius, *The History of the Order of Assassins*, p. 65, and Hammer-Purgstall, *The History of the Assassins*, p. 135.

1 Hodgson, "The Ismaili State," in Boyle (ed.), *CHI*, vol. 5, pp. 456–457.

CHAPTER SIXTEEN

The Death of Hasan and the Continuation of the Nizari State

> The basis of Sayyidna's manner and of his honor was rectitude, mysticism, piety, the promotion of virtue and the prevention of vice. —Rashid al-Din[1]

The Death of Hasan

DURING SANJAR'S REIGN, Hasan fell ill and summoned Buzurgumid from Lammasar to join him and take on the leadership of Alamut. He charged three other *dais* to act as a council with Buzurgumid. He told them to act together as one until the coming of the Imam. Rashid al-Din wrote:

> He appointed Kia Buzurgumid as his successor and installed him in his own position. He placed Dihdar Abu-Ali Ardistani on his right, and specifically surrendered to him the affairs of teaching and administration; he placed Hasan Adam Qasrani on his left, and Kia Ba Jafar, the military commander, in front. Hasan commanded that these four men move the work forward with discretion and good policy.[2]

Hasan passed away on May 23, 1124. His grave at Alamut was a pilgrimage site for Nizari faithful until it was destroyed by the Mongols in 1256.

Hasan-i-Sabah spoke to the idealistic passions of the spiritual seekers among the Ismailis—a sect of Islam particularly known for the uncompromising nature of its adherence to the religious needs of its faithful. By the time of the death of Caliph al-Mustansir, the

---

1 Rashid al-Din, appendix two, p. 330.

2 Ibid., pp. 339–340.

Ismailis' greatest success—the Fatimid movement—had been thoroughly discredited. Famine, military weakness, and an absence of will had resulted in the ultimate form of blasphemy: the usurpation of the integrity of the Imamate itself in the appointment of the pretender al-Mustali by a Turkish military dictator in place of the designated Imam. "The break with Cairo, and the transfer of allegiances to a mysterious hidden Imam, released the pent-up forces of Ismaili passion and devotion; it was the achievement of Hasan-i-Sabbah to arouse and direct them."[1]

Hasan was followed by seven more leaders who controlled the Nizari state apparatus from its headquarters in Alamut. Hasan had held the reins from 1090 to 1124. Buzurgumid, his trusted warrior companion, ruled until 1138. Buzurgumid was responsible for several important assassinations and led the Nizaris in important military exploits, including the defense of Nizari territories against campaigns launched by Sanjar in 1126 (probably to test the newly-ascended successor to Hasan). Sanjar had been prompted to this behavior by his wazir, Muin al-Din, who was killed in 1127 by Buzurgumid's *fidais*.[2] Buzurgumid also built the new castle of Maymundiz and acquired Talaqan.[3]

Buzurgumid was succeeded by his son Muhammad I, who reigned until his death in 1162. Muhammad's ambitions were far more limited in scope than those of his two predecessors. As noted, he did conduct several important assassinations. Surviving records of the time, however, describe raids against neighboring tribes and rulers, including listings of sheep and cows taken along with other booty. The empire-building ambitions of the Nizari Ismaili state had drawn to a close.

---

1 Lewis, *The Assassins*, p. 63.

2 Ibid., p. 65.

3 Wiley, *Eagle's Nest*, p. 35; Daftary, *The Ismailis*, p. 372.

MARSHALL HODGSON DIVIDES the 166 years of the Alamut state into three broad periods.[1] He characterizes the reigns of the first three leaders named above as the Revolutionary Period.

Hodgson calls the reign of Hasan II and his son Muhammad II the *Qiyama* Period. The leadership of the charismatic Hasan II was cut short after four years by his assassination in 1166.[2] He was succeeded by his son Muhammad II, whose forty-four year reign allowed him the time to consolidate his father's religious doctrine of the *Qiyama* and advance the concept of the Alamut Imamate.[3] The revolutionary teachings of the uniqueness of the Nizari community were carefully developed and embraced.

Hodgson goes on to define the final three reigns of the leaders of the Alamut state as the *Satr* (Concealment) Period, when the doctrine of *Qiyama* was placed in the background and there was a rapprochement with the larger Sunni community. This was especially true during the leadership of Hasan III, Jalal al-Din Hasan, who followed Muhammad II in 1210 and reigned until 1221. Jalal al-Din ordered a return to *sharia* practices among the Nizaris and was known as Jalal ad-Din *Naw-Musulman* (the New Muslim) as a result. He befriended the Abbasid caliph al-Nasir (r. 1180–1225) and was undoubtedly received into the chivalric *Futuwwa*, a Sufi order promoted by the caliph among his princes, nobles, and other close allies. It was called the way of "the brave, handsome youth" (*fata*) and included a code of loyalty, self-sacrifice, and righteousness.[4] Jalal al-Din Hasan was said by some Ismailis to be the father of Shams-

---

[1] Marshall Hodgson, *The Order of Assassins*, summarized in the chart on page 42, and extensive discussions passim. Daftary follows this model in *The Ismailis*, pp. 334–335.

[2] See chapter nineteen.

[3] See chapter nineteen.

[4] Muhammad ibn al-Husayn al-Sulami (trans. by Sheikh Tosun Bayrak), *The Book of Sufi Chivalry: Lessons to a Son of the Moment*, pp. 6–15. See also my *The Templars and The Assassins*, pp. 121–122.

i-Tabriz, the spiritual master of the poet and founder of the Mevlevi Order of Sufis, Jalal al-Din Rumi.[1]

Muhammad III, the son and successor of Hasan III, was also known as Aladdin (glory of the faith). Aladdin relaxed his father's strict enforcement of the *sharia* law and allowed for a quiet return to the *Qiyama* doctrines. He was the leader of the Nizaris named in the account of Marco Polo (where he is called the Old Man of the Mountain). He reigned during the very dangerous period from the beginning of the Mongol invasions until his death in 1255. Aladdin was a brave and resolute leader but he was also prone to great psychological instability and was considered dangerously unbalanced by many of the elders of Alamut. His drunken murder by a resentful lover averted the need to replace him prematurely with his son Rukh al-Din Khurshah—whose short-lived reign as the eighth Lord of Alamut was the catastrophic conclusion of the Alamut state.

The Mongol Invasions of Persia, Mesopotamia, and the Levant

Genghis Khan (perfect warrior) united his fellow Mongolians and conquered northern China before setting his sights westward.[2] By 1218, his armies had reached the Jaxartes River, the border of the Khwarazmian Empire, which he defeated in 1219, sacking the cities of Bukhara and Samarkand. He continued on to Balkh, Merv, and Nishapur in northeast Iran. Before returning east, he sent an army of eighty thousand men to Herat in modern Afghanistan. In 1222, after a six-month siege, they were said to have slaughtered a million peo-

---

1 Browne, *A Literary History of Persia*, vol. 2, pp. 516–517.

2 A fascinating historical note on Genghis Khan was reported by *National Geographic* on Valentine's Day in 2003 in an article by Hillary Mayell. She wrote that an international group of geneticists studying Y-chromosome data reported in the *American Journal of Human Genetics* that some eight percent of men in the region of the former Mongol Empire carry nearly identical Y-chromosomes. This suggests descent from a common ancestor for some sixteen million men. https://nationalgeographic.com/news/2003/02/mongolia-genghis-khan-dna/ [accessed April 28, 2019].

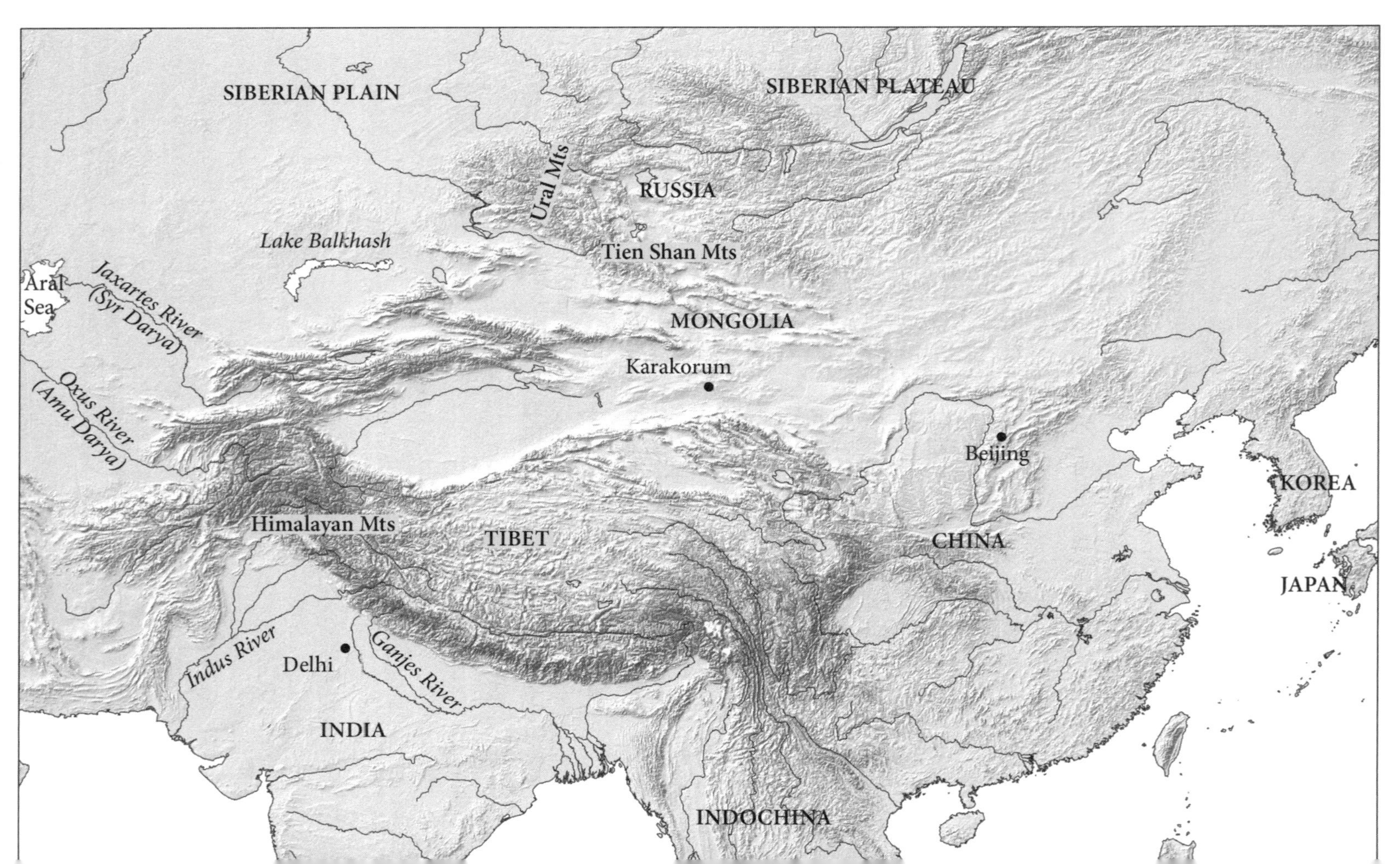
SIBERIAN PLAIN
SIBERIAN PLATEAU
Ural Mts
RUSSIA
Lake Balkhash
Tien Shan Mts
Aral Sea
Jaxartes River (Syr Darya)
MONGOLIA
Karakorum
Oxus River (Amu Darya)
Beijing
KOREA
Himalayan Mts
TIBET
CHINA
JAPAN
Indus River
Delhi
Ganjes River
INDIA
INDOCHINA

ple.[1] When Genghis Khan died in 1227, he left a powerful empire to his sons.

In 1238, the English historian Matthew of Paris described a failed diplomatic mission to Europe from Muslim leaders, "principally from the Old Man of the Mountain," in search of an alliance with the French and English against the Mongol invaders.[2] The Mongols were called "Tartars" by the Franks, a name derived from *Tartarus*, the Greek term for Hell.[3]

The End of Alamut

Huelgu, the grandson of Genghis Khan and brother of the supreme Mongol chieftain Mangu Khan, laid siege to Alamut in 1256. Recognizing the inevitability of capitulation to the Mongol power—and lacking the will, fortitude, and skill to resist—Khurshah wrote to offer his submission. On November 19, 1256, Khurshah entered Huelgu's camp to surrender. He was accompanied by his family, his entourage, and his treasure.

Huelgu received Khurshah graciously. He distributed the Assassin bounty to his Mongol warriors, but gifted the Imam with a hundred camels and a beautiful Mongol bride. He asked Khurshah to personally appeal for the surrender of the remaining Assassin castles. Approximately one hundred Nizari castles are said to have surrendered to the Mongol armies at the request of the weakened Imam.[4] Each fortress was evacuated and then destroyed. The commanders of Alamut and Lammasar initially refused to surrender, but Alamut capitulated in December of 1256. The garrison at Lammasar held out for a year longer.

The Mongols were rapt in amazement at the marvels of Alamut. Huelgu himself climbed to the fortress to observe the carefully-crafted brilliance of its design. Water ran through solid rock channels

---

[1] Franzius, *The History of the Order of Assassins*, pp. 126–127.

[2] Lewis, *The Assassins*, p. 5.

[3] Daftary, *The Assassin Legends*, p. 59.

[4] Franzius, *The History of the Order of Assassins*, p. 137.

and was stored in enormous tanks hollowed out from the massive rock. Food and weapons were stored in subterranean chambers also cut from solid rock. The impregnable fortress still contained viable supplies from the time of Hasan-i-Sabah. With much labor, the Mongols destroyed it all. Juvaini accompanied Huelgu's army and personally oversaw the burning of the Alamut library.

In 1257, Khurshah, accompanied by his Mongolian captors, embarked on the long journey to Karakorum to meet Mangu Khan. When he arrived, the Great Khan refused him audience because Lammasar and Girdkuh still held out against the Mongolian army. On the return journey, Khurshah's Mongol guards "caused him to rate the punishment for all that his forefathers had done to the people of God. He and his followers were kicked to a pulp and then put to the sword . . . So was the world cleansed which had been polluted by their evil."[1]

In 1258, Huelgu's armies conquered Baghdad. The Abbasid caliph al-Mustasim Billah surrendered as abjectly as Khurshah before him and was also put to death. The dynasty that had ruled Islam (at least in name) for half a millennium was crushed. In 1260, Huelgu seized the Ayyubid cities of Damascus and Aleppo. But in 1259, Mangu Khan had died. Upon learning of this, Huelgu returned to Persia, where he and his successors established the Ikhwan dynasty, which ruled until the fifteenth century. Huelgu left his general Ket-Buqa in charge of his Syrian forces. The ruthless and extraordinary Mameluke military leader Baybars defeated the Mongol army in 1260 at the Battle of Ain Jalut (south of Nazareth) and at last drove them from the Holy Land. The Syrian Nizaris, along with other Muslim forces, came to the aid of the Mamelukes in this decisive campaign.

---

[1] Juvaini, *Genghis Khan*, pp. 724–725.

CHAPTER SEVENTEEN

The Nizari Faith after the Fall of Alamut

Any discussion of Nizari survival must begin with the observation that despite the loss of many sectarians by immersion in the greater Islamic mass, the Nizari Ismailis have been able to maintain their unique perspective and traditional loyalty to their Imams. The core community managed to resist cultural dispersion and assimilation during the centuries following the loss of Alamut and Masyaf, and remains a vibrant and modern Muslim minority to this day.

The main concern of the post-Alamut Ismailis was smuggling Rukh al-Din Khurshah's son Shams al-Din Muhammad to safety. The Mongols began a ruthless campaign to wipe out all memory of the Assassins, which included their efforts to kill every Nizari man, woman, and child, particularly anyone related to Khurshah. Many were sold into slavery. The defenders of Lammasar and Girdkuh were obliterated when their castles fell, although the garrison in Girdkuh managed to hold out until 1270. In 1275, an Assassin force recaptured Alamut, but the Mongolian military reclaimed the castle within a year.

The surviving Nizaris in Persia became fugitives, hunted and pursued. The Persian Nizaris, unlike the Syrians, could not maintain even the illusion of political independence. However, their faith may have been stronger because of the presence—even if hidden—of the child Imam Shams al-Din Muhammad, the twenty-eighth Imam of the Nizaris.[1] He had been carried to the safety of the Azerbaijan region to the northwest of Alamut. Fortunately, just before the fall of Alamut, a Nizari community had developed in the remote upper Oxus region to the northeast. They remained unaffected by the Mongol invasion. This group preserved the bulk of the medieval Persian-language Ismaili literature which is available to contemporary scholars.

---

[1] Farhad Daftary, *A Short History of the Ismailis*, p. 161.

In Syria, lacking the leadership of the revealed Imam, there was more dissension among members of the Assassin community. The Syrians fell under the rule of the Mamelukes and their Sultan Baybars I. The crucial fortress of Kahf was the last to submit in 1273.[1] In addition, an ongoing state of warfare with the Nusayris (which continued into the twentieth century) further weakened the Syrian Nizaris, undermining any political ambitions they may have still entertained. The Syrian Nusayris are known today as the Alawis, "one of the most famous extremist Shia sects,"[2] the tribe of the contemporary reigning al-Assad dynasty.

The post-Alamut period has extended for over seven centuries. Only certain highlights will be mentioned here. A more detailed overview of this history is presented in *The Templars and the Assassins*. The interested reader is further referred to Dr. Farhad Daftary's encyclopedic study, *The Ismailis*, which presents an extensive discussion of the subject along with a plethora of references for further research, as well as his later volume, *A Short History of the Ismailis*, another invaluable (and less weighty) resource.

Post-Alamut Concealment

For two centuries after the fall of Alamut, the Imams shielded their identity from even their followers, living under intense conditions of *taqiyya* in an extremely hostile environment.

During this overtly leaderless phase, the Nizaris were separated from the mountain strongholds in which they had grown for over a century and a half. Disoriented and confused by the Mongol military devastation and subsequent persecution, the sect became fragmented and diffused, developing into a profusion of separate communities without central leadership. Many survivors migrated to remote parts of Persia, Afghanistan, Central Asia, and India, where Nizari *dais* had

---

1 Daftray, *The Assassin Legends*, p. 43.

2 Ibid., note 2 to Silvestre de Sacy, "Memoir of the Dynasty of the Assassins," p. 182.

paved the way.[1] As individuals arose to fill a teaching or leadership role (in the absence of a known Imam), the unified doctrine characteristic of the Alamut period became disconnected.

Many Persian Nizari survivors were able to gracefully conceal themselves within the esoteric currents of Iranian Sufism. Their training in the disciplines of a secret society no doubt saved many lives. The common elements shared by Sufism and Ismailism—mysticism, Gnosticism, speculative philosophy, techniques of self-development, and loyalty to a central teacher, *pir*, *murshid*, or shaykh—encouraged mutual interaction. Assumption of the Sufi mantle would later allow the Nizari Imams to cloak themselves as shaykhs who taught the esoteric meaning or *batin* to their disciples or *murids.*

The Imam Shams al-Din Muhammad died in 1310–1311 in Azerbaijan. (Some Ismaili legends identify him as Shams-i-Tabriz, the spiritual master of Rumi.)[2] Although the details are obscure, there was a dispute among members of his family over the succession, resulting in the first Nizari schism. Two separate lines of Imams arose — the Muhammad-Shahi and the Qasim-Shahi.[3] The Muhammad-Shahi line was more popular in Syria, although it had a large following in Persia until the second half of the fifteenth century. The last Imam of this line died in India in the late eighteenth century without a successor. The majority of Syrians transferred their allegiance to the Qasim-Shahi Imam Aga Khan III.

In the beginning of the fifteenth century, the Mongol Ilkhanate dynasty, established by Hulegu after the fall of Alamut and the Abbasid dynasty, had collapsed in Persia. Following the Ilkhanate disintegration, Persia remained politically fragmented for the better part of the next century. The Nizaris were able to take advantage of the more relaxed religious and political environment to expand their activities while still maintaining a rigorous *taqiyya*. Not surprisingly (in view

1 Daftary, *A Short History of the Ismailis*, p. 161.

2 Ibid., p. 162.

3 Daftary, *The Ismailis*, pp. 446–448.

of the *satr* period at Alamut) this included the outward embrace of *sharia*, and even the adoption of the guise of Twelver Shiism.[1]

Anjudan Revival

The period known as the "Anjudan Revival" began in the latter half of the fifteenth century when the Qasim-Shahi Imam Mustansir Billah II relocated to Anjudan in central Persia. He emerged from the two-century-long concealment of the Nizari Imams to proclaim the continuation of the Alamut Imamate. This inaugurated a renaissance in Nizari thought and philosophy as well as a revival of Nizari literary efforts. Succeeding Imams worked diligently to reassert their control of the far-flung and fractured Nizari population scattered throughout Persia, Syria, and India.

The steadily increasing influence of the Sufi *tariqas,* or orders, and the re-emergence of Shiism were important developments in Persia during the fifteenth century. The Safawi Sufi *tariqa* worked steadily to extend its political control and succeeded in 1501 in installing their shaykh as the ruler of Persia. Shah Ismail was the founder of the Safawid dynasty,[2] which governed the country for over two centuries. The Safawids established Twelver Shiism as the Iranian state religion. Soon after, they began to suppress some of the more popular rival Sufi groups, as well as the more extreme Shiites. Despite the growing intolerance of the Safawid dynasty, the Nizaris managed to fare well, for the most part, attesting to the success of their *taqiyya* practices.

One of the Sufi *tariqas* which helped bring the Safawid regime to power in 1501 was the Nimat Allahi Order. Their long-lived founder, Shah Nimat Allah Wali (1330–1431), traced his lineage through the Fatimids and Muhammad ibn Ismail. His success further helped to create a compatible environment in which the Nizaris could operate and cloak their *dawa* activities in the language of Alid Sufism.[3]

---

[1] Daftary, *A Short History of the Ismailis*, p. 176.

[2] Ibid., p. 175.

[3] Daftary, *The Ismailis*, pp. 463–464.

One important development during the Anjudan Revival was the Imam's emphasis on the importance of tithing—that is collecting a tenth of the annual income of adherents throughout the scattered Nizaris territories. Tithing served a two-fold purpose. Obviously, it helped to finance the Imam's activities. Equally important, however, it helped to re-establish his central control over the disparate groups that had developed during the two-hundred-year diaspora following Ȧlamut. The Imam was able to install his own representatives in each population center of the Nizari community. In the more remote areas, they conducted their collections and inspections through a hand-picked network of traveling representatives.

The Aga Khans and the Emigration to India

The modern period of the Nizari community begins with the relocation of the Nizari Imam to India in the mid-nineteenth century. By the mid-eighteenth century, the Nizari Imam moved his headquarters from Anjudan to Kirman in southeast Persia, closer to India and its expanding Nizari community. When the Qajar dynasty (1789–1925) fully established itself in Persia by 1794, the Nizaris were well-treated. The forty-fifth Nizari Imam, Shah Khalil Allah, married the daughter of a prominent Nimat Allahi Sufi. She would become the mother of his successor, Hasan Ali Shah, born in 1804. However, Khalil Allah was murdered by a Twelver Shiite mob in Yazd in 1817. In response to the murder, the Qajar ruler Fath Ali Shah gave the young Imam Hasan Ali Shah a grant of additional lands, as well as the hand of one of his daughters in marriage. He also bestowed on him the honorific title of *Aga Khan*, "Chief Commander." This is the title retained to this day by the Nizari Imam.[1]

Fath Ali Shah was succeeded by his grandson, whose ill treatment of the Nizaris caused Hasan Ali Shah (Aga Khan I) to organize an unsuccessful rebellion. He tried again some years later and again faced defeat. He, thus, traveled to Afghanistan in 1841, ending eight centuries of the Persian Imamate. He befriended the British in

[1] Ibid., pp. 503–505.

Afghanistan and came under their protection. In 1842, he continued on to India where he was enthusiastically welcomed.

The Nizari *dawa* in India had begun in the early thirteenth century during the later Alamut period. Nizari conversion efforts were increasingly successful during the fourteenth century under the leadership of a *dai* named Pir Sadr al-Din. The Indian Nizaris called themselves *Khojas,* "lords or masters."[1] One reason for the success of the *dawa* in India was the characteristic respect shown by the *dais* or *pirs* for the beliefs and traditions of their Hindu converts. In return, Indian Nizarism was enriched by its contact with Hindu religion and mythology.

Aga Khan I flourished in Bombay. He was a strong, effective, and well-organized administrator. But a group of dissident Khojas resented his efforts to centralize the Imamate. They brought a lawsuit against him in 1866 to prevent him from interfering in their affairs. A hearing was held before the British High Court of Bombay that lasted twenty-five days. Massive amounts of historical documents, genealogical data, and religious doctrines were examined. The Aga Khan was declared by Chief Justice Sir Joseph Arnould to be the legitimate descendent and heir of the Alamut Imams—and thus of the Fatimid Caliphate, and thus of the Prophet Muhammad through Fatima. Further, he ruled that the Aga Khan was entitled to the customary dues and tithes collected from the Khojas.

The Chief Justice's ruling is presented in full in A. S. Picklay's *History of the Ismailis*. It is a supremely interesting analysis and reveals the judge's great research efforts into the available materials of his day, as well as of the evidence presented by both parties. Arnould writes at some length about Hasan-i-Sabah and Alamut, as well as the Fatimid dynasty, the Ismaili religion, the rivalry between Aisha and Fatima, and the massacre at Karbala. The Chief Justice makes clear that the claims of the dissident Khojas that Pir Sadr al-Din was a Sunni proselytizer—and that the Khojas were therefore Sunnis—was both absurd and ahistorical.[2]

---

[1] Ibid., pp. 479–480.

[2] There was an execrable travesty in the lies of the dissidents who attempted

The Nizari Ismailis Today

The forty-ninth and present Nizari Imam is Karim al-Husayni, Aga Khan IV (b. 1936). Educated in Switzerland, Aga Khan IV moved to the United States and completed his undergraduate studies at Harvard, majoring in Islamic studies. He has pursued his predecessors' ambitious plans to improve the quality of life for his people.

He has provided numerous scholarships to eligible Nizari students to attend Western institutions of learning. He has expanded the indigenous educational opportunities for his people, creating some three hundred institutions worldwide, ranging from daycare centers and elementary schools to a medical college and nursing school in Pakistan. He has built six general hospitals. Both the Nizari schools and health services are open to people of all races and religions. He has worked diligently in rural support and health services, as well as refugee resettlement when political conditions demanded this action.

In 1984, he established the Aga Khan Fund for Economic Development as the umbrella organization for his Third World community self-development projects. He has instituted programs for promoting Islamic religion, architecture, and civilization among Western students by providing scholarships at such prestigious American universities as Harvard and MIT. He has worked to restore historical castles of the medieval Nizari period through the Aga Khan Cities Support Program and the Aga Khan Trust for Culture.[1] Aga Khan IV has also encouraged the growth of worldwide Ismaili scholarly research by founding the Institute of Ismaili Studies in London in

---

to overthrow the authority of the Aga Khan. Justice Arnould describes the solemnity, tears, and mourning of the Shia during the annual *Muharrum* day of remembrance of the martyrdom of Husayn ibn Ali at Karbala. He contrasts the excess of Shia sorrow with the wild celebrations, ribaldry, and mockery of the Indian Sunnis on that day. Picklay, *History of the Ismailis*, pp. 123–124. Arnould further notes that many of these dishonest dissidents had at least three times before been expelled and readmitted to the Khoja fold by the Aga Khan. See pp. 148–149, 152. (*Plus ça change, plus c'est la même chose.*)

1 Farhad Daftary and Zulfikar Hirji, *The Ismailis: An Illustrated History*, pp. 140–141.

1977, which remains actively engaged in research, archival acquisition and preservation, and publishing. The Nizari Ismailis thus describe their guiding principles:

> As in the developing world, the Ismaili Muslim Community's settlement and the establishment of community institutions in the developed world have been characterised by an ethos of self-reliance, an emphasis on education and a pervasive spirit of philanthropy.[1]

Aga Khan IV is recognized as the head of approximately twenty million Nizari Ismailis, scattered in more than twenty-five countries: the majority of Ismailis in the world today.[2] Each of the Aga Khans has been concerned with improving the socio-economic status of his people in the modern world, making ethical, intelligent, objective judgments, and standing apart from the corruption, poverty, illiteracy, and religious intolerance of much of the Islamic world.

The success of the modern Nizaris may serve as an object lesson for the continued merit of hard work and strongly-held moral values. Despite the loss of their state and their failure to attain world conquest and control of Islam, the modern Nizaris have accomplished much of the miracle envisioned by Hasan-i-Sabah, their illustrious founder and chief *dai* and *hujja* at Alamut ten centuries ago.

---

[1] For more on the cultural, humanitarian, financial, and education activities and accomplishments of the contemporary Nizari Ismailis under the leadership of Aga Khan IV, see: https://iis.ac.uk/about-us/ismaili-community [accessed July 28, 2019].

[2] https://the.ismaili/community-0 [accessed July 28, 2019].

PART THEE

The Gnosis of Hasan-i-Sabah

CHAPTER EIGHTEEN

The Doctrine of *Talim* or Authoritative Teaching

LET US START by reminding ourselves that the renowned library at Alamut was burned by Huelgu and Juvaini in 1256. We therefore have an extremely limited picture of Hasan's literary output—although, as we have discussed throughout this book, he is believed to have spent significant time in developing, writing, and communicating the Nizari Ismaili doctrine and teaching. We are very lucky to have the *Sar-Guzasht-i-Sayyidna* (*The Biography of Our Master*), but it is mostly autobiographical/biographical rather than doctrinal.

The only surviving known doctrinal writing of Hasan is an abridgement of the *al-Fusul-al arbaa* (The Four Chapters), no longer extant. It was originally written in Persian, and translated into Arabic and summarized by the medieval Persian Sunni scholar and heresiographer Muhammad al-Shahrastani (1086–1153). Hodgson reports, "There seems little doubt that Sharastani's claimed translation from Hasan-Sabbah is genuine."[1]

The basic thesis of *talim* is that the Imam is the ultimate source of Truth.[2] People are incapable of defining Truth for ourselves because

---

[1] Hodgson, *The Order of Assassins*, p. 43, note 9. Hodgson offers his English translation of these pages in appendix two of *The Order of Assassins*. He summarizes the doctrine of *talim* and Hasan's interpretation of the same in pages 52–61 of that book. He presents another summary of *talim* in his essay "The Ismaili State" on pages 433–437 of *The Cambridge History of Islam*, vol. 5, edited by J. A. Boyle. Al-Shahrastani's abridgement is also discussed by Farhad Daftary in *The Ismailis*, pages 368–371, where the author mentions that some of al-Shahrastani's medieval contemporaries believed he was secretly an Ismaili, including the renowned Nasir al-Din al-Tusi (d. 1274) who lived at Alamut for some years. See Daftary, *The Ismailis*, p. 368. See also Wilfred Madelung, "Aspects of Ismaili Theology: The Prophetic Chain and the God Beyond Being," in Nasr (ed.), *Ismaili Contributions to Islamic Culture*, p. 58. Rashid al-Din's summary in appendix two, pp. 311–312 and 333–337, is also instructive.

[2] The Nizaris are also known as *Talimiyya*. Daftary, "Hasan-i Sabbah and the

we do not have the divine link to the source of Knowledge itself that is enjoyed by the Imam. Therefore, the duty of the spiritual seeker is to connect with the sole Ismaili Imam of the time. The seeker does not choose the Imam; the Imam is chosen and directed by God. Those who fail to find or follow the Imam are sinners. As the Prophet was chosen by God to bring the Law, so the Imam is chosen by God to interpret the Law for those living in the present time.

Shiites long accused the Sunnis of having neglected this principle, beginning with the death of the Prophet when they chose Abu Bakr as their caliph. Mankind's spiritual ignorance demands that an authoritative teacher lead the community. Why else would God have needed to send the Prophet? Sunnis countered that the consensus of an educated majority, combined with accepted tradition, were sufficient. Shiites might answer that the combined opinion of unenlightened people to determine truth could merely compound error. Hasan's argument in favor of the authority of the Imam is unconditional.

A Summary of Hasan's Four Propositions:

One: One needs a teacher to know the truth of the Creator. One who rejects seeking a teacher therefore chooses himself as his own teacher. This proposition eliminates rationalism because, despite the views of the philosophers who deny the need for a teacher, human reason is inadequate as a source of the ultimate authority. If one does not have a teacher, one's opinion is only that, an opinion, and there are many opinions.

Two: If one accepts the need for a teacher, he must be an authoritative teacher, the Imam, the sole arbiter, one alone in every age. Otherwise, any teacher is as good as any other. The Sunnis accept many teachers as noted in Rashid al-Din's recap of Hasan's argument to the jurists

Origins of the Nizari Ismaili Movement," in Daftary (ed.), *Mediaeval Ismaili History and Thought*, p. 197.

in Mayyafariquin.[1] On what basis do they claim authority? What is the difference between true and false? What good is a teacher who may be wrong?

Three: Hasan goes on to critique the errors to which the Shiites may be prone. In order to be acknowledged as the proper teacher, the chosen Imam must demonstrate his qualifications. How can he do this? One must use reason to distinguish and determine his claims—thus acknowledging a contradiction: in the first proposition, reason was declared inadequate.

Four: Determining who the Imam is requires that the problem be solved by skepticism, dialectic, the pitting of opposites against each other to resolve all differences into a whole. (Think of 0=2 [1+-1].)[2] Something can be known only by knowing its opposite, its contradiction. "By our need we know the imam, and by the imam we know the measure of our need."[3] "Without the imam, reason leads to a blank. Without reason, the imam rests unproven, and so unknown."[4]

Hasan points to the existence of both truth and error in the world. "The sign of truth is unity, the sign of error is multiplicity . . . unity comes with *talim*, and multiplicity with reflection."[5] These form the opposition that is present, for example, in the *Shahada*. Here we have resolution of conflict by understanding contradiction. "There is no god but God and Muhammad is His Prophet" begins with negation (no god), what God is not. It continues with an affirmation, what

---

[1] See (in this book) Rashid al-Din, appendix two, p. 305, and especially notes 1–3 and 6.

[2] This formula is discussed by Aleister Crowley in several places, including *The Book of Thoth*, pp. 29–30.

[3] Shahrastani, "Hasan-i-Sabbah's Doctrine," trans. by Hodgson, *The Order of Assassins*, p. 326.

[4] Hodgson, *The Order of Assassins*, p. 56.

[5] Shahrastani, "Hasan-i-Sabbah's Doctrine," trans. by Hodgson, *The Order of Assassins*, p. 327.

God is. Then it asserts that the true God is the God of Muhammad, Allah, who sent His messenger to mankind so that we could be guided back to Him. The certainty and unity of this statement satisfies all the questions raised by the previous contradictions.

The *Kalami Pir* highlights this divine ambiguity in its discussion of God: "He has form and attributes, and, at the same time, has no form and no attributes."[1] Because God desires that He should be known by man, we must have something in common with our Creator. It is impossible to understand anything without a frame of reference. God created man in His own image.

"The proof of Hasan's imam is not extrinsic to the imam, but consists of the logical position of the imam himself. The very nature of his claims are their own proof."[2]

The fragment summarized here—by an outside party, if a contemporary of Hasan—only enhances our sense of loss that the vast majority of Hasan's writings were destroyed. May they one day be reclaimed.

---

1 Ivanow, *Kalami Pir*, p. 55.

2 Hodgson, *The Order of Assassins*, p. 56.

CHAPTER NINETEEN

Sufism and the *Qiyama*

> [Hasan-i-Sabah] deliberately chose austerity and renunciation. Because Hasan belonged to Sufism and according to Sufis, one cannot fly to the spiritual world unless he is free from the chains of desires which go on increasing unceasingly.
>
> —Jawad al-Muscati[1]

THE PRIMARY THESIS of this book is Gnosis, the aspirant's direct personal experience of God while within the human body.

> 29. This immortality is no vain hope beyond the grave: I offer you the certain consciousness of bliss.
> 30. I offer it at once, on earth; before an hour hath struck upon the bell, ye shall be with Me in the Abodes that are beyond Decay.[2]

The knowledge of God transcends all the doctrinal rigors and hierarchies of all the established religions of the world through time. Yet, each of the major religions contains its own mystic tradition by which the keys to make the initiate worthy of the divine experience are communicated to the sincere seeker.

It is difficult to trace the origins of esoteric doctrines within a faith because, in large measure, the esoteric group stands outside the faith. Thus the Essenes and kabbalists among the Jews are sometimes considered antedating Judaism itself, extending to a universal pre-literate time of spiritual unity. This is equally true of the Christian mystics and ascetics of the early years of that faith. They are believed to have tapped into a current of Gnosis that predated and greatly expanded upon the teachings of the Apostles. Similarly, Muhammad

---

1 Al-Muscati, *Hasan bin Sabbah*, p. 3.

2 Aleister Crowley, *Liber Tzaddi*.

is sometimes said to have been the first Sufi. He did, after all, experience direct knowledge of the Divine in the here and now. But the term "Sufi" was unknown at his time, and making too broad a statement about something leaves it as undefined as not saying anything.

I believe the first "Gnostics" were those who looked at the heavens and felt unity—a rather amorphous concept to be sure. Add the aspect of cultivating that experience of unity in a repeatable fashion over time, in a community of like-minded souls who share their methods and discoveries with each other while protecting themselves against the hostile, superstitious, and incurious—and you have defined the Gnostic secret society.

Within the larger Muslim faith, this gnostic position (*tasawwuf*) is held by the Sufis. The Nizari Ismailis have been identified with Sufism since their beginning. The proclamation of *Qiyama* by Hasan II in 1164 at Alamut appears to this writer as the primary evidence of the identification of the Assassins as a gnostic movement. The renowned and very strict Nizari scholar Farhad Daftary states unequivocally, "the doctrine of the *Qiyama* laid the ground for the coalescence between Nizari Ismailism and Sufism in Persia during the post-Alamut period."[1] We will discuss the *Qiyama* in the next section.

The Assassins of Alamut were not the first to reject the outward form of Islam (or *sharia*) as necessary for the aspirant to divine unity. The dismissal of mechanistic orthodoxy was the heresy at the root of Sufism and resulted in numerous periods of persecution.

Sufi masters (*pirs*) were often independent charismatic teachers who attracted numbers of disciples to their schools. It is thus difficult to define what it means to be a Sufi.[2] Some are fervent Sunnis and others Shiites. As worshippers of Unity, such divisions begin to recede into meaninglessness. Various Sufi groups sought to explore the esoteric meaning of Islam, and worked to develop and practice exercises to increase mystic awareness by penetrating the veil of

---

1 Daftary, *The Ismailis*, pp. 395–396.

2 The Arab term means, "one who wears woolen garments, a devotee, a *Santon* [Muslim holy man]." Burton, *Arabian Nights*, vol. 3, p. 140, note 1.

everyday consciousness and achieving communication with the transcendental mind.

The celebrated Sufi mystic Mansur al-Hallaj (ca. 858–921) was suspected of being an Ismaili[1] and even accused of being a Qarmati agent.[2] He was a disciple of Abul Qasim al-Junaid (ca. 825–910), a leader of the Baghdad school of Sufism.[3] Al-Hallaj had acquired great influence among certain members of the Abbasid royal family. Jealous enemies within the court arranged for him to be arrested, tried, tortured, crucified, and dismembered in Baghdad. His disciples were to found a number of mystical Sufi orders.[4] Mansur al-Hallaj experienced Gnostic union with God during which he was known to cry out *Ana'l-Haqq*, "I am the Truth."

Sufism as a term came into use by Muslims mystics of the eighth century AD.[5] The Abbasids actually encouraged the movement as it helped to strengthen their Sunni position. After the betrayal of their Shiite base, they needed something to obscure the cynicism of their own manipulative rise to power (as discussed in chapter three). Religion has always been a convenient cloak for the darker aspects of political intrigue. The purity, quiescence, and overall apolitical nature of Sufi mystics allowed the Abbasids a respite from religious and political rivalry, while lending them an aura of sanctity.

The orthodoxy of Islam precludes creativity in the same way as all establishment faiths. Religions' founders have that direct personal experience of the Lord which they share with others. Listen to the passionate biographies of Moses, Jesus, Muhammad, Buddha, and the rest. They inspire their followers into believing that an experience of the Holy awaits them as well. The revolutionary words of Jesus would prove an obstacle to those who preached lockstep obedience. People capable of contemplating the mysteries of the Bible ponder verses like this: "Verily, verily, I say unto you, He that believeth on

---

1 Daftary, *The Ismailis*, note 138, p. 609.

2 Ibid., p. 161.

3 S. H. Nasr, "Sufism," in Frye (ed.), *CHI*, vol. 4, p. 453.

4 Daftary, *The Ismailis*, pp. 160–161.

5 Foltz, *Iran*, p. 53.

me, the works that I do shall he do also; and greater works than these shall he do; because I go unto my Father."[1]

With that said, political and social power are often the consequence of religious success, and spiritual creativity thereby suffers. Burton speaks of this loss of vitality in his Terminal Essay to *The Arabian Nights*:

> Mohammed left a dispensation or rather a reformation so arid, jejune and material that it promised little more than the "Law of Moses," before this was vivified and racially baptized by Mesopotamian and Persic influences. But human nature was stronger than the Prophet and, thus outraged, took speedy and absolute revenge.[2]

He continues that this "revenge" was in the form of the gnostic vision of the Sufi that is craved by the spiritually an-hungered soul in search of a personal relationship with the Divine:

> Before the first century had elapsed [i.e., after Muhammad], orthodox Al-Islam was startled by the rise of *Tasawwuf* or Sufyism a revival of classic Platonism and Christian Gnosticism, with a mingling of modern Hylozoism; which quickened by the glowing imagination of the East, speedily formed into a creed the most poetical and impractical, the most spiritual and the most transcendental ever invented; satisfying all man's hunger for "belief" which, if placed upon a solid basis of fact and proof, would forthwith cease to be belief.[3]

As mentioned in chapters sixteen and seventeen, Shams-i-Tabriz was considered by some to be the son of Hasan III, and identified by others as Shams al-Din Muhammad, the son of Rukh al-Din

---

1 John 14:12, KJV.

2 Burton, *The Book of the Thousand Nights and a Night*, Terminal Essay, vol. 10, p. 116.

3 Ibid., Terminal Essay, vol. 10, p. 116.

Khurshah. If it is true that Shams-i-Tabriz was a Nizari Ismaili, and even a Nizari Imam,[1] the influence of the Ismailis on Sufism would be incalculable. His student was the Persian poet Jalal al-Din Rumi, the founder of the Sufi Mevlevi Order of the Whirling Dervishes. Their ecstatic trance-dancing is a well-known form of Sufi practice to this day. The *Qiyama* is also compatible with the spiritual creativity of contemporary well-known Sunni Sufi poets such as Rumi himself, Sanai, Farid al-Din Attar, and the renowned Sufi master Ibn al-Arabi—thus giving rise to claims by some Ismailis that these luminaries are among their co-religionists.[2]

We have pointed out earlier that the compatibility between Nizari Ismailism and Sufism allowed the Ismailis an almost seamless, life-saving integration within Sufism after Alamut. But it is also important to note the difference between the concept of the Sufi *pir* and the Nizari Imam. "[T]he Nizari imam was much more than a Sufi master, the latter being one among a multitude of such guides at any time. For the Ismailis, the imam was a single cosmic individual who summed up in his person the entire reality of existence; the perfect microcosm for whom a lesser guide or a Sufi *pir* could not be a substitute."[3] A highly developed Ismaili *dai* might be closer to the Sufi concept of a *pir*.

---

1 Hodgson, *The Order of Assassins*, p. 276; Daftary, *The Ismailis*, p. 415.

2 Hodgson, *The Order of Assassins*, p. 181.

3 Daftary, *A Short History of the Ismailis*, pp. 167–168.

The *Qiyama*

> The historical Qiyamat then, is a symbol—an imaginal fact—to be contemplated and subjected to *ta'wil,* used as a focus for perception, a mode of understanding, a means to consciousness. To consider it a religious dogma is simply inappropriate. Rather it is a gate of perception, permanently open. To walk through it one simply walks through it—and discovers that there was never a step to be taken. The Qiyamat is an affiliation without an organization, a sign for expressing a state of awareness.[1]

What then is the *Qiyama*? Let us begin with the history of its declaration in 1164. In chapter eleven, we mentioned that the first three Lords of Alamut were considered *hujjas*, that is "proofs" of the Imam. These included Hasan-i-Sabah himself, his successor Buzurgumid, and Buzurgumid's son and successor Muhammad I.

Muhammad I's son was also named Hasan. Born in 1126, he later became known as Hasan II after he succeeded his father and became the fourth Lord of Alamut, where he served from 1162 to 1166. Hasan II was a popular, charismatic, radical, and brilliant young man who devoted himself to the teachings of Hasan-i-Sabah, the Gnostic explorations of earlier Ismaili philosophers like Ibn Sana (Avicenna), the Epistles of the Brethren of Sincerity, and the mysticism of the Sufis. It was rumored that he drank wine to show that he was above the reach of the *sharia*,[2] and that he was the hidden Imam about to emerge and reclaim the spiritual pre-eminence of Alamut as the cutting edge of Islam.[3]

---

1 Wilson, *Scandal: Essays in Islamic Heresy*, p. 62.

2 Hodgson, "The Ismaili State," in Boyle (ed.), *CHI*, vol. 5, p. 458; Juvaini, *Genghis Khan*, p. 688.

3 Burzurgumid and Muhammad I had been careful and competent leaders, but Muhammad especially lacked the spiritual creativity and ambition that had enflamed the Assassin community in the past. People were impatient for the

Such speculation and adulation roused his father to fury. He insisted Hasan could not be an Imam because Hasan was his son. Since he (Muhammad) was not the Imam, Hasan certainly could not be the Imam. In a fit of anger, Muhammad punished Hasan's widespread supporters at Alamut and throughout the Rudbar Valley in a particularly bizarre manner. Muhammad killed 250 of Hasan's followers, then bound their corpses to the backs of another 250, and banished them all from the region.[1]

Hasan worked patiently to regain his father's trust and did so. He succeeded him at age thirty-five.

The Proclamation of the *Qiyama*

The first two years of Hasan II's reign were uneventful. Then on August 8, 1164, on the seventeenth day of the fasting month of Ramadan,[2] he made religious history. At noon, clad in white and wearing a white turban, he mounted a pulpit whose four corners were covered with white, red, green, and yellow banners. Nizari delegations from Alamut, Kuhistan, and Khurasan were assembled before him. He began by praying with his back to Mecca, a violation of the Muslim norm. While holding aloft his sword, he announced that the hidden Imam had sent a secret messenger to him with an epistle declaring the doctrines of their faith and proclaiming the *Qiyama*, the Resurrection, the New Dispensation:

> O ye, inhabitants of the world, Jinns, men and angels! Know that Mawlana *Qaim* of the *Qiyamat*—prostration and glorification be to him on his mention!—is the Lord of (all) things created, the Absolute Existence; he is, in every way, beyond all

---

promised appearance of the long-awaited Imam, who had now been in concealment (*satr*) for three generations at Alamut.

[1] Juvaini, *Genghis Khan*, p. 687.

[2] As noted in chapter three, the Ramadan fast is one of the Five Pillars of Islam. During the ninth month of the Islamic calendar, observant Muslims fast from sunrise to sunset to commemorate the reception of the Quran.

> negation of his existence, because he is more exalted than anything that sinners can associate with Him.[1]

He then read the Imam's letter aloud in Arabic while a translator at the foot of the dais gave the address in Persian. The Imam declared that Hasan II was his direct representative on earth, caliph of the Nizari Ismailis, and all must be obedient to him. Furthermore, that the burden of *sharia* was lifted for the faithful, and that the Resurrection and the end of the world were about to arrive. At the close of this breathtaking address, he conveyed the Imam's greeting and blessing to the people and descended from the pulpit and held a banquet, declaring the Ramadan fast was at its end.[2] This was a supreme act of blasphemy according to *sharia.* Additional accusations were made against the Alamut community of engaging in wine-drinking and sensual indulgences following the *Qiyama* proclamation.[3]

Ten weeks after the event at Alamut, a similar pronouncement was made in Kuhistan by Hasan's representative, who read aloud a formal message from the Nizari caliph, the Lord of Alamut.[4] Hasan II's statement that he was the divinely appointed ruler (caliph) of the Ismailis involved another break with tradition. Previous Shiite caliphs had claimed a bloodline to Ali (no matter how tortuous).

The *Qiyama* proclamation was repeated in Syria by Hasan's representative Sinan. We know that in 1176–1177, Sinan attacked the *al-Sufat* (the Pure), a group in the nearby Jazr region who interpreted

---

1 *Haft-babi Abu Ishaq*, quoted in Ivanow, *Kalami Pir*, p. 116

2 Hodgson, *The Order of Assassins*, pp. 149–151.

3 For example, by Juvaini in *Genghis Khan*, pp. 689–690, and 696. Silvestre de Sacy also seems to suggest the *Qiyama* as the source of the libertine accusations he levels against the Ismailis, Druze, and Qarmatis in his "Memoir on the Dynasty of the Assassins," translated in Daftary, *Legends*, p. 136. Respected modern Ismaili scholars dispute this: "However, the current view among some historians that the proclamation [of *Qiyama*] involved an abrogation of *Sharia* has never been substantiated." Esmail and Nanji, "The Ismailis in History," in Nasr (ed.), *Ismaili Contributions to Islamic Culture*, p. 249.

4 Hasan II therefore established a rival caliphate to that of the Sunni Abbasids, well after the Nizari breach with the faltering Fatimid Caliphate.

the *Qiyama* as their license for libertinism. He was strategically obligated not to arouse the ire of the nearby powerful Sunni Zangids in Aleppo with whom he had an accord.[1]

Hasan II does not seem to have ever publicly claimed to be the Imam. He called himself teacher (*dai*), proof (*hujja*), and divinely appointed ruler (*caliph*)—all positions that imply the representation of the Imam. However, Rashid al-Din stated that Hasan sent out secret letters after his public announcement in which he wrote that he was the *inward* Imam, the Imam in *haqiqa* (the realm of reality), if not so in the flesh, that he was the *spiritual* descendant of Nizar.[2]

Those Nizaris who persisted in the traditional practices of Islam and refused to follow the New Dispensation were chastised, stoned, and killed as blasphemers—exactly as those who had previously been found guilty of breaking the *sharia* were treated.[3]

Hasan II was murdered on January 9, 1166, a year-and-a-half after his proclamation, stabbed to death by his brother-in-law Husayn-i Namawar, a member of the Twelver Shia Buwayhid line.[4] He vigorously refused to follow the *Qiyama* teachings and apparently hoped to return the Nizari community to its pre-*Qiyama* faith.

Despite the intense controversy surrounding Hasan's religious activities, he is held in veneration by Nizari Ismailis today, always referred to as Hasan *ala dhikrhi al salam* (upon whose mention be peace). Hodgson notes that in the death of Hasan II the Ismailis do not suggest that suffering is a divine role. He was not mourned as a martyr—as we have seen to be the case with the death of Husayn ibn Ali. As Hodgson quips, Hasan II "washes no feet."[5]

Hasan's son and successor Muhammad II (r. 1166–1210) was a young man of nineteen at the time his father's death. He was another powerful personality. He immediately caused Hasan II's murderer, along with the rest of the culprit's family, to be executed. Muhammad II continued the *Qiyama* revelation of Hasan II and devoted consid-

---

1 Daftary, *The Ismailis*, p. 402; Hodgson, *The Order of Assassins*, p. 205.

2 Lewis, *The Assassins*, p. 74; Hodgson, *The Order of Assassins*, p. 152.

3 Bernard Lewis, *The Assassins*, p. 74; Juvaini, *Genghis Khan*, p. 696.

4 Hodgson, *The Order of Assassins*, p. 159; Juvaini, *Genghis Khan*, p. 697.

5 Hodgson, *The Order of Assassins*, p. 177.

erable personal energy for the rest of his life to a careful and sophisticated elaboration of its doctrine. Muhammad II erected his teaching on the premise that his father was the literal Imam and biologically descended from Nizar, thus, as his son, he proclaimed himself Imam.

Beginning with the *Qiyama* proclamation of Hasan II, the Lord of Alamut was recognized by the Nizaris as the Imam rather than his chief *dai* or *hujja*—"after a period of some seventy years following Nizar's death, the line of the Nizari Imams emerged openly."[1] All future Nizari leaders were and are recognized as members of the Prophet's family.

The Nizari Lineage

Muhammad first undertook to provide a proper Alid lineage for his father. We recall that Hasan II was originally believed to be the son of Muhammad I, the son of Buzurgumid, and that he had never claimed a physical descent from Nizar. However, Muhammad II created an alternate lineage for his father. While the details of his actual paternity remain confused, the Alid lineage of Hasan II is a formal article of faith in the Nizari canon.

As mentioned in chapter eleven, some believed that Nizar, himself, escaped from his Egyptian prison and reached the safety of Alamut. Here he was said to have married the daughter of Hasan-i-Sabah.[2] She would give birth to Nizar's successor, who remained in hiding until his descendant Hasan II revealed the Alamut Imamate in 1164. Others maintain that it was Nizar's baby son or grandson who had received the *nass* to become the next Ismaili Imam, and that he was smuggled out of Egypt and raised secretly under the care of Hasan-i-Sabah.[3]

---

1 Daftary, *The Ismailis*, p. 392.

2 As reported by historians Ibn al-Qalanisi and Fariqi, and mentioned by Hodgson, ibid., p. 66, note 16.

3 Hodgson, *The Order of Assassins*, p. 162. The Fatimid caliph al-Amir mocked the idea that a descendant of Nizar had been hidden by Hasan-i-Sabah in his 1122 pastoral epistle, *al-Hidaya al-Amiriyya*. This refutation remains an extraordinary confirmation by a hostile source of the possibility of the continuation of

Still others thought Nizar's pregnant concubine had been rescued from Egypt and brought to Persia.[1] She then gave birth in the Rudbar Valley, at the foot of the rock of Alamut, to a child who was secretly raised by Hasan. Other theories include the possibility that the Imam had a secret affair with the wife of Muhammad ibn Buzurgumid and that she became pregnant by him with Hasan II.[2] Some speculate that the Imam's bride gave birth at the same time as Muhammad's wife, and that the babies were switched within three days of their births, unbeknownst to Muhammad.[3]

The most likely story is the Nizari tradition that while Nizar was widely acknowledged to have two grown sons, there was a third who had been less publicly known. Born in Cairo in 1076, he was al-Hadi ibn Nizar. As noted, Nizar had fled to Alexandria after the treason of al-Afdal and al-Mustali. After Nizar's arrest, or defeat in battle, al-Hadi's brothers each mounted unsuccessful rebellions against the injustice done to their father.[4] Al-Hadi, on the other hand, was taken from Alexandria to Alamut by a *qadi* named Abul-Hasan Saidi. He was introduced to Hasan-i-Sabah, who kept secret his identity.[5] Al-Hadi reigned in occlusion till his death in 1136. He passed the *nass* to his son al-Muhtadi, who then passed it to his son al-Qahir.[6] "Hasan-i-Sabbah and his next two successors ruled as *dais* of Daylam and *hujjas*, or chief representatives, of the Nizari Imams who were then concealed and inaccesible to their followers."[7]

---

the Nizari lineage and of contemporary rumors. Picklay, *History of the Ismailis*, p. 36; Daftary, "Hasan-i Sabbah and the Origins of the Nizari Ismaili Movement," in Daftary (ed.), *Mediaeval Ismaili History and Thought*, p. 196.

1 Lewis, *The Assassins*, p. 49.

2 Juvaini, *Genghis Khan*, p. 692. Juvaini even records that Muhammad ibn Buzurgumid discovered the adultery and slew the Imam! p. 694.

3 Ibid., p. 693–694.

4 *Encyclopaedia of Ismailism* by Mumtaz Ali Tajddin, found at http://ismaili.net/heritage/node/10342 [accessed April 18, 2020].

5 Daftary, *The Ismailis*, p. 392.

6 Farhad Daftary and Zulfikar Hirji, *The Ismailis: An Illustrated History*, p. 129.

7 Ibid., p. 130.

The Effects of the *Qiyama*

The blasphemous proclamation by Hasan II, and the embrace and development of the *Qiyama* doctrine by his son Muhammad II, severed any remaining Nizari ties with both Sunnis and Shiites. By their own efforts, the Assassins had fully attained the uncontested status of *malahida* or heretics. No longer was the argument centered around simple issues like acceptance or rejection of this or that Imam. With *Qiyama,* the Nizaris had declared their independence from the Islamic community. Only the Nizaris were able to receive and comprehend spiritual truth. All others, including non-Nizari Muslims as well as all non-Muslims, "were henceforth cast into eternal Hell, which was in effect a state of spiritual non-existence. In sum, the Nizaris were now collectively introduced into Paradise on earth, while the rest of mankind was made non-existent and irrelevant."[1] Hodgson elaborates:

> Those who could respond were, spiritually, already in eternal life, and those who could not were spiritually lifeless. This was the long-awaited culmination; the faithful Ismailis who understood were to leave behind all material compromise and rise to the spiritual level which was the only true victory; that is, they were to become spiritually perfect; while the Sunnis were defeated in the most final sense possible, in that all their further efforts were rendered spiritually meaningless.[2]

"But at the same time it was an admission of defeat in the attempt to take over Islam at large."[3] One indication of this was the change in the *dawa* efforts of the post-*Qiyama* Alamut period. More emphasis was devoted to teaching the new doctrine to members of the Nizari community than to spreading the faith through proselytizing and conversion as had earlier been their focus.

---

1 Daftary, *The Assassin Legends*, p. 41.

2 Hodgson, "The Ismaili State," in Boyle (ed.) *CHI*, vol. 5, pp. 459–460.

3 Hodgson, *The Order of Assassins*, p. 157.

More on the *Qiyama*

The word *Qiyama* means "Resurrection."[1] It announced a New Dispensation and identified the Nizari Ismaili community as having been saved and collectively received into Paradise, while on earth and within their physical bodies. Further, they would experience immortal life upon the death of their bodies. Those who obeyed the Imam's declaration of spiritual liberty were henceforth freed from the *zahir*, the outward form of Islam. Instead, the Nizari community had been received into the *batin*, the inner meaning, and the true end of their religious quest, the attainment of *haqiqa*, the ultimate reality. The *sharia* practices prescribed by Muhammad, to both Sunni and Shiite, were no longer necessary for the Imam's chosen people. They were merely outward symbols of inner spiritual truth. To the newly-liberated Nizaris, *sharia* was, thus, blasphemy. One no longer needed to prostrate himself and pray to Allah five times a day in an act of symbolic union with God. Under the New Dispensation, one maintained a state of continuous prayer and union with Allah.

The *Kalami Pir* is a post-*Qiyama* religious writing. Discussing its doctrine, Ivanow describes it as a "purely Nizari system, already fully developed, and far removed from the original Fatimid ideas. The principle which here dominates the whole structure is that of the Great Resurrection, or *Qiyamatu'l-qiyamat*, which was proclaimed by Imam Hasan *ala dhikrhi al salam* in Alamut, and the worship of the Imam of the time."[2] Ivanow characterizes the *Kalami Pir's* author as a "devoted and highly inspired Ismaili, whose thorough knowledge of his religion is beyond doubt."[3] Ivanow goes on to explain:

---

[1] It is important to note that, unlike in certain sects of Christianity, the word "resurrection" does not imply "rising in the flesh" to the Nizaris. "Here the orthodox eschatological ideas are apparently concerned only in so far as the promise that the faithful will see God Himself in His Real Substance." Ivanow, *Kalami Pir*, p. xxxvi.

[2] Ivanow, *Kalami Pir*, pp. xiii–xiv.

[3] Ibid., p. xv.

> At the *Qiyamat* God becomes visible to all: He can be seen directly (by *nazar* [spiritual sight]) and no one will need indirect information, received through others (*talim*). At that moment, in reality, all will be one: the *Qaim*, the *Qiyamat*, the knowledge, the worship, the object of worship, the reward, etc. . . . The faithful will lose their individualities, their consciousness of their own being, and they will see only God. This is obviously very close to the Sufic state of *fana fil-Haqq* [mystic unity].[1]

The *Qaim* of the *Qiyama*

There is another dimension to the radical depth of Hasan II's proclamation of *Qiyama* and his suggestion (and his son's assertion) that he was the Imam. The Imam who would announce the Resurrection was a figure already known to the Ismailis as the Judge of the Resurrection, the *Qaim* of the *Qiyama*. The special role of the *Qaim* was to be the consummation of the teachings of the Prophet at the end of time. All Islamic doctrine points to him. The Prophet Muhammad is the last of six prophets of mankind who precede the *Qaim*. Therefore in a very real sense, the *Qaim* is greater than even Muhammad himself. It was the function of Hasan-i-Sabah as his *hujja* to prepare the way for the advent of the *Qaim*.[2]

The theological contribution of Muhammad II elevated the concept of the Nizari Imam far higher than it had been within earlier Shiite theology. The *Qaim* of the *Qiyama* brought Paradise directly to earth and therefore God was manifest in all His magnificence *through* the Imam. The author of the *Kalami Pir* hymns that being:

> And Our Lord, the *Qaim* of the *qiyamats*—prostration and glory be due to him!—is the Lord of all things in existence; he is the Lord who is Absolute Existence; He is all—there is no existence outside of him; all that is comes from him.[3]

---

[1] Ibid., p. xxxvi.

[2] See Hodgson, *The Order of Assassins*, pp. 153–157, for more on this.

[3] Ivanow, *Kalami Pir*, p. 61.

As mentioned earlier, the motif of the individual and personal quest for God had long been a feature of Shiism and especially Ismailism. The Imam brought Gnosis by which all could know God directly. The Imam became the very form of God, his attributes were the attributes by which God revealed Himself to the people of the time. The Imam was to be the spiritual center and focus of each Nizari's life. Through the practice of holy awareness upon the limitless virtue of the Imam, the disciple would be liberated from error and prepared for the personal attainment of godhead. Achieving the true inner spiritual vision of the Imam was the gateway to the ultimate reality, Paradise, for the Nizari disciple. Because of the collective entrance of the Nizaris to Paradise, God was more knowable. This belief is not dissimilar to the higher reaches of mystical Christianity nor to the practices of *guru bhakti* within Indian and Sufi traditions (although the Ismaili conception of the Imam might be considered more impersonal and universal). It is one of the reasons the Nizaris were able to blend so successfully into the Sufi movement nearly a century later. "The imam did for the believer what the Sufi shaykh, religious guide, did for his disciples; by focusing their attention on him, they could be made to forget themselves, and be led to the divine hidden within him."[1]

The *Haft Bab-i Baba Sayyidna* is a surviving Nizari text dating to the reign of Muhammad II, most likely around the year 1200.[2] It states that Hasan-i-Sabah had himself prophesied the future revealing of the Nizari Imam:

---

[1] Hodgson, *The Order of Assassins*, p. 165.

[2] *Haft Bab-i Baba Sayyidna*, trans. by Hodgson, *The Order of Assassins*, appendix I, "The Popular Appeal of the Qiyama," p. 279. Contemporary scholar Sean W. Anthony writes that in 2005, the *Haft Bab-i Baba Sayyidna* was dated to 1205 and attributed to the authorship of Salah al-Din Hasan-i-Mahmud, a Nizari *dai* and poet associated with Nasir al-Din al-Tusi. "The Legend of Abdallah ibn Saba and the Date of Umm al-Kitab," *Journal of the Royal Asiatic Society*, 2011, note 43, p. 12.

> Hadrat Baba Sayyid-na Hasan-i Sabbah (may his grave be hallowed and may we be blessed in him) was the greatest *hujja* of the *Qaim* of the *Qiyama*, and the Jesus of the period of the *Qiyama* who makes clear the work of his father [the *Imam-Qaim*]. Sayyid-na states, "… I have seen all this good news …"[1]

⁂

Peter Lamborn Wilson's quote at the beginning of this section should have alerted the reader that there are people who believe the *Qiyama* is far more universal than its origin among the Nizaris may suggest. I do not know whether an observant Nizari Ismaili might be open to this supposition or be offended. However, I interpret the *Qiyama* from the point of view of a Gnostic—someone interested in the cross-cultural antecedents of the spirituality that has been the basis of my life since adolescence. In my opinion, Hasan II made religious history in 1164 by opening the gates and shattering the barriers between God and the seeker. The *Qiyama* promises knowledge and unity with the divine to those courageous enough to embrace it. That community of courage extends well beyond adherents of the Nizari faith and practice—it may extend to people of all creeds who feel the call of the Transcendant—and who understand that the proper response to such a call demands they breach the restrictions of conditioning, culture, and habit, and cut their own way through to the Light.

---

1 *Haft Bab-i Baba Sayyidna*, trans. by Hodgson, *The Order of Assassins*, appendix I, pp. 301–302.

CHAPTER TWENTY

Hashish and the Derivation of the Word "Assassin"

"Nothing is true; everything is permitted. —Hasan-i-Sabah"[1]

HISTORIANS agree that the term *fidai* comes from the root word *fida*, to redeem something by money or other form of payment.[2] The bravery of the Nizari warrior, sacrificing himself for the survival of his religion and community from the ruthless Seljuk efforts to destroy both, definitely fits with idea of redemption through renunciation, the "sacrifice of life and joy."[3]

The word "Assassin" is commonly believed to come from the term *Hashishim* used to describe the Nizari Ismailis. The first known use of the term *Hashishiyya* was in an anti-Nizari tract issued in 1123, prepared during the reign of the Fatimid caliph al-Amir, son and successor of al-Mustali. No explanation was given for the use of the word.[4] It has long been thought to be a reference to legends of Assassin chiefs administering a drug to disciples during their sojourn in the Garden of Pleasure, as memorialized by Marco Polo. However, even the most hostile contemporary Islamic writers, both Sunni and Shiite, nowhere accuse the sect of drug use.

The greatest European Arabic scholar of his day, Silvestre de Sacy, demonstrated in 1809 that the word "Assassin" was derived from the Arabic word *hashish*.[5] Although de Sacy rejected the notion that the *fidais* were a group of drug addicts under the sinister power of their

---

[1] Opening credit to *Naked Lunch* by William Burroughs, a film by David Cronenberg, 1991.

[2] Al-Muscati, *Hasan bin Sabbah*, p. 103.

[3] Aleister Crowley, *Liber XV*, "The Gnostic Mass."

[4] Daftary, *The Assassin Legends*, p. 30.

[5] Etymology discussed by De Sacy, *Memoirs on the Dynasty of the Assassins*, translated in Daftary, *The Assassin Legends*, pp. 147–171.

ruthless and scheming master, he believed that a potion composed of hashish, perhaps mixed with other substances such as opium, was initially administered to the *fidais* to induce a definitive ecstatic experience—despite the lack of historical evidence for this.

From the eleventh century until at least the late fourteenth, hashish use was frowned upon by the Muslim majority who associated it with the lower classes, and believed it was inevitably accompanied by the moral weakness symptomatic of social outcasts.[1] It is thus quite likely that the name *Hashishiyya* was a term of abuse, a pejorative label of derision used by Sunni writers in describing the fallacious beliefs and wild behavior of the Nizari sect, contemptuously associating them with drunkards and drug addicts.[2]

That which may have been intended as a moral criticism by Muslims was seized upon by Western Orientalists as a ready explanation for the self-sacrificing behavior and willingness to accept martyrdom of the *fidais.* How else than by a form of drug-induced madness could one possibly explain such irrational, suicidal, and alien behavior?[3]

The earliest European mention of the intoxication of the *fidai* by his murderous master was in a chronicle by Arnold of Lubeck written before 1210.[4] As if anticipating Marco Polo, Arnold wrote:

> [H]e himself hands them knives . . . and then intoxicates them with such a potion that they are plunged into ecstasy and oblivion, displays to them by his magic certain fantastic dreams, full

---

[1] Daftary, *The Assassin Legends*, pp. 91–93.

[2] Lewis, *The Assassins*, p. 12. The Scythians, as described by Herodotus in the fifth century BC, made use of hemp fumes for intoxication and cleansing. Reminiscent of shamanic sweat lodges, they burned hemp (hashish) in a central fire inside a tent-like structure, howling with delight. Since they did not bathe with water, they afterward made a paste of the ashes and smeared it over themselves, causing a wonderful scent. The next day, removing the paste, their bodies would be "shining clean." Herodotus, in David Grene (trans.), *The History*, 4:73–75, p. 307.

[3] Daftary, *The Ismailis*, p. 19.

[4] Daftary, *The Assassin Legends*, pp. 104–105.

> of pleasures and delights . . . and promises them eternal possession of these things in reward for such deeds.[1]

ON THE OTHER HAND, the term *Hasaniyin* may have simply been used to define "followers of Hasan"[2] —like the terms "Christians," "Buddhists," "Ismailis," or "Rajaneeshis" for disciples of Christ, Buddha, Ismail, or Rajaneesh. The word *Hashiya* also means "bodyguard."[3] It is known that Hasan's disciples acted as guards during peacetime to protect local towns against thieves.[4] Tsugitaka also defines the term *Hashiyas* to mean "servants."[5] Finally, al-Muscati points out that "Assassin" may be a corruption of *Hassasin*, from the verb *hassa* (to eliminate by killing).[6]

Al-Muscati further posits that "Assassin" may come from the word *Asasin,* "the name which was given to the community on account of their belief in *Asas,* that is the Imam." He continues, "*Asas* means Imam and *Asasi* means one who follows the Imam." He explores the issue further, noting that, "Because the expression *Asas* [is] one of the peculiar Ismaili religious terms, it was difficult for historians to grasp properly its meaning."[7] "The appellation *Asasin* is synonymous with the name *Imamiyin*."[8]

Al-Muscati continues that *natiq* and *asas* are the fundamental doctrines of Ismailism—with Muhammad identified as the *natiq* (*aql*=intelligence) and Ali as the *asas (nafs*=soul).[9] I described these concepts earlier:

---

1 Lewis, *The Assassins,* pp. 4–5.

2 Al-Muscati, *Hasan bin Sabbah*, p. 103; Picklay, *History of the Ismailis*, p. 41.

3 Tsugitaka, *State and Rural Society in Medieval Islam*, p. 35.

4 Muscati, *Hasan bin Sabbah*, p. 103.

5 Tsugitaka, *State and Rural Society in Medieval Islam*, p. 20.

6 Al-Muscati, *Hasan bin Sabbah*, p. 104. (In the novel *Angels and Demons*, Dan Brown's hired killer is called the *Hassassin*.)

7 Ibid., pp. 104-105.

8 Ibid., p. 112.

9 Ibid., p. 106.

> The individual's impassioned search for truth is a recurrent Ismaili theme . . . The devotee thus expresses through his individual spiritual journey the cosmic desire of the *Nafs al-Kull* (the principle of Universal Animation, symbolized in humanity as the Imam Ali), to return to its origin, the *Aql al-Kull* (the principle of Universal Reason, symbolized in humanity as the Prophet Muhammad).[1]

As Muhammad (*aql*) is the Prophet, the *natiq* (the Exponent of *Sharia*); and as Ali (*nafs*) is the first Imam or *asas* (the Interpreter of *Sharia*); *asas* more broadly refers to the continuous presence of the Imams in the spiritual life of the Ismaili community.[2]

The argument that Hasan-i-Sabah drugged his disciples is not consistent with his character as we know it. He was an extremely abstemious person. As noted in chapter fifteen, he killed one of his own sons for drinking wine and exiled a musician for playing a flute. Far from being the kind of manipulative sensualist posited by the myth of the Garden of Paradise, or the cynical and amoral leader portrayed in the rather excellent, but pejorative, novel *Alamut* by Vladimir Bartol, it seems unlikely that he would countenance drug use, the seduction of young men by beautiful young women, or the running streams of wine described by Marco Polo.

In appendix one, I give several verses of the Quran that speak of flowing streams of wine in Paradise. On the other hand, there are three main injunctions against alcohol (and, by analogy, drugs) in the Quran. These include the surah entitled "Women." Here the Quran counsels against drunkenness in prayer: "O ye who believe! Draw not near unto prayers when ye are drunken." One can easily imagine an

---

1 Wasserman, *The Templars and the Assassins*, p. 93. See Hodgson, *The Order of Assassins*, pp. 16–18, for a better understanding of these terms and more on the mythic identification between the Prophet and Ali.

2 Al-Muscati, *Hasan bin Sabbah*, p. 106.

adept like Hasan concluding that one's entire life should be offered in prayer, therefore drunkenness at any time is a violation of religious vigilance. In the surah called "The Cow," it is written: "They question thee about strong drink and games of chance. Say: 'In both is great sin, and (some) utility for men; but the sin of them is greater than their usefulness.'" The surah known as "The Table Spread" is even more explicitly prohibitive against alcohol:

> "O ye who believe! Strong drink and games of chance and idols and divining arrows are only an infamy of Satan's handiwork. Leave it aside in order that you may succeed. / Satan seeketh only to cast among you enmity and hatred by means of strong drink and games of chance, and to turn you from remembrance of Allah and from (His) worship. Will ye then have done?"[1]

A number of *hadith* also proclaim the illegality of intoxicants to believers. It appears that this prohibition grew stronger during the lifetime of the Prophet. One of the many stories in this vein is attributed to Aisha. "The Prophet said, 'All drinks that produce intoxication are *Haram* (forbidden).'"[2]

There are also practical reasons that might give one pause when considering the use of hashish by the Assassins. Let us look at the mission of the *fidais*. They would be required to live under "cover identities" for extended periods of time, pretending to be people they were not. Pretending to hold opinions and beliefs they would otherwise have rejected as those of the enemy. Such role-playing might go on for weeks, months, or even years. For some missions they would need foreign language skills or, at least, the ability to mimic certain

---

[1] Pickthall (trans.), *The Meaning of the Glorious Koran*, "Women," verse 4:43, p. 98; "The Cow," verse 2:219, p. 52; and "The Table Spread," verses 5:90–91, p. 131. Divining arrows are a method of divination, as mentioned in chapter three discussing the pre-Islamic Pagan deity Hubal.

[2] *Sahih Bukhari*, 1:4:243. For an in depth listing of *hadith* regarding alcohol, the reader may consult https://wikiislam.net/wiki/Qur'an,_Hadith_and_Scholars:Alcohol [accessed Jan 5, 2019].

regional dialects. Clothing and other local habits would need to be scrupulously studied, known, and the details followed. The ability to recite Sunni prayers and blend in to every religious, ceremonial, social, and courtly setting could be the difference between life and death. They would need to be hyper-vigilant, consummate actors. And they would need to be able to move with ruthlessness and decisiveness on a moment's notice. Timing could mean everything when it came to accomplishing their mission.

The idea that their initiation ceremony included drugs to open their minds to alternate possibilities may or may not have been true. But even if it were, I think it is highly unlikely the *fidais* used drugs in their daily lives.

We should note that images of hashish and wine are shared by the Sufis and countless others in the Mystery Traditions. While alcohol and drugs are forbidden in Islam, intoxication is often a symbol or metaphor for the ecstatic experience of Divine Union. This—the central tenet of Gnosis, the direct knowledge of God—is such an overpowering and disorienting phenomenon that it is often compared in the language of mysticism with drunkenness. In fact, de Sacy writes that the full name *hashisha*, "herb," is *hashishat al-fuqara*, "the herb of the fakirs."[1] He later suggests that hashish may have been introduced to the Ismailis by Indian yogis and notes the similarities of some of the doctrines of both groups.[2]

[1] De Sacy, *Memoirs on the Dynasty of the Assassins*, translated in Daftary, *The Assassin Legends*, p. 161.

[2] Ibid., p. 171.

CHAPTER TWENTY-ONE

The Degrees of Initiation

> Basic to all religion . . . is, we believe, a unique experience of confrontation with power not of this world. . . . "Numinous" . . . the experience of a . . . confrontation with a "Wholly Other" outside of normal experience and indescribable in its terms; terrifying, ranging from sheer demonic dread through awe to sublime majesty; and fascinating, with irresistible attraction, demanding unconditional allegiance. It is the positive human response to this experience in thought (myth and theology) and action (cult and worship) that constitutes religion.
>
> —Thorkild Jacobsen[1]

SOMETHING SECRET, mysterious, and progressive took place in the conversion and initiation process administered by the Ismaili *dais,* and in the training program by which the *dais* were educated. This is undisputed by modern scholars, including the most orthodox and the most inclined to treat the Ismailis with the greatest deference and respect. We know without question that the Ismaili and Nizari mysteries included a graded ascent with increasing revelations of the inner doctrine.

Bernard Lewis unequivocally states that, "In form, the Ismailis were a secret society with a system of oaths and initiations and a graded hierarchy of rank and knowledge. These secrets were well kept, and information about them is fragmentary and confused."[2]

We find the idea of secrets and grades in the work of Marshall Hodgson, who also does not shy away from the concept of a graded hierarchy among the Ismailis:

---

[1] Jacobsen, *The Treasures of Darkness*, p. 3.

[2] Lewis, *The Assassins*, p. 48.

> Among the several Shii movements, that of the Ismailis was distinguished by being organized hierarchically and secretly. . . . Adherents were ranked in several grades, in principle according to the degree to which they had advanced in the esoteric teachings ascribed to the imam. An adherent of an upper rank was set over adherents of a lower rank in his own area. Set over all adherents in a given province was the *dai*, or head of the religious teaching.[1]

Hodgson adds that there was a special ceremony and an oath of secrecy regarding the wider community of the Ismailis attached to the process of becoming a member of the sect, all to be understood by the concept of *taqiyya*. The Ismaili teaching unveiled the inner meaning of the Quran, the *batin*, the indispensable truth of the Imam. He also acknowledges the use of numerical correspondences in the Ismaili doctrine, as will be discussed below, and the wealth of cosmological and symbolic speculation made use of by the sect.[2] This has all been extensively discussed earlier regarding the kabbalistic and Neoplatonic Gnostic doctrines of emanation, and spiritual ascent in the Near Eastern philosophies and beliefs of the Mediterranean, Mesopotamia, and Persia.

Professor of Islamic history and author Heinz Halm gives a meticulous summary of the introductory oath administered by the *dai* to his prospect during medieval Fatimid times.[3] He quotes several variations of the oath and the accompanying dialog between candidate and teacher. The prospective initiate swore to observe secrecy regarding the inner meaning, or *batin*, about to be revealed by the *dai*. All the oaths involved ritualized actions such as ablutions and fasting; recitation of formulae; pledges of loyalty to the Imam; swearing to respect the identity of co-religionists and the privacy of their conver-

---

1 Hodgson, "The Ismaili State," in Boyle (ed.), *CHI*, vol. 5, p. 425.

2 Ibid., p. 425.

3 Heinz Halm, "The Ismaili Oath of Allegiance and the 'Sessions of Wisdom' in Fatimid Times," in Farhad Daftary, *Mediaeval Ismaili History and Thought*, pp. 91–115.

sations; and the payment of dues or fees. The violations of such oaths involved severe consequences and punishments both in the spiritual and material world. The oath was the prerequisite to being given the secrets of wisdom (*hikma*) by the Imam or the *dai* as his representative. The teaching sessions included women. The author points out that similar oaths are administered to this day among the Bohra communities of India.

As we noted in chapter three, as early as the late eighth or ninth century, Abd Allah b. Maymun was accused of having organized a hierarchical system of seven degrees whose end was atheism and libertinism.[1] A slightly later model of the Ismaili wisdom teaching dates back at least to the tenth century, and has proven both controversial and long-lived. It consists of nine degrees. It will be remembered that this time period is that of the establishment of the Ismaili/Fatimid dynasty in Egypt in 909.

The nine-degree model is found in a tract from the tenth century called *The Book of the Highest Initiation* (*Kitab al-halagh al-alhar*), which openly mentions the degrees for the first time—and assumes the reader should have been familiar with them. Recent scholarship has identified this writing as an anti-Ismaili forgery whose purpose was to slander and discredit the sect.[2] As was the case with the accusations leveled against Abd Allah b. Maymun, the end of the teachings of *The Book of the Highest Initiation* was said to be a cult of lawless atheism and amorality. It was reputed to be a cynical, secret Ismaili indoctrination manual for *dais*. While it is undoubtedly a false and slanderous product, Samuel M. Stern, writing about the degree structure of *The Book of the Highest Initiation,* acknowledges that a progressive system of initiation took place. "It is, therefore, undeniable that Ismailism knew the idea of gradual initiation . . . The author of our pamphlet did not invent anything in the framework he used . . . what

---

1 Daftary, *The Ismailis*, p. 110.

2 Heinz Halm, discussing Samuel M. Stern's research in Daftary, *Mediaeval Ismaili History and Thought*, p. 91.

is to be put down to his malevolent invention is the *contents* he attributed to the doctrines taught on the different stages of the initiation."[1]

Stern continues, "It is, however, inherent in the nature of such libelous products to be *travesties* rather than mere phantasies; they would miss the greater part of their effect if the object of their caricature were unrecognizable."[2] The reader would do well to compare *The Protocols of the Learned Elders of Zion* or *The Report from Iron Mountain,* both of which have been believed to be real, the former partly responsible for millions of deaths during the twentieth century.

The Book of the Highest Initiation counsels the *dai* to talk in the language of his intended convert, distinguishing between Shia, Sunni, Sabaean, Zorastrian, Jew, Christian, Manichaean and other Dualists, and philosophers. Its advice is common-sense, taking one's time to observe reactions—like a modern business course in customer relations and techniques of persuasion.

However, much of the content of *The Book of the Highest Initiation* is scandalous and slanderous. Some examples include the following: negation of the attributes of God; denying the Imamate of Ali; abdication of Islam and all ceremonial behavior; encouragement to learn juggling and conjuring tricks to pass oneself off as a miracle worker; the incentivizing of incest with sisters and daughters; encouraging the taking of the wealth, goods, property, and women from disciples; and a completely cynical approach to the accumulation of personal power.[3]

We do not know reliably what was taught in the various degrees of the secret doctrine, although we can be reasonably certain it did not involve the scandalous attitudes and behaviors mentioned in the previous paragraph! What did the graded ascent through the ranks of the Ismailis involve?

1 Samuel M. Stern, "The 'Book of the Highest Initiation' and Other Anti-Ismaili Travesties," in Stern, *Studies in Early Ismailism*, p. 61.

2 Ibid., p. 58 [emphasis added].

3 Ibid., pp. 64–72.

In *The Templars and the Assassins*, I offered a sympathetic look at the purported Nine Degrees of Wisdom in a brief appendix.[1] My sources for that résumé were listed.[2] They all derived their ideas from the medieval anti-Ismaili Sunni polemicists who attacked the sect—in particular the newly-proclaimed Fatimid Caliphate—as a dangerous arch-heresy.

As mentioned in chapter three, the first of these was Ibn Rizam, whose work is lost, but became the basis of the anti-Fatimid tract issued in 1011 by the Abbasid caliph. The Sunni Akhu Muhsin later made extensive use of Ibn Rizam's treatise. Although his work is also lost, a significant portion survives in the *Nihayat al-arab,* circa 1332, of the Muslim historian al-Nuwayri.[3] All these writers built on the "black legend" of Abd Allah b. Maymun—accused of being a non-Alid follower of the Christian Gnostic Bardesanes, the progenitor of the Fatimid (and thereby false) Imamate, and whose ultimate goal was the destruction of Islam from within.[4]

Why should we be concerned about the charges leveled against the Ismailis and give credence to them by continuing to discuss the degrees? The reasons are clear from the opening discussions in this chapter. We know the Ismailis had a graded system of instruction with oaths to assure secrecy. As one who has spent his adult life studying and participating in hierarchical secret societies, I believe there is much to be said for the private, teacher-to-student communications about the nature of Truth. The reader is now fully aware of the dangers these people faced in their hostile medieval environment

---

[1] Wasserman, *The Templars and the Assassins*, appendix one, pp. 273–276.

[2] E. G. Browne, *A Literary History of Persia*, volume I, pp. 410–415; Joseph von Hammer-Purgstall, *The History of the Assassins*, pp. 34–37; Enno Franzius, *History of the Order of Assassins*, pp. 26–29; and De Lacy O'Leary, *A Short History of the Fatimid Khalifate*, pp. 21–32.

[3] Daftary, *The Assassin Legends*, p. 25.

[4] Ibid., p. 25. Daftary coined the term "black legend," with his customary genius, to represent the long history of slanderous accusation made against the Ismailis by Sunnis, Twelver Shiites, and Christian Crusaders. Their inaccuracies formed the basis of most Muslim scholarship in the West until about the 1930s.

so their need for secrecy and privacy can be appreciated. We have also spent a good deal of time in discussion of the Mesopotamian, Persian, and Gnostic beliefs that are ascribed to the "secret doctrine" of the Ismailis and are part of the graded path of ascent.

As I have mentioned in previous writings, the model of the seven or nine degrees of initiation partakes of a marvelous symmetry which points to an elevated and exalted spiritual teaching. Here is an outline of what I believe may have been communicated—based on a positive interpretation of some of the clues afforded by these writers and elsewhere. These are personal speculative musings, and the reader should understand that at the outset.

Hasan gives us a bird's eye view of the recruiting process in the autobiographical portion of *The Biography of Our Master*.[1] The trained *dais* were looking for potential converts who were not afraid to think for themselves. They tried to raise doubt within the minds of their targets and patiently and carefully observed the recipient's reaction.

If the person was offended, the recruiting effort would immediately cease without danger signals having arisen. If the door seemed open to further conversation, simple but unanswerable questions concerning life and Quranic doctrines would demonstrate to the seeker his own ignorance, and the need for an authoritative teacher and guide. "Why did it take God six days to create the world when He could have accomplished it in an instant?" "What do the recording angels mentioned in the Quran look like, and why can't we see them?" "Why does man alone of all the animals stand erect?"

If the process continued in a productive manner, the potential candidate was sworn to an oath as discussed above by Professor Halm and described by various authorities. "Bind yourself, then, by placing thy right hand in mine."[2] He or she was then admonished regarding the importance of continuing the normal outward observance of Sunni practice, *sharia*, so that no signals were aroused against them by neighbors, friends, or family.

---

1 Rashid al-Din, appendix two, pp. 302–304.

2 Browne, *A Literary History of Persia*, vol. 1, p. 413, quoting Silvestre De Sacy.

The first idea the newly-sworn initiate was exposed to was that the Quran has a superior esoteric meaning, the *batin*, which must be learned from an authorized interpreter. The *dai*, as a representative of the divinely-chosen Imam, was in a position to lead the disciple. Next, the errors of the Sunni position and its inadequacy to answer the deeper questions of Being would be addressed. We have certainly seen this play out in the widespread corruption of the Abbasid Caliphate, let alone the modern Saudi royal family.

If the candidate progressed, kabbalistic mysteries of number were revealed, particularly, at first, of the number seven. The seven heavens, planets, colors, metals, days of the week, cervical vertebrae, apertures of the head (two eyes, two ears, two nostrils and the mouth), etc. were noted. He was taught that this mystery applied to the seven divine Ismaili teachers, the Imams, as well. Here the *dai* was separating his teachings from those of the majority Shiites who continued their count of Imams well past that of Musa ibn Jafar (until they would reach twelve). Next, the Ismaili teaching that there are seven Prophets was revealed, the last of whom follows Muhammad as either Ismail or his son Muhammad ibn Ismail. Here is heresy because in standard Islamic doctrine, Muhammad is recognized as the final Prophet.

The elasticity of interpretation of the Quran was then raised. Its literal reading was reserved for the masses, not the spiritual elite who were given insights into its true concealed meaning. As such, the practices of *sharia* were considered fit solely for the uninitiated. It was important to conform to outward practice when necessary for safety, of course, but that was an example of *taqiyya*, rather than an acceptance of the value of rote behavior.

Next would be a discussion of the mysteries of the number twelve, which included the twelve signs of the zodiac, months of the year, tribes of Israel, dorsal vertebrae, etc. Practical magical instruction was said to have been given here.[1] The philosophical teachings of Pythag-

---

1 See, as mentioned in chapter fifteen of this book, the *Kittab al-Muqaffa al-kabir* of al-Maqrizi describing Hasan as "an astute, capable man knowledgeable in geometry, arithmetic, the stars, magic and other matters." Al-Maqrizi is quoted by Hillenbrand in "A Neglected Source on the Life of Hasan-i Sabbah,

oras, Plato, and Aristotle were introduced, and the use of reason to test religious truth was endorsed. We have seen this throughout the root philosophies of the region, and it seems to comport seamlessly with what we already know, especially from the discussion of the *Rasail Ikhwan al-Safa* at the end of chapter three.

The mystical doctrines of Dualism were next introduced from the Zoroastrian teachings. The doctrine of First and Second Causes (the Pre-Existent and the Subsequent) was said to challenge the belief in Divine Unity. Aristotle's theory of the eternity of matter was studied. Creation was explained to be the introduction of movement into matter, which produced time and change. The existence of a formless, nameless, unknowable Being anterior to and beyond all previous dualistic conceptions was then discussed.

I wrote a description in *The Templars and the Assassins* of the last stage or ninth degree of this system. In my opinion, it fully illustrates the goal of any religious or spiritual system worth discussing:

> The Ninth Degree Ismaili was a pure philosopher, a law unto himself. The teaching within this degree is the source of the oft-quoted statement attributed to Hasan-i-Sabah, "Nothing is true, everything is permitted." It is reflected in the modern revelation proclaimed through the twentieth century English magus Aleister Crowley, "Do what thou wilt shall be the whole of the Law." It assumes a level of ego surrender and moral aus-

---

the Founder of the Nizari 'Assassin' Sect," *Iran: Journal of the British Institute of Persian Studies*, 2017, p. 4. She quotes the same source referring to Hasan performing magic in front of his disciples, pp. 7–8. Lewis, in *The Assassins*, cites al-Maqrizi and Hasan's magic on p. 152, note 38. Lewis also quotes early thirteenth century historian Arnold of Lubeck, who wrote that the Assassin master used magic to influence rhe dreams of his *fidais* (pp. 4–5). Burman describes the *Rasail*, Epistles 40–51, as concerned with "the occult sciences," in *The Assassins*, p. 56. Franzius speaks of the teachings of the "magical value" of mathematics and numerology, in *The History of the Order of Assassins* p. 28. The most famous magician among the Nizari Ismailis was Rashid al-Din Sinan in Syria. For a résumé of his magical skills see Wasserman, *The Templars and the Assassins*, pp. 136–138, and Hodgson, *The Order of Assassins*, pp. 193–197.

> terity concomitant with a successful search for spiritual truth in which the initiate may at last rely on his own perceptions for an understanding of his mission.[1]

The idea of looking for esoteric meaning within scripture, exploring the higher reaches of philosophy to understand Truth, exploring numerology, Qabalah, and thaumaturgy, asking questions of commonly accepted ideas, seems a more than acceptable way for people to creatively expand their intelligence.

Although it speaks of heresy—even to this day—I would suggest that the words of Sir Richard Burton are the clearest indication of the ultimate spiritual goal of the Gnostic initiate. He wrote that a teacher named Sahib the Sufi declared that the secret of man's soul was first revealed when the Egyptian Pharaoh declared himself a god.[2]

Similarly, Wladimir Ivanow writes in his introduction to the *Kalami Pir*, "The highest class of mankind . . . are entirely absorbed in God, so that their will becomes the will of God, and their actions become the actions of God."[3]

---

[1] Wasserman, *The Templars and the Assassins*, p. 276.

[2] Burton, *The Book of the Thousand Nights and a Night*, vol. 6, note 2, p. 115.

[3] Ivanow, *Kalami Pir*, p. xlvi. He notes that Mansur al-Hallaj was an example of this idea.

APPENDICES

APPENDIX ONE

Marco Polo's Medieval Legend of the Garden of Delights

> Rousseau [head of a clandestine French counter-terrorism agency] nodded slowly. "The marriage between hashish and terrorism," he said, "is as old as time itself. As you know, the word *assassin* is derived from the Arabic *hashashin*, the Shia killers who acted under the influence of hashish." —Daniel Silva[1]

Marco Polo (1254–1324) was the author of this longest-lived (and undoubtedly false) legend of Alamut and the Nizari Imam, published in *The Travels of Marco Polo* circa 1300.[2] A Venetian, Polo had spent twenty-four years (1271–1295) on various journeys through the known world of his day, including several years at the court of Kublai Khan in China. He traveled through Persia in 1273, where he heard tales of the Old Man of the Mountain. Marco Polo's account was so tantalizing that it became the model for an Arabic novel, written in 1430, that has been mistakenly identified as a confirmatory source of Polo's story.[3] *The Travels of Marco Polo* remained the most popular (and almost sole) European source for the Assassin myth for over four hundred years.

Polo's Garden hearkens back to numerous promises in the Quran of the reward of time spent in a Garden filled with lush foliage and flowing streams for those of the faithful. (One cannot erase from the mind the contrast between the harsh desert environment of Muhammad's life and the tantalizing moist greenery of the Garden.) While

[1] Daniel Silva, *House of Spies*, p. 117. A bestselling novel published in 2017.

[2] Translated here from *Marco Polo's Travels: with an Introduction by John Masefield.*

[3] See Hammer-Purgstall, *The History of the Assassins*, p. 136; Daftary, *The Assassin Legends*, pp. 118–120. Thomas Keightley in *Secret Societies of the Middle Ages* quotes the relevant portion of the novel on pp. 74–78.

there are constant references to gardens throughout the Quran, here are some of the most reminiscent of Marco Polo's description of the Assassin Garden of the Old Man of the Mountain.

A detailed description is given in the surah called "Muhammad":

> A similitude of the Garden which those who keep their duty (to Allah) are promised: Therein are rivers of water unpolluted, and rivers of milk whereof the flavour changeth not, and rivers of wine delicious to the drinkers, and rivers of clear-run honey; therein for them is every kind of fruit, with pardon from their Lord.[1]

All this despite the multiple citations, mentioned in chapter twenty of the present book, that wine is forbidden, both by the Quran and in the reported stories of the Prophet's teachings (*hadith*). One does not, however, quibble with apparent contradictions in holy texts.

The beautiful women of Polo's Assassin Garden, the heavenly *houris,* are promised as companions for the "single-minded slaves of Allah" in the surah known as "Those Who Set the Ranks":

> And with them are those of modest gaze, with lovely eyes.[2]

The Garden is identified with the Garden of Eden in the surah called "Ṣad." It is complete with references to the couches mentioned in Polo's tale, as well as fruit and drink, and the *houris*, "those of modest gaze, companions"[3] promised to the righteous.

In "Ornaments of Gold," the slaves of Allah are told to:

> Enter the Garden, ye and your wives, to be made glad. Therein are brought round for them trays of gold and goblets, and therein

1 Pickthall (trans.), *The Meaning of the Glorious Koran*, surah 47:15, "Muhammad," pp. 523–524.

2 Ibid., surah 37:40–48, "Those Who Set the Ranks," p. 458.

3 Ibid., surah 38:50–57, "Ṣad," p. 469.

> is all that souls desire and eyes find sweet. And ye are immortal therein.[1]

See also the surah called "Smoke" for the wedding in the Garden promised to "those who kept their duty … unto the fair ones with wide, lovely eyes."[2]

Again, in the surah called "The Mount," the Gardens of Delight are mentioned, and those "who kept their duty" are pictured:

> Reclining on ranged couches. And We wed them unto fair ones with wide lovely eyes.[3]

"The Beneficent" (surah 55:50–78) follows these themes again with verses describing the couches, the virgins, the fruits, and the fountains. These promises will also be found in "The Event" (surah 56:12–40 and 88–91). The Garden as a reward for the righteous is described in some detail in "Time" (surah 76:12–22). The maidens and the full cup are also present in the enclosed Gardens in "The Tidings" (surah 78:31–36). In "Defrauding" (surah 83: 21–28), the pure wine is sealed with musk for the righteous, who rest on couches, gazing in delight. In "The Overwhelming" (surah 88:8–16), the reward of the Garden is contrasted with the punishment awaiting the evil ones.

Thus, the vision of Paradise in Polo's account of the Assassin Garden would be familiar to anyone schooled in the text of the holy book of Islam.

---

[1] Ibid., surah 43:70–71, "Ornaments of Gold," p. 507.

[2] Ibid., surah 44:51–57, "Smoke," p. 512.

[3] Ibid., surah 52:17 and 20, "The Mount," p. 545.

Of the Old Man of the Mountain: Of His Palace and Gardens, of His Capture and His Death.[1]

Having spoken of this country, mention shall now be made of the Old Man of the Mountain. The district in which his residence lay obtained the name of Mulehet, signifying in the language of the Saracens, the place of heretics, and his people that of *Mulehetites*,[2] or holders of heretical tenets as we apply the term of Patharini[3] to certain heretics amongst Christians.

The following account of this chief, Marco Polo testifies to having heard from sundry persons. He was named Alo-eddin,[4] and his religion was that of Mahomet.

In a beautiful valley enclosed between two lofty mountains, he had formed a luxurious garden, stored with every delicious fruit and every fragrant shrub that could be procured. Palaces of various sizes and forms were erected in different parts of the grounds, ornamented with works in gold, with hanging paintings, and couches and furniture covered in rich silks. By means of small conduits contrived in these buildings, streams of wine, milk, honey, and some of pure water, were seen to flow in every direction.

---

1 This is chapter 22 of Marco Polo's travelogue.

2 From the Arabic *mulhid*, plural is *malahida,* whose meaning is "deviant."

3 The Patarini were members of an eleventh-century religious movement (Pataria) in Milan which supported clerical reformation, pietism, and holy poverty. They became an influence on the later Cathar movement. They were accused of heresy by those who disputed their goals. https://en.m.wikipedia.org/wiki/Pataria [accessed May 23, 2019.] De Sacy calls them "Albigensians" in his "Memoir on the Dynasty of the Assassins" in Daftary, *The Assassin Legends*, note 44, p. 186.

4 Muhammad III (r. 1221–1255), the seventh Alamut Imam, also known as Aladdin.

The inhabitants of these palaces were elegant and beautiful damsels, accomplished in the arts of singing, playing upon all sorts of musical instruments, dancing, and especially those of dalliance and amorous allurement. Clothed in rich dresses, they were seen continually sporting and amusing themselves in the garden and in the pavilions, their female guardians being confined within doors and never suffered to appear.

The object which the chief had in view in forming a garden of this fascinating kind was this: that Mahomet, having promised to those who should obey his will the enjoyments of Paradise, where every species of sensual gratification should be found in the society of beautiful nymphs, he was desirous of its being understood by his followers that he also was a prophet and the compeer of Mahomet, and had the power of admitting to Paradise such as he should choose to favour. In order that none without his license might find their way into this delicious valley, he caused a strong and inexpugnable castle to be erected at the opening of it, through which the entry was by a secret passage.

At his court, likewise, this chief entertained a number of youths, from the age of twelve to twenty years, selected from the inhabitants of the surrounding mountains, who showed a disposition for martial exercises, and appeared to possess the quality of daring courage. To them he was in the daily practice of discoursing on the subject of the paradise announced by the prophet, and of his own power of granting admission; and at certain times he caused opium to be administered to ten or a dozen of the youths; and when half dead with sleep, he had them conveyed to the several apartments of the palaces in the garden.

Upon awakening from the state of lethargy, their senses were struck with all the delightful objects that have been described, and each perceived himself surrounded by lovely damsels, singing, playing, and attracting his regards by the most fascinating caresses, serving him also with delicate viands and exquisite wines; until intoxicated with excess of enjoyment amidst actual rivulets of milk and wine, he believed himself assuredly in Paradise, and felt an unwillingness to relinquish its delights.

When four or five days had thus been passed, they were thrown once more into a state of somnolency, and carried out of the garden. Upon their being introduced to his presence, and questioned by him as to where they had been, their answer was, "In Paradise, through the favor of your highness." And then before the whole court, who listened to them with eager curiosity and astonishment, they gave a circumstantial account of the scenes to which they had been witnesses.

The chief thereupon addressing them said: "We have the assurances of our Prophet that he who defends his lord shall inherit Paradise, and if you show yourselves devoted to the obedience of my orders, that happy lot awaits you." Animated to enthusiasm by words of this nature, all deemed themselves happy to receive the commands of their master, and were forward to die in his service.

The consequence of this system was, that when any of the neighbouring princes, or others, gave umbrage to this chief, they were put to death by these his disciplined assassins; none of whom felt terror at the risk of losing their own lives, which they held in little estimation, provided they could execute their master's will. On this account his tyranny became the subject of dread in all the surrounding countries. He had also constituted two deputies or representatives of himself, of whom one had his residence in the vicinity of Damascus, and the other in Kurdistan; and these pursued the plan he had established for training their young dependents.

Thus there was no person, however powerful, who, having become exposed to the enmity of the Old Man of the Mountain, could escape assassination. His territory being situated within the dominions of Ulati [Huelgu], the brother of the grand khan [Mangu], that prince had information of his atrocious practices, as above related, as well as of his employing people to rob travellers in passage through his country, and in the year 1252 sent one of his armies to besiege this chief in his castle. It proved, however, so capable of defense, that for three years no impression could be made upon it; until at length he was forced to surrender from the want of provisions, and being made prisoner, was put to death. His castle was dismantled, and his garden of Paradise destroyed.

And from that time there has been no Old Man of the Mountain.

APPENDIX TWO

The Biography of Our Master
(Sar-Guzasht-i-Sayyidna)

By Rashid al-Din Tabib[1]

Translated and annotated by
Aliasghar Taghipourteroujeni and James Wasserman

Jameoltavarikh (*Jami al-Tavarikh*, or *Collection of Histories*) was written by Rashidoddin Fazlollah Hamedani (Rashid al-Din Tabib). A Jewish convert to Sunni Islam, Rashid al-Din (1247–1318) was a Persian historian, physician, and politician. His *Jami al-Tavarikh* is a multi-volume, illustrated compendium of the known world of his day, compiled between 1307 and 1316. He was a high official of the Mongol Ilkhanate dynasty that ruled Persia from 1260 to 1335. He rose to became wazir or prime minister, but was executed after a power shift in the court allowed him to be accused of poisoning King Oljeitu in 1316.

Note from Aliasghar Taghipourteroujeni:

At the time of its writing (ca. 1310), Rashid al-Din's text was simple and understandable for ordinary people. Modern researchers consider it difficult since Rashid al-Din's full history includes more than twenty thousand loanwords from the Arabic, Turkish, and Mongolian languages. However, in comparison to its contemporary counterparts like the *Ta-rikh-i-Jahan Gusha* by Ata-Malik Juvaini,[2] we can state

[1] Rashidoddin Fazlollah Hamedani, *Jami al-Tavarikh*, or *Collection of Histories*, ca. 1310.

[2] Translated in English as Ata-Malik Juvaini, *Genghis Khan: The History of the World-Conqueror.*

that it was not a complicated or specialized style at the time it was written.

The Biography of Our Master is the only portion of Rashid's extensive *Jami al-Tavarikh* translated here. In this section of Hasan-i-Sabah's life, there are many unknown names which were associated with people or places that were mentioned in earlier chapters of the much larger book. There are also many Arabic sentences which are mostly religious quotations, because one part of Rashid al-Din's book is a history of the Ismaili religion. I have done my best to become familiar with the general narration, structure, and information of the book and to recognize the special grammatical features of that period. Naturally, these were different than current Persian grammar. I used the *Dehkhoda* dictionary, the most trustworthy source for the meaning of old words in Persian. I began this work by first translating the seven hundred year-old text into contemporary Persian, and then to English. My most-used resource for the work of the English translation was the *Oxford English Dictionary*.

One of the main characteristics of old Persian historical writings is that the style is not consistent, sequential, or cohesive. There is much back and forth in the narration, and many pronouns are used. There are frequently points or allusions made by the author which are not always directly related to the topic at hand. Thus, the overall feel of the text may seem disjointed or confused at times, especially to the modern reader.

I would like to thank and acknowledge Dr. Seyyed Mohammad Dabirsiaghi, the editor responsible for the 2006 Persian language book of Rashid al-Din's 1310 text on the Ismailis from which this translation was begun. Dr. Dabirsiaghi was born in Ghazvin, Iran in 1920. He is a researcher, writer, poet, and editor of ancient Persian books. He worked in the *Dehkhoda* Encyclopedia Institution for many years, and has edited and published more than eighty books. Some of his works include: *Shahname Ferdowsi, Divane Manouchehri, Nozhatolgholub,* and *Farhange Soruri*. His most recent project is a Persian dictionary of which several volumes have been published in recent years. Dr. Dabirsiaghi writes in the introduction to this work:

> In this book, I use *Jameoltavarikh* as my main source, plus the work of Vladimir Ivanow on his uncompleted project. Ivanow was a Russian researcher who did much work in the field of Persian local literature and the history of Ismailism in Iran. In 1958, he came to Iran to visit Alamut mountain. In addition to his field study, he took pictures from different manuscript versions of *Jameoltavarikh* around the world to preserve trustworthy information. Unfortunately, he did not have the opportunity to complete the project and was thus not able to publish his translation of the section on Hasan-i-Sabah in *Jameoltavarikh*.[1]

It is a great honor for me to have participated in this important rendering of a crucial seven-hundred-year-old text which had remained curiously unavailable to the English-speaking reader before this publication. I appreciate the editorial help and friendship extended to me by James Wasserman.

—Aliasghar Taghipourteroujeni
New York University

---

[1] Seyyed Muhammad Dabirsiaghi (ed.), *The History of Hasane Sabbah and His Successors: A Chapter of Jame o t.tavarix.*

The Biography of Our Master
(Sar-Guzasht-i-Sayyidna)

About the Teachings or the Faith of the *Dais*[1] and their Predecessor: Hasan-i-Sabah Himayari

He was Al-Hasan ibn[2] Ali ibn Muhammad ibn Ja'far ibn al-Hussein ibn Muhammad ibn al-Sabbah Himyar[3] al-Yamani. He was originally from the Himyarite tribe, the tribe of the kings of Yemen. When his followers wrote out his genealogy and showed it to him, he threw that paper in the water. He showed them his dissatisfaction and said: "I would prefer to be the special servant of the Imam rather than his perverse son."

His father came from Kufa to Qum, and then left Qum, and finally resided in Rayy. Hasan-i-Sabah was born in Rayy. It has been narrated in his story that he said:

> In my childhood, and at the age of seven, I was interested in learning various sciences and I wanted to be a religious scholar. I was seeking this knowledge until I was seventeen years old. I was faithful to Shiism, *Ithna ashariyya*,[4] the religion of my ancestors.

---

[1] A *dai* (Arabic) is someone who engages in *dawa*, the act of inviting people to Islam. But it is more specifically an important religious office amongst the Ismaili Shia Muslims.

[2] Arabic word which means "the son of."

[3] An important tribe in the ancient Sabaean kingdom of southwestern Arabia. See chapter four of this book.

[4] An Arabic word meaning "twelve Imams," the faith of the majority of Shiites, known as Twelver Shiites. The Ismailis believe in seven Imams and are known as Sevener Shiites or *Sabiyya.* See chapter three of this book for more on this important topic.

Later, I met a man named Amira Zarrab through my friends. He was speaking about the excellence of the Egyptian caliph's faith, the Ismaili sect.[1] Before him, Nasir-i Khusraw,[2] who was the Ismaili propagandist [*hujja*] of the Khurasan district, introduced me to the Ismaili belief, although he was not successful in this work. Abu Ali Simjur[3] and a group of other people accepted and believed in that faith during the reign of Sultan Mahmud.[4] Also Nasr ibn Ahmad Samani and a group of elders in Bukhara accepted that religion.

I never thought I would have any doubt regarding my faith in Islam. Whereas there is a God, the living, almighty, all-hearing and all-seeing God, and also his Prophet, Imams, the lawful and the unlawful, Paradise, Hell, the duty to promote virtue and prevent vice. I thought that the rightful faith is the faith which is believed by the majority of the populace, especially [Twelver] Shiites. I never thought that it would be advisable and worthy to seek the truth outside of Islam. The faith of the Ismailis seemed to me to be a *philosophy*, and I believed the caliph of Egypt was a philosopher.[5]

Amira Zarrab was a kind man. First, he spoke with me and introduced me to the Ismaili belief. I said: "Oh, my friend! Do not talk about them. They are outside the circle of truth and they are against the faith." We were discussing and debating together. He was challenging my thoughts and disparaging them. I had not given up, but his words impressed my heart.

---

1 The Fatimid caliph in Egypt was the head (Imam) of the Ismaili faith.

2 See chapter five of this book for more on Nasir-i Khusraw.

3 A Samanid *emir* (a noble commander or minister).

4 Sultan Mahmud (r. 1002–1030) of the Ghaznavid Empire in Afghanistan conquered eastern Persia. Toward the end of his life, he fought against the Seljuk invaders from Central Asia.

5 "Philosopher" was considered a pejorative term, the opposite of spiritual or religious.

As part of our conversation, I said: "Whenever someone who believes the Ismaili faith happens to die, people will say, 'It is the corpse of an infidel man.'" This is because most of the populace lied about the Ismailis and defamed them. But I saw that the group of Nizaris were pious and devout, abstinent, and anxious about drinking wine. I was scared of wine because it is a teaching of Islam that, "There is a great sin and uncleanness" in drinking. Amira told me: "At night, when you reflect in your bed, you will know that what I say is necessary for you."

Then we were separated from each other for a while. I found many arguments regarding the Imamate of Ismail[1] in their books. Again when I was faced with the topic of the hidden Imams,[2] I was astonished. I agreed that the Imamate belongs to the rule of the *nass*,[3] but I did not know who they are.

In the meanwhile, I suffered a severe illness. God wanted to turn meat and skin into something else. "God made his meat to a better meat and made his blood to a better blood."[4] I had begun to believe that the religion of the Ismailis is the Truth, but I did not affirm that due to my utmost anxiety. I said to myself: "If I pass away, I will perish while not acquiring the Truth." Eventually, I was healed.

I found another person named Abu-Najam Sarraj of the Ismailis. I asked him some questions about the faith and he gave me a complete exposition. So I learned about the complexities

---

1 Ismaili Muslims recognize Ismail as the rightful and true seventh Imam after Imam Jafar al-Sadiq, while the Twelver Shia recognize Musa al-Kazim, Ismail's half-brother as the seventh Imam.

2 The Ismaili teachers were divided into two groups after Muhammad ibn Ismail (grandson of Jafar al-Sadiq): some of them were the hidden Imams themselves, while their *dais* were openly inviting selected people to the Ismaili faith.

3 *Nass* refers to the spiritual designation (transmission) to his successor by the Imam.

4 *Hadith* of the Prophet Muhammad.

and truth of that religion. Another person was called Mumin. He had been allowed to preach the faith by Shaykh Abd al-Malik ibn Attash.[1] I asked Mumin to give me the covenant and allow me to make the promise. He said: "You, Hasan, are more faithful than I, Mumin.[2] So how can I give you the covenant and take [the vow of] allegiance to the Imam from you?" Finally, he swore me to the covenant.

During Ramadan, 464 AH [May–June 1072 AD],[3] Abd al-Malik ibn Attash came to Rayy. He was the chief *dai* of Iraq. He liked me, appointed me a deputy in the *dawa,* and told me that I should go to the court of Caliph al-Mustansir Billah.[4]

[Hasan's Travels] [5]

Shaykh[6] traveled from Rayy to Isfahan in 467 AH [1074–1075 AD]. After being appointed to the position of deputy by Abd al-Malik ibn Attash, he decided to travel to Egypt in 469 AH [1076–1077 AD].

Hasan went first from Isfahan to Azerbaijan. After some dangerous travel, and concealing his fear, he arrived at Mayyafariquin.[7] One

---

[1] He was one of the greatest Persian Ismaili *dais.*

[2] Mumin is referring to the meaning of the word "Hasan" in Arabic. Hasan was the name of the son of Ali and means "good." The Arabic meaning of Mumin is "believer." Thus, Mumin is said to have, at first, humbly deferred to Hasan. (See J. A. Boyle, notes to Juvaini, p. 668.)

[3] Ramadan is observed in the ninth Arabic lunar month.

[4] The head of the Ismaili faith, the Fatimid Imam.

[5] Until this point, the story has been written in the first person by Hasan-i-Sabah. The balance of the *Sar-Guzasht-i-Sayyidna* is a narrative about Hasan, undoubtedly written by a trusted disciple. As we will see, Rashid al-Din will insert himself into the text as well.

[6] "Shaykh" refers to Hasan-i-Sabah. Shaykh is an Arabic word meaning the elder of a tribe, a revered old man, or an Islamic scholar. It is a source of the legendary title "Old Man of the Mountain."

[7] A city and district in the Diyarbakır province of Turkey.

of the city's leading jurists went to see Hasan. They debated together about the *hadith* on *ijtihad* (reasoning).[1] Hasan said: "One *faqih's* (jurist's)[2] reasoning is not superior to another jurist's reasoning.[3] It is therefore not worthy for one jurist to argue about the *Shafii* religion[4] [with another] because both of them are only *mujtahids.*[5] How should the people choose religion when they do not have the ability to discern the true religion?"[6] When this discussion reached the ears of the *qadi* (chief judge), he said: "We have to expel him as soon as possible. Because it will be harmful for us if those speeches come to the attention of the governor and to the ears of the people."

So Hasan traveled from Mayyafariquin to Mosul. Then he rode from there and continued from near Rahabah (?) to the Samawah desert,[7] which was a terrible and arduous desert. He navigated by the stars until he arrived at Damascus on a feast day.

---

1 *Ijtihad* is an Islamic legal term referring to independent reasoning, or the thorough exertion of a jurist's mental faculty in order to find a solution to a legal question. The *hadith* (saying of the Prophet) on *ijtihad* reads: "Amr ibn al-As reported: The Messenger of Allah, peace and blessings be upon him, said, 'If a judge makes a ruling, striving to apply his reasoning (*ijtihad*) and he is correct, then he will have two rewards. If a judge makes a ruling, striving to apply his reasoning and he is mistaken, then he will have one reward.'" *Sahih Muslim* 1716.

2 A *faqih* (Persian) is a jurist or a divine. He is a member of the Sunni *ulema* and an expert in *fiqh* (Islamic jurisprudence and Islamic law), the Quran and its interpretation, Muslim history, logic, rhetoric, and philosophy.

3 In other words, the learning of one jurist is not necessarily superior to the learning of another jurist because neither one really knows Truth. As the *hadith* on *ijtihad* (quoted in note 2 above) makes clear, no matter how sincere he is, the judge may be in error.

4 *Shafii:* One of four schools of Sunni Muslim law, founded in the early ninth century. Among other characteristics, it relies on the consensus of scholars of the *ulema* for its guidance.

5 A *mujtahid is* a person who has been accepted as an authority in Islamic law.

6 Hasan's meaning is that the only true spiritual authority belongs to the Imam. A normal person cannot find the truth alone and unaided. See chapter eighteen on the doctrine of *talim.*

7 Modern Samawah is a city in Iraq, located halfway between Baghdad and

A Turkish man named Afsar had traveled to Moazie (Cairo)[1] with warlike intentions. He escaped to Damascus where he was defeated. Afsar had caused much insecurity in Damascus. Then Sayyidna[2] went to Beirut from Damascus. He traveled on to Sidon, Tyre, Acre, and Caesarea. He wanted to go to Egypt by sea, so he went to the harbor and shipped out from there. The sea was stormy. He arrived at Tennis city[3] within seven days, and continued to Qusats city, which is near to Moazie Cairo.

A group of elders and nobles of the Caliph al-Mustansir welcomed him—for example, Abu Dawud, who was the *Dai al-Doa,*[4] and Sharif Taher Qazwini, who was famous among the people. On Wednesday, Safar 18, 471 AH [August 30, 1078 AD], Sayyidna arrived in Cairo. Al-Mustansir Billah sent his chosen and closest friends to Sayyidna to greet him, professing affability and affection, expressing great favor, kindness, and respect to him.

Hasan stayed there for a year and a half. Although he did not visit the court of al-Mustansir while he was in Egypt, Mustansir was informed of his situation and praised him several times. The Imam's relatives were jealous of Sayyidna and worried about his rank and position. The Commander of the Forces Badr al-Jamali was the absolute ruler and suzerain of the country. He supported [the succession of] al-Musta'li, who had been chosen by a second *nass* as the crown prince by al-Mustansir. Badr feared that al-Mustansir might give Hasan a higher position than Badr or his supporters. Al-Mustali could not do anything without the permission of his father. Sayyidna

---

Basra. The Euphrates River runs through the city. It is otherwise surrounded by desert.

[1] The city of Cairo was called Moazie Cairo in the past, because it was conquered and ruled by Commander al-Moaz-al-Din Fatimid (931–975), who lived during the time of third Fatimid caliph.

[2] This Arabic honorific is attributed to Hasan-i-Sabah. It means our "overlord" or "master."

[3] Tennis or Tinnis was a medieval city in Egypt.

[4] Arabic word, meaning the "elder of *dais*."

proselytized in favor of Nizar[1] with his manner of teaching the faith. So the Commander of the Forces Badr was extremely angry with Hasan and proposed killing him.[2]

Badr decided to send Hasan from the land of Egypt to the isle [of Damietta] and throw him into prison forever in the name of the government. Fellow Daylamis[3] told Sayyidna: "We will kill Badr if you order us." But Sayyidna did not consent to that. Al-Mustali supported the decision to send Hasan to Damietta, but al-Mustansir did not consent. In the meantime, in the same week, the tower and fence of Damietta, which was built on the water, collapsed and failed.

The elders supposed it was a strange occurrence. They imagined the momentous event [was caused by] the miracles of al-Mustansir and the munificence of Sayyidna. Then, they entertained Hasan and sent him with a crowd of elders to the west by ship. In Rajab, 472 AH [January, 1080 AD], they brought Sayyidna to Alexandria. Suddenly, a storm arose and a hard wind began to blow. Parts of the ship broke up and people became anxious and worried, but Sayyidna remained calm. Someone asked him: "How you are so relaxed in this situation?" He said: "Mustansir told me about the incident and said that I should never be afraid because no harm will come to me. That is why I am not afraid."

Then the ship arrived at Jableh [in Syria], which is a Christian city. The judge of Jableh met Sayyidna as he disembarked from the ship and hosted him. He continued on by ship from there around the Levant in stormy seas. Then Hasan went to Swidia[4] and from there

---

1 The Imam's eldest son and original holder of the *nass* as his successor.

2 Please see chapter eleven of this book for a closer look at the Nizar/al-Mustali succession issue that led to Hasan's founding of the Nizari Ismailis in 1094. The discussion here by Rashid al-Din appears to be out of the proper chronological sequence by over a decade.

3 Daylam is the mountainous region in northern Persia along the southern shore of the Caspian Sea in which Hasan established his capital. The Daylamis were a particularly fierce and independent people.

4 Modern As-Suwayda, a Druze city in southwest Syria.

he went to Aleppo. He had spent seventeen months in Cairo, and then seventeen months in Alexandria, and wandered at sea.

He went to Isfahan by way of Baghdad and Khuzistan at the end of Dhi, 473 AH [June, 1081 AD]. He then visited Yazd and Kirman, promoting the faith. Again, he returned to Isfahan. He then visited Farim and Shahkouh. He stayed for four months there and again he went to Khuzistan. After three months he returned to Damghan traveling through a desert and wilderness. He stayed and prosecuted his mission in Damghan, Gorgan, and Janashk for three years.

Then, he returned to Shahkouh, and sent a group of *dais* to Andajroud and other provinces near Alamut. The *dais* included Hassanka Ghasrani, Khajeh[1] Ali Khaledan Qazvini, Khajeh Ismail Qazvini, Mohammad Jamal Razi, Kia Bul-qasem Larjani, Ali Namadgar Damavandi, and Alawi Razi. They all had responsibility for inviting people to the faith. Hasan traveled to Gorgan, Tarz, Sohad, Janashk, and wanted to go on to Daylaman. But he returned because he did not want to go by way of Rayy.[2]

Nizam al-Mulk, the prime minister, ordered Abu Moslem Razi to arrest Sayyidna. He worked hard in his search. Hasan arrived in Sari and wanted to go to the Damavand Road. Along the way, his mule became obstinate and motionless, so Hasan and his comrades returned to the road at night [when the mule was more cooperative]. They settled in a village. In the morning, they arrived at Damavand by way of Ghazi Bashm (?). Some said that Abu Moslem Razi, who was looking for Sayyidna, was coincidentally on the same road.[3] Then, Hasan arrived at Khar Rayy and went to Qazvin. He stayed away from Rayy itself and settled in Qazvin for a few days. He sent the men who were with him separately to Alamut. Finally, he went toward Alamut.

---

[1] Khajeh: a Persian word meaning "master."

[2] Because he was afraid of falling into the hands of Nizam al-Mulk and Abu Moslem Razi. See below.

[3] This is confusing, but appears to suggest that the mule's obstinacy saved Hasan from being arrested by Abu Moslem Razi.

[Hasan Acquires Alamut]

In those days, Mahdi the Alid was the ruler of Alamut. He had been appointed by Sultan Malikshah. Husayn Qaini invited Mahdi to the [Ismaili] faith, and a group of people in Alamut accepted his preaching. Mahdi also accepted. But his heart was not concurrent with his language. He wanted to betray those who accepted the teaching.[1] He sent his people down [from the rock] and finally closed the door of the castle, declaring that Alamut belonged to the Sultan. But after much conversation and discussion, he acquiesced to readmitting the residents back to the castle. After that adventure, the people of the castle did not listen to the Alid's words and commands.

Sayyidna sent Ab Ol Ghasem to Shahkouh.[2] Also Deh-Khoda[3] Khosrow Shah went from Janashk. In Rajab, 483 AH [September, 1090 AD], Sayyidna went to Daylaman from Qazvin through the roads of Bireh and Anboh. Then he went from Selasko Ashkur (?) to Andajroud,[4] which was nearby Alamut. Sayyidna stayed for a time at Andajroud.

Due to his high level of piety, many people fell into his trap and accepted his proselytizing.[5] Finally, on the night of Wednesday, Rajab 6, 483 AH [September 4, 1090 AD], Hasan arrived at Alamut and entered the castle secretly. He stayed there in disguise under the pseudonym Dehkhoda.

Of old, the castle used to be called "Alah Amout." That means "the eagle's teaching."[6] Wonderfully, the letters of Aluh-Amut indicate the date of Hasan's arrival at the castle according to *abjad*.[7] The

---

[1] He had lied so he could identify those who accepted the Ismaili faith.

[2] The name of a mountain range near Alamut.

[3] A Persian word, meaning "headman" (of a village).

[4] One of the valleys of the Qazvin province near Alamut.

[5] Remember that the Sunni Rashid al-Din was writing as an employee of the Ilkhanate Mongol dynasty. Despite his occasional expression of disapproval, his attitude to Hasan is far friendlier than that of Juvaini.

[6] This is also translated as "the eagle's nest."

[7] *Abjad* is the Arabic equivalent of the Hebrew *gematria*. Both languages are

comrades transported Hasan secretly to the castle. Mahdi had no choice but to accept all of this when was he was informed about the presence of Hasan. Then he was allowed to leave the castle. Sayyidna wrote a paper for Rais[1] Muzaffar, the governor of Girdkuh and Damghan, asking him to pay the Alid three thousand dinars[2] as the price of the castle. Rais Muzaffar had secretly accepted the Ismaili preaching. Hasan, due to his excessive virtue and piety wrote a small and brief note, explaining the paper was a draft: "Rais Muzaffar (God bless him), should pay three thousand dinars, the cost of Alamut castle, to the Alid Mahdi. Peace be upon Muhammad and his family. God is enough for us, and He is our best protector."

Mahdi received the draft and thought to himself, "Rais Muzaffar is a great man, he is the successor to Amirdad Habashi, son of Altontagh. So, how will he pay him something by a letter from an unnamed and vile man?" After a while, residing in Damghan, the Alid was in need of funds. He took the paper to Rais Muzaffar as a test. Rais Muzaffar kissed the handwriting and paid the money to Mahdi as soon as he received the draft.

Alamut was a stable castle, although the building was old and timeworn. The air was smelly because of the dryness, except for the Shahrud waterway which did not provide enough water for daily usage. Sayyidna commanded [the Ismailis] to build an irrigation raceway from the Andajroud and Mahrout mountains to Alamut. He built many villages around Alamut, and planted a lot of willow trees and cultivated the agricultural lands. Thereupon, the air of the castle became desirable. Hasan ordered many buildings to be built on that great rock. Thereafter, in the days of the rule of Kia Buzurgumid, water was brought into Alamut, and the stream of water trilled constantly through the castle.

---

alpha-numeric so letters do double duty as numbers. The spelling of Aluh-Amut (ALH AMWT) = 1 + 30 + 5 + 1 + 40 + 6 + 400 = 483. Hasan entered Alamut in 483 AH. (See Juvaini, p. 670 and chapter eight of this book.)

1 *Rais* is a Persian word meaning chief.

2 Past currency of Iran.

[Hasan's Teachings]

When Sayyidna settled there, he sent his *dais* to areas around the castle. He restricted his life to the teaching of the faith. He clarified his religious message, which was called *al-dawa al-jadida.*[1] He said his religious forerunners had based their faith on the inner and outer meaning of the texts, especially about similar verses, strange verses, verses that held textual mysteries. These older teachers said: "There are interpretations (*tawil*) about the meaning of verses (*tanzil*)."[2]

Sayyidna restricted his life completely to the teaching of religion. He said:

> Theology is not accessible by intelligence and opinion. It is only accessible through the teaching of the Imams. Because most people in the world have intelligence, everyone has a theoretical opinion about religion. If knowledge of God was accessible just by intelligence and thought, religious people should not have any disagreement. And all of them would be equal. Because they are all religious in terms of *nous.*[3] Therefore, most people need to follow their religion since the doors of disagreement and hostility are open to them. But some men should have true authority in religion. The religion which is based on true teachings says that the intellect alone is not an adequate instrument for truth. The Imams of the time must teach the faith to their followers and disciples.

---

1 An Arabic phrase meaning "new propaganda" or "new preaching."

2 *Tawil* refers to the process of discovering the inner or esoteric meaning (*batin*) within the outer expression (*zahir*) of a religious text, especially the Quran, through hermeneutical exegesis. *Tanzil* means "descent," or the "sending down" of revelation, the transmission of divine guidance for humanity through the prophets—beginning with Adam and culminating in the mission of Muhammad.

3 From the ancient Greek. In classical philosophy, *nous* means intellect, intelligence, understanding, reason, and intuition.

Sayyidna spoke simply to encourage understanding and attract people [to the teaching]. One of his most precise statements—which caused doubt for the protesters about their religion—was: "Is intelligence enough for theology or not?" It means that if reason is an adequate instrument for reaching certainty in religious knowledge, anyone who has reason [may be correct] and we must allow everyone to act according to his reason.[1] On the other hand, if the protester says: "Reason is not enough," the need for learning in any time cannot be denied. Religion demands an answer to the question of whether Reason is enough or not. The correct answer is: Learning, faith, and reasoning are obligatory together. The true religion opposes the theory that learning and reasoning are not obligatory together. When they are not together, true theology cannot be obtained.

The people's religion explains that reason by itself is not enough. Making use of the reason must be done in a special way. Teaching and guidance should be prescribed for most of the wise. On the other hand, some of them do not need this learning. The Prophet Muhammad (peace be upon him and his family) said: "I have been commanded to fight against the people until they are ready to say, 'There is no god but God.'" This means that it is obligatory for us to learn this truth. This is the meaning of schooling. In the abstract, Sayyidna was inviting people with these simple comparisons and doctrines.

[Expansion and Battles]

He struggled mightily to free the areas around Alamut and all the places close to it. He liberated the countryside peacefully and bloodlessly, wherever possible, by teaching the faith. When this was not possible, he obtained his ends by war. He acquired castles when he could by conversion. He built castles wherever he found stone that was suitable for the construction of buildings and where he found flowing water.

Sayyidna sent Husayn Qaini, one of his best *dais* to Kuhistan and around Khurasan in 484 AH [1091–1092 AD]. Khajeh Adib Muham-

[1] Nobody can deny his enemy's reasoning.

mad ibn Taher Sajzi had earlier been the chief of *dais* in the region. Muhammad ibn Abdul Rahman followed him in that position in 412 AH [1021–1022 AD]. He had chosen Hasan ibn Ahmad as his deputy. Hasan ibn Ahmad lived during the time of Sultan Malikshah's rule. Many people accepted the teachings of Husayn Qaini and rejoiced in their faith. Thereafter, Sayyidna appointed him as his deputy to rule there, while Sayyidna spent his time governing Alamut. Husayn Qaini was in Kuhistan revealing *dawa,* liberating the surrounding areas and districts, and acquiring fortresses.

Amir Turan-Tash, who was given the Alamut area by Sultan Malikshah,[1] attacked Alamut repeatedly and looted there. He killed everyone who accepted and obeyed Sayyidna's preaching. The inhabitants of the castle were very worried and distressed because Alamut had not yet been stockpiled with supplies and food. They decided to entrust the fortress to some brave and intrepid men and quietly leave and scatter themselves in the area. But Sayyidna told them that he was informed from the court of Imam al-Mustansir Billah that the comrades[2] should not leave there, and that fortune and felicity would favor them. Sayyidna created a situation by duplicity and hiding the truth so his people would acquiesce in the pains and stand their ground firmly at Alamut.[3] They then called Alamut *Baladat-al-Iqbal*[4] due to this saying: "The misery of darkness inherits the pleasure of fortune."

Sultan Malikshah granted Kuhistan to a person in his service named Ghizil Sarigh. His first task was to defeat the Nizaris. Sultan Malikshah sent troops to Khurasan to assist and support Ghizil Sarigh as soon as the narrative of Sayyidna's teaching was revealed and his reputation was spread around. There was no shelter for the

---

1 Turan-Tash was the governor of the Seljuk fief that included the Rudbar district.

2 In this book, the people who accepted the *dawa* teachings of Hasan-i-Sabah and served in his court were called *Rafiqan*, which means "comrades."

3 In view of the outcome, one wonders if "duplicity and hiding the truth" is editorially accurate.

4 Arabic phrase meaning "the city of luck."

castle inhabitants except the town of Hesar Darreh, which was connected to Sistan.[1] Ghizil Sarigh surrounded the area and started to fight there.

In the early days of 485 AH [1092 AD], Sultan Malikshah chose his emir Arslan-Tash to be the commander of the army sent to fight against Alamut and overthrow Sayyidna and his followers. In Jumada 1 [June-July] of the same year, the emir had assembled his troops to surround Alamut. At that time, there were not more than seventy men among the comrades beside Sayyidna. And they had a trifling amount of supplies, subsisting on the bare minimum amount of food required to prevent them from losing their lives. Yet they fought bravely and killed as many of their enemies as they could.

Bu-Ali Dihdar, was the governor of the nearby rural districts Zavareh and Ardestan. He was chosen as *dai* by Sayyidna and lived in Qazvin. Numerous people from Qazvin responded to his teachings. Also, many people in Taleqan, Kouhbar, and the province of Rayy, who accepted the message of Sayyidna and obeyed him were connected with Bu-Ali. Sayyidna asked Bu-Ali for help during the siege. So Bu-Ali sent three hundred troops with weapons of warfare and food from Kouhbar, Taleqan, Qazvin, and Rayy provinces. They arrived at Alamut with help for the castle inhabitants. Some people of the Rudbar also assisted them from outside the castle. They attacked the army of Arslan-Tash in a night raid at the end of Shaban [February]. They killed a group of his soldiers; others were demoralized and retreated. The Nizaris found many bows and arrows, cereals, furniture, foods, and drinks. Their own supplies in the castle had become so scarce by this time.

[The Assassination of Nizam al-Mulk]

Sultan Malikshah thought about what happened and consulted with anyone he could about planning and strategizing for another cam-

---

[1] In southeastern Persia.

paign against Alamut. Nizam al-Mulk Hasan ibn Ali ibn Isaac al-Tusi (may Allah be merciful to him), was the prime minister of Malik-shah. He was an intellectual and a farsighted advisor. He understood the danger of Sayyidna and his followers and the signs of sedition, disturbance, and destruction from their status as an independent community.

He firmly and resolutely decided to end these threats. He did not withhold any effort in equipping and supplying an army for the repression and conquering of the Ismailis. But due to predestination, his plan did not work. Sayyidna tapped a strategy of malice and mischief to catch such a unique prey as Nizam al-Mulk in the perdition trap. He devised a species of trick and deception with his devotees. He said, "Which man amongst you will rid this country of the evil Nizam al-Mulk?"

A comrade named Bu-Tahir Aranni, put his hand on his chest in the sign of consenting. While he was searching for the bliss of doomsday,[1] he came from around Mount Damavand and traveled along the road to Sahneh[2] while assuming the disguise of Sufi. He approached the litter of Nizam al-Mulk as he traveled from the Sultan's palace toward Baghdad. It was the night of Friday, Ramadan the twelfth, 485 AH [October 22, 1092 AD]. Bu-Tahir plunged his knife into the flesh of Nizam-al-Mulk, who was martyred by that attack. Nizam al-Mulk was the first person to be killed by the devotees of Alamut. Sayyidna deserves every calamity that happened to him. He said: "Killing this devil is the first step to reaching bliss." Nizam-al-Mulk had lived more that eighty years, and Sayyid Ajal (Aziz ibn Hab-Allah Alawi) wrote four couplets lamenting the death of Nizam al-Mulk and criticizing his killers:

---

1 This sentence alludes to the idea that the *fidai* or assassin would be able to enter Paradise through the slaying of the enemies of the community.

2 In southwest Persia, on the route between Mt. Damavand (near Alamut) and Baghdad.

Do not be surprised by the killing Nizam al-Mulk, that a blond
manly guy will become black.[1]
Surprisingly, they allowed his killing, hoping the king would be
obedient.
That was a big mistake, they did not know the rule that the
sword will corrode when it is unsheathed.
It will take a thousand years to birth another wise man like
Nizam al-Mulk among competent people.

[The Tale of the Three Schoolfellows and Hasan at the Seljuk Court]

The hostility and fear between Hasan-i-Sabah and Nizam al-Mulk originated from their childhood. Sayyidna, Hakim Omar Khayyam, and Nizam al-Mulk were in the same school in Nishapur. As a childhood tradition, they became faithfully intimate. They took a solemn vow in each other's blood that whichever of them should reach power and wealth, he should reinforce and strengthen the other two by sharing the opportunity of his high position.

As reported in the historical writings of the Seljuk dynasty, Nizam al-Mulk was the first to gain a high position in the ministry. Omar Khayyam went to him and reminded him of their childhood covenant. Nizam al-Mulk remembered his duty from the past and said: "The governorship of Nishapur and its districts is for you." Omar was a great and wise man and replied: "I do not want to rule and govern people. Set an annuity for me instead." Nizam al-Mulk set ten thousand dinars and ordered his servants to pay him yearly, without fail, in Nishapur.

Sayyidna also went to him from Rayy and said: "A gracious man is one who can be faithful to his promise and keep his covenant." Nizam al-Mulk said: "Choose the governorship of Rayy or Isfahan." Sayyidna, who was an ambitious man, was not convinced and did not

---

[1] This ancient Persian poem uses "black" to describe the shame of wrongdoing. A "blond man" (respected good man) become a "black man" (i.e. a bad person) by committing sin.

accept. He wanted to join the Sultan's court and become a part of the ministry. Nizam al-Mulk said to him: "You will then be in service of the king for a while and stay with him." Then Nizam al-Mulk avoided Sayyidna because he was informed that Hasan was seeking to take Nizam's place and rank.

After a few years, the sultan became worried about the affairs of Nizam al-Mulk and demanded that he render an accounting of the budget. Nizam al-Mulk asked the sultan to give him some time to carry out the project. At the same time, Sayyidna told one of the government officials that he could finalize the budget calculations in two weeks.[1] He worked diligently and accomplished the auditing in two weeks as he had undertaken. On the date when his report was due, he was taking his account book to Sultan Malikshah. Because the servants of Nizam al-Mulk and Sayyidna had a friendly and hearty relationship, Nizam al-Mulk had told his servant: "Before Hasan is able to show his calculation to the sultan, go to a corner with the valet of Sayyidna for some minutes and contrive to mix up the sheets of his book. I will entertain him for some minutes. Then I will emancipate you and give you a thousand dinars as a reward."

On the due date, the servant disrupted that book according to his conversation and pact with Khajeh (Nizam al-Mulk). At the time of showing the calculations to the sultan, Hasan could not deliver his accounting from the book. He just leafed through the [disordered] pages. The sultan got angry and asked him for the cause of the delay and his anxiety. Hasan said the sheets of book had become mixed up. Nizam al-Mulk gloated and said to the sultan: "I have already told you that his nature is a combination of levity and incompetence, and there is no credit in his words and speeches."

[Rais Abufasl]

Hasan was inwardly troubled and went out from the court of the Sultan. Nizam al-Mulk prepared to kill him. Sayyidna escaped. He went to Rayy and then to Isfahan. He took refuge in the house of

1 Elsewhere, forty days. See chapter six of this book.

Rais Abulfasl. Hasan resided there for a while since he was a fugitive from the agents of Nizam al-Mulk. Rais Abufasl accepted Sayyidna's teaching. The two men used to have conversations with each other during their time together. One day, as Hasan complained about the world and told the story of the sultan's prejudice and of his betrayal by the sultan's officials, he sighed and said: "Alas! Oh! If two people were united with me, I could answer the iniquity of that Turkish village man."[1]

Rais Abulfasl supposed that Hasan had become infected with melancholia due to the abundance of his prayers, nightly worship, and continuous fasting. Otherwise, how could he believe he could disturb the king's dominion, a king whom the world celebrated with praises, high reputation, and coins from Egypt to Kashgar? A king with several thousand troopers and infantry under his banner overturned by just two collaborators! Abulfasl was troubled by this idea. He told himself that since Hasan was not an intemperate braggart, he was undoubtedly suffering from a mental disease. Due to his belief in this diagnosis, he started to cure the illness without telling Hasan anything. He brought fragrant syrups, saffron, and nutritious foods during Iftar[2] for Hasan.

Sayyidna immediately understood the thoughts and intentions of Rais Abulfasl as soon as he saw the fragrant syrups and saffron foods. He left the home of Abulfasl, although the chief begged him to stay. Then, he continued on to Egypt. After some time, he returned and settled in Alamut. He commanded his devotees to kill Nizam al-Mulk. Then Sultan Malikshah was poisoned forty days after the death of Nizam al-Mulk.[3] He died on Saturday night, Shawwal 18, 485 AH

---

[1] Sultan Malikshah.

[2] An Arabic word for the sunset meal during which Muslims end the daylong Ramadan fast.

[3] Malikshah's death was not ascribed to the Nizaris. They never used poison for their assassinations, nor any weapon other than the dagger. See chapter six for more on Malikshah's death and the possibility of the involvement of the Abbasid caliph Muqtadi.

[November 27, 1092 AD]. Amir Moazi wrote a poem of eulogy for the Sultan, and here are two of the couplets:

> The old minister went to Paradise in one month, the young
> king followed him in another month
> Suddenly, the wrath of God revealed the disability of the king,
> see the wrath of the Lord God and look at the disability of
> the king.

Due to the deaths of Nizam al-Mulk and the sultan, the country was disrupted and anarchy arose. During this time, Sayyidna became strong. Anybody who was afraid of anything took refuge with him. Rais Abulfasl profited by this opportunity and went to Alamut and became one of Sayyidna's comrades. One day, Sayyidna asked him: "Hey chief! Was I sick from melancholia or was it you? Should I eat the fragrant syrups and saffron soup or should you? Now, do you understand how I kept to my word when I got two collaborators?" Rais Abulfasl fell to his feet and begged Hasan to pardon him and asked his forgiveness.

[The Battles Continue]

After the assassination of Nizam al-Mulk, the comrades knifed both of his two sons.[1] One of them, Ahmad, was crippled in Baghdad. The other, Fakhr al-Mulk, was injured in Nishapur. Afterward, commanders, ministers, generals, aristocrats, and nobles were killed by the devotees, one after another. Anyone who worked with Hasan and advocated for him was busy with these adventures.

Ghizil Sarigh and Arslan-Tash ended their sieges and were scattered when the news of the death of the Sultan was revealed to them. Therefore, their armies were dispersed, and following that, the cruel people[2] encroached against them on each side.

---

1 The sons of Nizam al-Mulk.

2 The Ismailis.

On Muharram 13, 486 AH [February 13, 1093 AD], Resamoj, Lamsalar his cousin, Kalmahdha, the king of Asin, and Abu-al-qasem went to Alamut to profess their obedience. Sayyidna cherished them and gave them gifts. On Safar 22 [March 30, 1093 AD], the devotees conquered Andajrud and killed many of their enemies. The son of Zaefarani, a lawyer and erudite scholar of Rayy, took a thousand irregular soldiers to Taleqan. A thousand comrades were sent to overthrow them. In Rabi al-awwal 5, 486 AH [November 15, 1093 AD], they arrived at the town of Taleqan, and started to fight. Finally, they defeated the army of Zaefarani's son. After a difficult battle, a group of the defeated soldiers threw themselves into the river, fearing for their lives, and drowned. Six thousand people were killed in that war and massacre.

Then, the comrades went to Qazvin's villages and took blood money of Khaldar and returned. An army had been gathered for killing comrades in Taleqan, but the devotees routed them in a single action and dispersed them. They captured King Shir Khosrow. Ali Noshtgin[1] assembled an army of swordsmen who tried to deceive and kill the comrades. The devotees lined up for battle. Their enemies were ambushed. But survivors rose from the ambush, got back into the queue of battle, and killed the devotees who were in the first lines—including Kjakeidar, Mawaih, Calhadar, Calhadha, and Kianur Hashavar. Ali Noshtgin killed the swordsman and then sat on the ruling seat in Falis.[2]

[The Liberation of Lammasar Castle]

Lammasar castle is in the Rudbar Valley near Alamut. Its inhabitants—Resamoj, Lamsalar, and their relatives—had previously followed Hasan. But they rebelled and wanted to give the castle to Ali Noshtgin. Sayyidna offered to give the castle's stocks to Resamoj and

---

[1] One of the Seljuk chiefs.

[2] Ali Noshtgin, thus, betrayed his allies. He killed them so he could take over Falis without any rival.

keep the castle for himself, but Resamoj did not accept. Then Sayyidna sent out Kia Buzurgumid, Kia Ba Jafar, Kia Bu Ali, and Kiagar Shasef to take possession of the castle. They arrived during the night of Wednesday, Dhu al-Qidah 20, 489 AH [November 9, 1096 AD] and started fighting. Resamoj and Kalkhodha came forth with their bows and arrows, but both of them were killed by Kia Buzurgumid. The Ismailis took the castle without suffering any casualties.

However, the castle was like a destroyed mountain with several dilapidated houses placed on top. There was no water, no plant life, and its weather was very warm. Sayyidna ordered the construction of a mansion there, and they built a stone irrigation raceway from the Ninehrud River, which was two and a half parsangs[1] away from the castle. This brought a water supply to the castle. They constructed several gardens, mills, and cold storage areas throughout the castle, and extended the gardens all around the castle as well. The weather became nice and pleasant from all the water and foliage. Because of their efforts, the fortress of Lammasar became stable and solid. No one knew of any castle more beautiful than that in all the universe. Now the people of the Lammasar area, who had not obeyed Hasan, obeyed him. Sayyidna conquered all the surrounding villages and gave that castle to Kia Buzurgumid, who remained there for twenty years until Hasan summoned him.

[The War Between the Sons of Sultan Malikshah: Barkiyaruq and Muhammad]

When Sultan Malikshah died, his two sons Barkiyaruq and Muhammad [Tapar] disputed with each other for the rule of the kingdom. There were a series of mutinies and much concern among the people. Rais Moayed al-Din Muzaffar ibn Ahmad ibn Qasem, with the title of Abi al-Reza, who was also famous as al-Mustoufi from Isfahan, was the ruler and revenue officer of Isfahan in the time of Sultan Malikshah's government. He had secretly accepted the religion of

1 A Persian parasang is about 5,400 meters (5,905 yards or 3.35 miles).

the Nizaris through the proselytizing of Abd al-Malik ibn Attash. When his troopers learned of his beliefs, he traveled from Isfahan to Damghan due to the invectives and obloquy of the people. He bought estates and furniture in Qum, Mazandaran, Saveh, and Khurasan, and settled there.

[Rais Muzaffar and the Taking of Girdkuh]

The castle of Girdkuh, which was called Gonbazan Dez at the time, was useless and destroyed. In 429 AH [1037–1038 AD], a small mansion, several pools, and houses had been built there. They were taken by Sultan Malikshah. Girdkuh was then given to a servant of the sultan who was named Khordak. He ruled over the slaves of Malikshah and the government officials, and was a man of authority. Later Amirdad Habashi ibn Altontagh, who had a high position in Sultan Barkiyaruq's government, asked the king to give him Girdkuh. Sultan Barkiyaruq ordered his secretary to write the guardianship order. But Khordak told the secretary that if he wrote the transfer deed, Khordak would decapitate him. The secretary thus delayed writing the paper until the minister angrily told him to write. Finally, he wrote the paper and hid himself due to his fear of Khordak. The next day, Khordak was killed by Barkiyaruq.

Amirdad arrived at the castle in Jumada al-Thani, 489 AH [June, 1096 AD]. He conducted a week long unsuccessful negotiation for possession of the castle with a deputy of Khordak who was the castellan. He returned angry and frustrated. He assembled an army and went back to the castle on the fifth of Rajab [July 5, 1096 AD]. When the castellan had been apprised of the death of his master, he compromised with Amirdad because the castle lacked any means to resist. Finally, he abdicated in the middle of Shaban [August, 1096 AD]. Amirdad put the castle in the custody of his deputy there,[1] and went on to Damghan. He sent a qualified engineer to the castle who supervised the construction of a new foundation and a new building.

---

[1] Rais Muzaffar.

Rais Moayed al-Din Muzaffar was a high ranking noble and aristocrat. He had great riches and abilities and supported a lot of senior Seljuk officials, especially Amirdad, who held Damghan and bought most of its lands. But the Seljuk ministers and governors were unkind to him and coveted his riches. There were none who spoke well of him in the court of the Sultan. Amirdad had grown up under the protection of Rais Muzaffar who accepted him as his child. Rais Muzaffar helped Amirdad [with his construction efforts] and managed and brought in servants for the castle. Amirdad ordered that Damghan's wealth and assets be spent on the expenses of building the mansions of Girdkuh and paying the rations of the servants.

Muzaffar served at Girdkuh as the deputy of Amirdad Habashi.[1] He transferred all his treasuries to the castle. He did not take any funds from Amirdad, but paid all the costs of the castle and building construction from his own treasuries. Amirdad was killed by Bergish[2] in 493 AH [1099–1100 AD] in Pouzhgan.[3] In the same year, Rais Muzaffar dug a well to a depth of three hundred *gaz*[4] through the rock in Fasil Girdkuh. But he gave up when he had not reached water. A few years after his death, a spring sprung up in that well due to a massive earthquake.

Apart from the estates and gifts which Rais Muzaffar had sent to Alamut, he spent thirty-six thousand dinars on the Nizari mission: including sending twelve thousand dinars in cash to Alamut, spend-

---

1 We might ask why this wealthy aristocrat would act as "the deputy" of Amirdad. The criteria here is not his social, financial, or political background. His strong beliefs play a more important role. Rais Muzaffar and Amirdad were both Nizaris. Rais Muzaffar, as a patron and supporter, undertook Amirdad's succession in Girdkuh castle. Both men chose to sacrifice their great political positions to be able to promote their beliefs. This point will be observable in the following pages, especially in the conversation recorded at a feast between Rais Muzaffar and one of Sultan Sanjar's ministers.

2 A commander of the Seljuk army.

3 Currently named Torbat-e Jam.

4 A *gaz* is 104 centimeters (41 inches). The well was thus 1,025 feet deep.

ing twelve thousand dinars on a state guest house,[1] and twelve thousand dinars to dig two wells. When the lord of castle[2] was killed, Rais Muzaffar handed the castle to the Nizaris. He stayed on as the leader of Girdkuh on behalf of Sayyidna for forty years. With the help and support of the high-ranking and valuable Muzaffar, Hasan-i-Sabah became even more prosperous and strong.

Sultan Sanjar[3] had a meeting with Rais Muzaffar on his way from Khurasan to Iraq. Muzaffar gave donations to the sultan. Sultan Sanjar was in a hurry and did not inspect the castle. On his return journey to Khurasan, Sanjar reached Damghan. Rais Muzaffar arranged a reception feast at the suggestion of Hasan. He offered many gifts and awards to the sultan and all his nobles, emirs, and ministers. Rais Muzaffar was brought to the sultan, being carried in a litter due to his bodily weakness caused by aging. The sultan honored him and increased his rank higher than all the nobles of his entourage. A minister scornfully addressed Rais Muzaffar and said: "Do you not regret obeying a misbeliever in your old age and giving the property of the Amirdad to him?" Muzaffar replied quickly: "No, because I found him right. I have never craved wealth or status, neither in the past nor at present, and do not need it now. See how I am called with exalted titles and great honors in letters from the court of the sultan. And they [the Nizaris] address me so simply without any formalities. If the reason for my obedience was securing money or status, I would certainly have never have left the court of the sultan."

A man who was the Rais' secretary put letters in front of the minister. The minister observed that the letters from the sultan's court were full of the titles of respect. While the letters and papers from Alamut were short and brief, such as: "Rais Muzaffar, may the Lord increase his virtues, and may he do this or that." The minister was surprised and said: "Bravo, commander and I am obedient! And what could I say except that?" The government officials asked the sultan to get back the money and property of Amirdad. Rais Muzaffar said: "I

---

[1] Girdkuh castle.

[2] Amirdad Habashi.

[3] The ruler of Khurasan and the half-brother of Sultan Barkiyaruq.

and the inhabitants of the castle are the servants of the sultan. We have been living on his benevolence and kindness, and we have grown under his kind protection." At the same time, the sultan shouted at the officials and rewarded Rais Muzaffar with great honor and kindness. Rais Muzaffar died at the beginning of Shawwal, 498 AH [1105 AD], having lived for 101 years and five months. His son, Sharaf al-Din, the secretary of the court of the Sultan, was appointed as surrogate and keeper of Girdkuh.

[Isfahan and the Castle of Shahdiz]

Sultan Barkiyaruq was a lover and a believer of the Nizaris.[1] He did not deny their religion. One of the comrades, who was named Fakharavar Asadabadi, was in the service of Barkiyaruq. He had spoken to people and invited them to the faith. The minister ordered that he be killed without the permission of the sultan. Sayyidna sent out a servant to take out that evil minister in Isfahan. This same year, the Ismailis became famous in Baladeh, Isfahan. The reason was that one day a woman saw some cassocks and footwear in the house of an Ismaili man. She told the people. So a crowd in Isfahan broke in the door and looted the house.[2]

---

1 As with much else in this history, there is some ambiguity here. According to Rashid al-Din in his *History of the Seljuk Turks* (another portion of the *Jami al-Tavarikh* [ed. C. Edmund Bosworth]), Barkiyaruq (r. 1094–1105) was a Shiite (see note 62, p. 171). However, he had also survived an attempt on his life by "the heretics." Edmund G. Browne, in *A Literary History of Persia*, vol. 2, tells us that Barkiyaruq "was accused of being in sympathy with them [the Assassins], or at least allowing them a large measure of toleration in return for their support or benevolent neutrality," and that he was taunted by enemy forces as "*Ya Batiniyya* [i.e., Ismaili]." (p. 312) Sultan Barkiyaruq was, however, responsible for a massacre of the Assassins in 1101. See chapter twelve.

2 The rest of this story is told by Nashmud Din Rawandi and discussed in *The Literary History of Persia* by E. G. Browne, vol. 2, pp. 314–315. It is also told by Rashid al-Din in *The History of the Seljuk Turks* (ed. Bosworth), pp. 74–75. A blind beggar claiming to be a Nizari was said to have lured strangers to their deaths in a house in Isfahan that served as the Assassin meeting place. When

The castle of Shahdiz, which had been built by Sultan Malikshah near Isfahan, was occupied by Ahmad ibn Abdul Malik Attash. Sultan Muhammad brought him to the base of the castle with an oath and killed him. The story goes as follows: Ahmad had a close friendship with the castellan of Shahdiz. When the castellan moved, Ahmad was appointed to replace him. He ruled over the residents there. He was also in charge of all the treasures troves, slaves, and the servants who remained there due to the seraglio tradition of the sultan.[1] He killed some of them. In Isfahan, the Batinis[2] appointed Ahmad as their chief *dai*. By the assistance of Ahmad, they placed taxes on estates and the treasures of the people. The sultan and Seljuk officials were anxious to eradicate this evil.

During the period of civil war between Sultan Barkiyaruq and Sultan Muhammad, Ahmad supplied the castle and made it habitable with stores of food, treasures, instruments, weapons, and furniture. He also rebuilt the fortress and the surrounding areas. When Muhammad [Tapar] was declared the sole Seljuk sultan,[3] and nobody else remained as his enemy, he decided to attack Shahdiz.

Life became hard for the castle inhabitants. They transmitted messages out of the fortress saying: "What will the Imams say about the case of a tribe who believe in the unity of Almighty God, confess to His mission, the prophecy of Muhammad, the commandments of the heavenly Quran, and recognize it as right and true. But the King of Time should allow reconciliation to the tribe who has dissented

---

the townspeople initially discovered the crime, they broke into the house and found some four to five hundred people in the cellar, most dead, some having been tortured, some crucified, a very few still being alive. The townspeople burned the owners of the house in the town square, and rioting followed against the Ismailis throughout the city. This story sounds highly improbable for any number of reasons!

[1] The seraglio was the concealed women's quarters. When the sultan traveled, most of his wives and concubines would remain at one or another of his many castles. The servants who remained were there to serve and protect the women and children.

[2] Literally means "inward," another name for the Nizari Ismailis.

[3] Upon the death of his half-brother and rival, Sultan Barkiyaruq, in 1105.

about the identity of the correct Imam [i.e., the sole Ismaili Imam] of the time, accept their obedience, and protect them from incidents and disasters." The Imams [i.e., wise men][1] who were present supported extending the permission and protection for these people. But Abul-Hasan Ali ibn Abdul Rahman al-Samenjani, who was an elder of the Shafii shaykhs, said: "Accepting their credo is not permissible. The Imam, in whom they have trusted, has forbidden what is lawful according to canon; and that is proscribing the religious laws. Otherwise, they will come to disputing and arguing."[2]

The sultan and the Imams agreed that Ghazi Abu-al-Ala Saed ibn Yahya Hanafi should go to the castle and have a full discussion with the castle inhabitants. But this beginning did not lead to a favorable outcome. Because the real purpose was to delay and stall. The sultan was seeking to increase the pressure of the siege. He knew that a battle for the castle would not be a beneficial strategy.[3] Instead, he turned over to them the fortress of Khalinjan.[4] He then put a pigeon on his arm and put his hand on the wall of the castle. He swore to God, that he would keep his vows as long as he would live. The castle inhabitants went to the base of the castle and swore allegiance to the sultan.

The sultan ordered them to go to Alamut to Sayyidna with news that they [the sultan's army] had destroyed the fortress. Then, the subaltern of the sultan set Ahmad ibn Attash on a camel with disrespect and disgrace, walked him around the city, and eventually cut off his skin and stuffed him with straw. But he remained silent and did not cry out in pain. They also killed his son and sent both their heads to

---

1 Note several different usages of the word "Imam."

2 This theological dispute is discussed in more detail in chapter twelve.

3 Sultan Muhammad did not want to battle and kill people in the castle. Maybe because he had invested so much money in equipment, manpower, and time. Instead, he offered a compromise and swore to honor it. He gave safe passage to the inhabitants of the castle.

4 This castle is located east of the Zayandeh Rood River in the Lanjan district. Its basic building belonged to the Sasanian period. Some parts of the castle were later added by the Seljuks during their occupation.

Baghdad. His wife threw herself down from the top of the castle. The period of Ibn Attash inhabiting the castle was about twelve years.

[After Shahdiz]

Sultan Muhammad crucified his minister (wazir), who was named Saad al-Molk Abu al-Mahasen. This was due to accusations of heresy and friendship with the infidels[1] that had been made against him in Isfahan. He appointed Ahmed ibn Nizam al-Mulk to replace the slain minister.

Other Batini castles were these: Tabas, which belonged to a descendent of Simjur;[2] Simin Kuh castle near Abhar province; Khalinjan castle, which was close to Isfahan; Ardahan castle, governed by Abu al-Fath, the nephew of Sayyidna; Nazer castle in Khuzistan; Tanburak castle, which was two parasangs away from Arrajan; Yasasi castle in the Samawe Mountains; and Masyab castle. They built another castle near Qazvin. Ildogoz[3] could not invade this castle. In Rabi al-awwal, 490 AH [February–March 1097 AD], Hasan ordered them to build the castle of Maymundiz, which was very secure and sturdy.[4] The Ismailis also built another castle named Joran-Dez near that.

[Sultan Sanjar]

In 498 AH [1104–1105 AD], the chief of Beihaq[5] was killed by Damghan devotees, and a legion of the Ismailis revolted from Tarsit. Ismailis massacred and marauded in the province of Beihaq. A group

---

1 Ismailis.

2 The Simjurids were a Turkic family that served the Samanid emirs.

3 Founder of the Atabakan dynasty of Azerbaijan.

4 However, according to several reliable modern historians, Maymundiz was built in 1126 by Buzurgumid. See Daftary, *The Ismailis*, p. 372; Hodgson, *The Order of Assassins*, p. 102; and Wiley, *Eagle's Nest*, p. 35.

5 Beihaq is the old name of modern Sabzevar in Khurasan province.

of them seized Khar in Rayy. They became brigands on the roads and killed people.

In order to make peace offering and seek reconciliation, Sayyidna sent messengers several times to Sultan Sanjar. A group of elders praised Sayyidna in the presence of the Sultan. The elders[1] colluded and collaborated with a specific servant. One night, a dagger was planted in the ground close to the bedstead of Sanjar as he lay in a drunken sleep. When he woke up and saw the dagger, he was disturbed and anguished. Since he could not accuse anyone, he ordered that the incident be concealed from all.

Later Sayyidna sent him a message: "That dagger could have been thrust into your soft heart that night, if I had not affection and trust for you." The sultan became fearful and anxious and was willing to make peace with him. The sultan offered peace on three conditions: first, the Ismailis should not build a new castle; second, they should not buy and retain weapons and equipment; third, they should not invite the people to their religion. But the court lawyers did not approve of the conciliation. They accused Sultan Sanjar of collaboration with the Ismailis.

Yet the Ismailis thrived in their works and succeeded and increased in their proselytizing efforts due to the kindness and leniency of Sultan Sanjar in his time. Sanjar ordered that they be paid about three thousand or four thousand dinars as a pension from the tribute of the region of Qum, which he assigned to them and where they ruled. He also allowed them to collect a tax from the travelers and caravans along the hillside of the Girdkuh fortress as a fee for their protection. From the charters and orders which were written by Sultan Sanjar, there were several whose contents demonstrate affability, kindness, and soothing language. Those were kept in their formal archives,[2] and these letters determined and confirmed the benevolence of Sultan Sanjar.

---

1 The elders who were the comrades of Hasan-i-Sabah.

2 The library at Alamut.

[Hasan at Alamut]

During this time, an Alid man, who was named Zaid Hasani, was soliciting people secretly and confidentially, and saying to them: "I am the Imam who is entrusted to you." He sought the overthrow, eradication, and killing of Sayyidna and his closest comrades. As a result, he initially arranged to kill Husayn Qaini at the hands of Ahmad of Dunbavand. The people imputed the bloodshed to Ustad Husain, the son of Sayyidna, and to Ahmad of Dunbavand. Sayyidna commanded the killing of both. After a time, he learned the truth of the situation. He killed the Alid Zaid Hasani and his son.

Sayyida had another son who was named Muhammad. He was accused of drinking wine. Sayyida ordered that he be killed as well. The purpose of murdering his two sons was to demonstrate that establishing a dynasty was not his goal. He did not preach the teachings of the faith on their behalf and never intended that.

Another confirmation of his sincerity is that during the time of a siege,[1] he sent his wife and his daughters to Girdkuh to Rais Muzaffar. He wrote him: "They must work the spindle due to my engagement in preaching. Give them what they need as wages therefore." This was because he did not want to have any women in the castle during a period of war, especially if they held a prominent position. So thereafter they did not have women with them during sieges.

The basis of Sayyidna's manner and of his honor was rectitude, mysticism, piety, the promotion of virtue, and the prevention of vice. No one in the realm during the period of his rule drank wine openly nor played music. One person who played the flute in the fortress was sent down from Alamut and never readmitted.

[More Campaigns Against Alamut]

The strength of the Ismailis was continually on the increase. Ali Noshtgin went to the court of Sultan Muhammad [Tapar] and made a petition, saying: "If you do not prepare to eradicate them, just as

[1] The siege of Alamut by Muhammad Tapar's army lasted eight years.

soon will you loss the power of controlling the issues." Because of these words, Sultan Muhammad sent his armies under the command of Ahmad ibn Nizam al-Mulk that he might avenge the murder of his father. Sultan Muhammad dwelled at Golpayegan[1] with his government officials. He was waiting for news of victory. Ahmad laid siege to Alamut from the early spring until the fall, burning and destroying their grain. But it did not work. Finally, they departed from Rudbar in winter due to the extreme rain and snow. When Ahmad arrived in Baghdad, the devotees knifed him in a mosque. The year 487 AH [1094–1095 AD] saw the death of the Abbasid caliph Muqtadi, and the beginning of al-Mustazhir's caliphate.

In the castle of Alamut was a great famine and the people lived on grass. That is the reason the women and children were sent to secure and fertile places. Sayyidna had already sent his wife and daughters to Girdkuh. Anyone who had argued or threatened him would have been killed by the devotees. It was said that those who had bad feelings toward him would be destroyed by destiny.

In Jumada al-awwal, 500 AH [January–February 1107 AD], Sultan Muhammad sent Qaren ibn Shahriar, the governor of Tabarestan, who had assembled an impressive force from Gil and Daylam, to reinforce the armies and overthrow the Nizaris. He was going with Ali Noshtghin and Amir [. . .] The full army of twelve thousand men arrived in Rudbar. Then they regularized and organized the troops into formations. In the forenoon the comrades began fighting. The sun blazed against the eyes of their enemies below, blinding them with heat and discomfort. Suddenly clouds emerged in the sky [over the castle] and blocked the heat of the sun. Although the battlefield remained melting hot, the wind blew on the comrades higher above on the rock of Alamut.

Sultan Muhammad's army incinerated a field of grain, and its smoke rose toward the comrades. But the wind blew the smoke back on the army when it intensified. The saying "Everyone who digs a pit for his brother, will finally fall into it himself"[2] was appointed for

---

[1] The city is located in Isfahan province.

[2] *Hadith* of the Prophet Muhammad.

them. The assembled troops fell into the disaster they had hoped to cause their enemies. The lawyer Muhammed Haskani shot an arrow toward the commander of Sultan Muhammad´s army and killed him. The rest of the army acknowledged defeat and scampered away from the Rudbar.

The army of the comrades went to Taleqan, toward Falis castle which was governed by Ali Noshtgin. Ali Noshtgin was afraid of Sultan Muhammad (because of his military loss). The comrades encompassed and arrested Ali Noshtgin. After a while, they brought him to the base of the castle and put him to death.

When the sultan heard about failure of his corps, he called all the government officials and commanders, and said: "There is not any work more important than to overthrow this group. I will spend all the army and treasure for this issue. I have no wish except fighting and defeating them." All the knowledgeable officials were silent, knowing that they would not profit from disputing.

Anushtagin Shirgir, who was a fearless and brave man, said: "This work can be done under my command and authority." So, the Sultan made him the commander of the army, handed over all treasures and stores to the army, and sent endless amounts of food and grain for them to Alamut. Shirgir arrived at the gate of the city of Qazvin in the beginning of Muharram, 511 AH [May, 1117 AD]. Many scattered armies from various places were gathered together there. They raided Lammasar but were not successful. Then they returned to the gate of Qazvin and reorganized the army and rearranged themselves. In Safar, 511 [June–July, 1117 AD], Shirgir launched nightly raids against Lammasar with help from the armies of Gilan, Daylam, and a group of allies. These included his son named Omar, Amir Ellfast, Ahmad Yal Maraqi, Barsaagh, Javali Saghawo, Qaracheg Saqi, Aram the son of Toqyabak, Esfandiar ibn Baqra, and Ayas. All of these warriors were the special companions of Sultan Muhammad.

They attacked Alamut on Rabi al-awwal 11 [July 20, 1117 AD] and encompassed it, set up a catapult to attack the castle, and were fighting ferociously against the Assassins. They killed a total of sixty of the devotees. They also killed the mother of Mardavij. She was seventy years old and they enjoyed killing her. From there, they went to the base of Bireh castle. Ahmad Yal deceived the castellan, who was named Amir Isaac, by deceitful and unfounded words, proclaiming there was a friendship between them. Ahmad said to Isaac: "We will arrange [a grant of] property for you from the court of the sultan so you can use the revenue. Also, I will do other valuable services for you." Isaac was misled by Ahmad's words and handed over the fortress to him. Then, all the commanders continued to lie and make promises to Isaac. When they arrived at the court of the sultan, he confirmed their oaths. The sultan said to Isaac: "Do not worry about safety and property, these are certified for you. I will grant you several parts of property." But he secretly called Ilqafshat and told him to send Isaac to Qazvin. So they took him there and betrayed their oaths, and took him to the base of Bireh castle and killed him.

[Religious Discussions in the Midst of the Battle of Alamut]

The sultan sent a religious scholar, named Abu al-Abbas Arjani, to have a discussion with the Ismailis. He said to them: "There are many people in the world who are of the Ismaili faith. But they do not kill even one Muslim. Numerous people have had your faith, but they do not do what you are doing."

Sayyidna answered: "People can be saved by the Book of God and the Tradition of His Messenger. The idea and belief of our enemies is that people know God only by reason and intellect. They say the religious man, the believer, will never go to Hell. Now, I speak about the Holy Book and the Tradition of Muhammad, while they speak various words about intellect, thought, opinion, analogy, and jurisprudence."

The religious scholar asked: "Is the Quran created or not?"

Sayyidna replied: "Almighty God said in his Holy Quran: 'And if any one of the polytheists seeks your protection, then grant him protection so that he may hear the words of Allah.'[1] Qadrian[2] and other

---

1 Surah At-Tawbah (9:6).

2 Qadriya is one of the oldest sects of Islam. It thrived in the second half of the first century AH (seventh–eighth century AD).

innovators in religion have said that it is created. 'Every invention results in aberrance, and aberrance results in fire.'[1] In all the world, there is no true adherent of *hadith*[2] except us. All the others are theorizers."

(In forty days, they turned three times around Lammasar with an aggregate army and appointed there some castellan.)[3]

Subsequently, a religious scholar, Abu Nasr Labib, came from the court of the sultan to speak with the *dais* and answer their questions. He said: "Why do you shout from the walls of fortresses, saying: 'You must say, "There is no god but God," otherwise the Prophet will behead you.' We all say the same thing that other Muslims have said. You deny intellect and reason while the one who has not intellect would be crazy."

Kia Buzurgumid replied:

> You should not look for [the explanation of] our beliefs from our enemies. The basis of our faith is that people must have intellect and thought. But they also must use the intellect of the Prophet Muhammad (peace be upon him and his progeny). Of course, someone who has no intellect would be an idiot. He would be an infidel if he does not hear the allocutions of the Prophet. For example, the eye is necessary to sight to observe and know the world. But it is only possible by using light. A man cannot see anything in darkness, although he has eyes for seeing. And vice versa: if a person has light but no eye [he also cannot see]. Thus, we suppose that people should be believers in a faith which God has taught by the words of the Prophet in the great

---

[1] Imam Sadiq's *hadith* about the heretics in Islam.

[2] The *hadith* is the record of the sayings of the Prophet Muhammad and the Imams.

[3] The sentence in parentheses does not belong to this part of the book, or perhaps, several lines have been deleted before this passage.

> Quran. We also must rise up for right and wrong, lawful and forbidden, until there is no one left who is an infidel.

Abu Nasr said: "People can know God by using their intellect. It would be obligatory for them to know God, even if God did not send the prophets. Now, all Muslims are infidels?"

The *dais* replied:

> Listening to the speeches of the Prophet Muhammad is an essential part of Muslim identity. If people do not need prophets for religion, how would they be faithful to Islam? If people would be faithful to Islam without the Prophet, needing only their intellects and thoughts, then who would be an infidel? Because all Jews, Zoroastrians, Christians, and the Pagans are wise and intellectual. The Prophet, peace be upon him and his progeny, said: "My nation will divide into seventy-three sects. All of them will be in the Fire except for the one which is saved." The audience asked him about that saved sect. He said: "Those who adhere to the *sunnah*[1] of the Prophet." Finally, they asked him more about the identity of the sect of the men of the *sunnah*. He replied to them: "It is the one sect that follows the journey that I and my companions are upon now."

The scholar said: "Now, we are that saved sect."

The *dais* replied: "We will identify the saved sect, if we refer to the primary rule of Islam. You will be a Muslim and prosperous, if you retell that which was told by the Prophet Muhammad (peace be upon him and his family). The infidel is the one who knows God only by using his intellect."

Sayyidna sent his statement about the result of this discussion from the castle, saying:

> This large group of people believed that it is not permissible to catechize and teach the creatures of God. But if you asked them

1 Tradition of Muhammad.

who created them, they would surely say, "Allah."[1] Not to mention that there are basics and rules about every issue which the Imams of various sects of Islam express. Their followers refer to their words, ask, and learn.

Also, in our congregation, there is an Imam who is one of the descendants of Mustafa,[2] *peace be upon him and his progeny. The followers ask him about various issues and learn from him the facts.*[3] [emphasis added]

If the religious scholars find something forbidden or not forbidden, they would quickly put out a *fatwa* to make the Muslims united against their enemies. Then they can eliminate the great sedition and cause the victory of Muhammad's religion. If we—all the congregation of Islam (God increase our population)—join together, our enemies and opponents will be but contemptible and despicable. If people oppose us, we will tolerate them as much as possible. If it was not efficacious, the opponents must be sure "who warns would be excused."[4]

We say: "There is a right way. There are people on this right way, and a man must accept and learn the right way from these people." What is right? "There is no god but God, and Muhammad is the Messenger of Allah."[5] His deputy in time, who teaches and commands this word must be accepted. If our opponents do not accept it, their belief would not be acceptable to God. At the blessed time of the Prophet Muhammad (peace be upon him), the Jews, elders, and the other infidels said those words. But they did not accept the speech of the Muslims. So

---

1 Surah Al-Zokhrof [Ornaments of Gold] (43:87).

2 Mustafa is a name and title of Muhammad. It means "chosen man."

3 This is a direct confirmation of the presence of an Imam at Alamut, after the death of Imam al-Mustansir. For more on this important subject, please see chapters eleven and nineteen.

4 This is an old statement from Muawiya Abu Sufyan, the first Umayyad caliph (r. 661–680).

5 The *Shahada* (The Second Testimony). The two phrases of this proclamation are the gate by which unbelievers may embrace Islam.

> God did not accept their faith. Our community will never give up proclaiming the slogan "There is no god but God." This "no" is a hidden paganism which has appeared among the Ummah of the Prophet Muhammad (peace be upon him).[1] "May Allah"[2] this is a confirmed commandment. "There is not forgiveness in their fate."[3]
>
> I hear our enemies threaten us many times. This community will not earn victory and have no credit if all the world will be gathered, "but Allah refuses except to perfect His light, although the disbelievers dislike it."[4]

They went on discussing and debating for several days, while the army of soldiers were insulting and cursing them from outside the castle. Sayyidna told them: "Between you and us, the curse of the righteous, the devout, and the worshipers may be put on whoever is further from the rules of Islam—whoever betrays and oppresses the Lord's creatures, tells more lies, and rebels against the righteous sultan. All say amen."

For eight years, Sultan Muhammad continued to send support for the siege [against Alamut]. The army of the Sultan Muhammad was burning the fields where the castle's inhabitants secured their cereal and besieging the fortresses. But still the comrades were fighting, suffering disaster and calamity, and enduring poverty. Daily, each of the men ate only about one hundred masses of dirham[5] of barley while he was standing on the wall. At the same time, he was obliged to not stop the battle. They spent days eating little pieces of wood and the seeds of plants. They knew their hardships as the reason for

---

[1] The meaning of this "no" is to reject the proselytizing and discussions of the Muslim religion by innovators or infidels.

[2] This is an Arabic phrase.

[3] An Arabic sentence attributed to Imam Tahawi, a religious scholar of the Hanafi school.

[4] Surah At-Tawbah [Repentance] (9:32).

[5] A unit of mass in medieval times, equivalent to 47.661 troy grains (3.088 g or 0.11 oz).

the reward against doomsday. They were comforting each other: "We endure these disasters for God, His Messenger, the Imam, and the Religion of Truth. The success of religion is near to us, since all the prophets suffered from ignorant people and their shared desire to merit the satisfaction of the omnipotent God." The castle inhabitants became stronger and more courageous in battle every day. They were nightly attacking their enemies and raiding them. Their enemies wondered and exclaimed: "Well done, by steadfast men!" when they saw their patience, stability, and courage.

Meanwhile, Sultan Muhammad was suffering from colic disease in the first days of Muharram, 511 AH [May, 1117 AD]. His armies in Lammasar were informed of that. They were arguing and disagreeing with each other. They started leaving behind their tents, weapons, pack animals, cereals, and the sheep which they had brought to the fortress as their subsistence. Before this adventure, most of the militiamen of the sultan's army were singing and ridiculing the comrades, taunting them: "Our lord has sent sheep and cereals for you. Come and take them." One of the comrades, who was named Solomon, replied to them and said: "God willing! We will do it in time when your army fails." Right at this time, Shirgir put his hand on his thigh and said: "Solomon's speech proved to be the truth and the reality."

By reasoning and induction, the comrades knew that Sultan Muhammad had died. The comrades sent some messengers towards the castles to make the announcement. Their enemies were fleeing, throwing down their weapons and [tossing] their fighting uniforms aside. The comrades killed a group of them, and drowned them in water. They continued to follow them to the town of Taleqan.

[The Coming of Peace]

After this adventure, the power of the Nizaris and Ismailis was increased. Many provinces and people obeyed them. Ismailis dominated large areas of Iraq, Azerbaijan, Khurasan, Mazandaran, Rustamdar, Saveh, Sahan, Georgia, and Guilan. They took crucial governmental positions in those regions. Finally, they were united and allied with those provinces. (At least until the time of the reign of the blessed king of the world, Huelgu Khan,[1] who destroyed Khurshah.[2] The government of the Ismailis was put to death forever.)

In Dhu al-Hijjah, 511 AH [March, 1118 AD], Sultan Sanjar sent Ebrahim Sahlawi to Alamut to make peace offerings and strengthen their friendship pact. After [the death of] Sultan Muhammad, his son Sultan Mahmud was appointed as the Seljuk sultan. The Iraqi commanders provoked him to oppose Sultan Sanjar. So Sultan Sanjar went to Iraq and fought with them and defeated the Iraqi army. After that, Sultan Sanjar was confirmed in the position of [Supreme] Seljuk Sultan. He sent his nephew Sultan Mahmud to Iraq to act as his representative and returned to Khurasan.

During Ramadan of 515 AH [November/December, 1121 AD], the Commander of the Army in Egypt, who was named al-Afdal,[3] was killed by three comrades from Aleppo. Sayyidna ordered a great celebration at Alamut and entertained the comrades for seven nights.

[The Death of Hasan]

Hasan-i-Sabah became fatally ill in Rabi al-Thani 518 AH [May–June 1124 AD]. He did not display his illness to others for some time, and worked according to his usual routine. When the illness became dangerous, he sent someone to Lammasar for Kia Buzurgumid. He appointed Kia Buzurgumid as his successor and installed him in his own position. He placed Dihdar Abu Ali Ardistani on his right, and

---

1 He was the Mongol ruler who conquered much of western Asia including all the Nizari Ismaili fortresses in 1256, ending the state founded by Hasan-i-Sabah 166 years earlier.

2 The final Alamut Imam, who was killed by the Mongols.

3 As chief minister and Commander of the Army of the Fatimid court, al-Afdal (the son and successor of Badr al-Jamali who died in 1094) was the main authority of Egypt. He had been responsible for the succession travesty after the death of Caliph al-Mustansir in 1094. Al-Afdal had bypassed Nizar, the chosen successor of al-Mustansir, in favor of his younger half-brother al-Mustali. Hasan avenged this usurpation of the Imamate.

specifically surrendered to him the affairs of teaching and administration; he placed Hasan Adam Qasrani on his left, and Kia Ba Jafar, the military commander, in front. Hasan commanded that these four men move the work forward with discretion and good policy.

He died during the night of Wednesday, 6th Rabi al-Thaani 518 AH [May 23, 1124 AD].

As has been previously mentioned: from the day Hasan entered Alamut, until thirty-four years later when he left the world, he never descended from the castle. He only came out from the house, which was his domicile, two times, both times going up to the roof. The rest of the time, he stayed in his house, fasted, prayed, read books, wrote the words of his preaching, and administered the tasks of his kingdom. He was a virtuous man.

The story of Sayyidna is over, and the success is from God.

APPENDIX THREE

Purported Letter Exchange Between Sultan Malikshah and Hasan-i-Sabah

Translated and annotated by
Aliasghar Taghipourteroujeni and James Wasserman

Note from Aliasghar Taghipourteroujeni:

Professor Nasrallah Falsafi has an interesting chapter in his book *Eight Essays.* Titled "Four Historical Letters of Three Great Men of History," it includes this letter from Sultan Malikshah Seljuki to Hasan-i-Sabah along with Hasan's reply. While this exchange of letters has been disputed by some historians as forgeries, Professor Falsafi also adds a letter [not included here] from Khajeh Nizam al-Mulk Tusi to Sultan Malikshah and the sultan's response to him. Nizam al-Mulk gave a comprehensive description of Hasan-i-Sabah and then mentioned the exchange of letters below between the sultan and Hasan. He also gave Malikshah some information on the Seljuk military campaign against Alamut.

Professor Falsafi points out that the text of the exchange of letters between Malikshah and Hasan-i-Sabah was transcribed from a handwritten collection. He states that these letters were published after checking with the book *Majles Al-Momenin* by Judge Nur Allah ibn Sharif Marashi Shoshtary, which seems to be the only reference to the two letters in the manuscript collection. The handwritten collection is part of a rare and unique archive that was assembled in 1099 AH [1687–1688 AD] in Isfahan. It contains official proclamations, writings, and letters from kings, ministers, and other historic men of Iran. The original items in this precious collection had been gathered by one of great men of the Safavid court named Haidarbeig Ayo Oqli. He was the son of Abu al Qasem Beig Ayo Oqli, the protocol chief of the Safavids at the beginning of the reign of King Safi, grandson and successor of King Abbas. Haidarbeig Ayo Oqli succeeded his father as protocol chief. Thus both father and son had access to the royal library.

This collection now belongs to Dr. Mehdi Bayani, director of National Library of Iran.

Letter from Sultan Jalaluddin Malikshah Seljuk to Hasan-i-Sabah

You, Hasan, have founded a new religion and a new nation. You deceive people and you have been a traitor to the rulers of the land. You have gathered some ignorant people, hill dwellers, and have said kind words to them. Then, they have gone on to kill people with the dagger. You blame the Abbasid caliphs, who are the caliphs of Islam and responsible for the order of the domain and the people and the system of religion and government. You must cease this aberrant behavior and be a true Muslim. Otherwise, we have ordered that many corpses will be created. We will, however, wait until you present yourself at the court or your reply to this letter has been received. Beware! Beware! Have mercy on your own life and that of your followers. Do not lead yourself or your followers to destruction. Do not be proud of the strength of your castle. Be aware that if your castle of Alamut was the castle of the fortress of heaven, we would destroy it by the grace of God.

Reply of Hasan-i-Sabah to the Letter of Sultan Malikshah Seljuk

When Chief Minister (Sadar-i-Kabir) Zia-ud-din Khaqan arrived to this place and delivered the sultan's letter, I appreciated it and placed the letter on my eyes.[1] It is my pleasure that the sultan has talked about me. Now I will write a statement of my activities and my own beliefs. I hope the sultan will listen to my thoughts and arguments.

Regarding my activities, please do not consult with courtiers around you who are my enemies, especially Nizam al-Mulk, who is

1 A Persian custom that means offering many respects to the sender.

known to be hostile to me. Then I will completely accept whatever would be the Sultan's opinion about my words. If I disobey the sultan's judgment it will mean that I have blasphemed the religion of Islam and rebelled against the Lord and the Prophet. However, if the sultan listens to what my evil-wishing enemies say about me and my activities, I should have a full right to vindicate my thought. Because I have some perilous adversaries who always show wrong what is right and show right what is actually wrong. I personally have been harassed by these people. Maybe this is not a secret to the sultan.

Now, I will describe my life. My father was a true Muslim man of the Shafii school of thought.[1] When I was four-years-old, I went to school. I began to study in various sciences. I mastered many branches of knowledge from the age of four to my adolescence, especially the science of the Quran and the apostolic traditions. Then I discovered my interest in religion. I found many references in Shafii's books about the virtues of the descendants of Prophet (peace be upon him and his family) and their claim to the Imamate. I was so impressed that I began continually looking for the Imam of the time.

However, I was obliged to involve myself in worldly affairs by the tyranny of time. I forgot my enthusiasm. Dedicating myself towards the affairs of the world and people, I relinquished my duty to the Creator of this world. God did not accept my work and he enflamed enemies against me continually. They ejected me stressfully from my duty. Therefore, I was forced to abscond [from the court]. I moved through towns and deserts where I faced many difficulties. The sultan has been informed of the contention between me and Nizam-al-Mulk.

When the Lord God freed me from this disaster, I knew that all those calamities had been the result of my preference for the affairs of the people. I manfully dedicated myself to my religion and eschatology. I went to Baghdad from Rayy. I remained there for a while. I became acquainted with the affairs of the people, and investigated the caliphs and Imams of the Muslim religion. I found that the activities

---

1 As noted in chapters six and nine, this statement is likely an example of *taqiyya.* Hasan's father was a Twelver Shiite and the Shafii school is of the Sunnis.

of the Abbasid caliphs were far from the Islamic ideals of justice and truth. Also, I concluded that if the basis of Islam and its faith were those embodied by these caliphs and Imams, atheism would be better than such a faith.

Then, I traveled from Baghdad to Egypt where the rightful caliph, Imam al-Mustansir, lived. I investigated his affairs. I compared the caliphate and Imamate. I found his leadership was more legitimate and spiritual than that of the Abbasids. I avouched that I hated the Abbasid Caliphate completely. The Abbasid caliph knew of my conviction and appointed people to arrest me. God saved me from this disaster. I reached Egypt safely.[1] Following this incident, the Abbasid caliph sent three mules laden with gold to Badr al-Jamali who was the Commander of the Forces of Egypt to deliver "Hasan dead or alive." Since the benevolence of the rightful caliph and the enduring Imam al-Mustansir was in my favor, I was not seized.

However, the Abbasid caliph had enflamed the general Badr al-Jamali against me. Later he appointed me to convert the Frankish infidels. This information reached the ears of rightful Imam al-Mustansir. He supported me and gave a proclamation that I should guide Muslims to the right path, and inform them about Imamate of the Egyptian caliph and his legitimacy as much as I could.

If the sultan has the good fortune to obey the Quranic command to promote virtue—"Obey Allah and obey the Apostle and those in authority from among you"—then he should not deny my speeches. As if Sultan Mahmud Ghazi ibn Sebuktigin[2] raised himself to eradicate the Abbasids, so similarly should the sultan rise to save Muslims from these evildoers. Otherwise a time will come when another will do this work and reap all the benefit for it.

On the other hand, the sultan has said that I have founded a new religion and a new nation. May a curse fall upon Hasan if this be true. The religion in which I believe is the same religion that was preva-

---

[1] This sentence, in context, is confusing.

[2] Founder of the Ghaznavid empire in Afghanistan (r. 388–421 AH / 998–1030 AD). However, he was known to be a staunch defender of the Abbasid Caliphate.

lent among the Companions of Prophet, and which will remain the true faith until the Day of Judgment. At this time my religion is the religion of the Muslim: "I testify that there is no god but God, and Muhammad is the Messenger of God." I have no attachment to this world and its concerns. The work that I have done and the speeches that I have made are all offered honestly for the true faith.

It is my belief that the children of the Prophet are more qualified for the caliphate of their father than the children of Abbas. If you, Sultan Malikshah—after the many dramas that you have had in governing your territory, fighting from west to east and from the North Pole to the bounds of India to extend your empire—accept that the country be out of your sons' control and in the hands of the sons of Harun,[1] then perhaps their [Abbasid] Caliphate is justified. But I say that the children of Abbas are corrupt! I hope no land will have such leaders. However, there are some people who ignore these facts. They believe in the Abbasids and think the caliphate is their unquestionable right. But I have been aware of their action and treatment; so how can I believe that their caliphate is right?

If the sultan does not act to eradicate their evil after knowing their treatment, how would he answer and how he would have any hope for salvation on the Day of Judgment? My religion has been constant, and will always remain so. I do not deny that. My friendship and affection for the Four Righteous Caliphs and the Ten Blessed Companions[2] are in my heart and will always remain there. I have not believed a new faith. I have followed the same faith that existed before. My religion is the same religion that was followed by the Companions of the Prophet in their time and it will continue to be the true religion until the Day of Judgment.

---

1 Harun al-Rashid (r. 149–193 AH / 786–809 AD) was the fifth and most famous Abbasid caliph. He flourished during the golden age of Islam and was a contemporary of the Frankish emperor Charlemagne. Many of the stories of *The Book of the Thousand Nights and a Night* are set in his court.

2 The Ten Blessed Companions were those early Muslim stalwarts promised Paradise by the Prophet. The Four Righteous Caliphs were the first leaders after his death.

Some people say that my followers and I oppose the Abbasids. Whoever is a true Muslim and is conscious of his faith and people, should criticize those whose behavior always remains, from beginning to end, full of duplicity and treachery. Their activities are exposed to the entire world. I will conclude shortly in order that sultan stays in no shadow of doubt.

First, let us discuss the life of Abu Muslim,[1] a man who brought justice to the world and worked hard to eradicate the tyranny of Bani-Marwan and his family. But the Abbasids used treason against him and against the Prophet's good family. You know that the Abbasids gathered several thousand descendants of the Prophet and put them to martyrdom. They habitually indulged in wine-drinking, fornication, and other wanton evil acts. It was said that Harun al-Rashid, the most virtuous and educated among them, had two sisters. One of them was always present in his wine ceremony. He had not forbidden his companions to join in the debauchery until Jafar Yahya, one of the permanent attendees of Harun´s parties, perpetrated corruption with her. Harun's sister gave Jafar a son. The boy was hidden from Harun until the year Harun went on the *Hajj* and saw his sister's son there. Then he killed Jafar. Harun's younger sister, who was named Mohseneh, was very beautiful. Harun approached her and fornicated with her. A famous jest tells that after the death of Harun, his son Amin fornicated with his aunt Mohseneh. Amin had thought she was virgin, but she was not. Amin asked her: "O, aunt, you were not a virgin?" Mohseneh replied: "Your father had sex with all women without any exception!"

Secondly, the Abbasids ordered torture against a great and respected man, namely Abu Hanifa,[2] who is considered a pillar of

---

[1] Abu Muslim defeated Bani-Marwan, the last of the Umayyad dynasty, and installed the Abbasid dynasty in the person of Abu al-Abbas in 132 AH / 750 AD in Baghdad. He was executed because his popularity was seen as a threat to the new rulers, especially after they betrayed their Shiite base. See chapter three.

[2] Abu Hanifa (80–150 AH / 699–922 AD) was one of the founders of the major schools of Sunni Islamic jurisprudence. The four schools are mentioned briefly in chapter six.

Islam. They also killed Mansur al-Hallaj.[1] If I should start to count their despicable actions, even a lifetime would not be enough. These were not the Rashidun caliphs[2] and the pillars of Islam, the pivot of the Islamic state and nation and religion. If I, or anybody else, blames them, would not that disobedience be justified?

Some people have slandered me by saying that I have been inciting ignorant people to kill and raid others. It is obvious to any discreet person that nothing is more precious than life. Therefore, it is not logical that people would imperil their own life at the bidding of a poor man such as myself. Some employees and administrators of the government have deviated from the right way, which was followed in the past by the Muslims in Khurasan and around it. Some of these Abbasids have encroached upon Muslim women, the wives of pious and religious people. They have killed women in the presence of their husbands. When a complaint is submitted to government officials, it is usually turned down and the plaintiff carries the entire blame. Nizam al-Mulk, the chief administrator of the government, killed Khawja Abu Nasr Kunduri[3] under the pretext of his having embezzled government funds. But Khawja Abu Nasr Kunduri was a worthy man. No king in any country in all of history had such a qualified man as an administrator.

Today, Nizam al-Mulk collaborates with cruel people. Khawja Abu Nasr Kunduri collected ten dirhams and deposited them in the treasury. But Nizam al-Mulk collects fifty dirhams, of which not even half a dirham is spent on the sultan's behalf. Then he gives an insignificant amount to his collaborators, and spends the rest on his own sons, daughters, and sons-in-law. It is a fact which is clear to everybody that he wastes governmental funds by building worthless buildings of brick and clay throughout the kingdom. Where were the sons and daughters of Khawja Abu Nasr? When did he spend one dinar

---

1 Mansur al-Hallaj (244–309 AH / 858–922 AD), the Sufi martyr killed by the Abbasids is discussed in chapter nineteen.

2 The first four caliphs after the death of the Prophet, the Rightly Guided Ones.

3 The famous minister of Toghril Beg Seljuk. He was killed by a conspiracy of Nizam al-Mulk and under the command of Alp Arslan in Dhu al-Hijah, 456 AH / 1064 AD.

for clay and brick? People are in a state of misfortune and they have no hope of liberation. It is entirely understandable then that some people would devote themselves and risk their lives to assassinate the forces of evil; and it is not unlikely that if they are themselves killed in this process, they will be excused.

When there is not any solution, the keen sharp blade comes to the aid of mankind.[1] What profit will Hasan-i-Sabah gain by these adventures, and what kind of advantage does he seek in deceiving anyone? Why should he incite anyone in this respect? Every event happens at a specific moment and manner as fated by Heavens.

As far as your warning that I should leave my activities, otherwise you will punish me. God forbid. Save us! I, Hasan, could never be guilty of any act which would be opposed to the sultan's opinion. However, there is a group of people at the sultan's court trying to misrepresent me. So I have acquired this retreat to be beyond their access. My followers are, however, willing to serve the sultan. After I finish my works against my enemies, I will present myself in the court of the sultan and serve the king like so many others in your court. I will devote myself to the best of my ability to the betterment of your worldly affairs and to the spiritual salvation of the sultan. If I did any action opposed to my promises and did not obey the orders of the sultan, then I should deserve obloquy and retribution in this world. I should be anathematized by people from far and near. They would say that I had revolted against the governor and that I had disobeyed the command of the Quran: "Obey Allah, His Messenger, and whoever is in authority from among you."

Such [behavior on my part] would strengthen the unjust and spurious stories [of my enemies] of which I would be unaware. Whatever I do about my religion and my teaching of the faith (*dawa*), they would distort the facts about me. They would undo my good name. If—despite my hostility to Nizam al-Mulk, since he still oppresses me—I would present myself at the court of the sultan as a servant to the king, keep my heart at peace and free from the fear of him—there are other factors which require my consideration. I know that the

[1] From a distich by Sadi Golestan

sultan is forced to obey the Abbasid caliphs and that he cannot disobey their orders. I also know that the sultan is aware of their enmity toward me. They tried to arrest me. But they could not, although they sent many agents and valuable gifts to secure my arrest to the Commander of the Forces of Egypt during my travels over there. Finally, the Commander decided to kill me. If I had not the loving kindness of al-Mustansir, who is the true caliph, I would have gotten into great difficulty.

The commander-in-chief sent me amongst the Frankish people on a sea voyage and commanded me that I should preach the faith amongst Frankish unbelievers. By the grace of God, I was successfully saved from this whirlpool. After tolerating several years of hardship and difficulty, I reached Iraq. The Abbasids still persisted in my pursuit. Today I have reached this position.

I keep promoting the faith, *dawa,* of the Alid caliph. I have obtained several strongholds in Tabaristan, Kuhistan, and in the mountains. I am surrounded by many comrades and friends, and followers of the Alid faith. This all means that the Abbasids fear me. They always try to turn the opinion of the sultan against me. They try to pursue me. It is possible that they would have asked the sultan to secure my arrest. During that time, it is not certain how the matter could be resolved. Whichever way the situation would be solved; it would be open to criticism. If the sultan accommodates their request, it would undoubtedly be considered a slur against his manliness. On the other hand, if he did not fulfill their request, those uninformed amongst the people will speak ill of him, saying his action is like "Walking on foot when there was horse available to ride." And "Why has not Hasan-i-Sabah surrendered himself instead?" It is probable that those two sides would squabble and it would be unclear how best the conflict could be resolved.

With reference to the statement of the sultan: "If this fortress were the one fortress of Heaven, we will level it to the ground." The inhabitants of this fortress trust to speeches of truth from the Imam of our time.[1] They believe that this fortress will be safe for a long time

[1] Imam al-Mustansir.

because of his loving kindness; its safety is dependent on the grace of God. Now, I take refuge in this place so that I may accomplish all the duties with which I am charged. I pray to God and his Messenger that the sultan and his government officials may come to the right path, that God Almighty will show them the true path, and that the degeneration and debauchery of the Abbasids may disappear from the world.

If the sultan is destined to achieve salvation in his faith, and on the day of Judgment, and in his worldly affairs, he must arise against the Abbasids. He should do such action that the Sultan of Islam Mahmud Ghazni "God's Blessings on him" did, who eradicated their evil, called Sayyid Ala-al-Mulk from Termez,[1] to entrust the caliphate to him. The sultan has to arise for this duty which may detract from their evil amongst the people of God Almighty. Otherwise another time, a righteous king will rise up and accomplish this duty and rescue Muslims from the oppression of the Abbasids.

Lastly, I pray that God may guide those who follow the right path.

---

[1] These two names present a problem. Did this letter refer to Sultan Mahmud of Ghazni (r. 998–1030)? This seems unlikely, as he was a strong ally of the Abbasids. However, he may have selected an individual named Ala-al-Mulk to be the ruler of Khurasan.

On the other hand, the Khwarazmian Shah during the time of Genghis Khan was Sultan Muhammad Ala-al-Din (r. 1200–1220). He had a fierce dispute with the Abbasid caliph an-Nasir li-Din-Allah (r. 1180–1225). Juvaini writes that around 1217–1218, Sultan Muhammad declared the Abbasids had no right to the caliphate and that the leadership of Islam belonged to the descendants of the Alid line. Furthermore, "that whoever had the power to do so was under an obligation to redress wrongs" (Juvaini, pp. 364–365). Sultan Muhammad designated Sayyid (i.e., Alid) Ala-al-Mulk of Termez to be proclaimed as caliph. As the sultan's army battled its way to Baghdad in pursuit of this goal, they encountered blizzards in the mountains which killed many soldiers and ended their campaign (Juvaini, pp. 366–367). The problem with this history—in the context of this letter—is, of course, that Hasan-i-Sabah would have died some nine decades earlier.

APPENDIX FOUR

Timeline

All dates BC (UNLESS OTHERWISE NOTED)

ca. 10,000 BC	Beginning of the Holocene Epoch and end of last Ice Age
ca. 5300	First cities in Mesopotamia
ca. 4500	Civilizations begin in Susa in Elam and Kish in Sumer
ca. 3760	Beginning of the Jewish calendar
ca. 3500	Old Kingdom in Egypt
ca. 3300	Written language (cuneiform) in Sumer
ca. 3200	Written language (hieroglyphic) in Egypt
ca. 2600	Period of the reign of King Gilgamesh of Uruk
ca. 2357	Sumerian city of Ur conquered by Persian Elam
ca. 2330	Akkadian Empire under Sargon the Great conquers Sumer
ca. 2200	Assyrian Empire begins
ca. 1800	Birth of Abraham in Ur
ca. 1792–1750	Reign of King Hammurabi of Babylon
ca. 1750	Defeat of Sumer
ca. 1479–1447	Reign of Pharaoh Thutmose III in Egypt
ca. 1250	Birth of Moses and later Exodus from Egypt
ca. 1000	Capture of Jerusalem by King David
ca. 1000	Birth of Zoroaster
ca. 957	Completion of the Temple of Solomon

ca. 705	Nineveh becomes capital of Assyria
ca. 612	Nineveh conquered by Babylon and Media
ca. 586	Capture of Jerusalem and destruction of the First Temple
ca. 580	Birth of Pythagoras
549–330	Persian Achaemenid dynasty
ca. 539	Persian conquest of Babylon by King Cyrus II
ca. 538	Cyrus allows Jews to return to Jerusalem
ca. 525	Persian conquest of Egypt under King Cambyses
ca. 515	Second Temple completed in Jerusalem
ca. 500	Birth of Buddha
ca. 334	Capture of Jerusalem by Alexander the Great
ca. 331	Alexander conquers Persia
247 BC–224 AD	Parthian/Arsacid dynasty in Persia
ca. 4 BC	Birth of Jesus

All dates AD

224–651 AD	Sasanian dynasty in Persia
380	Conversion of Himyar kingdom in Arabia to Judaism
565	Sasanian conquest of Himyar
ca. 570	Birth of Muhammad
613	Muhammad begins to receive surahs of the Quran
614	Capture of Jerusalem by Sasanian Persians
630	Muhammad conquers Mecca
632	Proclamation by Muhammad at Ghadir Khumm in support of Ali's succession
632	Death of Muhammad and beginning of Sunni/Shia split

638	Capture of Jerusalem by Caliph Omar
651	Fall of Persia to Arab Muslim armies
656	Ali becomes fourth caliph
661	Ali murdered in Iraq and establishment of Umayyad Caliphate
680	Murder of Husayn at Karbala by Umayyads, formal split of Shiites
685	Muktar proclaims Muhammad ibn al-Hanifiyya as Mahdi
749	Establishment of Abbasid Caliphate and betrayal of Shiite supporters
762	Abbasids establish Baghdad as their dynastic capital
765	Jafar al-Sadiq dies. Ismail does not succeed his father, producing the Ismaili/Shia split
813	Death of Muhammad ibn Ismail and *satr* of Syrian Ismaili *dawa*
870	Hamdan Qarmat becomes the leader of Iraqi Ismaili *dawa*
899	Hamdan Qarmat breaks with Fatimid Ismailis
909	Proclamation of Fatimid Caliphate by Ubayd Allah
922	Death of Mansur al-Hallaj
930	Qarmatis attack Mecca and seize the Black Stone
945	Shiite Buwayhids conquer Baghdad but retain Abbasid caliph al-Mustakfi as figurehead
951	Qarmatis return Black Stone
969	Fatimids take Egypt and build the city of Cairo as their capital
988	Fatimids establish al-Azhar, the world's first university
1005	Fatimid caliph al-Hakim founds *Dar al-Hikma*, or House of Wisdom, in Cairo

1009	Caliph al-Hakim destroys Church of the Holy Sepulcher in Jerusalem
1011	Sunni and Twelver Shiites condemn Ismailis as heretics
ca. 1050	Birth of Hasan-i-Sabah
1055	Sunni Seljuks take Baghdad from Shiite Buwayhids, freeing Abbasid caliph
1071	Hasan elevated to deputy *dai* of Persia by Abd al-Malik ibn Attash
1071	Seljuks defeat Byzantines at the Battle of Manzikert
1076	Hasan travels to Isfahan
1078	Hasan arrives in Egypt
1090	Hasan takes Alamut
1092	Assassination of Nizam al-Mulk
1092	Death of Malikshah
1094	Death of Fatimid caliph al-Mustansir
1094	Nizari/Mustali split
1095	Europe launches the Crusades
1099	Capture of Jerusalem by Crusaders
ca. 1100	Mission to Syria launched by Hasan-i-Sabah
1118	Sunnis of Aleppo massacre Ismailis
1121	Assassins kill the wazir and Commander of the Armies al-Afdal who had deprived Nizar of the caliphate
1124	Death of Hasan-i-Sabah (first Lord of Alamut)
1124–1138	Reign of Buzurgumid (second Lord of Alamut)
1129	Sunnis of Damascus massacre Ismailis
1130	Assassins kill the Fatimid caliph al-Amir
1131	Buri, governor of Damascus, slain in retaliation for massacre of 1129

1135	Abbasid caliph al-Mustarshid assassinated
1138	Abbasid caliph al-Rashid assassinated
1138–1162	Reign of Muhammad I (third Lord of Alamut)
1148	Second Crusade begins
1152	Count Raymond II becomes the first Crusader victim of the Assassins
1162–1166	Reign of Hasan II *ala dhikrhi al salam* (fourth Lord of Alamut)
1162	Rashid al-Din Sinan established as chief *dai* of Syria
1164	Proclamation of the *Qiyama* by Hasan II
1166–1210	Reign of Muhammad II (fifth Lord of Alamut)
1171	Saladin establishes his Ayyubid dynasty in Egypt, overthrowing two centuries of the Fatimid dynasty
1187	Capture of Jerusalem by Saladin
1192	Assassination of Conrad of Montferrat by Sinan
1193	Death of Sinan in Syria
1193	Death of Saladin
1194	The Khwarazmians end the Seljuk dynasty at the battle of Rayy
1207–1273	Life of Jalal-al-Din Rumi
1210–1221	Reign of Hasan III (sixth Lord of Alamut)
1215	Genghis Khan takes Beijing
1219	Mongol invasion of Islamic lands begins
1221–1255	Reign of Muhammad III (Aladdin) (seventh Lord of Alamut)
ca. 1226–1283	Life of Ata-Malik Juvaini, author of the *Ta-rikh-i-Jahan Gusha.*
1227	Death of Genghis Khan

1247–1318	Life of Rashid al-Din Tabib, author of *Jami al-Tawarikh*
1250	King Louis IX of France receives Assassin ambassador from Masyaf
1255–1256	Reign of Rukh ad-Din Khurshah (eighth Lord of Alamut)
1256	Destruction of Alamut and Nizari Ismailis by Huelgu's Mongols
1258	Destruction of Baghdad and Abbasid caliphate by Huelgu's Mongols
1260	Defeat of Mongols at Ain Jalut by Baybars
1291	Fall of Acre and effective end of the European Crusades

APPENDIX FIVE

Glossary of Names

Abbas: Seljuk governor in Rayy who ordered a massacre of Ismailis in retribution for the slaying of Sultan Daud. The Supreme Seljuk Sultan Sanjar sent the head of Abbas to Isfahan as a peace offering in 1146 or 1147.

al-Abbas (Abbas ibn Abdul-Muttalib): The uncle of Muhammad and progenitor of the Abbasid Caliphate. He was initially opposed to the teaching of the Prophet and served in the Meccan army sent against the early Muslims.

Abd-al-Malik: In 691, this Umayyad caliph erected a group of structures on the Temple Mount of Jerusalem. Known as the Venerable Sanctuary, it includes the Dome of the Rock and the al-Aqsa Mosque.

Abd al-Malik ibn Attash: Chief of the Ismaili *dawa* in western Persia and Iraq, he visited Rayy and met Hasan-i-Sabah in 1072. He elevated Hasan to the position of deputy *dai* and instructed him to travel to the caliph's court in Egypt.

Abd Allah b. Maymun al-Qaddah: Accused of being a heretic and a magician who corrupted the Ismaili message of the Fatimids in clandestine collusion with his father, Maymun al-Qaddah. He is also accused of instituting the secret hierarchy of degrees of initiation among the Ismailis.

Abd Allah ibn Unays: One of the first Muslims to heed the Prophet's call to assassination. He killed the chief of a hostile tribe and thereby saved the Islamic community of Medina from a powerful and dangerous enemy.

Abdan: Brother-in-law of Hamdan Qarmat, he was sent to Syria in 899 to investigate Fatimid doctrinal changes.

Abraham: (c.1800 BC) The founding patriarch of monotheism, born in the ancient city of Ur, he migrated to Israel. He is considered the father of Judaism, Christianity, and Islam.

Abu al-Abbas al-Saffah: (r. 750–754) The first Abbasid caliph, he was the half-brother of Ibrahim al-Imam. He established the first Abbasid capital in Kufa in Iraq. His armies defeated the Umayyads in Egypt.

Abu Bakr: Muhammad's father-in-law and friend, father of Aisha, and the first nobleman of Mecca to accept Islam. He was immediately accepted as Muhammad's successor or caliph (prince of the faithful) by a group of elders in Medina in 632.

Abu Hamza (the Shoemaker): An Ismail *dai* and contemporary of Hasan-i-Sabah, he had also been trained in Egypt. He established the regional center in the Zagros Mountains of southwestern Iran near Khuzistan.

Abu Hashim: Son of Muhammad ibn al-Hanifiyya, accepted as Imam by the Abbasids.

Abu l-Mahasin Ruyani: A vehement anti-Ismaili Sunni teacher who was assassinated in 1108.

Abu Muhammad: Chief *dai* of the Syrian Assassins, succeeded by Sinan.

Abu Muslim (Behzadan): A Persian Abbasid general instrumental in defeating the Umayyads, elevating the Abbasids to power, and then being executed as a troublemaker by the Abbasids.

Abu-Najam Sarraj (the Saddler): One of Hasan-i-Sabah's early Ismaili instructors in Rayy.

Abu Tahir al-Jannabi: Qarmati leader in Bahrain. He attacked Mecca in 930, massacred some thirty thousand Meccans and Muslim pilgrims, and seized the sacred Black Stone from the Kaaba. The Qarmatis held the stone until 951, when the Abbasids arranged to ransom it.

Abu Tahir (the Goldsmith): He succeeded al-Hakim al-Munajjim as the chief *dai* of the Syrian Assassins. He was captured by Tancred and forced to ransom himself. He was later executed by Alp Arslan, the governor of Aleppo.

Abufasl: Ismaili teacher of Hasan-i-Sabah while he was in Isfahan during his long journey to Egypt. Years later, Rais Abufasl would become Hasan's disciple at Alamut.

Abul Fath: Assassin leader who arranged the purchase of the fortress of Qadamus in the Jabal Bahra mountain range in 1132.

Abul-Hasan Ali: Sunni legist who convinced the *ulema* in 1107 that the Ismaili arguments of Ahmad ibn Attash were fallacious and that the Ismailis were not to be considered Muslims.

Abul-Khattab: A disciple of Jafar al-Sadiq who zealously upheld the authority of the Imam, but whose radical religious and political views caused Jafar to publicly curse him.

al-Adid: (r. 1160–1171) The fourteenth and final Fatimid caliph who died of illness at the age of twenty-three, soon after being overthrown by Saladin.

al-Afdal: Son of Badr al-Jamili, he succeeded his father as Fatimid Commander of the Armies, appointed al-Mustali as Fatimid caliph supplanting Nizar, and was killed by *fidais* sent by Hasan-i-Sabah in 1121.

Ahmad ibn Attash: The son of the head of the Persian *dawa*, Abd al-Malik ibn Attash, he succeeded his father as the *dai* of Isfahan. He seized Shahdiz for the Nizaris in 1100.

Ahmad ibn Nizam al-Mulk: He succeeded his father as the Seljuk wazir. He led a second unsuccessful Seljuk expedition against Alamut in 1107.

Ahriman: The Dark Lord, in contrast to Ahuramazda, the Zoroastrian Lord of Light.

Ahuramazda: The Wise Lord, the supreme deity of the Persian royalty.

Aisha: Daughter of Abu Bakr and said to have been Muhammad's favorite wife, she held longstanding grudges against both Fatima and Ali. When Ali became the fourth caliph, she led a revolt against him.

al-Ajami: Bahram's successor as Syrian chief *dai*, he wrote to King Baldwin II of Jerusalem with an offer to surrender Baniyas in exchange for safe haven from his Sunni persecutors. He died in exile among the Franks in 1130.

al-Akhram: (d. 1018) Fatimid *dai* who proclaimed the divinity of Caliph al-Hakim and was executed. Those who embraced his doctrine became known as the Druze.

Aladdin: (See Muhammad III)

Alexander the Great (356–323 BC): Greek general and king who conquered most of the known world of his time. He introduced Hellenism to the Near East.

Alexius Comnenus: (r. 1081–1118) In 1095, during the Council of Piacenza, he is said to have offered to join the Byzantine to the Roman Church in return for Western aid against the Muslims—thus setting the stage for the Crusades.

Alf ibn Wafa: Assassin leader who joined forces with Raymond of Antioch in an unsuccessful battle against the Zangids in 1149, during which both he and Raymond were killed.

Ali ibn Abu Talib: Muhammad's cousin and son-in-law, believed by Shiites to have been Muhammad's legitimate successor. He reigned as the fourth caliph until 661, when he was murdered in Iraq. He is viewed by Shiites as second in holiness only to the Prophet.

Ali ibn Husayn (Ali Zayin al-Abid): Great-grandson of the Prophet. While a young child, he miraculously survived the massacre at Karbala. His critical role as the sole lineal descendant of the Prophet remains significant to this day.

Ali ibn-Muhammad: Father of Hasan-i-Sabah.

Alp Arslan: (r. 1063–1072) The second Seljuk sultan, he succeeded his uncle Toghril Beg after a brief battle of succession for the throne. He was later victorious over the Byzantine Christian forces at the Battle of Manzikert in 1071.

Governor Alp Arslan: Son of Ridwan, he succeeded his father in Aleppo in 1113. Bowing to pressure from Seljuk sultan Muhammad Tapar, he sanctioned the destruction of the Aleppine Nizari community.

al-Amir: (r. 1121–1130) The tenth Fatimid caliph, under whose reign the Fatimid Caliphate grew progressively weaker and more isolated. In 1130, he was murdered by Assassins sent by Buzurgumid.

Amira Zarrab (the Coiner): A comrade, or *rafiq*, in Rayy who introduced Hasan-i-Sabah to the Sevener or Ismaili doctrines of the Fatimid Imamate.

Amirdad Habashi: High-ranking Seljuk official and Ismaili sympathizer who was given charge of Girdkuh.

Anjudan Revival: The reemergence of the Nizari Imamate in Central Persia in the latter half of the fifteenth century under the leadership of Imam Mustansir Billah II.

Anushtagin Shirgir: He launched a third Seljuk effort against Alamut in 1109, a siege which continued until 1118. With the Assassins on the verge of defeat, his assault was interrupted by news of the death of Sultan Muhammad Tapar.

Aqa Ali Shah (Aga Khan II): (r. 1881–1885) He was particularly concerned with establishing a modern school system, maintaining good relations with the British, and reaching out to Nizari communities in the upper Oxus, Burma, and East Africa.

Ardashir I: (r. 224–239/40) Founder of the Sasanian dynasty in Persia.

Aristotle: (384–322 BC) Greek philosopher and student of Plato, whose philosophy celebrated the rational faculties, and thereby stimulated the development of science and mathematics.

Sir Joseph Arnould: The British chief judge in India who declared that Aga Khan I was the legitimate descendent and heir of the Alamut Imams—thus of the Fatimid Caliphate and the Prophet Muhammad.

Arsaces: (r. ca. 250–211 BC) Founder of the Parthian dynasty in Persia.

al-Ashraf: Son and successor of the Mameluke sultan Qalawun, he swore to continue in his father's footsteps. He took Acre in 1291.

Arslan-Tash: A Seljuk amir of Sultan Malikshah who attacked Alamut in 1092.

Artabanus IV: (r. 213–224) Final king of the Parthian dynasty, defeated by Ardashir.

Artaxerxes III: (r. 359–338 BC) One of the last Achaemenid kings, he faced an invasion from Philip II of Macedonia, the father of Alexander the Great.

Ashurbanipal: Mid-seventh century BC king of Assyria and conqueror of Elam.

Astyages: (r. ca. 585–559 BC) The last king of the Median Empire, the son of King Cyaxares. He was defeated by Cyrus the Great.

Saint Augustine of Hippo: (354–430) A hugely influential early Church Father and philosopher, he had been a member of a Manichaean sect for some ten years before converting to Christianity in 386. He wrote extensively of his experience.

Aybeg: A former slave and royal consort of Shajar-al-Durr, founder and queen of the Mameluke dynasty. He acted as the first Mameluke sultan. In 1257, he was murdered by the queen, after which she was beaten to death by his slaves.

Ayyub: Father of Saladin, he was the governor of Baalbek under Zangi, and then of Damascus under Nur al-Din.

al-Aziz: (r. 975–996) Fifth Fatimid caliph during whose reign the Fatimids reached their greatest territorial extension.

Badr al-Jamali: (1015–1094) In 1074, al-Mustansir appealed for help against his rebellious troops to this Armenian general. Badr acted quickly. His troops suppressed the revolt and restored order. He also took control of Egypt.

Bahram: Syrian chief *dai* whose Nizari soldiers provided critically needed military support to Tughitigin, ruler of Damascus, against the Franks in 1125. The Assassins were given the frontier fortress of Baniyas.

Bahram I: (r. 273–276) Sasanian Persian king, son and successor of Shapur I. He imprisoned and executed the philosopher Mani, in contrast to his father's policy of religious tolerance.

Baldwin I: (r. 1100–1118) King of Jerusalem who sought to build its Western population as a safeguard against the surrounding Muslim enemies.

Baldwin II: (r. 1118–1131) King of Jerusalem during the formation of the Knights Templar. He awarded them lodging in the al-Aqsa mosque near the Dome of the Rock, the original site of the Temple of Solomon.

Baldwin III: (r. 1143–1162) King of Jerusalem and son of Melissande and Fulk. His army was defeated by Nur al-Din in 1150 when he rushed to reinforce the area after the defeat of Raymond of Antioch and his Assassin ally Alf ibn Wafa.

Baldwin IV: (r. 1174–1185) King of Jerusalem, he suffered from what was believed to be leprosy. As he became weaker, he appointed his brother-in-law Guy de Lusignan to rule the kingdom and lead the army. In 1177, his forces defeated Saladin at Mont Gisard with Templar help.

Bardesanes: (b. 154) A Christian Gnostic in Syria who taught emanationist doctrines that placed the Christ figure within a familiar pattern of cosmic spiritual hierarchies.

Barkiyaruq: (r. 1092–1105) Son and successor to the Seljuk sultan Malikshah. During his reign, the empire was plunged into chaos and civil war as he battled his half-brother, Muhammad Tapar, who succeeded him.

Baybars: (r. 1260–1277) Sultan of the Mameluke dynasty, he was born a Turkish slave who rose to become a general in the Egyptian army. A brilliant military leader, he was responsible for the defeat of the Syrian Assassins, the Mongols, and the Crusaders.

Saint Bernard of Clairvaux: (1090–1153) He was the most influential and politically powerful Catholic theologian of his time. Known as the

"Conscience of Christendom," he was of enormous help to the Templars both spiritually and materially.

Bohemond IV: (r. 1175–1233) Count of Tripoli and Prince of Antioch. He was involved in an ongoing series of hostilities with the Hospitallers, who, in 1230, were aided by the Assassins.

Bohemond V: (r. 1233–1252) Prince of Antioch. He wrote to Pope Gregory IX complaining of the alliance between the Hospitallers and Assassins. Gregory demanded that both the Templars and Hospitallers cease any dealings with them.

Brocardus: A German priest who warned King Philip VI of France in 1332 about the dangers posed by the Assassins.

Bu-Ali Dihdar: The Ismaili *dai* of Qazvin who rushed to the aid of Alamut with three hundred soldiers during the attack by Seljuk emir Arslan-Tash in 1092.

Bu Najm Sarj: Another Ismaili *dai* who assisted in Hasan-i-Sabah's conversion.

Bu-Tahir Arrani: The *fidai* who assassinated the powerful Seljuk wazir Nizam al-Mulk in 1092, and thereby saved Alamut from almost certain destruction.

Burchard of Strassburg: An envoy of Holy Roman Emperor Frederick Barbarosa, he was one of the earliest European chroniclers of the Syrian Assassins, about whom he reported in 1175.

Buri: Son of Tughitigin. He succeeded his father as governor of Damascus in 1128. When an anti-Ismaili wave arose in the city, he murdered his pro-Nizari wazir, al-Mazdaqani, and publicly exposed his severed head. He was assassinated in 1131 by two *fidais* sent from Alamut.

Burton, Sir Richard: (1821–1890) Famed traveler and writer whose editorial work and translation of *The Book of a Thousand Nights and a Night* is a remarkable testament to his understanding of Islamic culture. He successfully made the *Hajj* to Mecca (forbidden to any but Muslims) in disguise in 1853.

al-Busasiri: In 1057, this rebellious Turkish general sought Fatimid caliph al-Mustansir's alliance against the Seljuks and Abbasids. He took Baghdad in 1058. However, in 1059, he was defeated and slain by the Seljuks.

Buzurgumid: (r. 1124–38) (Second Lord of Alamut). Chief disciple of Hasan-i-Sabah who seized the strategically important castle of Lammasar in 1096 or 1102. He succeeded Hasan and confounded the expectations of his enemies by providing strong leadership.

Pope Clement V: (r. 1305–1314) Successor to Pope Benedict XI, he had been the archbishop of Bordeaux. He served as King Philip IV's accomplice in the conspiracy to destroy the Knights Templar.

Conrad of Montferrat: This powerful German marquis arrived in the Holy Land 1188 to fulfill his crusading vow. He established a legitimate claim to the throne of Jerusalem by marrying Isabel, daughter of Amalric. He was slain by Syrian Assassins in 1192.

Constantine the Great: (r. 312–337) Roman emperor who embraced Christianity and established it as the state religion. In 324, he founded Constantinople (modern Istanbul) on the site of the ancient city of Byzantium.

Cyaxares: (r. 625–585 BC) This Median king formed an alliance with the Babylonian king Nabopolassar against Assyria. In 612 BC they were victorious.

Cyrus II (the Great): (r. 559–530 BC) King of Persia and founder of the Achaemenid dynasty. In 538 BC, he defeated the Babylonians and allowed the Jews, led by Zerubbabel, to return to Jerusalem.

Darius I: (r. 522–486 BC) Achaemenid king who greatly expanded the empire, but lost the famous Battle of Marathon with Greece in 490 BC.

Darius III: (r. 336–330 BC) The last of the Achaemenid kings, he was defeated by Alexander the Great.

Sultan Daud b. Mahmud: A grandson of Muhammad Tapar and Seljuk sultan of Azerbaijan, he was slain in 1143 by Assassin *fidais* after having persecuted the sectarians.

King David: Warrior/poet king who established Jerusalem as the capital of Israel in the tenth century BC, respected equally by Muslims, Christians, and Jews.

Dihdar Abu-Ali Ardistani: Appointed by Hasan-i-Sabah to manage the teaching and administrative affairs of Alamut in conjunction with Kiya Buzurgumid.

Duqaq: He was a son of Tutush and the Seljuk governor of Damascus. His brother Ridwan governed in Aleppo.

Ea: Babylonian deity associated with creation, wisdom, magic, and incantations. Equivalent of the Sumerian Enki.

Edward I: (r. 1272–1307) King of England. He was a powerful ruler and staunch defender of the Templars. In 1271, while still a prince, his arrival in Acre contributed to Baybars' willingness to offer the Franks a ten-year truce.

Edward VII: (r. 1901–1910) King of England who befriended Aga Khan III.

Enheduana: (c. 2330 BC). The daughter of Sargon the Great, she was the Akkadian priestess of the Moon god Nanna. She authored history's first signed writings, a series of liturgical prayers.

Enki: Sumerian deity associated with creation, wisdom, magic, and incantations. Equivalent of the Babylonian Ea.

Enlil: Mesopotamina deity and head of the Sumerian pantheon.

Fakhr ad-Din al-Razi: A Sunni scholar who had begun a vigorous lecture campaign against the Nizari doctrine. Threatened (and bribed) by a *fidai* send by Muhammad II, he ceased his vilifications.

Fakhr al-Mulk: He was a son of Nizam al-Mulk and supplanted his brother Muayyid al-Mulk as wazir under Sultan Barkiyaruq.

Fath Ali Shah: Qajar ruler of Persia who bestowed the title of Aga Khan on the young Nizari Imam Hasan Ali Shah after the murder of the

Imam's father by a Twelver Shiite mob in 1817. He also gave him a grant of land and the hand of one of his daughters in marriage.

Fatima: Muhammad's sole surviving child and the wife of Ali, she was the mother of Hasan and Husayn.

Saint Francis of Assisi: (1181–1226) Famed thirteenth-century founder of the Franciscan monastic order, he attempted to negotiate a treaty with the Fatimid sultan al-Kamil during the siege of Damietta.

Frederick I Barbarosa: (r. 1155–1190) Holy Roman Emperor. He led an army during the Third Crusade, but drowned along the way in the Saleph River in Turkey.

Frederick II: (r. 1212–1250) Holy Roman Emperor. He was the controversial leader of the Sixth Crusade. In 1225, he was married to Isabel, daughter of John of Brienne and Queen Maria, thereby establishing his claim to the throne of Jerusalem.

Gabriel: Archangel said to have delivered the Quran to Muhammad.

Genghis Khan: (d. 1227) Powerful Mongol leader who began the conquest of Central Asia.

Shah Ghazi Rustam: (r. 1140–1163) When his son was murdered by Assassins in Isfahan in 1142, this Bavandid leader was turned into a bitter and powerful foe of the Nizaris.

Ghizil-Sarigh: A Seljuk emir of Sultan Malikshah, sent against Husayn Qaini in Kuhistan in 1092.

Gilgamesh: The Sumerian king who ruled in Uruk, ca. 2600 BC, and is immortalized in *The Epic of Gilgamesh.*

Girdbazu: Son and designated successor of Shah Ghazi Rustam, killed by the Assassins in 1142.

al-Hadi ibn Nizar: Son and successor of Nizar as twentieth Imam.

al-Hafiz: After the death of Fatimid caliph al-Amir, he was acknowledged as the Imam and successor, rather than the Imam's son al-Tayyib.

Pope Gregory IX: (r. 1227–1241) He ordered Frederick II to begin a crusade, excommunicating him on his premature return. He denounced the dualist Cathars as worshippers of Satan, and laid the groundwork for the Inquisition by assigning the Dominicans to pursue heresy.

Hagar: Servant of Abraham by whom he fathered Ishmael, progenitor of the Muslim peoples.

al-Hakim: (r. 996–1021) Sixth Fatimid caliph. In 1005, he founded the *Dar al-Hikma*, or House of Wisdom, as a training center for *dais*. In 1009, he ordered the destruction of the Church of the Holy Sepulcher, a contributing cause of the later Crusades.

al-Hakim al-Munajjim: Known as the "physician-astrologer," he was the Assassin leader in Syria and an ally of Ridwan in Aleppo.

Hamdan Qarmat: The leader of the Ismaili *dawa* in Iraq since 870. He refused to acknowledge Ubayd Allah and his revisionist teachings on the Imamate. In 899, he denounced the Fatimid Imam and disappeared from history.

Hammer-Purgstall, Joseph von: (1774–1856) The first popular European chronicler of the Assassins, whose history was published in German in 1818 and in English in 1835.

Hammurabi: (r. ca. 1792–1750 BC) Powerful Babylonian king and founder of the Amorite dynasty, his famous law code is credited as the origin of Western common law.

Harun al-Rashid: (r. 786–809) Abbasid caliph of near-legendary fame, immortalized in *The Thousand Nights and a Night*. He is believed to have poisoned Musa al-Kazim.

Hasan (son of Ali and Fatima): The eldest of two brothers, he abdicated his leadership to Muawiya. He was murdered by one of his wives in 669. (See Husayn.)

Hasan II *ala dhikrhi al salam*: (r. 1162–66) (Fourth Lord of Alamut) Born in 1126, he was devoted to the teachings of Hasan-i-Sabah, the occultism of earlier Ismaili philosophers, and the mysticism of the Sufis.

In 1164, he proclaimed the advent of the millennium, the Resurrection or *Qiyama*.

Hasan III: (r. 1210–21) (Sixth Lord of Alamut) The son of Muhammad II, he was also known as Jalal al-Din Hasan. He caused the Assassins to embrace Sunni orthodoxy and publicly and ceremonially cursed his forefathers for their sins.

Hasan Adam Qasrani: Appointed by Hasan-i-Sabah as part of a leadership council to manage the affairs of Alamut in conjunction with Kiya Buzurgumid.

Hasan Ali Shah (Aga Khan I): (b. 1804) After his father was killed by a Twelver Shiite mob, he was acknowledged as Aga Khan I by the Qajar ruler Fath Ali Shah and presented with his daughter as a bride. Ultimately relocating to India, he won legal recognition in the British High Court of Bombay in 1866.

Hasan-i-Sabah: (r. 1090–1124) (First Lord of Alamut) Founder and chief *dai* of the Nizari Ismailis. He built a successful state and community in an otherwise hostile environment.

Henry: (d. 1197) Count of Champagne, later King of Jerusalem. Nephew of both King Richard of England and King Philip of France, Richard arranged for him to marry Conrad of Montferrat's widow Isabel within days of Conrad's death and supplant Guy de Lusignan as King of Jerusalem. He visited the Syrian Assassins in 1194.

Henry III: (r. 1216–72) King of England, approached by Assassin envoys in 1238 for help against the Mongol invasion. He was the father of Edward I.

Heraclius: Byzantine emperor who defeated Khosrow II in 628. He negotiated the return of Egypt, Palestine, Syria, Asia Minor, and western Mesopotamia, as well as the fragment of the True Cross. He rebuilt the Church of the Holy Sepulcher.

Herodotus: (c. 484–425 BC) Greek historian, aptly named "the father of history" by the Roman orator Cicero. He wrote extensively about Persia and Mesopotamia.

Hezekiah: (r. ca. 716–687 BC) Judean king who defeated the Assyrian invasion led by King Sennacherib in 700 BC.

Pope Honorius II: (r. 1124–1130) He was represented by his legate at the Council of Troyes, which recognized the Knights Templar, where their Rule was written, and where they were awarded a distinctive dress.

Hubal: Chief deity of the Arab pagans before the coming of Islam. His image was housed in the Kaaba and was removed by Muhammad.

Huelgu: Mongol grandson of Genghis Khan and younger brother of Mangu Khan, he set out against the Nizaris in 1252, defeating them in 1256. In 1258, he took Baghdad, ending the Abbasid Caliphate. His armies were defeated by Baybars in 1260.

Hughes de Payens: (r. 1119–1136) Founder and first Grand Master of the Knights Templar, he was a French knight who took religious vows upon the death of his wife. He is known to have been an austere man of deeply held spiritual values, humility, and uncompromising valor.

Humban: Elamite deity, and head of the pantheon, ca. 2200 BC. See Pininkir.

Husayn ibn Ali: Grandson of Muhammad, the younger son of Ali and Fatima, he was murdered in 680 by the Umayyad caliph. His death is regarded as the pivotal event that gave birth to Shiism as a formally separate faith and dogma.

Husayn Qaini: Hasan-i-Sabah's trusted *dai* who helped him to secure Alamut. He later served as the head of the Nizari mission in Kuhistan.

Iamblichus: (ca. 250–330) Greek Neoplatonist whose writings were preserved by being translated into Arabic in the ninth century and became a formative influence in the development of Ismaili philosophy.

Iblis: The Arabic name for Satan or Lucifer.

Ibn al-Athir: (1160–1234) Respected medieval Muslim historian and author of *al-Kamil fil Tarikh*.

Ibrahim al-Imam: Son and successor of Muhammad ibn Ali, he died in a Umayyad prison in 749, just months before the Abbasid-led victory against the Umayyads at Kufa.

Inanna: Sumerian goddess of fertility associated with Venus. She traveled to the Underworld, from which she successfully returned.

Isabel I: (r. 1192–1205) Queen of Jerusalem. She was the daughter of King Amalric. She married Conrad of Montferrat, later slain by the Assassins. She then married Henry, Count of Champagne.

Isabel II: (r. 1212–1228) Queen of Jerusalem. She was the daughter of John of Brienne and Queen Mary of Jerusalem. She married Holy Roman Emperor Frederick II, thus establishing his claim to the throne.

Ishtar: Akkadian/Semitic name of the Sumerian goddess Inanna.

Ishmael: Oldest son of Abraham with Hagar. He is regarded as the father of the Arab peoples and thus of Islam.

Ismail: Eldest son of the sixth Imam Jafar al-Sadiq, who is believed by the majority of Shiites to have either predeceased his father or to have been disinherited. The Ismaili schism arose from the dispute over succession and the true identity of the seventh Imam.

Isaac: Second son of Abraham through his aged wife Sarah. He is regarded as the father of the Jewish people.

Ivanow, Wladimir: (1886–1970) Pioneering Russian-born scholar of Ismailism who collected, recovered, preserved, translated, and published a large number of texts that had been previously unknown. He revolutionized the modern field of Ismaili scholarship.

Jacques de Molay: (r. 1293–1314) Twenty-third and final Templar Grand Master. Born in France in 1244, he joined the Order in 1265. He was burned at the stake while proclaiming the Order's innocence.

Jafar al-Sadiq: The sixth Imam, who succeeded his father in 732. This deeply spiritual and brilliant Imam was the last to be recognized as such by all Shiites. His learning and piety were so unique that he was (and continues to be) accepted as an authority by Sunnis.

Jalal al-Din Rumi: (1207–1273) Founder of the Mevlevi Sufi Order, the Whirling Dervishes, he was a poet and disciple of Shams-i-Tabriz.

Janah al-Dawla: The ruler of Homs and a rival of Ridwan, the Assassins were accused of murdering him in 1103.

Julian "the Apostate": (r. 361–363) Roman emperor who tried to reverse the embrace of Christianity by Constantine and reintroduce a refined paganism as the religion of Rome. He invaded Persia where he was killed in battle.

Justinian: (r. 527–565) Roman emperor who codified the laws of Rome and declared Christianity the sole legal faith of the empire. He rebuilt Constantinople in one of the most ambitious architectural enterprises in history.

Juvaini: (1226–1283) This Persian historian, who hated the Assassins, accompanied Huelgu during the destruction of Alamut in 1256. He personally oversaw the burning of the famed library of Alamut and wrote the first history of Hasan-i-Sabah and the group.

al-Kamil: Ayyubid sultan visited by Francis of Assisi in Egypt in 1219 during the Fifth Crusade. In 1229, he negotiated a ten-year treaty with Frederick II, ending the Sixth Crusade.

Karim al-Husayni (Aga Khan IV): (r. 1957–) He is recognized as the current head of some twenty million Nizari Ismailis, scattered in more than twenty-five countries. He has worked tirelessly on behalf of his people.

Kavad I: (r. 488–496 and 499–531) Sasanian Persian king who supported the Mazdakites in an attempt to weaken the power of the aristocracy. He was imprisoned before fleeing the country. He later returned to power.

Ket-Buqa: Mongolian general who served under Huelgu in Syria. He was defeated by Baybars in 1260 and the hated Mongols were finally forced out of the region.

Khadijah: Muhammad's first wife, his business partner, the mother of his children, his friend, and the first Muslim.

Shah Khalil Allah: The forty-fifth Nizari Imam married the daughter of a prominent Nimat Allahi Sufi. He was murdered by a Twelver Shiite mob in Yazd in 1817.

Khawla: After Fatima passed away, she became the wife of Ali. She was a member of the Prophet's tribe, the Banu Hanifa, and was the mother of Muhammad ibn al-Hanafiyya.

Khosrow I: (r. 531–579) King of Persia. Founded the college of Jund-i-Shapur in southwest Iran. After Justinian closed the Neoplatonic academy in 529, it became a great educational center, attracting Neoplatonist exiles, Jews, and Christians.

Khosrow II: (r. 590–628) King of Persia. He declared war on Byzantium, and a holy war against Christianity. In 614, he sacked Jerusalem, massacred thousands of Christians, burned the Church of the Holy Sepulcher, and carried the fragment of the True Cross to Persia.

Khurshah: (r. 1255–1256) (Eighth and final Lord of Alamut) Rukh al-Din Khurshah was the twenty-seventh Nizari Imam. He offered his submission to the Mongols. He was beaten to death by Mongol soldiers after being refused an audience with Mangu Khan at Karakoram.

Kia Ba Jafar: Appointed by Hasan-i-Sabah as part of a leadership council to manage the affairs of Alamut in conjunction with Kiya Buzurgumid.

Kiririsha: Mother goddess of the southern Elamite pantheon in Susa, wife of Napirisha, and rival of Pininkir.

Pope Leo IX: (r. 1049–1054) Battled for the supremacy of the Roman Church against Constantinople. He issued a bull of excommunication against the Eastern Patriarch Michael Cerularias on July 16, 1054. He was also an active Church reformer.

Louis IX: (r. 1226–1270) King of France, who led the last great crusading effort in 1248. He was an intensely spiritual man, later canonized. He met with an Assassin delegation in 1250.

Mahdi the Alid: Sultan Malikshah had granted Alamut to this Shiite nobleman. Hasan-i-Sabah paid Mahdi three thousand gold dinars for the property, despite the fact that he already controlled it as the result of a careful strategy.

Mahmud: Son and designated successor of Muhammad Tapar as Seljuk sultan. However, Muhammad's younger brother Sanjar actually held the reins of power.

Mahmud of Ghazni: (r. 998–1030) Powerful ruler of Afghanistan and a strong supporter of the Abbasid Caliphate.

Malikshah: Seljuk sultan, under whom Nizam al-Mulk served. His death from illness in 1092, soon after the latter's assassination, suspended the Seljuk campaign against Alamut.

al-Mamun: Twelver Shiite wazir of the Fatimid caliph al-Amir after the death of Commander of the Armies al-Afdal. He was unhappy with the caliph's rapprochement efforts toward the Assassins. In 1122, he arranged for an assembly of supporters of the Mustalian succession to refute Nizari claims.

Mangu Khan: Grandson of Genghis Khan, he was elevated as supreme Khan of the Mongols at Karakoram in 1252. He ordered his younger brother Huelgu to set out against the Nizaris and destroy them utterly.

Mani: (216–272) Dualist Persian Gnostic mystic who proclaimed himself messiah in 242. Crucified by Persian authorities in 272, his martyrdom fueled the spread of his teachings, known as Manichaeism.

Mansur al-Hallaj: (858–922) Celebrated Sufi mystic who had acquired great influence among members of the Abbasid royal family. Jealous enemies arranged for him to be arrested, tried, tortured, crucified, and dismembered. His disciples would found a number of mystical Sufi orders.

al-Maqrizi: (1364–1442) An Egyptian historian of the Mameluke dynasty who wrote about Hasan-i-Sabah in his two histories of the Fatimid dynasty: the *Kittab al-Muqaffa al-kabir* and the *Ittiaz al-hunafa*.

Marco Polo: (1254–1324) Famous European chronicler whose account of his travels in the fourteenth century popularized the Assassins and their legendary Garden of Delights.

Marduk: King of the gods of ancient Babylon, who replaced the Sumerian Enlil about 1100 BC.

Masud: Regional successor to Seljuk sultan Mahmud (under the Supreme Sultan Sanjar), he defeated, captured, and imprisoned the Abbasid caliph al-Mustarshid in Isfahan in 1135.

Matthew of Paris: (ca. 1200–1259) Medieval English historian of the Crusades whose works included numerous invaluable illustrations.

Maymun al-Qaddah: Called by an anti-Ismaili tenth-century tract the progenitor of the Fatimids, he was slandered as a non-Alid Gnostic follower of Bardesanes. He was the father of Abd Allah b. Maymun al-Qaddah.

al-Mazdaqani: Chief Seljuk wazir under Tughitigin. He was partial to the Nizaris and encouraged his leader's largesse toward the sect.

Michael Cerularius: (r. 1043–1058) Patriarch of the Eastern Orthodox Church, he battled the Roman Church under Pope Leo IX, closed Roman churches in Constantinople, excommunicated the Latin clergy, and widely criticized the pope on doctrinal grounds.

Mithridates I: (171–139/8 BC) Powerful Parthian king who expanded the empire.

Mithridates II: (124/3–88/7 BC) Parthian king who established relations with China and thereby enhanced the cultural, spiritual, and commercial stature of Persia.

Mithra: Persian deity of the first century AD whose faith spread rapidly, particularly among the Roman army. He was the son of Ahuramazda (God of Light), who battled his antagonist Ahriman (God of Darkness). Mithra came to mediate in favor of mankind.

Moses: (c. 1200 BC) Ancient lawgiver of the Jews, who delivered the Ten Commandments to the West.

Muawiya: Othman's cousin and the governor of Syria, he refused to recognize Ali as caliph, declared civil war against him in 657, and announced himself as a rival caliph.

Muayyid al-Mulk: He was a son of the assassinated emir Nizam al-Mulk and served under Sultan Barkiyaruq until he was supplanted by his brother Fakhr al-Mulk. He later strangled the sultan's mother and was killed in retaliation by Barkiyaruq.

Muhammad (the Prophet): (ca. 570–632) He began his teachings of submission (Islam) to Allah in about 613. He stamped out the influence of earlier idolatrous Arab religions. Islam introduced a sense of national and racial unity among the scattered tribes of Arabia.

Muhammad: Son of Hasan-i-Sabah, he was executed by his father for drinking wine.

Muhammad I: (r. 1138–1162) (Third Lord of Alamut) A conservative man whose ascension to power indicated a new phase for the Nizari state. His overall ambition for expansion was limited.

Muhammad II: (r. 1166–1210) (Fifth Lord of Alamut) Son of Hasan II, he was a powerful personality who declared his father to have been the spiritual and physical Imam, and thus proclaimed himself Imam. He elaborated upon the doctrine of the *Qiyama.*

Muhammad III: (r. 1221–1255) (Seventh Lord of Alamut) Son of Hasan III, he was also known as Aladdin. He quietly returned Alamut to the Shiite/Ismaili fold, announcing that his father's Imamate was to be viewed as a period of occultation.

Muhammad al-Baqir: Son of Ali ibn Husayn, who succeeded his father in 714 as the fifth Imam. He is credited with being the first to perform the charismatic role of authoritative and inspired teacher, firmly establishing the Imamate tradition within Shiism.

Muhammad al-Mahdi: (r. 775–785) The Abbasid caliph who declared the Prophet had never appointed his cousin Ali as his successor, but instead had bestowed that role upon his uncle al-Abbas.

Muhammad al-Mahdi: Twelfth Shiite Imam who disappeared in 873 (or 878). His reappearance at the end of the world, in triumph as the Mahdi, is still awaited by the majority of Shiites.

Muhammad b. Abd Allah: (1393–1464) (called Nurbakhsh) Founder of the Nurbakshiyya Persian Sufi order which became a haven for displaced Nizari Ismailis.

Muhammad ibn al-Hanafiyya: Proclaimed by Muktar as the Imam and Mahdi, he was the son of Ali and Khawla, thus not a lineal descendant of the Prophet. He died around 700. Many Shiites believed he had actually gone into hiding and will return as the Mahdi.

Muhammad ibn Ali: Distant cousin of Muhammad ibn al-Hanifiyya and great-grandson of al-Abbas, an uncle of the Prophet, he assumed the Abbasid leadership in 716, posing as a Shiite revolutionary.

Muhammad ibn Ismail: Son of Ismail, he was the grandson of Jafar al-Sadiq, who reputedly withdrew the *nass* from Ismail and transferred it to Musa al-Kazim. Ismailis believe this is not the case, and either Ismail or Muhammad ibn Ismail is the true Seventh Imam.

Muhammad Shah (Aga Khan III): (r. 1885–1957) His seventy-two-year reign included providing written constitutions, establishing administrative councils, regularizing religious practices, and supporting education, welfare, and health care for the Nizaris.

Muhammad Tapar: (r. 1105–1118) Half-brother of Sultan Berkiyaruq whom he succeeded, ruling as the undisputed supreme Seljuk sultan until his death. He initiated campaigns against the Nizaris throughout the Persian territories.

Muin al-Din: Wazir to Sultan Sanjar. He advised the sultan to attack Alamut after Hasan-i-Sabah's death rather then retain the state of peace that existed. He paid for this advice at the hands of Buzurgumid's *fidais* in 1127.

al-Muizz: (r. 953–975) Fourth Fatimid caliph who seized Egypt from the Abbasids and built the city of Cairo (al-Qahirah) as his capital in 969. His doctrinal modifications helped extend Fatimid influence among the larger Ismaili community.

Muktar: A Shiite leader who formed the Army of Penitents, composed of Husayn's followers. In 686, he defeated Yazid's Umayyad forces in battle. He imbued Shiites with an invincible faith in the power of the Imam and the advent of the Mahdi.

Mumin (the Believer): One of Hasan-i-Sabah's Ismaili instructors in Rayy before whom he swore the oath of allegiance to the Fatimid caliph al-Mustansir.

al-Muqtadi: (r. 1075–1094) Abbasid caliph who may have poisoned Seljuk sultan Malikshah over a succession dispute and an insult to the sultan's daughter.

Musa al-Kazim: Younger son of Jafar al-Sadiq, who is recognized as the seventh Imam by most Shiites. Musa's line continued through the Twelfth Imam, Muhammad al-Mahdi.

al-Mustali: (r. 1094–1121) Ninth Fatimid caliph, he was the younger brother of Nizar. Commander of the Armies al-Afdal arranged for him to become his son-in-law and appointed him caliph, usurping the position of Nizar.

al-Mustansir: (r. 1036–1094) Eighth Fatimid caliph, he began his reign at age seven, and ruled for nearly sixty years. For one brief moment during his term, the Fatimids gained titular control of the Abbasids and therefore all Islam.

Mustansir Billah II: An Imam of the Qasim-Shahi line, he relocated to Anjudan in central Persia and openly proclaimed the continuation of the Alamut Imamate in the latter half of the fifteenth century, ending two centuries of occultation.

al-Mustarshid: Abbasid caliph murdered in Isfahan by twenty-four *fidais* from Alamut in 1135.

al-Mustasim Billah: The final Abbasid caliph who surrendered as abjectly as Khurshah to the Mongolian army in 1258. After revealing the hiding place of the Abbasid fortune, he was put to death.

Muwaffaq al-Dawla Ali: Grandfather of historian Rashid al-Din, he stayed at Alamut and may have had access to additional material from its library.

al-Muwaffaq an-Naysaburi: Famed Imam of Nishapur, whose school was said to have been attended by Hasan-i-Sabah, Nizam al-Mulk, and Omar Khayyam. He is mentioned in the *Wasiyat* of Nizam al-Mulk and in the *Sar-Guzasht-i-Sayyidna* of Rashid al-Din.

Rais Muzaffar: A Seljuk governor who was a secret Ismaili. He stocked and fortified the castle at Girdkuh at Seljuk expense, after which he declared himself a disciple of Hasan-i-Sabah. He continued to rule the castle for forty years.

Nanna: (Sin) Sumerian/Babylonian Moon god, the son of Enlil and Ninlil.

Napirisha: Head of the southern Elamite pantheon in Susa, husband of Kiririsha, and rival of Humban.

Nabopolassar: (r. 626–605 BC) Founder of the Neo-Babylonian or Chaldean dynasty and father of Nebuchadnezzar II. His alliance with Cyaxares of Media brought down the Assyrian dynasty in 612 BC.

al-Nasir: (r. 1180–1225) Abbasid caliph who led a revitalization of the Sunnis. He promulgated a chivalrous ceremonial order of which he had become Grand Master. He was friends with Hasan III, Lord of Alamut, during the Nizari period of rapprochement with the Sunnis.

Nasir al-Dawla: During the reign of al-Mustansir, open warfare broke out near Cairo between dissident elements in the army in 1062. This Turkish commander became the effective leader of Egypt until he was assassinated in 1073.

Nasir al-Din Aftekin: Ismaili governor of Alexandria who supported the Imamate of Nizar.

Nasir al-Din al-Tusi: Islamic philosopher who wrote at Alamut as the guest of Aladdin. His teachings served as the philosophical lifeline that helped the Nizaris maintain their identity rather than amalgamate with the Sunnis or Twelver Shiites.

Nasir-i Khusraw: (ca. 1004–ca. 1088) Persian poet, philosopher, traveler, and Ismaili *dai*, he was widely respected as the *hujja* of Khurasan. He was the first to introduce the Ismaili doctrine to Hasan-i-Sabah.

Nebuchadnezzar I: (r. ca. 1125–1104 BC) The Babylonian king who returned the statue of Marduk from Elam to Babylon around 1100 BC.

Nebuchadnezzar II: (r. 605–562 BC) The Babylonian king who conquered Jerusalem in 586 BC and destroyed the Temple of Solomon.

Nimat Allah: (1330–1431) Long-lived founder of the Nimat Allahi *tariqa*, he traced his lineage through the Fatimids to Muhammad ibn Ismail.

Nizam al-Mulk: Seljuk wazir and lifelong enemy of Hasan-i-Sabah (after a reputed friendship during their youth). He was a brilliant and capable administrator. He became the first victim of Hasan's *fidais* in 1092.

Nizar: Son of Caliph al-Mustansir, Nizar had been proclaimed as heir, received his father's *nass*, and been accepted as the nineteenth Ismaili Imam. His succession was overturned in 1094 by Commander of the Armies al-Afdal.

Nur al-Din: (1118–1174) Zangid general headquartered in Aleppo, he was the second son of Zangi. In addition to his political and military activities, he set up a system of *madrassa* schools throughout the Holy Land designed to foster a unified approach to the Sunni faith.

Omar (Umar): Successor as the second caliph to Abu Bakr in 634. During Omar's reign, the entire Arabian Peninsula was brought under Muslim control.

Omar Khayyam: (1048–1131) Known to the West mainly for his exquisite poetry (especially *The Rubaiyyat*), he was one of the greatest mathematicians of medieval times. He was reputed to have been a friend of Hasan-i-Sabah during their youth.

Othman (Uthman): Successor as the third caliph to Omar. During his rule, the aggressive expansion of Islam had come to an end, leaving behind a group of unemployed and discontented military personnel. In 656, Othman was murdered by a group of mutineers from the Arab army.

Philip IV (r. 1285–1314): King of France, grandson of Louis IX, he had become the most powerful king in Europe. With the help of the pope he helped elect, he destroyed the Knights Templar Order and seized their assets.

Pininkir: Elamite mother goddess and wife of Humban.

Plotinus: (205–70) Greek Neoplatonist whose writings were preserved by being translated into Arabic in the ninth century and became a formative influence in the development of Ismaili philosophy.

Porphyry: (234–305) Greek Neoplatonist whose writings were preserved by being translated into Arabic in the ninth century and became a formative influence in the development of Ismaili philosophy.

Proclus: (ca. 410–485) Greek Neoplatonist whose writings were preserved by being translated into Arabic in the ninth century and became a formative influence in the development of Ismaili philosophy.

Ptolemy I: Greek general and rival of Seleucus I, he established the Ptolemaic dynasty which ruled Egypt and North Africa long after the death of Alexander the Great.

Qalawun: (r. 1277–1290) Successor to Baybars, he continued the inexorable Mameluke campaign against the Crusader states.

Ralph of Merle: He was a knight who was slain by the Assassins, outside the gates of Tripoli, with Count Raymond II in 1152.

al-Rashid: Abbasid caliph, son and successor to al-Mustarshid, slain by Nizari fidais while he was in Isfahan.

Rashid al-Din Sinan: (see Sinan)

Rashid al-Din Tabib (aka Rashidoddin Fazlollah Hamedani): (1247–1318) Persian historian, born in Hamadan in western Iran, who wrote an extensive history of the known world, *Jami al-Tavarikh*. It included a section on the Ismailis and a biography of Hasan-i-Sabah (ca. 1310, and included here in appendix two in its first English translation).

Raymond II: (1116–1152) Count of Tripoli. He fought against Zangi and was briefly imprisoned. He was the first Frankish victim of the Assassins. This led to war with the Knights Templar and the imposition of an annual tribute on the Syrian Assassins.

Raymond of Antioch: (d. 1213) Eldest son and heir of Bohemond IV, Prince of Antioch and Count of Tripoli. Assassinated by Syrian *fidais* in the cathedral of Tortosa, possibly at the behest of the Hospitallers.

Raymond of Poitiers: (d. 1149) Prince of Antioch. In 1136, King Fulk of Jerusalem arranged his marriage with Alice of Antioch's nine-year-old daughter. He was killed in battle against the Zangids along with his ally, the Assassin leader Alf ibn Wafa.

Renaud de Vichiers: Grand Master of the Templars, he met with Assassin envoys in 1250 after they had made veiled threats against King Louis IX of France. He and Grand Master of the Hospital William of Chateauneuf encouraged the Assassins to enter into a nonaggression pact with Louis.

Richard I: (the Lionhearted) (r. 1189–1199) King of England. This legendary warrior king established his reputation in the Holy Land. He was of enormous help to the Templars. Together they defeated Saladin at Arsuf in a well-executed battle strategy.

Ridwan: (r. 1095–1113) He was the son of Tutush and served as the Seljuk governor of Aleppo. The initial success of the Syrian Assassin mission was greatly facilitated by his support.

Sacy, Silvestre de: (See Silvestre de Sacy.)

Pir Sadr al-Din: The most successful Nizari *dai* in India during the fourteenth century. He chose the name *Khojas*, which means "lords" or "masters," for the Indian Nizaris.

Saladin: (1138–1193) "Righteousness of the Faith." In 1174, he had himself crowned as the first king of the Ayyubid dynasty. He was the most successful proponent of Muslim unity since the Prophet. He dreamed of a single Islamic society governed by the purest religious principles.

al-Salih: The last sultan of the Ayyubid dynasty who died in 1249. His widow, Shajar-al-Durr, arranged for the murder of his son and heir, proclaimed herself queen, and inaugurated the Mameluke dynasty.

Sanjar: (r. 1118–1157) Son of Malikshah, half-brother of Sultan Barkiyaruq, and full brother of Muhammad Tapar. Sanjar became the overall Seljuk leader until his death. He established good relations with Hasan-i-Sabah.

Sargon the Great: (r. ca. 2334–2279 BC) Akkadian king considered the world's first great empire-builder. He was hidden in a basket of rushes by his mother and cast upon the water for his protection, almost a thousand years before the story of Moses.

Sennacherib: (r. ca. 705–681 BC) Assyrian king who battled Judah and Babylon and rebuilt the city of Nineveh, earlier the Akkadian capital.

Shahrastani: Twelfth-century Sunni heresiologist who preserved Hasan-i-Sabah's critique of the doctrine of *talim* (authoritative teaching) by carefully summarizing and commenting on the work. See chapter eighteen of this book.

Shahriyar: Leader of the Bavandid Ispahbadhs of the Daylami region, he refused to participate in Sultan Muhammad Tapar's assault against Alamut in 1107.

Shajar-al-Durr: When al-Salih, the last sultan of the Ayyubid dynasty, died in 1249, his widow, a former slave, arranged for the murder of her stepson and proclaimed herself the first queen of the Mameluke dynasty.

Shalmanessar III: (r. 858–824 BC) Assyrian king who conquered southern Mesopotamia.

Shalmanessar V: (r. ca. 727–722 BC) Assyrian king who conquered northern Israel in 722 BC. He was the son of Tiglath-Pileser III.

Shams al-Din Muhammad: Son of Rukh al-Din Khurshah, he was smuggled to safety in the Azerbaijan region by the surviving Assassins after the fall of Alamut. The modern Aga Khan is descended from this child Imam.

Shams-i-Tabriz: An Alamut survivor, he was the famed spiritual master of the Persian poet Jalal al-Din Rumi, founder of the Mevlevi Sufi Order, the Whirling Dervishes.

Shapur I: (r. 240–270) Sasanian son and successor of Ardashir, he was victorious in battle with the Romans and was a protector of the prophet Mani.

Shirkuh: (d. 1169) Military commander under Nur al-Din. He became the wazir of the Fatimid caliph al-Adid in Cairo after he returned to Egypt in 1169. He was the uncle of Saladin and gave the young man his first command.

Silvestre de Sacy: European Arabic scholar who demonstrated in 1809 that the word "assassin" was derived from the Arabic word "hashish."

Sinan: (r. 1162–1192) The most famous of the Syrian Assassin chiefs, the quintessential Old Man of the Mountain, another legendary Nizari spiritual leader.

King Solomon: King of Judea and son of King David, he built the First Temple, which housed the mysterious Ark of the Covenant, in the mid-tenth century BC.

Tahir: An Ismaili carpenter in Sava (between Rayy and Qum) who was the son of a local religious teacher. He was executed by Nizam al-Mulk for his role in the death of the local *muezzin*.

Taj al-Din: Syrian Assassin chief *dai*, and probably the Nizari leader, visited ca. 1250 at Masyaf by the friar Yves the Breton. Yves was sent on a diplomatic and religious mission by King Louis IX.

Taj al-Mulk: The chosen of Tarkan Khatun to replace Nizam al-Mulk as chief wazir of the Seljuk dynasty after the death of Malikshah. Their plot failed.

Tammuz: Sumerian shepherd god and agricultural deity, he was the husband and consort of Inanna/Ishtar. He was the Mesopotamian predecessor of the Greek Adonis, lover of Aphrodite.

Tancred: Prince of Antioch, who attacked the newly acquired Nizari castle of Apace outside of Aleppo. The Christians defeated the Nizaris and leveled a tribute against the sect.

Tarkan Khatun: A wife of Sultan Malikshah, who campaigned aggressively with the Abbasid caliph al-Muqtadi for her son Mahmud to succeed his father. She disputed against Barkiyaruq, eldest son of Malikshah.

al-Tayyib: Infant son of Fatimid caliph al-Amir, who may or may not have survived to succeed his father as Fatimid Imam. (See al-Hafiz.)

Tiglath-Pileser III: (r. ca. 745–727 BC) Assyrian king who conquered southern Israel in 736 BC. His conquests ranged throughout Mesopotamia and all the way south to Arabia and north to the Black Sea and Caucasus Mountains.

Toghril Beg: (r. 1038–1063) The Turkish Seljuk sultan who converted to Islam and freed the Abbasid caliph from the grip of the Shiite Buwayhids in 1055 and the Ismaili Fatimids in 1060. He was appointed "King of the East and the West" in 1058 by the caliph, who wed Toghril's niece.

Toghril III: Last of the Turkish Seljuk rulers, he was slain in 1194 in Rayy by the Khwarazmian Turks.

Tughitigin: Seljuk ruler of Damascus who gave the Assassins the frontier fortress of Baniyas in appreciation for their help against the Franks. They were also given a mission house in Damascus to serve as their urban headquarters.

Turan-Tash: Seljuk emir who held the district which included Alamut as a fief from Sultan Malikshah. He led the first Seljuk attack against Hasan-i-Sabah's early community.

Tutush: (r. 1092–1094 as Sultan of Damascus) He was the Seljuk emir of Damascus from 1078–1092 and the brother of Malikshah. He proclaimed himself sultan on the latter's death and died in battle against Barkiyaruq in 1095.

Ubayd Allah: (r. 909–934) Ismaili Imam who proclaimed the Fatimid Caliphate in North Africa. His choice of dynastic name expressed the regime's assertion of Alid lineage.

Untash-Napirisha: (r. 1340–1300 BC, or 1275–1240 BC) Elamite king who attempted to reconcile the northern and southern pantheons. He was the builder of the Choga Zanbil Ziggurat.

Pope Urban II: (r. 1088–1099) In November 1095, he convened the Council of Clermont and issued his call for the First Crusade. This was one of history's inexplicably perfect moments when an idea inflamed an entire population.

Urukagina: King of Lagash in Sumer (r. ca. 2900 BC). He introduced history's first written legal code.

Ustad Husain: Son of Hasan-i-Sabah, he was executed by his father for his part in a conspiracy to murder Husayn Qaini, of which he was innocent.

Utu-hegal: A Sumerian king from Uruk who defeated the Gutian conquerors of Akkadia around 2100 BC.

Wah Sudan ibn Marzuban: Daylamese king who built the castle at Alamut about 860.

Walter de Mesnil: In 1172, this Templar knight killed the Assassin ambassador who had been sent by Sinan to King Amalric. The possibility of an alliance with the Assassins was lost.

William of Chateauneuf: Grand Master of the Hospital, he met with Assassin envoys in 1250 after they had made veiled threats against King Louis IX of France. He and Grand Master of the Templars Renaud de Vichiers successfully encouraged the Assassins to enter into a nonaggression pact with Louis.

William of Rudrick: Franciscan friar and ambassador of Louis IX, who traveled to Karakoram in 1254 in an effort to enlist the support of Mangu Khan against the Muslims.

Archbishop William of Tyre: (1130–1186) A contemporary historian of the Crusades, he lived in Syria during the reign of Sinan and the campaigns of Saladin. He had little good to say of the Templars but was the most accurate early European historian on the Assassins.

Xerxes I: (r. 486–465 BC) Achaemenid king who invaded Greece and defeated the Spartans at Thermopylae.

Yasur: The Mongol commander who preceded Huelgu and first demanded the surrender of Khurshah.

Yazdgird I: (r. 399–421) Sasanian king who recognized the Persian Christian church in 410. A group of radical Christians rejected the idea of a nationalized church and revolted.

Yazdgird III: (r. 632–651) The last Sasanian king. He was assassinated by his rivals as the Umayyads conquered Persia.

Yazid: Son and successor of Umayyad caliph Muawiya. He murdered Husayn, grandson of the Prophet, at Karbala in 680.

Yves the Breton: Arabic-speaking friar sent to the Assassin fortress at Masyaf by King Louis IX, ca. 1250, on a diplomatic and religious mission.

al-Zahir: (r. 1021–1036) Seventh Fatimid caliph He gave permission to the Byzantines to reconstruct the Church of the Holy Sepulcher.

Zaid Hasani: A traitor at Alamut who murdered Husayn Qaini, an important *dai* and friend of Hasan-i-Sabah.

Zangi: (ca. 1085–1146) A former Kurdish slave of the Seljuk sultan Malikshah. In 1127 he became governor of Mosul and then of Aleppo. By 1130, he was the master of northern Syria and founder of the Zangid dynasty.

Zerubbabel: He led the Jews in their return to Jerusalem from Babylon. They completed the construction of the Second Temple in 515 BC.

Zoroaster: The Persian prophet who lived approximately 1000 BC. He taught the religion of Dualism, the struggle between Light and Darkness, Good and Evil, Ahuramazda and Ahriman.

APPENDIX SIX

Glossary of Terms

Abbasid Caliphate: Reigned in Baghdad for some five hundred years as the titular leaders of Sunni Islam. Descended from al-Abbas, an uncle of the Prophet, they came to power in 749, and were destroyed by the Mongols in 1258.

Abjad: Arabic numerology. Like Hebrew and Greek, Arabic is an alphanumeric language. Letters do double duty as numbers. Thus, words of equivalent value are interpreted as related—as they are in the Qabalistic tradition of gematria.

Achaemenid Empire: The first Persian dynasty founded by Cyrus II, the Great, which lasted from 549 to 330 BC.

Aga Khan: (loosely, "Chief Commander") An honorific title bestowed on the Nizari Imams in the nineteenth century.

Ahl al-Bayt: ("People of the House") Descendants of the Prophet's bloodline through the marriage of his daughter Fatima and his nephew Ali.

Al-Aqsa Mosque: Located in Jerusalem on the Temple Mount near the Dome of the Rock, it was built by the Umayyad caliph al-Walid in the eighth century. It served as the Templar headquarters until 1187 when Jerusalem was reclaimed by Saladin.

Al-dawa al-jadida: ("New Preaching") The term by which Hasan-i-Sabah identified the Nizari Ismaili doctrine.

Alamut: Built on a narrow ridge on a high rock in the heart of the Elburz Mountains of Persia, it was the capital of the Nizari state. *Aluh amut* means "eagle's teaching" or "eagle's nest" in the Daylami language.

Alid lineage: The lineal descendants of Ali and Fatima.

Al Jazireh: Mesopotamia, the land between the Tigris and Euphrates Rivers.

Amir: (See Emir)

Ansar: (The Helpers) Those first Arabs in Medina who accepted Islam after Muhammad and his followers were forced to flee Mecca. (See *Muhajreen.*)

Aql al-kull: The term used in Ismaili philosophy to signify the principal of Universal Reason, the origin, symbolized in humanity as the Prophet Muhammad.

Ark of the Covenant: The gold-plated wooden chest that housed the two Tablets of the Law, given to Moses by God, and later housed in the Temple of Solomon in the mid-tenth century. Its fate has been unknown since the sixth century BC destruction of the Temple by Nebuchadnezzar.

Army of Penitents: Formed by Muktar, they were composed of the martyred Husayn's followers. In 686, they defeated Yazid's Umayyad forces.

Asas: Successor to the speaking Prophet. Imam. (See *natiq, wasi,* and *samit.*)

Ashura: The annual Shia commemoration of the death of Husayn on the tenth day of the month of *Muharram.*

Atabeg: A trusted advisor, a guardian, often a governor, charged by the monarch with raising the crown prince.

Avesta: Also called *Zend Avesta*, the scriptures of Zorastrianism. The earliest known full copy seems to date to the third century AD in the Sasanian dynasty, but is likely far older in manuscript fragments and oral tradition.

Ayyubid Dynasty: Founded by Saladin in 1174. After his death in 1193, a virtual civil war erupted between dynastic leaders in Egypt and Syria, with smaller sultanates variously allied with larger combatants. Overthrown by the Mamelukes in 1250.

Baladat-al-Iqbal: (The Town of Good Fortune) A name applied to Alamut after it survived the first Seljuk campaign.

Banu Hanifa: (or Banu Hashim) The Prophet's sub-tribal clan of the Quraysh.

Batin: The inner meaning of Islam, only capable of being revealed by the Imam, who is often referred to as the "speaking Quran."

Batinis: (Followers of the *batin*) A name for the Ismailis.

Black Stone: This holy object, some seven inches in diameter, was built into the east wall of the Kaaba and was said to have been given to Abraham by an angel. Muhammad taught that it had been pure white, but the sins of mankind turned it black.

Bohras: Modern name of Mustalian or Tayyibi Ismailis in India and Yemen.

Brethren of Sincerity: (See *Ikhwan al-Safa.*)

Buwayhids: A Persian Shiite dynasty from the Daylami region who ruled over the Sunni Abbasid caliph in Baghdad from 946 to 1055.

Caliph: Prince of the Faithful. The religious and secular leader of Sunni Islam.

Carmations: (See Qarmati.)

Cathars: Mystical Christians in the Languedoc whose origins trace back to the dualist Bogomils. Both groups had much in common with the Persian Manichaeans of the fourth century.

Church of the Holy Sepulcher: Built in Jerusalem by Constantine and his mother St. Helena in 336 upon the site believed to be the tomb in which Jesus was crucified, buried, and rose from the dead.

Companions of the Prophet: The first Muslims who accompanied Muhammad on the journey from Mecca to Medina in 622. Later more broadly applied to anyone who saw him in life.

Comrade: (See *Rafiq.*)

Coptics: Egyptian Christians who embraced Monophysite beliefs in the fifth century and resisted Muslim acculturation.

Council of Piacenza: Byzantine Patriarch Alexius Comnenus appealed to the West in 1095 to come to the aid of the Christian East. He is said to have offered to join the Eastern to the Western Church in return for aid against the Muslims.

Council of Troyes: Convened in 1128 (or 1129), the Knights Templar Order was recognized by the Church under Pope Honorius II, a Rule was ordered to be written for the knights, and they were awarded their plain white robe.

Dais: The Imam's direct representatives, missionaries carefully trained and trusted to spread the Ismaili *dawa* to worthy candidates.

Dar al-Hikma: (House of Wisdom) Established in 1005 by Fatimid caliph al-Hakim as a training center for *dais*. Its library housed some two hundred thousand books on theology, astronomy, and medicine.

Dawa: The Ismaili teaching of Truth, the divinely inspired wisdom of the Imam spread by his *dais*.

Daylam: The northern region of Persia along the southern shore of the Caspian Sea which includes the Elburz Mountains. The term "Daylami" is often used to describe the fierce mountain people who embraced Ismailism and the teachings of Hasan-i-Sabah.

Dehkanan: The class of small Persian landowners encouraged by Khosrow I to balance the wealthy aristocracy.

Deviationists: One of the pejorative terms used by Sunni historians for the Ismailis.

Dome of the Rock: The oldest Islamic monument, built in 691 on the Temple Mount in Jerusalem. It houses the Rock where Abraham was to sacrifice Isaac, Moses received the Ark of the Covenant, and Solomon built the First Temple. Muhammad ascended to Heaven from here and met with Abraham, Moses, and Jesus.

Druze: This movement arose in 1017 as a number of al-Hakim's *dais* began to preach extremist ideas concerning the physical divinity of the Fatimid Imam. Today there are some three hundred thousand Druze, who continue to await the return of al-Hakim.

Dualism: The religious and philosophical understanding of the world as divided between forces of Light and forces of Darkness. There have been innumerable variations of this idea across many cultures. Variations in the conception of the balance of power between Good and Evil are a key to the identity of various adherents.

Eid al-Ghadeer: Annual Shiite festival celebrating Muhammad's designation of Ali as his successor at Ghadir Khumm.

Emanationist doctrines: The teachings, often confused with polytheism, by which Deity divides tasks and the rulership of spiritual realms to a hierarchy of consciousness. This model of "universal management" has been the philosophical standard for many races and climes.

Emir: Prince, military commander, high official such as a governor or independent ruler.

Faciens misericordiam: Papal bull issued by Clement V in 1308 listing the charges made against the Knights Templar, among which was collaboration with their Muslim opponents (often interpreted as the Assassins).

Faqih: A Persian word denoting a jurist, a member of the Sunni *ulema*, an expert in *fiqh* or Islamic jurisprudence and law.

Fata: Meaning "a handsome, brave youth" in Arabic, it became the idealized basis of the *Futuwwa* teachings of the chivalric order founded by Caliph al-Nasir.

Fatimid Caliphate: The Ismaili dynasty established in 909. It was the first successful Ismaili state, renowned for its respect for learning and cultural and religious achievements. It fell to Saladin in 1171.

Fertile Crescent: Near Eastern lands periodically inundated by the Tigris, Euphrates, Jordan, and Nile Rivers, whose rising waters brought silt to nourish the soil or were otherwise capable of being productively utilized.

Feudal system: The economic and political organization of agricultural territory in which the land is owned by the king in Europe or sultan or caliph in the Mideast, and assigned to nobles with carefully defined administrative and fiducial responsibilities. In turn, a peasant or farming class is sustained and able to work the land with a portion of their production paid as a form of rent or taxation.

Fidai: ("faithful") The name by which Nizari assassins were known.

Fiqh: Islamic jurisprudence and Islamic law

Fitra: An income tax among the Qarmatis. (Followed by *hijra*, and *bulgha* taxes.)

Five Pillars of Islam: These include belief in Allah and acceptance of Muhammad as His Prophet and the four duties of prayer, almsgiving, fasting, and pilgrimage.

Franks: Generic name applied to the European Crusaders.

Futuwwa: The way of *fata* (see above). Refers to the ideal, noble and perfect man; one who would give all, including his life, for the sake of his friends.

Garden of Delights: Popularized by Marco Polo, it refers to a secret mythic garden at Alamut, said to resemble Muhammad's description of Paradise, and used to inspire the young *fidais* to loyalty to their Master.

Ghadir Khumm: Arabian town along the Red Sea where Muhammad is said to have proclaimed Ali his successor.

Ghulat: (Exaggerators) Shiite religious extremists whose views were particularly offensive to their co-religionists.

Ghurids: A tribe from the Hindu Kush which had converted to Islam and gained control of Afghanistan.

Girdkuh: An Assassin castle in the eastern Elburz region, acquired in 1096.

Gnosticism: Loosely applied to the body of beliefs especially associated with the Mediterranean regions from the second century BC to the sixth century AD. It incorporated the wisdom teachings of Egypt with the Greek Mysteries and much original teaching. Derived from *gnosis*, the Greek word for "knowledge."

Gondeshapur: The college founded by Khosrow I in southwest Iran. After Justinian closed the Neoplatonic academy in 529, it became a great educational center attracting Neoplatonists, Jews, and Christians, who infused Persian culture with Gnostic spirituality and philosophy.

Great Schism: The final break between Western Roman Catholicism and Eastern Orthodox Catholicism when the Patriarch Michael Cerularius was excommunicated by Pope Leo IX in 1054.

Gutian: A barbarous tribe from the Zagros Mountains which conquered the Akkadian Empire, ca. 2150 BC.

Hadith: The traditions associated with the Prophet's behavior and sayings, recorded during his lifetime and held as an example and guide to the righteous way of life for all Muslims.

Hafizi Ismailis: A short-lived schism after the death of the last Fatimid caliph al-Amir and the usurpation by a cousin of the regular succession of his infant son al-Tayyib.

Hajj: The annual pilgrimage to Mecca and the Kaaba, considered mandatory at least once in the lifetime of those who are able.

Haqiqa: The inner Truth, concealed by external appearance.

Hashishim: ("users of hashish") Term applied to Nizari Ismailis by Sunni and Twelver Shiite enemies. It is the etymological derivation of the term "Assassin." It may apply to either their use of the drug, or to their unusual beliefs being unfavorably compared to those of drunkards or drug users.

Hellenism: The cultural values characterized by the embrace of Greek aesthetic ideals in art, sculpture, architecture, classical philosophy, individualism, education, myth, and the celebration of physical prowess.

Heyssessini: ("Those who live without law") Term applied by Burchard of Strassburg against the Syrian Assassins in 1175.

Hieros Gamos: The ancient magical nuptials performed by the king and a goddess whose effect was the fertility and well-being of the land. Sacred sexuality generally.

Hijrah: The historic journey from Mecca to Medina in 622, the event that marks the beginning of the Muslim calendar.

Himyars: The ancestral tribe of Hasan-i-Sabah. The Semitic Himyars established a kingdom in Yemen that lasted from 110 BC–525 AD.

Hospitallers: The Order of the Hospital of Saint John of Jerusalem, established around 1080 as a charitable group to provide medical care and shelter for pilgrims. It received papal recognition in 1113 and became a military order. Known today as the Knights of Malta.

Houris: Beautiful angelic women said to reside in Paradise in the Garden of Delights.

House of Wisdom: (See *Dar al-Hikma.*)

Hujja: The proof or source of knowledge and authorized teaching, the immediate representative of the concealed Imam, and custodian of the Nizari *dawa* until the Imam chose to reveal himself.

Ibaha: Libertinism

Ijtihad: Refers to a judge's independent reasoning, or the thorough exertion of a jurist's mental faculty, in order to find a solution to a legal question.

Ikhwan al-Safa: (Brethren of Sincerity) This group appeared in Basra at the end of the tenth century, They followed a revolutionary Gnostic teaching preserved in the anonymous and encyclopedic *Rasail Ikhwan al-Safa*.

Ilhad: (arch heresy) Twelver Shiites and Sunnis accused the Ismaili Imams of pursuing a course of sinister evil.

Ilkhanate Dynasty: Mongol rulers of Persia from 1256–1353. They were established by Huelgu and embraced Islam in 1295.

Ilm: Gnosis, direct spiritual wisdom, bestowed by Allah and transmitted through the Ismaili Imam to the community of believers.

Imam: The Ismaili spiritual leader is viewed as heir to the Prophet, the chosen of God, and the sole leader of mankind. Descended from the bloodline of Ali and Fatima, he carries a genetic link to the spiritual stature and mission of the Prophet.

Inquisition: The militant anti-heresy purges of the Catholic Church which judged religious orthodoxy and imprisoned or executed those found in violation. It functioned roughly from the twelfth through as late as the eighteenth century.

Iqta: The name of the Islamic feudal system of land grants and tax farming. It included, as in Europe, the reciprocal responsibility of providing properly equipped troops to the sultan or caliph. See also *Muqti.*

Islam: Means "submission" to the will of God. It is an optimistic faith. Adherence to its strict requirements is rewarded in an afterlife whose appeal is universal.

Ismailis: Shiite sect which remained loyal to the succession of Ismail (eldest son of Jafar al-Sadiq) as the true Seventh Imam.

Ithna Ashariyya: Twelver Shiites, the majority branch of Shiism that has been the official religion of Iran since the sixteenth century. The twelfth Imam disappeared ca. 873 and his reappearance. in triumph as the Mahdi, is still awaited by most Shiites

Jami al-Tawarikh: Rashid al-Din's extensive world history (produced from 1307–1316), which includes the history of Hasan-i-Sabah, the *Sar-Guzasht-i-Sayyidna* (*The Biography of Our Master*), and much else.

Jihad: The spiritual duty of the Muslim to battle against the infidel, whether viewed as an internal process of cleansing the character or is applied to external enemies of the faith.

Jinn: Spirits—both angels and demons.

Jund-i-Shapur: (See Gondeshapur)

Kaaba: The sacred building in Mecca that houses the Black Stone. It had been a spiritual center for the Arab peoples even before the advent of Islam.

Karbala: The holy city of the Shiites in Iraq. It was the scene of the martyrdom of the Prophet's grandson Husayn in 680.

Khojas: The name by which modern Nizari Ismailis are known in India. It means "lords" or "masters."

Khutba prayer: Traditional weekly Muslim prayer, said on Friday, including a blessing for the rulers of Islam.

Koran: (See Quran.)

Khwarazmian Dynasty: A Turkish warrior clan which defeated the Seljuk Turks in 1194. They were themselves defeated by the Mongol invasion in 1231.

Krak des Chevaliers: In 1142, the Hospitallers received this castle, becoming hostile neighbors of the Syrian Assassins.

Lammasar: This strategically important early Persian Nizari castle, some twenty-five miles west of Alamut, was taken by Kiya Buzurgumid in 1096 or 1102.

Lugalene: ("Big Men") In the third millennium BC, these nobles and military leaders in Kish in Sumer gave rise to the concept of kingship.

Madrassa: The system of Sunni Islamic religious schools designed to teach uniformity of belief among the young.

Mahdi: Shiites believe he is "the rightly guided one," the messianic Imam chosen by Allah who will emerge at the proper time, triumph over his enemies, make the inner doctrine public, and usher in the age of truth, justice, and equality.

Malahida: (Heretics, deviators) A term by which the Ismailis were slandered. Plural of *Mulhid*.

Mameluke Dynasty: The Mamelukes ("owned") were former Turkish white slaves who were the palace guards of the Ayyubids. They seized power in 1249 and ruled Egypt until their defeat by the Ottoman Turks in 1517.

Manichaeism: Dualistic religion founded in 242 when the Persian mystic Mani proclaimed himself messiah. He divided the world into good and evil, identifying the earth as the kingdom of Darkness under the reign of Satan. Man's hope lay in the ascetic practices by which one could ascend to the kingdom of Light.

Masyaf: Syrian Assassin castle acquired in 1140.

Mawali: ("clients") Persian and Iraqi converts to Islam. The fact that their social, political, and religious status was inferior to that of the Arab ruling class became a source of enormous resentment among them.

Mawlana: Arabic, Our Lord/Master.

Mazdakism: A new religion introduced to Sasanian Persia during the fifth century AD, a radical religious and cultural socialism that included the equal sharing of food, property, and women.

Mesopotamia: ("Between Two Rivers") The center of civilization between the Tigris and Euphrates Rivers.

Mevlevi Order: The Whirling Dervishes. A still-flourishing Sufi order founded by Jalal al-Din Rumi, ca. 1250.

Muezzin: A town crier who issues the Call to Prayer five times each day in support of *sharia*.

Muhammad-Shahi: After the Imam Shams al-Din Muhammad died in 1310–1311, a dispute over the succession resulted in the first Nizari schism—between the Muhammad-Shahi and the Qasim-Shahi. The last Imam of the Muhammad-Shahi line died in the late nineteenth century without a successor.

Muhajirun: (The Emigrants) Those first Arabs who accepted Islam in Mecca. (See *Ansar*.)

Muharrum: The month of the annual Shiite commemoration of the martyrdom of Husayn ibn Ali at Karbala in 680. (See *Ashura*.)

Mujtahid: A person who has been accepted as an authority in Islamic law.

Mulhid: (Heretic, deviator) A term by which the Ismailis were slandered. Plural is *Malahida.*

Munafiqun: (The Hypocrites) Arabs in Medina who falsely asserted they had accepted Islam.

Muqti: Landholder in the Islamic feudal system. (See *Iqta* and *Qati.*)

Murid: A Sufi term for disciple.

Murshid: A Sufi term for teacher.

Mustalian Ismailis: Followers of the lineage of the ninth Fatimid Imam al-Mustali, as opposed to followers of his brother Nizar, the Nizari Ismailis. (See Bohras and Tayyibi Ismailis.)

Nafs: The soul.

Nafs al-kull: The term used in Ismaili philosophy to signify the principal of Universal Animation, symbolized in humanity as the Imam Ali.

Nass: The spiritual essence of the reigning Imam. The bestowal of the *nass* upon the designated successor is the process by which the current Imam transfers his *ilm* to the next Imam.

Natiq: A speaking or law-giving prophet who brings forth a new religious doctrine. The Ismailis accept seven such beings as extensively discussed. (See *asas*, *samit*, and *wazi.*)

Neoplatonism: The Gnostic teachings of the third to fifth centuries included an emanationist cosmology, along with meditative practices and techniques of theurgy by which the disciple was able to attain higher states of consciousness.

New Preaching: (See *Al-dawa al jadida.*)

Nimat Allahi: Persian Sufi order founded in the fourteenth century by Nimat Allah. Initially adapting the outward behavior of a Sunni order, the rise to power of the Shia Safawids allowed it to reveal its Shia roots. The order became a haven for displaced Nizari Ismailis.

Nizari Ismailis: The majority Ismaili sect founded by Hasan-i-Sabah which accepted the Imamate of Nizar, son and designated successor of Caliph al-Mustansir.

Noruz: The Persian New Year celebration at the spring equinox.

Nubuwwiyya: Sunni vigilantes who fought against Shiites and Ismailis in Syria at the time of the Crusades.

Nur: The mystical radiance of the Divine Light.

Nurbakshiyya: Persian Sufi order founded by Muhammad b. Abd Allah (called Nurbakhsh) in the early fourteenth century. It was a Shia *tariqa* which sought to fuse both Sunni and Shia under the umbrella of Sufism. The order was a haven for displaced Nizari Ismailis.

Nusayris: Heretical tribe living in the Jabal Bahra mountain region of Syria during the Crusades. They resented the newly-arrived Syrian Assassin community and fought them well into the twentieth century. Known today as Alawis, they currently rule Syria.

Old Man of the Mountain: A title of Hasan-i-Sabah and the subsequent leaders of the Assassin communities in Persia and Syria.

Ottoman Dynasty: Turkish rulers who defeated the Mamelukes in 1517 and ruled until 1922, when the modern state of Turkey was established.

Outremer: ("Beyond the Sea") A generic name for the Holy Land during the Crusades.

Parthian Dynasty: Ruled Persia from 247 BC to 224 AD.

Pir: The Sufi term for enlightened spiritual teacher or shaykh.

Ptolemaic Dynasty: Descended from Ptolemy I, a successor of Alexander the Great and rival of Seleucus I, which ruled in Egypt from 305 BC to 30 BC.

Qadi: (Arabic) A judge or magistrate in an Islamic court.

Qati: Private land held in return for tithe revenue (*usher*) rather than military service. (See *Iqta.*)

Qaim: ("The Last One") Ismailis believe in the coming of an Imam who will bring to earth the final perfection of Islam. (See also *Qiyama*)

Qajar Dynasty: Ruled Persia from the fall of the Safawids in 1794 until 1925.

Qarmatis (Carmatians): The followers of Hamdan Qarmat whose preaching efforts had spread through Iraq, Persia, Transoxiana, Syria, Bahrain, Yemen, Sind, and North Africa. They were finally absorbed under the Fatimid umbrella by 1077 after some two centuries of activity.

Qasim-Shahi: Contemporary line of the Nizari Imams. (See Muhammad-Shahi.)

Qiyama: The culmination of all historical and religious cycles proclaimed in 1164 by Hasan II, fourth Lord of Alamut. The practices of the *sharia* were declared outward symbols of inner spiritual truths and no longer necessary. One was to experience spiritual union with Allah directly.

Quran (Koran): The Muslim holy book received by Muhammad from the archangel Gabriel.

Quraysh: Muhammad's ancestral tribe. Meccan nobility long in charge of the Kaaba.

Rafiq: (Comrade) The first level of Ismaili instructor below the rank of *dai.*

Rais: The leader of a town. He was both the town's representative to the sovereign and acted as a representative of the sovereign to the people. The office was often passed from father to son.

Ramadan: Month long fast from dawn to sunset in honor of the reception of the Quran.

Rasail Ikhwan al-Safa: A collection of fifty-one epistles published at the end of the tenth century by the Brethren of Sincerity. It discussed all known science of the time, in addition to philosophical and religious speculation on cosmology, theology, and eschatology.

Rayy: Northern Persian city near modern Tehran. According to the *Sar-Guzasht-i-Sayyidna,* it was the birthplace of Hasan-i-Sabah.

Rashidun: (See Righteous Caliphs.)

Righteous Caliphs: (*Rashidun*) The first four Caliphs who had each accompanied Muhammad on the *Hijrah.*

Rudbar Valley: Location of Alamut. Rudbar means "by the River," referring to the Shahrud River which provided water to Alamut and the valley.

Sabiyya: Sevener Shiites or Ismailis. Those who support the claim that Ismail, son of Jafar al-Sadiq, is the true Seventh Imam, succeeded by his son, Muhammad ibn Ismail. The larger Shiite group is known as *Ithna ashariyya* or Twelver Shiites.

Safawids: This Sufi *tariqa* succeeded in installing their own shaykh as the ruler of Persia and founder of the Safawid dynasty in 1501. They governed until 1736, establishing Twelver Shiism as the state religion.

Samit: Silent successor to the sole Imam incarnate on earth. He may be present during the lifetime of the Imam in anticipation of his future role. (See *natiq*, *asas*, *wasi*.)

Sar-Guzasht-i-Sayyidna (*The Biography of Our Master*): A manuscript discovered by Ata-Malik Juvaini in the Library of Alamut containing a biography of Hasan-i-Sabah. Juvaini quoted it extensively. Rashid al-Din Talib published a more complete version. (See appendix two.)

Sasanian Dynasty: Rulers of Persia from AD 224 to 651. They supported the Zoroastrian faith and welcomed displaced pagan philosophers fleeing Christian persecution. They were overthrown by the Muslim Arab conquests.

Satr: This term meaning "concealment" is used to describe a time when the identity of the Imam or the nature of the doctrine are hidden.

Sayyidna: (Our Master) A term of respect by which Hasan-i-Sabah (and other Muslim luminaries) were known.

Seal of the Prophets: Muslim belief that Muhammad was the last of the line of prophets that included Adam, Noah, Abraham, Moses, and Jesus before him.

Seleucid Dynasty: Founded by the Greek general Seleucus I, one of the successors of Alexander the Great, they ruled Persia from the death of Alexander in 330 BC to 247 BC. They cemented the legacy of Hellenism.

Seljuk Turks: They began their conquest of Persia in the beginning of the eleventh century, and sent a deputation to the caliph in Baghdad announcing their conversion to Islam. They were the true power behind the Abbasid throne until the late twelfth century.

Sevener Shiites: (See *Sabiyya.*)

Shafii School: One of the four schools of Sunni jurisprudence—favored by Nizam al-Mulk. The others are the Hanafi, Maliki, and Hanbali schools.

Shahada: The Muslim creed summarized in the statement, "There is no god but God and Muhammad is the messenger of God."

Shahnameh, The Persian Book of Kings: A mythic history of the land compiled during the tenth century.

Shaykh: Elder, chief of a tribe, wise man, spiritual guide, *murshid*, or *pir*.

Sharia: Divinely revealed law. This is the set of religious commandments by which the Muslim guides his life personally, socially, and politically. The canon of *sharia* was fixed around the ninth century.

Shiiatu Ali: The party of Ali, later simply Shiites. According to Shiite doctrine, Muhammad declared Ali his successor in 632 at Ghadir Khumm when he took Ali's hand and said to the assembled faithful, "He of whom I am the patron, of him Ali is also the patron."

Shia: (See *Shiiatu Ali*)

Silk Road: An ancient trade route linking the Orient to the Mideast and West. Its earliest form dates back to the second millennium BC. It was greatly expanding by the Persian Parthian and Chinese Han dynasties in the third century BC. It represents the beginning of international cross cultural and commercial interactions among civilizations.

Sufis: Muslim mystics grouped around independent spiritual teachers, who sought to explore the esoteric meaning of Islam and worked to develop and practice exercises to increase mystical awareness.

Sunnah: The "well trodden path" for the majority of Muslims who aspire to follow the tradition of the Prophet's righteous behavior, codified by the tenth century. (See also *Hadith.*)

Sunnis: Those who supported the succession of Muhammad's father-in-law Abu Bakr (as opposed to Shiites, who supported Muhammad's son-in-law Ali). They tend toward a consensus-driven view of the proper direction for both religion and society. Approximately ninety percent of Muslims are Sunnis.

Talim: (authoritative teaching) This fundamental Shia/Ismaili/Nizari doctrine essentially states that human beings are incapable of determining religious truth for themselves; we do not possess the required expertise with which to judge.

Talimiyya: A term by which the Nizaris are known because of their acceptance of *talim*.

Tanasukh: Reincarnation

Tanzil: "Descent," or the "sending down" of revelation, the transmission of divine guidance for humanity through the prophets—beginning with Adam and culminating in the mission of Muhammad.

Taqiyya: Introduced by Imam Muhammad al-Baqir and enlarged upon by his son Jafar al-Sadiq, this important Shiite survival skill involves dissimulation as precaution, allowing sectarians to conceal their true beliefs without entering a state of sin.

Tariqas: Sufi orders.

Tasawwuf: Sufism

Tawhid: The doctrine of the unity of God.

Tawil: The Imam's ability to interpret and distinguish between the inner meaning (*batin*) and the outer teaching (*zahir*).

Tayyibi Ismailis: This is the modern term for followers of the Mustalian Ismaili succession. Also known as Bohras.

Twelver Shiites: (see *Ithna ashariyya*)

Ufa: The common fund of the shared assets of the Qarmati community.

Ulema: The councils of scholars—educated and trained Sunni theologians charged with interpreting and transmitting religious knowledge and Islamic law.

Umma: The community of Muslim believers.

Umayyad Dynasty: (651–750) Caliph Umar (Omar) was the successor of Abu Bakr, who had succeeded Muhammad. The Umayyads ruled Islam for nearly a century and were active in Spain for many years after that. They were replaced by the Abbasids.

Usher: Ten percent of income (tithe) that Ismailis donate to the Imam or his representative for the furtherance of the goals of the community. The tithe was also used by Sunni Arabs as a property tax under the Abbasids.

Venerable Sanctuary: A group of structures on the Temple Mount in Jerusalem built by Caliph Abd-al-Malik in 691. It includes the Dome of the Rock.

Vizier: (See Wazir)

Wasi: Immediate successor of a Prophet, charged with explaining and interpreting the teachings of the *natiq*.

Wasiyat: ("Testimony") A book by Nizam al-Mulk, although his authorship is disputed. It states that Nizam was a childhood friend of both Omar Khayyam and Hasan-i-Sabah.

Wazir: (Vizier) The chief minister of an Islamic state or dynasty, the prime minister.

Zahir: The outward meaning of Islam, the letter of the Law, as distinguished from the inner meaning, or spirit of the Law (*Batin*).

Zangid Dynasty: Formed by Zangi, a former Kurdish slave, they were a short-lived but fierce enemy of both the Franks and the Nizaris.

Zend Avesta: See *Avesta.*

Zoroastrianism: Ancient Persian religion combining monotheism and dualism dating at least back to the sixth century BC. It survives in India among the Parsees and in Iran among the Gabars.

Acknowledgments

My appreciation to Professor Ogden Goelet, who introduced me to Aliasghar Taghipourteroujeni, translator of the Rashid al-Din biography of Hasan-i-Sabah (and the purported letter exchange between Sultan Malikshah and Hasan). Aliasghar's gentleness and humility only added to the joy of working with a wonderful young man who has offered this crucial seven-hundred-year-old work to an English-speaking readership for the first time. And, as always, my thanks to Bill Corsa, who helped us navigate the intricacies of intellectual property, as he has so many times before.

Thanks to Yvonne Paglia, who acquired this for Ibis Press after I shared my enthusiasm with her one day. She has offered constant encouragement and guidance ever since. Tobias Churton has humbled me with his friendship and efforts on this book's behalf. His meticulous scholarship also revealed a significant clue of great value to this story.

Lisa Wagner was an ally in the conceptual and editorial stages of this work and understands that power by which I have been possessed. Richard Kaczynski's superb copyedits made this book both more readable and coherent. Jay Cumming's editorial review was invaluable, as was that of Nathan Schick. Ed Weech, librarian of the Royal Asiatic Society provided excellent source materials and confirmed important facts. Rachel Wasserman helped me obtain a copy of Professor Jawad Muscati's excellent and extremely rare biography of Hasan.

Jon Graham started this all by securing my manuscript of *The Templars and Assassins* for Destiny Books before it was even formally submitted. Ehud Sperling and Jeanie Levitan brought that book to life two decades ago. Daniel Pineda shares my love for Hasan and his vision one day helped confirm the direction of this effort. Peter Levenda has done so much research into this topic I am honored by his enthusiasm.

I thank Dr. Nelson Klaus whose technical expertise, patience, and ability to listen were of invaluable assistance. Magdalena Grogg's quiet faith has meant so much to me, as have the interest, advice, and efforts on its behalf by Jamie Francey. Thanks to Stuart Weinberg, Satra Wasserman, Marco Rodriquez, David Vagi, Kent Finne, Amir Modak, Stella Grey, and Keith Readdy for their help, and to my oldest and dearest friend Claire Deem for her support.

Bill Breeze, as ever, made intelligent comments and recommendations and has set a standard of excellence in his own work that I admire. Ricardo Brown-Salazar saw a very early draft of a few pages of the manuscript and offered a structural critique that dramatically improved this book. He also opened an avenue to source material of which I had been unaware. Marie Herman, Shannon Steuart, and Lindy Wisdom were all inspirations because they "got" why a nine-hundred-year-old mysterious and distant figure remains so crucial today.

Anthony Derajja generously shared his talents on the web on behalf of this book. I appreciate the skills and professionalism of David Knipfer and Don Larson of Mapping Specialists, Ltd., Fitchburg, WI, who provided the topographic base map art. And thanks to Fred Kirkhart of Stuart Photography for his skills.

I pay tribute to the three English-speaking scholars I think of as the Lions of Ismailism: Marshall Hodgson, Bernard Lewis, and Farhad Daftary. The reader has seen their names in so many footnotes because I have found them to be the most trustworthy sources. I am honored to acknowledge my debt to them.

Nancy Wasserman patiently and with quiet support helped guide and sustain me and this project to completion. Without her love, wise counsel, partnership, and friendship, I would never have been able to accomplish this.

Though this book focuses much attention on death and murder, I hope the reader will agree that its underlying message is one of the celebration of life. I am grateful to the subject of this tome for his guidance, protection, and affirmation throughout.

Bibliography

The Assassins and Islam

Al-Muscati, Jawad (trans. Abbas H. Hamdani). *Hasan Bin Sabbah.* Karachi: The Ismailia Association Pakistan, 1953; rpt. 1958.

Al-Sulami, Muhammad ibn al-Husayn (trans. Sheikh Tosun Bayrak al-Jerrahi al-Halveti). *The Book of Sufi Chivalry.* New York: Inner Traditions International, 1983.

Anthony, Sean W. "The Legend of Abdallah ibn Saba and the Date of Umm al-Kitab." *Journal of the Royal Asiatic Society* 21 (third series), no. 1 (2011): 1–30.

Bartol, Vladimir (trans. Michael Biggins). *Alamut: A Novel.* Originally published in Slovenian, 1938. English translation, Berkeley: North Atlantic Books, 2007.

Bowen, Harold. "The *sar-gudhashti-i sayyidna*, the 'Tale of the Three Schoolfellows' and the *wasaya* of the Nizam al-Mulk." *Journal of the Royal Asiatic Society* 63, no. 4 (1931): 771–782.

Boyle, J. A. (ed.). *The Cambridge History of Iran, Volume 5: The Saljuq and Mongol Periods.* London: Cambridge University Press, 1968.

Browne, Edward G. *A Literary History of Persia* (4 vols.). London: Cambridge University Press, 1902; rpt. 1977.

Burman, Edward. *The Assassins: Holy Killers of Islam.* Wellingborough UK: Aquarian Press, 1987.

Burton, Richard F. (trans. and ed.). *The Book of the Thousand Nights and a Night: A Plain and Literal Translation of the Arabian Nights Entertainments.* In sixteen volumes, privately printed by the Burton Club, 1885.

Corbin, Henri. *The Voyage and the Messenger: Iran and Philosophy.* Berkeley: North Atlantic Books, 1998.

Daftary, Farhad. *The Assassin Legends* (includes the first English translation of *Memoir on the Dynasty of the Assassins* by Silvestre de Sacy originally published in French in 1818). London: I. B. Tauris & Company, 1995.

Daftary, Farhad. *The Ismailis, Their History and Doctrines.* Cambridge: Cambridge University Press, 1994.

Daftary, Farhad (ed.). *Mediaeval Ismaili History and Thought.* Cambridge: Cambridge University Press, 1996.

Daftary, Farhad. *A Short History of the Ismailis: Traditions of a Muslim Community.* Princeton: Markus Wiener Publishers, 1998.

Daftary, Farhad and Zulfikar Hirji. *Islam: An Illustrated Journey.* London: Azimuth Editions, in association with The Institute of Ismaili Studies, 2018.

Daftary, Farhad and Zulfikar Hirji. *The Ismailis: An Illustrated History.* London: Azimuth Editions, in association with The Institute of Ismaili Studies, 2008.

FitzGerald, Edward (ed. Daniel Karlin). *Rubaiyat of Omar Khayyam.* Oxford: Oxford University Press, 2009.

Franzius, Enno. *History of the Order of Assassins.* New York: Funk & Wagnalls, 1969.

Frye, R. N. (ed.). *The Cambridge History of Iran, Volume IV: The Period from the Arab Invasion to the Saljuqs.* New York: Cambridge University Press, 1975.

Hammer-Purgstall, Joseph von. *The History of the Assassins.* New York: Burt Franklin, originally published 1835; rpt. 1968.

Hillenbrand, Carole. "A Neglected Source on the Life of Hasan-i Sabbah, the Founder of the Nizari 'Assassin' Sect." *Iran: Journal of the British Institute of Persian Studies* vol. 55, no. 1 (2017): 3–10.

Hodgson, Marshall G. S. *The Order of Assassins.* The Hague: Mouton, 1955.

Ivanow, Wladimir (ed. Farhad Daftary). *Fifty Years in the East: The Memoirs of Wladimir Ivanow.* London: I. B. Taurus Publishers, in association with The Institute of Ismaili Studies, 2015.

Ivanow, Wladimir (ed. and trans.). *Kalami Pir: A Treatise on Ismaili Doctrine, Also (Wrongly) Called Haft-Babi Shah Sayyid Nasir.* Islamic Research Association: Series No. 4, 1935. Calcutta. Baptist Mission Press. (https://archive.org/details/in.ernet.dli.2015.227582)

Juvaini, Ata-Malik (trans. and ed. J. A. Boyle). *Genghis Khan: The History of the World Conqueror (Ta-rikh-i-Jahan-Gusha).* Manchester, UK: Manchester University Press/UNESCO, 1958, 1997.

Keightley, Thomas. *Secret Societies of the Middle Ages.* London: M.A. Nattali, 1846. Reprinted, with an introduction by James Wasserman. York Beach, ME: Red Wheel Weiser, 2005.

Khayyam, Omar (trans. and ed. Edward FitzGerald). *The Rubaiyat.* New York: Collier Books, 1962. See also FitzGerald (ed. Daniel Karlin).

Levy, Reuben. "The Account of the Isma'ili Doctrines in the *Jami' Al-Tawarikh* of Rashid Al-Din Fadlallah." *Journal of the Royal Asiatic Society of Great Britain and Ireland* 3 (1930): 509–536.

Lewis, Bernard. *The Assassins, A Radical Sect in Islam.* New York: Basic Books, 1968.

Lewis, Bernard, *The Origins of Ismailism.* Cambridge: W. Heffer & Sons, Ltd, 1940; rpt. New York: AMS Press, 1975.

Lewis, Bernard. "Saladin and the Assassins." *Bulletin of the School of Oriental and African Studies* 15, no. 02 (1953): 239–245.

Lings, Martin. *Muhammad, His Life Based on the Earliest Sources.* New York: Inner Traditions International, 1983.

Lockhart, Laurence. "Hasan-i-Sabbah and the Assassins." *Bulletin of the School of Oriental Studies* 5, no. 4 (1930): 675–696.

Maalouf, Amin (trans. John Rothschild). *The Crusades Through Arab Eyes.* New York: Shocken Books, 1984.

Nasr, Seyyed Hossein (ed.). *Ismaili Contributions to Islamic Culture.* Tehran: Imperial Iranian Academy of Philosophy, 1977.

Newby, P. H. *Saladin in His Time.* New York: Dorset Press, 1992.

O'Leary, De Lacy. *A Short History of the Fatimid Khalifate.* Delhi: Renaissance Publishing House, 1923; rpt. 1987.

Picklay, A. S. *History of the Ismailis.* N.P., Bombay, originally published 1940; rpt. India: Facsimile Publisher, 2016.

Pickthall, Marmaduke (trans. and ed.). *The Meaning of the Glorious Koran.* New York: Alfred A. Knopf, originally published 1930; rpt. 1992.

Polo, Marco. *Marco Polo's Travels: with an Introduction by John Masefield.* London: J. M. Dent Sons, Ltd., 1908.

Rajput, Dr. Ali Mohammad. *Hasan-i-Sabbah: His Life and Thought.* UK: Xlibris LLC., 2013.

Rashid al-Din (Xajeh Rasido'd.din Fazlo'l.lah) (ed. Dr. Seyyed Muhammad Dabirsiaghi). *The History of Hasane Sabbah and His Successors: A Chapter of Jame o t.tavarix.* Tehran: Khojasteh Press, 2006.

Rashid al-Din (ed. Bosworth, C. Edmund, trans. Kenneth Allin Luther). *The History of the Seljuq Turks: From the Jami al-Tawarikh.* London and New York: Routledge, 2001.

Rashid al-Din (trans. and ed. Aliasghar Taghipourteroujeni and James Wasserman). *Sar-Guzasht-i-Sayyidna (The Biography of Our Master).* See appendix two of this volume.

Rosebault, Charles J. *Saladin, Prince of Chivalry.* New York: Robert M. McBride & Co., 1930.

Sacy, Silvestre de. *Memoir on the Dynasty of the Assassins.* (See Daftary, *The Assassin Legends.*)

Shah, Idries. *The Sufis.* Garden City: Doubleday, 1964.

Stern, Samuel M. "The Epistle of the Fatimid Caliph al-Amir (al-Hidaya al-Amiriyya)—Its Date and Its Purpose." *Journal of the Royal Asiatic Society* 82 (1950): 20–31.

Stern, Samuel M. *Studies in Early Ismailism.* Jerusalem: The Magness Press–The Hebrew University/Leiden: E. J. Brill, 1983.

Tawfik, Younis. *Islam.* New York: Konecky & Konecky, 1998.

Tsugitaka, Sato. *State and Rural Society in Medieval Islam: Sultans, Muqtas, and Fallahun.* Leiden: E. J. Brill, 1997.

Wasserman, James. *The Templars and the Assassins: The Militia of Heaven.* Rochester, VT: Destiny Books, 2001.

Wasserman, James. *Templar Heresy: A Story of Gnostic Illumination.* Rochester, VT: Destiny Books, 2017.

Waterson, James. *The Ismaili Assassins: A History of Medieval Murder.* London: Frontline Books, 2008.

Willey, Peter. *Ismaili Castles in Iran and Syria.* London and New York: I. B. Tauris Publishers, in association with The Institute of Ismaili Studies, 2005.

Wilson, Peter Lamborn. *Sacred Drift: Essays on the Margins of Islam.* San Francisco: City Lights Books, 1993.

Wilson, Peter Lamborn. *Scandals: Essays in Islamic Heresy.* Brooklyn, NY: Autonomedia, 1988.

The Knights Templar and the Crusades

Barber, Malcolm. *The New Knighthood.* Cambridge: Cambridge University Press, 1994.

Barber, Malcolm. *The Trial of the Templars.* Cambridge: Cambridge University Press, 1978.

Bernard of Clairvaux (trans. Conrad Greenia). *The Cistercian Fathers Series: Number Nineteen, The Works of Bernard of Clairvaux: Volume Seven, Treatises III.* Kalamazoo: Cistercian Publications, 1977.

Billings, Malcolm. *The Cross and the Crescent.* New York: Sterling Publishing, 1990.

Bradford, Ernle. *The Knights of the Order.* New York: Dorset Press, 1972; rpt. 1991.

Burman, Edward. *The Templars: Knights of God.* Wellingborough, UK: Aquarian Press, 1986.

Coss, Peter. *The Knight in Medieval England 1000–1400.* Conshohocken: Combined Books, 1993.

Encyclopedia Americana. 1979 edition.

Eschenbach, Wolfram von (trans. with introduction by Helen M. Mustard and Charles E. Passage). *Parzival.* New York: Vintage Books, 1961.

Holy Bible. King James translation. Camden, NJ: Thomas Nelson, Inc., 1970.

Howarth, Stephen. *The Knights Templar.* London: Collins, 1982.

Lambert, Malcolm. *The Cathars.* Oxford: Blackwell Publishers, 1998.

Legman, G. *The Guilt of the Templars.* New York: Basic Books, 1966.

Marshall, Christopher. *Warfare in the Latin East, 1192–1291.* Cambridge: Cambridge University Press, 1992.

Michelet, Jules (trans. A. R. Allinson). *Satanism and Witchcraft.* New York: Citadel Press, 1946.

Partner, Peter. *The Murdered Magicians, The Templars and their Myth.* Oxford: Oxford University Press, 1981.

Payne, Robert. *The Dream and the Tomb: A History of the Crusades.* Chelsea: Scarborough House, 1991.

Riley-Smith, Jonathan (ed.). *The Atlas of the Crusades.* New York: Facts on File, 1990.

Robinson, John J. *Born in Blood.* New York: M. Evans & Company, 1989.

Robinson, John J. *Dungeon, Fire and Sword.* New York: M. Evans & Company, 1991.

Runciman, Steven. *A History of the Crusades,* 3 vols. London: The Folio Society, originally published 1951; rpt. 1994.

Simon, Edith. *The Piebald Standard.* London: White Lion Publishers Limited, 1976.

Strayer, Joseph R. *The Albigensian Crusades.* Ann Arbor: The University of Michigan Press, 1992.

Wasserman, James. *An Illustrated History of the Knights Templar.* Rochester, VT: Destiny Books, 2006.

Weston, Jessie L. *From Ritual to Romance.* Garden City: Doubleday Anchor Books, 1957.

General Reference Works

Balfour, Henry. "On the Structure and Affinities of the Composite Bow." *Journal of the Anthropological Institute of Great Britain and Ireland,* vol. 19 (1890): 220–250.

Barnes, Ian. *The Historical Atlas of the Bible.* New York: Chartwell Books, Inc., 2006, rev. 2010.

Beitzel, Barry J. *Biblica, The Bible Atlas: A Social and Historical Journey Through the Lands of the Bible.* Hauppauge, NY: Barron's Educational Services, 2007.

Bowersock, G. W. *The Throne of Adulis: Red Sea Wars on the Eve of Islam.* New York: Oxford University Press, 2013.

Brook, Kevin Alan. *The Jews of Khazaria: Second Edition.* Lanham, MD: Rowman & Liitlefield Publishers, Inc., 2006.

Brosius, Maria. *The Persians: An Introduction.* London and New York: Routledge, 2006.

Bryce, Trevor and Jessie Birkett-Rees. *Atlas of the Ancient Near East: From Prehistoric Times to the Roman Imperial Period.* New York and London: Routledge, 2016.

Cantor, Norman F. *The Civilization of the Middle Ages.* New York: Harper Perennial, 1994.

Cerow, Don. *The 8th Seal: Its Time Is Now!* Lake Worth, FL: Ibis Press, 2017.

Cohn, Norman. *The Pursuit of the Millennium.* New York: Oxford University Press, 1957, rev. ed., 1961, 1970.

Crowley, Aleister. *The Book of Thoth: A Short Essay on the Tarot of the Egyptians.* New York: Samuel Weiser, Inc., 1969.

Crowley, Aleister. *The Holy Books of Thelema.* York Beach, ME: Samuel Weiser Inc., 1983.

Crowley, Aleister. *777 Revised.* New York: Samuel Weiser Inc., 1970.

Crystal, David (ed.). *The Cambridge Biographical Encyclopedia.* Cambridge: Cambridge University Press, 1994.

Cumming, James H. *Torah and Nondualism: Diversity Conflict, and Synthesis.* Lake Worth, FL: Ibis Press, 2019.

Cumont, Franz. *The Mysteries of Mithra.* Chicago: Open Court Publishing Company, 1903; rpt. New York: Dover Publications, 1956.

Dalley, Stephanie (trans. and ed.). *Myths from Mesopotamia: Creation, The Flood, Gilgamesh, and Others.* Oxford: Oxford University Press, 1989, rev. ed. 2000.

Darmesteter, James (trans.). *The Zend-Avesta* (3 vols.). Sacred Books of the East Series, Delhi: Motilal Banarsidass, 1883; rpt. 1969.

De Waele, An. "Composite Bows at ed-Dur (Umm al-Qaiwain, U.A.E.)." *Arabian Archaeology and Epigraphy* 16, no. 2 (2005): 154–160.

Durant, Will. *Our Oriental Heritage: The Story of Civilization,* vol. 1. New York: Simon and Schuster, 1935.

Durant, Will. *The Life of Greece: The Story of Civilization,* vol. 2. New York: Simon and Schuster, 1939.

Durant, Will. *The Age of Faith: The Story of Civilization,* vol. 4. New York: Simon and Schuster, 1944.

Encyclopedia Britannica, 15th edition, 32 volumes published on CD, Chicago, 1998.

Epstein, Steven A. *An Economic and Social History of Later Medieval Europe, 1000–1500.* New York: Cambridge University Press, 2009.

Ferdowsi, Abolqasem (trans. Dick Davis). *Shahnameh: The Persian Book of Kings.* New York: Viking Penguin, 2006.

Foltz, Richard. *Iran in World History.* New York: Oxford University Press, 2016.

Foltz, Richard. *Religions of Iran: From Prehistory to the Present.* London: Oneworld Publications, 2013.

Garraty, John A. and Peter Gay (eds.). *The Columbia History of the World.* New York: Harper & Row, 1972.

Gershevitch, Ilya (ed.). *The Cambridge History of Iran, Volume 2: The Median and Achaemenian Periods.* London: Cambridge University Press, 1985.

Graves, Robert and Raphael Patai. *Hebrew Myths: The Book of Genesis.* Garden City, NY: Doubleday and Company, 1964.

Hanegraaff, Wouter J. (ed.). *Dictionary of Gnosis & Western Esotericism.* Leiden: Brill, 2006.

Herodotus (trans. David Grene). *The History.* Chicago: University of Chicago Press, 1987.

Iamblichus (trans. Thomas Taylor). *On the Mysteries of the Egyptians, Chaldeans and Assyrians.* London: Stuart and Watkins, originally published 1821; rpt. 1968.

Jacobsen, Thorkild. *The Treasures of Darkness: A History of Mesopotamian Religion.* New Haven and London: Yale University Press, 1976.

James, E. O. *The Ancient Gods: The History and Diffusion of Religion in the Ancient Near East and the Eastern Mediterranean.* New York: G. P. Putnam's Sons, 1960.

Johnson, Scott (ed.) *The Oxford Handbook of Late Antiquity.* New York: Oxford University Press, 2012.

Khan Sahib Khaja Khan. *The Secret of Ana'l-Haqq.* Lahore Pakistan: Sh. Muhammad Ashraf, originally published 1926; rpt. 1976.

Knight, Stephen. *Robin Hood: A Mythic Biography.* Ithaca and London: Cornell University Press, 2003/2009.

Koestler, Arthur. *The Thirteenth Tribe: The Khazar Empire and Its Heritage.* New York: Random House, 1976.

Kramer, Samuel Noah. *History Begins at Sumer: Thirty-Nine Firsts in Recorded History.* Philadelphia: University of Pennsylvania Press, 1956, rev. ed. 1981.

Kramer, Samuel Noah. *The Sumerians: Their History, Culture, and Character.* Chicago: University of Chicago Press, 1963.

Kriwaczek, Paul. *Babylon: Mesopotamia and the Birth of Civilization.* New York: Thomas Dunne Books/St. Martin's Press, 2010.

Levenda, Peter. *Tantric Temples: Eros and Magic in Java.* Lake Worth, FL: Ibis Press, 2011.

Lewis, Franklin D. *Rumi—Past and Present, East and West: The Life, Teachings, and Poetry of Jalal al-Din Rumi.* Oxford: Oneworld Publications, 2008.

Patai, Raphael. *The Hebrew Goddess.* N.P.: KTAV Publishing House, 1967.

Podhoretz, Norman. *Why Are Jews Liberals?* New York: Doubleday, 2009.

Quirke, Stephen and Jeffrey Spencer (eds.). *The British Museum Book of Ancient Egypt.* London: British Museum Press, 1992.

Ridpath, John Clark. *History of the World: Being an Account of the Principal Events in the Career of the Human Race from the Beginning of Civilization to the Present Time.* Cincinnati: The Ridpath Historical Society, Inc., 1936.

Robinson, Andrew. *The Story of Writing: Alphabets, Hieroglyphs, and Pictograms.* London: Thames and Hudson, Ltd., 1995.

Robinson, James M. (ed.). *The Nag Hammadi Library*, rev. third edition. San Francisco: Harper & Row, 1988.

Sandars, N. K. (trans. and ed.). *The Epic of Gilgamesh.* London: Penguin Books, 1960, rev. 1972.

Shaw, Ian (ed.). *The Oxford History of Ancient Egypt.* Oxford: Oxford University Press, 2000.

Smith, William (rev. and ed. F. N. and M. A. Peloubet). *A Dictionary of the Bible.* Philadelphia and Toronto: The John C. Winston Company, 1948.

Stanley, Thomas (eds. James Wasserman and J. Daniel Gunther). *Pythagoras: His Life and Teachings.* Lake Worth, FL: Ibis Press, first published 1687, rev. and exp. edition, 2010.

Steindorff, George and Keith C. Steele. *When Egypt Ruled the East*, rev. 2nd ed. by Keith Steele. Chicago and London: The University of Chicago Press, 1957.

Ulansey, David. *The Origins of the Mithraic Mysteries: Cosmology and Salvation in the Ancient World.* New York and Oxford: Oxford University Press, 1989.

Van De Mieroop, Marc. *A History of the Ancient Near East ca. 3000–323 BC, Third Edition.* Malden, MA: John Wiley & Sons Ltd., 2016

Van der Toorn, Karel, Bob Becking, and Pieter W. van der Horst (eds.). *Dictionary of Deities and Demons in the Bible (DDD)*, 2nd extensively rev. ed. Leiden: Brill Academic Publishers, and Grand Rapids, MI/ Cambridge UK: Wm. B. Eerdmans Publishing Company, 1999.

Wasserman, James. *The Slaves Shall Serve: Meditations on Liberty.* New York: Sekmet Books, 2004.

Wasserman, James. *The Temple of Solomon: From Ancient Israel to Secret Societies.* Rochester VT: Inner Traditions International, 2011.

Wasserman, James and Nancy Wasserman. *To Perfect This Feast: A Performance Commentary on the Gnostic Mass* (3rd ed.). Newburyport, MA: Sekmet Books, 2013.

Westcott, William Wynn (trans.). *Collectanea Hermetica.* London: Theosophical Publishing Society, 1895; rpt. R. A. Gilbert (ed.), Yorke Beach, ME: Samuel Weiser, Inc., 1998.

Yarshater, Ehsan (ed.). *The Cambridge History of Iran, Volume III (1 and 2): The Seleucid, Parthian, and Sasanian Periods.* New York: Cambridge University Press, 1983.

Yates, Frances A. *Giordano Bruno and the Hermetic Tradition.* Chicago and London: The University of Chicago Press, 1964.

Yates, Frances A. *The Rosicrucian Enlightenment.* London: Routledge & Kegan Paul, 1974.

Index

About the Author

James Wasserman is a lifelong student and practitioner of the Mystery Traditions. A book designer by trade, he has been intimately involved with the teachings of Aleister Crowley and the orders he promoted. This is his fourth book on the Crusades and the interaction between the military orders of East and West. His first essay on this topic was published in 1986 in *Equinox* III:10.

For more on the the author and a sampling of his other books, essays, lectures, and media appearances, please visit:

JamesWassermanBooks.com

Other Titles of Interest from Ibis Press

Pythagoras

His Life and Teachings

Thomas Stanley
Preface by Manly P. Hall;
Introduction by Dr. Henry L. Drake;
Edited by James Wasserman;
Study of Greek Sources by J. Daniel Gunther

Pythagoras is known as the Father of Philosophy. He was one of the most influential figures of all time. While he lived some 2,600 years ago, he is as much a part of today's world as he was of classical Greece.

His contributions encompassed a wide spectrum of knowledge. Mathematics, in particular geometry, is perhaps the area in which he is best known today. However, he did much original work in such diverse fields as Religion, Mysticism, Symbolic Numbers, Philosophy, Music, Astronomy, Politics, Health, and Nutrition. He founded a spiritual academy in which an active intellectual curriculum was augmented by a highly disciplined program of character development—making it one of the true Mystery schools of the ancient world. He sought to develop a superior human being through the cultivation of morality, intellectual learning, self-discipline, spiritual sensitivity, and good citizenship.

The timeless brilliance of Thomas Stanley's study of Pythagoras is as relevant today as it was when first published over three hundred years ago. Stanley's text and typography have been updated for a modern audience by editor and book designer James Wasserman. This edition features a biographical sketch of Stanley by renowned esoteric philosopher Manly P. Hall, an in-depth overview of the teachings of Pythagoras by classical scholar Dr. Henry L. Drake, and a study of Greek and Latin sources by J. Daniel Gunther.

$24.95 • Paperback • ISBN: 978-0-89254-160-7
416 pp. • 6 x 9 • Illustrated

Other Titles of Interest from Ibis Press

Secret Societies

Illuminati, Freemasons, and the French Revolution

Una Birch,

Enlarged, edited, and introduced by James Wasserman

The greatest success of the Bavarian Illuminati conspiracy was the French Revolution of 1789. The profound impact of that Revolution is felt to this day in the political destinies of billions of people worldwide. The Illuminati had declared war against Church and State a decade earlier and worked feverishly to spread their new gospel of Liberty and Reason. Although the Order was officially suppressed on the eve of the Revolution, its efforts were not in vain.

Secret Societies is an invitation to the clandestine world behind the veil of daily events. In its pages you will meet the legendary Cagliostro and the Comte de Saint-Germain as they traveled through the royal courts and Masonic lodges of eighteenth-century Europe, fomenting Revolution and working to overturn the social order of their day. Alchemists, magicians, adepts, mystics, and Freemasons joined forces with politicians, journalists, scientists, writers, philosophers, and libertines in a movement that forever altered the cultural landscape of Western Civilization.

What message does the triumph of these secret societies carry for the modern world? English historian Una Birch attempts to answer this question from the point of view of the very early twentieth century. Writing just a hundred years after the event, her closeness in time, and sympathy for the Revolution, offer a unique perspective to the modern reader. Editor James Wasserman adds a contemporary perspective that takes into account the later events of the twentieth century. He has also added a guide to the history and personalities of the French Revolution to help clarify the text.

$18.95 • Paperback • ISBN: 0-89254-132-6 • 288 pp. • 6 x 9

In the Center of the Fire
A Memoir of the Occult 1966–1989

James Wasserman

In this daring exposé by a survivor of a unique era in the New York occult scene, James Wasserman, a longtime proponent of the teachings of Aleister Crowley, brings us into a world of candlelit temples, burning incense, and sonorous invocations.

The author also shares an intimate look at the New York Underground of the 1970s and 1980s and introduces us to the company of such avant-garde luminaries as Alejandro Jodorowsky, Harry Smith, and Angus MacLise. A stone's throw away from the Velvet Underground and Andy Warhol's Factory, William Burroughs' "bunker," and the legendary Chelsea Hotel was a scene far more esoteric than perhaps even they could have imagined.

When the author joined the O.T.O. in 1976, there were fewer than a dozen members. Today the Order numbers over 4,000 members in 50 countries. Wasserman founded New York City's TAHUTI Lodge in 1979. He chronicles its early history and provides a window into the heyday of the Manhattan esoteric community.

He also breaks decades of silence concerning one of the most seminal events in the development of the modern Thelemic movement—detailing his role in the 1976 magical battle between Marcelo Motta and Grady McMurtry. Long slandered for his effort to heal the temporary breach between the Orders of A.·.A.·. and O.T.O., James Wasserman sets the record straight.

$35.00 • Hardcover • ISBN: 978-089254-201-7 • 336 pp. • 6 x 9
with 24 pages of glossy photos and numerous magical diagrams